DIVINE ELOQUENCE AND HUMAN TRANSFORMATION

DIVINE ELOQUENCE AND HUMAN TRANSFORMATION

RETHINKING SCRIPTURE AND HISTORY THROUGH GREGORY OF NAZIANZUS AND HANS FREI

BEN FULFORD

Fortress Press

Minneapolis

DIVINE ELOQUENCE AND HUMAN TRANSFORMATION

Rethinking Scripture and History through Gregory of Nazianzus and Hans Frei

Cover design: Alisha Lofgren

Library of Congress Cataloging-in-Publication Data is available

Print ISBN: 978-1-4514-6548-8

eBook ISBN: 978-1-4514-6960-8

The paper used in this publication meets the minimum requirements of American National Standard for Information Sciences — Permanence of Paper for Printed Library Materials, ANSI Z329.48-1984.

Manufactured in the U.S.A.

This book was produced using PressBooks.com, and PDF rendering was done by PrinceXML.

For Alison.

CONTENTS

Abbreviations

I cite Gregory's texts by the standard oration, epistle, or poem number and by edition, using the following abbreviations (for full references, see the bibliography):

PG   J.-P. Migne, ed., *Patrologia Graeca*

SC   *Sources Chrétiennes*

Some of Hans Frei's writings are available online as part of the *Unpublished Pieces*, edited by Mike Higton. I have also included their catalogue numbers in the Yale Divinity School archive, using the abbreviation *YDS* for Yale Divinity School.

Acknowledgements

The writing of this book has been a lengthy affair, and I have incurred many debts during its long gestation.

The research and writing of the thesis from which this book has been developed was made possible by awards of a Crosse Studentship from the Faculty of Divinity, University of Cambridge, by a Domestic Research Scholarship from the University of Cambridge, and by a doctoral award from the Arts and Humanities Research Council, and I am grateful to all these bodies for their support.

I also owe considerable debts to a number of people. Anna Williams first introduced me to both Gregory and Frei, fostered a love of theological texts, and supervised the dissertation on which this book is based. Denys Turner supervised me during Anna's research leave in 2005 and provided much-needed encouragement and insight. Mike Higton read and commented on a draft of the Frei material in the thesis, and he and Morwenna Ludlow also gave me feedback on the whole thesis with a view to publication. Tim Hull has read both the original dissertation and drafts of revised material and provided encouragement, stimulating criticism, and intellectual comradeship. I owe a great deal to the late Dan Hardy, who generously read and gave time to discuss drafts of the thesis and continued to do so even after he was diagnosed with what turned out to be a fatal illness. I am grateful too to David Ford and Frances Young, who examined the thesis and whose constructive feedback has been in my mind as I revised it for publication, and to the late Brevard Childs, who kindly discussed Hans Frei with me. Thanks too to Christine Ainsley, then librarian at St. John's College, Nottingham, who miraculously obtained a copy of Frei's doctoral dissertation. I'm grateful also to Suzanne Abrams Rebillard for allowing me to see a copy of her chapter on "Historiography as Devotion" before it was published.

I have also benefited from conversations and encouragement from many people along the way: Ed Morgan, Brett and Ali Gray, John Hughes, James Walters, Tom Greggs, Nick Adams, Ben Quash, Susannah Ticciati, Rachel Muers, Greg Seach, Jamie Hawkey, Simeon Zahl, Andy Angel, David Neaum, Rachel Greene, Philip McCosker, Doug Ingram, Karen Kilby, Willie Young, Jim Fodor, Chad Pecknold, Imogen Atkins, Angela Bryan, Michael Leyden, Dawn Llewellyn, Craig Hovey, David Runcorn and Andii Bowsher, to name a few. St John's College, Nottingham gave me research leave in Michaelmas 2011, and the department of Theology and Religious Studies at the University of Chester has made me very welcome and, with the support of Professor David Clough, enabled me to find time to finish the manuscript. I benefited from being able to discuss some of the ideas developed here in research seminars at the University of Cambridge, King's College London, and St. John's College, Nottingham.

My deepest debts are to my family: my Mum and Dad and sister Nancy; Robin and Carol, my parents-in-law; my sons, Matthew and Nathan, and above all to Alison whose patient and loving support, unfailing encouragement, commitment to theology, and friendship have sustained me when I thought the project would never end. To her the book is dedicated.

Introduction

The contemporary movement in theology that seeks to recover ways of understanding and reading the Bible as Christian Scripture has, in large part, been constituted over against a captivity of the Bible to the hegemonic claims of historical criticism.[1] These claims are often taken to delimit the ways in which meaning can be found in biblical texts and to be destructive of Christian uses and readings of those texts as Scripture.[2] Much thinking in this movement challenges therefore that understanding of meaning or reframes the issue in terms of a theological account of the Bible as Holy Scripture. Historical-critical inquiry, in all its variety, however, is informed by a more basic sensibility, a sense of the historical character of reality, which poses serious challenges for Christian theology and for the whole project of the theology and theological interpretation of Scripture. Yet this challenge goes largely unaddressed in much of the literature, and where addressed, its full force does not seem to have been registered. What follows, therefore, lays out one way of beginning to address these challenges, drawing on the theology and exegesis of a fourth-century theologian-bishop, Gregory of Nazianzus, and the thought of a twentieth-century theologian, Hans Frei. At its heart is the proposal that the ontology, meaning, and meaningfulness of Scripture can be located within a properly theological historical sensibility centered upon Jesus Christ as the one who in his historical existence is the luminous presence of God and the focal center of God's ordering of all of history, in all its contingency and complexity. The force of this meaning as the frail bearer of the presence of Christ is mediated through a scripturally wrought rhetoric, deploying the story of Christ and other texts in connection to him, to further the transformation of human beings and the slow and tenuous reshaping of human society.

1. Such, for example, seems to be the tenor of the contributions to Carl E. Braaten and Robert W. Jenson, eds., *Reclaiming the Bible for the Church* (Edinburgh: T. & T. Clark, 1995).

2. Jon D. Levenson argues cogently for the destructive consequences for Jewish and Christian scriptural interpretation of making historical context primary in biblical interpretation. See his "The Hebrew Bible, the Old Testament, and Historical Criticism" in his book of the same name (Louisville: Westminster John Knox, 1993), 1–32.

I

The sense of history as a vast, complex network of interrelated phenomena that are, in principle, explicable in terms of their mutual relations lies at the heart of Ernst Troeltsch's careful, critically realistic account of historiography. It also provides, on his account, a strong objection to belief in the manifestation of the absolute in history, and this difficulty has profound consequences for the theology of Scripture, as I explore in Chapter 1, and hence for the current movement for the recovery of the theological interpretation of Scripture.

The signs are abundant of the vitality now long-lived and broad tendency in recent theology to seek to recover theological and ecclesial ways of reading Scripture, supported by theological accounts of Scripture's reality, meaning, and significance.[3] Several accounts of this tendency situate it explicitly over against a putative hegemony of historical critics with respect to the legitimate, scholarly reading of biblical texts. Others seem to presuppose this hegemony and the claims about the nature, meaning, and significance of biblical texts. We can tentatively distinguish three overlapping approaches here.[4]

The first takes the canon of biblical texts as its focus, and proposes that understood rightly it evinces a powerful coherence that allows it to serve as the vehicle of the divine will. Here we might instance Brevard Childs's

---

3. Besides the literature cited below, which is by no means an exhaustive survey, there are a number of other indicators. First, there are now several undergraduate-level introductions to the subfield of the theological interpretation of Scripture. Examples include Stephen E. Fowl, *Theological Interpretation of Scripture* (Eugene, OR: Cascade Books, 2009); Daniel J. Treier, *Introducing Theological Interpretation of Scripture: Recovering a Christian Practice* (Nottingham: Apollos, 2008); J. Todd Billings, *The Word of God for the People of God: An Entryway to the Theological Interpretation of Scripture* (Grand Rapids: Eerdmans, 2010); and Alexander Jenson, *Theological Hermeneutics* (London: SCM, 2007). A second indicator is the several series of theological commentary on the books of the Bible being published by Westminster John Knox (*Belief*), Brazos/SCM (*Theological Commentary on the Bible*), and Eerdmans (*Two Horizons*). A third is the revival of interest in premodern exegesis (and in the mid-century enterprise of *ressourcement* among Catholic writers of the so-called *nouvelle théologie*) evidenced not only by some of the literature cited below but also by the publication of collections of patristic and medieval commentary on biblical books by Eerdmans (*The Bible in Medieval Tradition, The Church's Bible*), InterVarsity Press (*Ancient Christian Commentary on Scripture*), and by the publication of Mark Sebanc's multivolume translation of Henri de Lubac's *Exégèse medievale* in the series *Ressourcement: Retrieval and Renewal in Catholic Thought* by Eerdmans (1998, 2000, 2009). The growth of graduate courses in the subfield, the development of dedicated journals and scholarly aids like K. J. Vanhoozer et al., eds., *The Dictionary for Theological Interpretation of the Bible* (Grand Rapids: Baker, 2006), are further signs.

4. For an alternative and more extensive analysis, see Daniel J. Treier, "What Is Theological Interpretation? An Ecclesiological Reduction," *International Journal of Systematic Theology* 12, no. 2 (2010): 144–61.

proposal that the canonical shaping of scriptural texts and of the canon as a whole is determinative of the meaning of the texts whereby they express God's intentions.[5] George Lindbeck's proposal that biblical narratives instantiate normatively the semiotic code of Christian communities, and propose a world of meaning that "absorbs" the world in which we live so that in it we live and move and have our being, and may conform our lives to the ultimate reality of God, is another example.[6] Francis Watson also privileges the final form of the scriptural texts in their canonical context, subject in turn to the constraints of the church's rule of faith, as capable of addressing the realities of the world in which the church finds itself and responding to the critiques that arise from that context.[7] All these accounts resist the constriction of biblical meaning to original authorial intentions or ancient receptions or reconstructions of the pasts to which they refer, without letting go of historical referentiality, but none grapple substantially with the issues raised by historical consciousness.

The second likewise concentrates on the final form of the texts in their canonical collection, but seeks to make its peculiar modes of truthfulness intelligible in light of philosophies of textual meaning and reference. On the one hand are accounts indebted to hermeneutical philosophies of Hans Georg Gadamer or Paul Ricoeur (or both), such as Sandra Schneiders's account of the New Testament's picture of Jesus Christ in terms of God's symbolic self-expression, which, through the semantic meaning of the text in its final form, discloses to the reader possible ways of being and seeing in the world for them to actualize.[8] The distanciation, through writing, of texts from the original authors and the circumstances they addressed is the condition of possibility of this kind of reference. Historical criticism is useful in attending to the semantic meaning, but the reference projected by that meaning exceeds its concerns and requires a lived appropriation. Werner Jeanrond is another example of this approach. Here, Gadamer and Ricoeur are supplemented with reader response theory and a critical appropriation of David Tracy's theological method to argue the strong affinity of Christian theology and hermeneutics so understood. On this account, the dynamic potential of biblical texts and their capacity to disclose God's Word in new ways are unleashed as we interpret them in new contexts, selecting appropriate styles of reading from a plurality of approaches, and so exercising our freedom and responsibility as fallible interpreters to enter

5. See Chapter 1.

6. *The Nature of Doctrine: Religion and Theology in a Postliberal Age* (Louisville: Westminster John Knox, 1984), 116ff.

7. *Text, Church and World* (Edinburgh: T. & T. Clark, 1994).

8. See Chapter 1.

into critical conversation with them.[9] These accounts acknowledge historical consciousness, but, as I argue later, fail to address the full force of its challenge.

Various appropriations of speech-act theory to understand biblical texts and the canon at large as God's speech also belong here, such as those of Nicholas Wolterstorff or the early constructive work of Kevin Vanhoozer.[10] Here the intended meanings of biblical authors are realized in the communicative actions of the texts and are appropriated by God as his own speech acts in respect of later readers and communities. Such theories seek to guard against problems of indeterminacy of meaning but also construe meaning in such a way that it is not limited to the ancient past. Here, too, the issue of history is not really a prominent concern.

The third approach rethinks meaning and understanding in terms of readers' agency. One version of this approach likens biblical interpretation to artistic performance.[11] Nicholas Lash's programmatic essay illustrates the main thesis.[12] The interpretation of texts depends on the text and its use, he argues; some texts require performance for the realization of their meaning. Such is the case with New Testament texts as relating the story of Jesus and the first Christian communities. The primary form of their Christian interpretation consists in the life, activity, and organization of the believing community as a witness to the one whose words, life, and suffering rendered the truth of God in our history. Interpretation is a corporate act bound in creative fidelity to the original meaning, concerns, and claims of the texts.[13] This approach resists the dominance of historical-critical biblical scholarship without abandoning its contribution. It incorporates a degree of historical sensibility, for the metaphor of performing the Scriptures seems to make biblical interpretation historically

9. *Text and Interpretation as Categories of Theological Thinking* (London: Gill & Macmillan, 1986).

10. Wolterstorff, *Divine Discourse: Philosophical Reflections on the Claim That God Speaks* (Cambridge: Cambridge University Press, 1995); Vanhoozer, *Is There a Meaning in This Text? The Bible, the Reader and the Morality of Literary Knowledge* (Leicester: Apollos, 1998), and his *First Theology: God, Scripture and Hermeneutics* (Downers Grove, IL/Nottingham: IVP Academic/Apollos, 2002).

11. See Stephen Barton's account of this approach in his "New Testament as Performance," *Scottish Journal of Theology* 52, no. 2 (1999): 179–208.

12. "Performing the Scriptures: Interpretation through Living," The Furrow 33, no. 8 (August 1982): 467–74.

13. Frances Young has developed this theme in conversation with early Christian uses of Scripture in her *The Art of Performance: Towards a Theology of Holy Scripture* (London: Darton, Longman & Todd, 1990). Kevin J. Vanhoozer takes up the metaphor and extends it considerably in his *The Drama of Doctrine: A Canonical Linguistic Approach to Christian Theology* (Louisville: Westminster John Knox, 2005).

located and contingent, but it has not been pursued in relation to the deeper issues raised by historical consciousness.

A similar emphasis on readerly agency and praxis is offered by Stephen Fowl. For Fowl, textual interpretation varies with the aims, interests, and practices of interpretations.[14] Such an "underdetermined" account allows Christians to specify the diversity of their interpretations and performances of specific scriptural texts. Biblical interpretation, for Christians at least, will be the occasion of complex interactions between the biblical text and the varieties of concerns that are part of the everyday lives of Christians "struggling to live faithfully before God in the contexts in which they find themselves," which no method can specify in advance.[15] Here readers' virtues and communal practices are central to shaping the interpretation of Scripture in any given context, whether in avoiding abusive readings, discerning questions of inclusion, offering counter-conventional readings, and learning how to disagree.[16] There is much to be admired in this account. It too refuses the hegemony of a concern with original meanings without forsaking critical scholarship, and again it is pervaded by a sense of historicity with respect to readers' contextualized agency. The saving purposes of the triune God provide the overarching theological framework, but there is no engagement with the questions historical consciousness poses to that schema.

Finally, though all these approaches invoke divine revelation and contextualize biblical interpretation within divine saving action in some sense, several recent works have offered more developed ontologies of Scripture, placing the texts, its origin, and its reception by the church within the field of God's saving economic action. John Webster's *Holy Scripture* is exemplary here.[17] For Webster, Holy Scripture has certain properties in virtue of its relation to God's communicative activity, and to describe it we must talk of the triune God's saving and revelatory acts, for it belongs to the saving economy of God's loving and regenerative self-communication—which is not to diminish

14. *Engaging Scripture: A Model for Theological Interpretation* (Oxford: Blackwell, 1998), 57.

15. Ibid., 60.

16. These concerns are also reflected in Fowl and L. G. Jones, *Reading in Communion: Scripture and Ethics in Christian Life* (London: SPCK, 1991).

17. *Holy Scripture: A Dogmatic Sketch* (Cambridge: Cambridge University Press, 2003). See also Telford Work, *Living and Active: Scripture in the Economy of Salvation* (Grand Rapids: Eerdmans, 2002); Angus Paddison, "Locating Scripture," in his *Scripture: A Very Theological Proposal* (London: T. & T. Clark, 2009), 5–32; Richard R. Topping, *Revelation, Scripture and Church: Theological Hermeneutic Thought of James Barr, Paul Ricoeur and Hans Frei* (Aldershot: Ashgate, 2007); and Mark Alan Bowald, *Rendering the Word in Theological Hermeneutics: Mapping Human and Divine Agency* (Aldershot: Ashgate, 2007).

its human character. Scripture denotes a set of fully human texts sanctified for, and taken up into, service of God's saving communicative agency, which graciously establishes covenant fellowship with human beings. This ontology forms the basis for thinking about Scripture in the church, the character of ecclesial reading, and the nature of theology, all understood in relation to the hearing of the Word through Scripture and its creative, vivifying, and mortifying functions. Webster's position makes divine action primary but inclusive of the creatureliness of Scripture and its readers and is hospitable to a historical sensibility but, like other similar works, does not substantially address the questions raised by historical consciousness.[18]

The account I develop later in dialogue with Frei and Gregory shares commonalities with many of these accounts—for instance, on the importance of the final form of the text, of readers' practices and character, of a theological ontology of Scripture and its reception. These works have other concerns besides the question of history. Nevertheless, the relative lack of detailed engagement in this field with the issues raised by historical consciousness seems strange when so many contributors seek to emancipate theological reading from the limitations of historical-critical reading, and especially when, as I will show in Chapter 1, the issues are explicitly or implicitly acknowledged by some leading contributions.[19] Nor is it easy to point to a publication or debate in which the question was settled long ago. One might object that history as a discipline has become theoretically problematic in recent decades, but to read Troeltsch on historiography is to become aware that it has long been possible to offer an account of the discipline that takes account of the selective, perspectival, and constructive nature of historical analysis and history writing without giving up on the whole exercise.

II

Why, though, turn to Gregory or Hans Frei, and why combine them in respect of this issue? A brief précis of their biographies only sharpens this question, for their historical contexts and the concerns they pursued in those contexts are quite diverse.[20] Gregory pursued an ascetic life in uneasy relation with a turbulent ministry of pastoral leadership and authoritative Christian

---

18. Murray Rae's work is a notable exception in discussing the problem of history in great depth, and is examined in Chapter 1. See his *History and Hermeneutics* (London: T. & T. Clark, 2005).

19. It is also striking that Mark Noll's article on "History" in *The Dictionary for the Theological Interpretation of the Bible*, ed. Kevin J. Vanhoozer, Craig G. Bartholomew, and Daniel J. Treier (Grand Rapids: Baker, 2005), 295–99, omits the issues Troeltsch raises.

teaching in Nazianzus, a small town in provincial Cappadocia, and briefly in Constantinople, the imperial capital, in the fourth century CE. He was one of a number of pro-Nicene theologians seeking to uphold faith in the Trinity and in the full divinity and humanity of the one Jesus Christ, to promote and model forms of holiness, and to further the transformation of Greek cities in the East in respect of their philanthropic practices and the Christianization of their literary culture. His mode of leadership and influence here drew on the accepted public function of rhetors in those cities and on the rhetorical forms of the "Second Sophistic," the revival of rhetoric in the Greek-speaking world under Roman rule in the second and fourth centuries CE. His theology is conveyed in the form of orations, poems, and letters. It is largely rhetorical in form and pastoral in function. Its content focuses on the proclamation and defense of the doctrine of the Trinity, of the God made manifest in the economy of salvation, and especially in the incarnation and the gift of the Spirit, in respect of human beings as microcosms of the spiritual and material realms.

Hans Frei, by contrast, was a Jewish convert to Christian faith and an immigrant from Nazi Germany to the United States of America, who settled there with his parents in the late 1930s and was drawn into academic theological study through the influence of another immigrant, the theologian H. Richard Niebuhr, who became his doctoral supervisor. Frei's world was that of the largely secular modern university, one in which the academic study of religion was formally and institutionally distinguished from the training of people for Christian ministry. His concerns have to do with the nature of Christian theology in the modern world, and with its intellectual history, but also with the teaching and formation of theologians and the relationship of Christian theology to its institutional academic context. His theology is largely in the form of commentary upon other theologies (with the exception of *The Identity of Jesus Christ*), and is often set forth in dense, difficult formulations. Jesus Christ is its principal concern, and how theology may be constituted in relation to

---

20. On Gregory's life, see John McGuckin, *Saint Gregory of Nazianzus: An Intellectual Biography* (Crestwood, NY: St. Vladimir's Seminary Press, 2001); Christopher Beeley, "Introduction," in his *Gregory of Nazianzus on the Trinity and the Knowledge of God: In Your Light We See Light* (New York: Oxford University Press, 2008), 1–62; Jean Bernardi's more introductory *Saint Grégoire de Nazianze: Le Théologien et son temps (330–390)*, (Paris: Éditions du Cerf, 1995); and Paul Gallay's classic, *La vie de saint Grégoire de Nazianze* (Paris: Emmanuel Vitte, 1943). On Frei's biography, see John F. Woolverton, "Hans W. Frei in Context: A Theological and Historical Memoir," *Anglican Theological Review* 79, no. 3 (1997): 369–93; Mike Higton, *Christ, Providence and History: Hans W. Frei's Public Theology* (London: T. & T. Clark, 2004), 15–20; Paul J. DeHart, *The Trial of Witnesses: The Rise and Decline of Postliberal Theology* (Oxford: Blackwell, 2006), 1–31.

other disciplines and to the scriptural text so as to attend to him as rendered to us in the stories of the New Testament about him. In connection with this concern, he seeks also to articulate a Christocentric theology of history and an account of how Christian theologians ought to exercise a public function, especially in his own context of the United States, its fragile power, and its global responsibilities.

Despite these marked differences, however, Gregory and Frei share some significant similarities, especially in relation to the theology of history and the theology of Scripture. Both understand history to be providentially governed without prejudice to creaturely freedom. They each have high Christologies that emphasize the oneness of Jesus Christ, divine and human, and make him the center of human (and cosmic) history. Both, furthermore, understand the nature and function of Holy Scripture in relation to the presence of Jesus Christ by way of the text of Scripture. For both, this account of Scripture relies on an understanding of divine action as so transcending creaturely interactions and freedoms as to ground and order them without competing with them, and yet in ways that exceed our understanding or full explanatory capabilities.

These broad similarities make possible a constructive dialogue between the theologians in respect of the challenges posed by historical consciousness to the theology of Scripture. In this dialogue I analyze Gregory's theology first, and draw out lines of thought and theological strategies for addressing those challenges. I then show how, in his own way, Frei pursues similar lines of thought, similar strategies. Gregory thus appears to "prefigure," in a premodern way and without anachronism, a strategy that can with modification be applied to a historically conscious theology of Scripture. Frei instantiates that strategy in chastened terms, in ways that explicitly take account of the challenge of historical consciousness. The virtue of combining their accounts, besides showing a significant measure of similarity across very different conceptualities and forms of theological writing, does not lie therefore in a simple application of premodern theology to modern theological problems. The particular way Frei realizes the strategies he and Gregory broadly share enables him to address those problems in ways Gregory's thought cannot. Yet the similarities allow Gregory's thought and practice to suggest ways of supplementing and enriching Frei's approach, so that by placing their accounts alongside one another we begin to see possibilities that combine their strengths without blurring their differences.

It would have been possible to undertake such an exercise with a number of patristic exegetes, and Gregory is not especially known for his exegesis. He is, however, known for the excellence not only of his theology but also of his rhetoric, and it is his understanding of the rhetorical character of the exposition of Scripture and his exemplification of its use in rhetoric that make him especially useful here.[21] For a historically conscious theology of Scripture, I will argue, ought to emphasize the significance of such rhetorical mediation.

Chapters 2 and 3, therefore, draw out from Gregory's orations his theology of history, providentially ordered, shaped by God's saving action centered upon the incarnation and drawing human beings into participation with that saving action in Jesus Christ by the incorporative work of the Spirit. Chapters 4, 5, and 6 analyze Gregory's theology of Scripture as the textual embodiment of Christ in his teachings, the way he understands those teachings as inscribed in the letter of the text and drawn from it in a movement conforming to the dynamics of God's action in history, and his account and practice of the deployment of scriptural pedagogy through Christian rhetoric. Chapter 7 turns to Frei's theology of history as providentially ordered in Jesus Christ in all its creaturely contingency and complexity, and suggests several ways of taking it forward in light of Gregory's pneumatology and concerns with divine pedagogy and persuasion and human transformation. Chapter 8 completes the argument by examining Frei's theology of Scripture in its connection to his theology of Scripture in virtue of his Christocentric account of Christian reading and of the truth of Scripture, and again proposes similar theological modifications in light of Gregory. I conclude by arguing that a truly historically conscious theology of Scripture ought to seek the rhetorical mediation of the significance of Jesus Christ for particular contexts and situations.

III

This account thus offers a contribution to wider debates about the theology and theological interpretation of Scripture in respect of the problems raised for that project by modern historical consciousness. In virtue of the approach taken here, however, it also makes contributions to three further fields of inquiry.

First, it extends our understanding of Gregory's theology of Scripture and how it relates to his use of Scripture in the orations. There is no developed account of this topic, though there are a number of studies and surveys of Gregory's exegesis. Many of these treat Gregory in terms of the somewhat tired categories of literal, typological, and allegorical interpretation or related terms.

21. See George A. Kennedy, *Greek Rhetoric under Christian Emperors* (Princeton: Princeton University Press, 1983), 215: Gregory was the "most important figure in the synthesis of classical rhetoric and Christianity." He adds that Gregory is rightly regarded "as the greatest Greek orator since Demosthenes" in his *New History of Classical Rhetoric* (Princeton: Princeton University Press, 1994), 261.

Here Gregory is variously characterized as an exponent, even an apologist, of Origen's Alexandrian allegorical "method."[22] Sometimes this description is qualified by reference to his recourse to typology.[23] Sometimes Gregory is seen as more typological than allegorical in approach and hence betraying the influence of the school of Antioch.[24] Others see him pursuing a middle path between literalism and overspeculative allegorism or between Alexandrian and Antiochene traditions.[25] Richard Hanson's praise of Gregory's relatively "realistic" doctrinal exegesis also belongs to this outlook on patristic exegesis.[26] More recently, scholars have begun to move beyond using these categories to summarize early Christian use of the Bible in general, and Gregory's in particular. While Origen's influence continues to be noted, what Gregory takes from Origen is not only a lively figural imagination and an aversion to literalism (Brian Daley observes), but a concern for the reader's participation in the world disclosed by Scripture; Gregory understood exegesis to be concerned with healing and transformation of the hearer.[27] Daley also notes how Gregory's scriptural allusions are intrinsic to the rhetoric of his orations.[28] Similarly Frances Young, who has done so much to advance the study of patristic exegesis

22. So Robert Grant, *A Short History of the Interpretation of the Bible* (London: A. & C. Black, 1965), 97–98, cited in K. Demoen, *Pagan and Biblical Exempla in Gregory of Nazianzen: A Study in Rhetoric and Hermeneutics* (Turnhout, Belgium: Brepols, 1996), 250–51; Jean Pépin, *Mythe et allégorie: Les origines grecques et les contestations judeo-chrétiennes* (Paris: Études Augustiniennes, 1976).

23. So Demoen, *Pagan and Biblical Exempla*.

24. Rosemary Radford Ruether, *Gregory of Nazianzus, Rhetor and Philosopher* (Oxford: Clarendon, 1969).

25. J. Plagnieux, *Saint Grégoire de Nazianze Théologien* (Paris: Éditions Franciscaines, 1951), 39ff.; P. Gallay, "La Bible dans l'oeuvre de Grégoire de Nazianze le Théologien," in *Le monde grec ancien et la Bible*, vol. 1, ed. C. Mondésert (Paris: Beauchesne, 1984), 313–34.

26. In his "Biblical Exegesis in the Early Church," in *The Cambridge History of the Bible*, vol. 1, ed. P. R. Ackroyd and C. F. Evans (Cambridge: Cambridge University Press, 1970), 442, and his "The Interpretation of the Bible in the Early Church," in R. P. C. and A. C. Hanson, *The Bible without Illusions* (London: SCM, 1989), 30. Arguably Donald Winslow's critique of Gregory's Christological exegesis as bifurcating the divinity and humanity of Christ belongs here too. See his "Christology and Exegesis in the Cappadocians," *Church History: Studies in Christianity and Culture* 40, no. 4 (1971): 389–96.

27. Brian Daley, "Walking Through the Word: Gregory of Nazianzus as a Biblical Interpreter," in *The Word Leaps the Gap*, ed. J. Ross Wagner et al. (Grand Rapids: Eerdmans, 2008), 514–31. Pierre C. Bouteneff likewise treats Gregory as a critical student of Origen's theological hermeneutics in his *Beginnings: Ancient Christian Readings of the Biblical Creation Narratives* (Grand Rapids: Baker, 2008), 140–51. Frederick Norris notes the communal and confessional context that shapes Gregory's exegesis, and its sacramental quality, in his "Gregory Nazianzen: Constructing and Constructed by Scripture," in *The Bible in Greek Antiquity*, ed. P. Blowers (Notre Dame: University of Notre Dame Press, 1997), 149–62.

in its complex concerns, contexts, and various procedures, observes in Oration 1 a highly developed and subtle "intertextuality," for which the categories of literal, typological, and allegorical are inadequate.[29] The reading of Gregory presented here extends those insights through close study of his use of Scripture in connection with Gregory's theology of Scripture and his hermeneutics.

Second, it also extends our understanding of Hans Frei's theology of Scripture. Many accounts of Frei treat him as a foil for alternative theological constructions. In such accounts, Frei is often taken to propose an account of Scripture in which the text is self-referential, or even to propose an anti-realist account of theology, or which at least fails to secure adequately the reference to historical events and transcendent realities intended in the text.[30] Several excellent works have adequately refuted these claims in the course of advancing our understanding of Frei as a theologian with a profound interest in history, among other concerns. George Hunsinger rightly traces how Frei's analysis of Jesus' identity leads to the assertion of his risen presence, as a self-warranting fact, in the context of Frei's nonapologetic description of the logic of Christian belief as an alternative to modern liberal theologies, while raising questions as to whether Frei needed a higher Christology.[31] More significant still is Mike Higton's *Christ, Providence and History*, which successfully argues that Frei offers a Christocentric theological account of history.[32] Here Christianity has a proper historical consciousness of its own, one that emerges from who Jesus is in the

28. As Paul Gallay had observed in his earlier "La Bible dans l'oeuvre de Grégoire de Nazianze le Théologien," 321.

29. Frances Young, *Biblical Interpretation and the Formation of Christian Culture* (Cambridge: Cambridge University Press, 1997), 195.

30. Scholars troubled about a lack of concern for reference include: Brevard Childs, *Biblical Theology of the Old and New Testaments* (London: SCM, 1992), 19; Francis Schüssler Fiorenza, "History and Hermeneutics," in *Modern Christian Thought: The Twentieth Century,* ed. James Livingstone, F. Schüssler Fiorenza, Sarah Coakley, and James H. Evans (Minneapolis: Fortress Press, 2006), 376; Mark I. Wallace, *The Second Naiveté: Barth, Ricoeur, and the New Yale Theology* (Macon, GA: Mercer University Press, 1990), 104–9; Francis Watson, *Text Church and World* (Edinburgh: T. & T. Clark, 1994), 25–29. Francesca Aran Murphy seems to take Frei for an anti-realist in her *God Is Not a Story: Realism Revisited* (Oxford: Oxford University Press, 2007), 113ff.

31. "Hans Frei as Theologian: The Quest for a Generous Orthodoxy," *Modern Theology* 8, no. 2 (1992): 103–28. In his reply, John Webster argues that Frei's Christology is high but needs more explicit statement by way of a more developed conceptuality ("Response to George Hunsinger," *Modern Theology* 8, no. 2 [1992]: 129–32). See also the excellent analysis in Charles L. Campbell's *Preaching Jesus: New Directions for Homiletics in Hans Frei's Postliberal Theology* (Grand Rapids: Eerdmans, 1997), to which I am indebted in the conclusion to this book.

32. *Christ, Providence and History: Hans Frei's Public Theology* (London: T. & T. Clark, 2004).

gospel narratives: at once immersed in history and just so identified in unity with God in bodily resurrection.[33] His identity is inclusive of all others through the relation of fulfillment to figure. This relation preserves the distinction between them and the historicity, unsubstitutability, and contingency of both; its display allows us to see the public world in which humans are situated as agents in its secularity as mysteriously providentially governed and directs us to careful, progressive political engagement in it. My own argument is in substantial agreement with and indebted to Higton's analysis, though I seek to show that Frei can be seen to address Troeltsch's principle of correlation, which seems to go to the heart of the challenge of history.

Higton also gives a useful overview of Frei's theology of Scripture as being concerned to clarify the resilience at the heart of the scriptural text, found in the narrative portrayal of Jesus of Nazareth, and grounded in a Barth-like doctrine of the Word.[34] Jason A. Springs has argued more forcefully that Frei's moves to frame reading Scripture in social, practical terms are grounded in a Barthian doctrine of revelation.[35] It is God's use of the scriptural witness to mediate Christ's presence that gives rise to embodied practices, to which the theologian must attend. Such arguments are in sharp contrast to those of Mark Alan Bowald and Richard Topping who, while sympathetic readers of Frei, fault him for not realizing the need for a more thoroughgoing or explicit theological approach to Scripture and its interpretation. Frei's account suffers, they argue, from not making divine agency prior to and all-encompassing of human processes involved in the production and reception of the scriptural text.[36] I take the side of Higton and Springs and seek to show in more detail the thoroughly theological character of Frei's account of Scripture, but more importantly to connect his theology of Scripture with his theology of history in order to show its potential for addressing the issues raised by historical consciousness for the theology of Scripture. In doing so I seek to take account of important (and surely related) critiques made by John David Dawson and David Demson, namely that Frei fails to attend sufficiently to the transformation of

33. Another useful correction to misreadings of Frei on the historicity of the resurrection can be found in Jason A. Springs, *Toward a Generous Orthodoxy: Prospects for Hans Frei's Postliberal Theology* (Oxford: Oxford University Press, 2010).

34. "Hans Frei," in Justin S. Holcomb, *Christian Theologies of Scripture: A Comparative Introduction* (New York: New York University Press, 2006), 220–39.

35. Springs, *Toward a Generous Orthodoxy*, 234.

36. So Richard R. Topping, *Revelation, Scripture, and Church: Theological Hermeneutic Thought of James Barr, Paul Ricoeur and Hans Frei* (Aldershot: Ashgate, 2007); Mark Alan Bowald, *Rendering the Word in Theological Hermeneutics: Mapping Divine and Human Agency* (Aldershot: Ashgate, 2007).

disciples and that he fails to specify adequately the relation between Jesus and the disciples, and in relation to them all the rest of us.[37]

Finally, by combining Gregory and Frei, I make a contribution to the particular venture of drawing on premodern theology and theological exegesis of Scripture—and patristic forms in particular—for the theological interpretation of Scripture in the present. There have been several important contributions to this subfield, combining careful analysis of early Christian thought and practice on Scripture with the elucidation of its possibilities for the present.[38] However, most of these do not seem to take account of the challenge of modern historical consciousness to the theological interpretation of Scripture and to the recovery of premodern approaches. In its concern with the theme of history, the present work shares a significant measure of common concern with Matthew Levering's *Participatory Biblical Exegesis*.[39] While I also share common concepts with his argument—especially divine pedagogy and history as participation—Levering's reframing of history as participation in the economy of salvation fails to grapple with the challenge posed by Troeltsch.

In formal terms, the present project also resembles David Dawson's *Christian Figural Reading*. He draws critically but constructively on Frei to view Christian figural readings of scriptural texts as extensions of their literal meaning. Such readings do not entail the erasure of the identity of Jewish readers or Jewish ways of reading. Frei's understanding of figural reading is in turn challenged by Origen's more fully developed account of the reader's transformation. Dawson leaves the contrast between Frei's high Christology and low account of the reader's transformation, on the one hand, and Origen's more developed account of the reader's transformation premised on a less absolute distinction between Christ and the disciple, on the other, unresolved. I seek to reconcile a high Christology and an account of readerly transformation

37. See David Demson, *Hans Frei and Karl Barth: Different Ways of Reading Scripture* (Grand Rapids: Eerdmans, 1997); J. David Dawson, *Christian Figural Readers and the Fashioning of Identity* (Berkeley, Los Angeles, London: University of California Press, 2002).

38. See, for example, Andrew Louth, *Discerning the Mystery: An Essay on the Nature of Theology* (Oxford: Clarendon, 1989), or David Steinmetz's famous article, "The Superiority of Pre-Critical Exegesis," in *The Theological Interpretation of Scripture: Classic and Contemporary Readings*, ed. Stephen E. Fowl (Oxford: Blackwell, 1997), 26–38; Robert Louis Wilken, "In Defense of Allegory," in L. Gregory Jones and James J. Buckley, *Theology and Scriptural Imagination* (Oxford: Blackwell, 1998), 35–50; Graham Ward, "Allegoria: Reading as a Spiritual Exercise," *Modern Theology* 15, no. 3 (1999): 271–95; Jason Byassee, *Praise Seeking Understanding: Reading the Psalms with Augustine* (Grand Rapids: Eerdmans, 2007).

39. *Participatory Biblical Exegesis: A Theology of Biblical Interpretation* (Notre Dame: University of Notre Dame Press, 2008).

within a more developed theology of history drawn from Frei and Gregory, one that entails a more rhetorical account of the deployment of Scripture to historical human beings.

1

The Theological Interpretation of Scripture and the Question of History

The questions raised for theology by modern historical consciousness go to the very heart of Christian faith and its core tenets. For that reason they are of profound import for the doctrine of Scripture and the practice of reading Scripture theologically. Yet although the issue of history is often recognized in connection with the claims of historical criticism, these deeper questions rarely receive extensive or adequate theological investigation in recent literature on the theological interpretation of Scripture. The present chapter sets the scene for that conversation. I draw on Ernst Troeltsch's classic account of modern historiography and the challenges it poses for Christian theology to draw out the implied difficulties for the theology of Scripture. I then show how four prominent, contrasting proposals in this field, for all their other strengths, fail to adequately address these challenges, even where they acknowledge their pertinence. Brevard Childs, Sandra Schneiders, and Kevin Vanhoozer represent the most theologically developed accounts of Scripture in terms of a canonical approach to biblical theology, theological hermeneutics, and the self-communication of the triune God, respectively, which I take to be the three most prominent ways of pursuing the theology of Scripture at present. Finally, Murray Rae has offered one of the most developed responses to the challenges posed by Troeltsch for the theological interpretation of Scripture, incorporating the strengths of a wide range of theological resources. The limitations of these authors in respect of the problem posed by Troeltsch are both indicative of the need for further work and help clarify the nature of that task.

HISTORICAL METHOD AND DOGMATIC THEOLOGY: ERNST TROELTSCH

Ernst Troeltsch offers a thoroughgoing analysis of modern historical consciousness and historical method and the profound challenges of enduring significance they pose to Christian theology, not least for theology and the interpretation of the Bible.[1] A brief examination of his account of these challenges will clarify the nature of the problems they pose for the theology of Scripture and its theological interpretation today.

On Troeltsch's account, the development of historical method is one of a number of shifts that have transformed the context for modern religious thought.[2] The critical historiography that has flourished since the Enlightenment has resulted in the full development of modern historical reflection.[3] From this perspective, the history of humanity is thoroughly enmeshed with natural history—it "merges in the evolutionary history of the earth's surface"—and is inextricable from the impact of its physical contexts and its changing social life.[4] It forms "an unspeakably complex, yet altogether coherent, whole of immeasurable duration both in the past and in the future" in which we must discover ourselves and the origin and reason for our existence. When we see ourselves in this way as so thoroughly immersed in history, historical inquiry becomes a vital, existential concern.

As Troeltsch explains, modern historical inquiry evinces three interrelated methodological procedures that follow from the way of seeing history he has just articulated. The first of these is that of analogy. This procedure is based on the claim that we have a key to understanding, explaining, and reconstructing what might have happened in the past on the basis of the similarity that obtains between events we observe, both within and without

---

1. As Roy Harrisville and Walter Sundburg claim in their useful overview of his context and thought in *The Bible in Modern Culture: Baruch Spinoza to Brevard Childs*, 2nd ed. (Grand Rapids: Eerdmans, 2002), 146–68. They point, for example, to Peter Stuhlmacher, *Historical Criticism and Theological Interpretation of Scripture*, trans. R. Harrisville (London: SPCK, 1979). Edgar Krentz remarks that Troeltsch's essay "On Historical and Dogmatic Method in Theology" (discussed below) "still haunts theology," in his *The Historical-Critical Method* (London: SPCK, 1975), 55. Troeltsch is also given a prominent position in expositions of the problem of history in a number of more recent works, e.g.: C. Stephen Evans, *The Historical Christ and the Jesus of Faith: The Incarnational Narratives as History* (New York: Clarendon, 1996), 185ff.; Murray Rae, *History and Hermeneutics* (London: T. & T. Clark, 2005), 16 and 154–55. See also Gregory Dawes, *The Historical Jesus Quest: The Challenge of History to Religious Authority* (Louisville: Westminster John Knox, 2001), 196.

2. "Historiography," in *Contemporary Religious Thinkers: From Idealist Metaphysics to Existentialist Theologians*, ed. J. Macquarrie (London: SCM, 1968), 76–77.

3. "Historiography," 80–81.

4. "Historiography," 81.

ourselves. Elsewhere Troeltsch is careful to qualify this assumption. In an earlier article, "The Historical and Dogmatic Method in Theology," he explains that while allowing all possible room for difference, the principle presupposes "a common core of similarity that makes the differences comprehensible and empathy possible."[5] It likewise presupposes that we are capable of understanding the nature and function of "apparently alien situations" because of definite points of correspondence between them and us.[6] The practice of analogy, then, does not entail the reduction of all events to a homogenous mass. Indeed, the fairly minimal condition of some similarity amid possibly great diversity allows for considerable growth in experience and understanding of the kind of things that can happen in history. As Van Harvey points out, analogical reasoning draws on a scientific worldview but also on much more than that, as historians make judgments about human motives, values, institutions, political trends, and events—and, we might add, an enormous variety of social and cultural phenomena.[7] It involves a wide variety of assumptions, employed as warrants for historical judgments.[8] It does not preclude but informs an imaginative entry into the mentalities and worldviews of past human beings.[9] Such a broad, flexible account of analogy also seems to allow for a great variety of historical methods and approaches and assumptions about historical phenomena, including the great expansion of approaches and use of theoretical instruments in historiography that have flourished since Troeltsch wrote.

That flexibility is important to note, for the principle of analogy provides the basis for the practice of criticism, which involves making judgments of probability about the testimony of the traditions concerning the past that we have inherited. On the one hand, "the illusions, distortions, deceptions, myths, and partisanships we see with our own eyes enable us to recognize similar features in the material of tradition."[10] Our present experience tells us that at

5. "Historical and Dogmatic Method in Theology," in *Religion in History*, ed. James Luther Adams (Edinburgh: T. & T. Clark, 1991), 14.

6. *The Absoluteness of Christianity and the History of Religions*, trans. D. Reid (London: SCM, 1972), 89.

7. Van Harvey, *The Historian and the Believer: The Morality of Historical Knowledge and Christian Belief* (London: SCM, 1967), 78–84. So great is Harvey's debt to Troeltsch that it is hard to see how Terrence Tilley can claim that Harvey renders "the Troeltschian problematic" untenable. See his *History, Theology and Faith: Dissolving the Modern Problematic* (Maryknoll: Orbis, 2004), 48.

8. Drawn, we might add, from more than the historian's commonsense knowledge of the world, which Harvey emphasizes: sociological, anthropological, economic, psychological, psychoanalytic, linguistic, hermeneutical discoveries and theory all now inform historical judgments in various, often contested, and sometimes mutually exclusive ways.

9. Harvey, *The Historian and the Believer*, 90–91.

10. "Historical and Dogmatic Method," 13.

times testimony is not always entirely reliable and needs critical scrutiny, and that experience of scrutinizing and sifting others' reports informs our treatment of the traditions we have received.[11] On the other hand, agreement with "normal, customary, or at least frequently attested happenings and conditions as we have experienced them is the criterion of probability for all the events historical criticism can recognize as having actually or possibly happened."[12] In other words, by basing judgments of probability on present experience, broadly conceived, the historian can make affirmations about the past on a reasonable basis, without claiming to define what kind of thing can happen or what did happen in the past.[13]

Both analogy and criticism are rooted in a further underlying idea about history, the principle of correlation. As we discern similar processes at work in the past and the present and see in both "the influence and intersection of various cycles of human life," Troeltsch writes, "we gain at length an idea of an integral continuity, balanced in its changes, never at rest, and ever moving towards incalculable issues."[14] This sense of a dynamic, ordered, ever-changing continuum involves an understanding of the complex causal interconnections that embrace all events. All phenomena come about through their causal interaction with other phenomena and in turn affect other events, he writes in the earlier article, "so that all historical happening is knit together in a permanent relationship of correlation, inevitably forming a current in which everything is interconnected and each single event is related to all others."[15] The causation in question, Troeltsch explains in "Historiography," is both natural and psychological; the investigation of human motive distinguishes historical

---

11. Troeltsch is therefore not skeptical about the value of testimony.

12. "Historical and Dogmatic Method," 13–14.

13. As Van Harvey argues, this principle involves what he calls historians' "radical autonomy" and logical candor in exhibiting the grounds for their historical judgments. The judgments involved are inferential on the basis of traces of evidence, and the arguments that justify them are, as he shows, quite diverse and involve a variety of warrants so that one cannot generalize about the presuppositions of historians. See *The Historian and the Believer*, 41–62. The diversity of approaches to historiography that have mushroomed in the last forty years only underlines his point.

14. Troeltsch, "Historiography," 82.

15. "Historical and Dogmatic Method," 14. Terrence Tilley claims that Troeltsch confuses assumptions with the defeasible presumptions that guide practice; see *History, Theology and Faith*, 40. However, Troeltsch's principles seem more fundamental than presumptions: it is difficult to see how historical research would be possible without them. Historical hypotheses, however, are defeasible, though many historians have other more fundamental ideological or theoretical commitments that are more difficult to defeat.

knowledge, but is not sufficient to explain historical events, for there are other forces involved than those in the soul.[16]

Wolfhart Pannenberg accuses Troeltsch of assuming the fundamental homogeneity or uniformity underlying all historical phenomena as the basis for an "omnipotence of analogy," which constricts historical inquiry, whereas the historian who attends to the individuality, uniqueness, and contingency of events will see they are not homogenous, which cannot be comprehended entirely by the analogy.[17] This criticism seems unfair. It is certainly difficult to see how the historian, in Troeltsch's view, could affirm the probability, or make sense, of the absolutely unique, in the sense of an event without any remotely plausible analogy with other events known to us: an event unrelated to the continuum of causally correlated occurrences.[18] Nevertheless, Troeltsch does make the novel and the particular central to the method of historical knowing. The method of historical knowledge, he writes, "is determined by the object of selecting from the flux of phenomena that which is qualitatively and uniquely *individual*, whether on a larger or on a smaller scale, and of making this intelligible in its concrete and specific relations."[19] History therefore, while drawing on abstract universal laws, has to operate with the notion of the individual case. The historian has to tailor his or her explanation to the particular phenomena, rather than subordinate them simply to a general law, for such laws fail to explain its "peculiar and concrete elements."[20] Explanation attends to the individual case, therefore, which "because of their infinite complexity produce the unique."[21]

What Troeltsch calls uniqueness here is a quality of individuality: a phenomenon that cannot be wholly or adequately explained as another instance of a universal principle, whose complexity bestows on it a configuration distinct from any other. Elsewhere Troeltsch argues that the reason for such individuality has to do with involvement of the higher, creative element in the perceptions, thoughts, and desires "that accompany man as a physical entity," an autonomous element that may intervene and oppose those physically grounded tendencies, and is not reducible to universal causal principles (here Troeltsch's

16. "Historiography," 87. Here Troeltsch is correcting the unbalanced emphasis on psychology he finds in Wundt, Dilthey, Windelbrand, and Rickert.
17. "Redemptive Event and History," in Pannenberg, *Basic Questions in Theology*, vol. 1 (London: SCM, 1970), 45–47.
18. See also Dawes, *Historical Jesus Quest*, 197–98.
19. "Historiography," 88.
20. "Historiography," 88.
21. "Historiography," 88.

idealism is in evidence).[22] He stresses the interplay of natural causes and human freedom and personality.[23] It is the need to understand such phenomena that justifies historians' selectivity of the material for their inquiries.[24] Such "uniqueness," however, does not remove a phenomenon from the web of causal relations, nor is it inconsistent with some degree of similarity with other events: an event may be irreducibly individual without being wholly unlike any other, as Troeltsch argues in the earlier article.[25]

In order to make such phenomena intelligible, history works with concepts. The overarching category here is that of causality in the specific form of individual causality, but the subjects of historical inquiry are also conceptual unities: phenomena bundled under the unitive force of a concept, we might say, or "historical aggregates," as Troeltsch calls them, such as "a human life," "a nation," "the spirit of an age," "a legal constitution," "a state of affairs," or "an economic condition."[26] Included in those concepts is that of the development of such aggregates, the principle that organizes aggregates and the forces at work in them, focusing the causes toward the progressive realization of a result. Such development is capable of regress as well as progress and is subject to contingency: "the convergence of a series of mutually independent causes," including climate, atmosphere, fertility, geographical position, natural wealth, physiological events, and conditions and the distribution of individual qualities.[27]

Troeltsch's point here is significant in two ways. First, his enumeration of the concepts historians employ helpfully amplifies the sense of contingency, interconnectivity, and contextuality inherent in the vision of history he articulates. Second, he acknowledges that concepts play a constructive part in

---

22. *The Absoluteness*, 64. He links this explicitly to the topic of individuality and uniqueness on page 88. Here his idealism, his commitment to the priority of consciousness over other forms of reality, shines through. See further Dawes, *Historical Jesus Quest*, 171.

23. *The Absoluteness*, 74. On Troeltsch's concern to refute naturalism in this way, see Mark D. Chapman, *Ernst Troeltsch and Liberal Theology: Religion and Cultural Synthesis in Wilhelmine Germany* (New York: Oxford University Press), 75ff. and 111ff.

24. And as Van Harvey points out, you do not have to unravel the entire chain of causes to identify certain causal links accurately; different events have various characteristics relevant to different kinds of inquiry. See *The Historian and the Believer*, 210.

25. "Historical and Dogmatic Method," 14. This account of individuality in history and the interplay of natural causes and human freedom shows how unjustified is Tilley's claim that "[t]he Troeltschian axioms of correlation and analogy treat history as if it were a Galilean science or a subsidiary of the hard sciences." See *History, Theology and Faith*, 44.

26. "Historiography," 89.

27. "Historiography," 90–91.

producing knowledge of the past, and it seems entirely consistent with what he says to add that such concepts are themselves open to critical evaluation of the efficacy and appropriateness of their purchase on phenomena, of their explanatory power, and of their capacity to distort or obfuscate. Indeed, Troeltsch has a fine appreciation of the limitations and fallibility of the conceptual description of history, especially where historical aggregates are combined under the concept of humanity itself. Humanity can never be seen all together all at once, and so the conception of it can never be more than "an incomplete work of the imagination."[28] Historical inquiry depends not only on the existence of a tradition to be examined—the past cannot be thought about independently of traditions—but also on the imaginative and synthetic powers of the historian, which are limited. Historians cannot recompose objects in their entirety or depict them in their simultaneous interaction, but must analyze. Therefore the historian's work must ever be taken up afresh and be subject to revision. It is never complete, comprehensive, or definitive, but suffices nevertheless to enable human beings to understand themselves as far as possible or necessary, Troeltsch argues. Although historiography is now much more sophisticated and diverse in the range of approaches and theoretical commitments and tools employed, these features of Troeltsch's account evince a nuanced evaluation of the role of "theory" and the provisional, exploratory, and imaginative character of historical inquiry characteristic of recent historical research.[29]

The strength of Troeltsch's analysis of modern historiography, together with the explanatory power of that vision evident in modern historiography, is that it lends force to his examination of its consequences for Christian faith. Historical inquiry "once admitted at any point, necessarily draws everything into its train and weaves together all events into one great web of correlated effects and changes."[30] Hence the adoption of historical method entailed the task of understanding ancient Israel's history and religion, Judaism, and primitive Christianity in relation to the history of their context in the Ancient Near East. This extension of historical method to the origins of Jewish and Christian faith has several consequences for Christianity, as Troeltsch explains.

---

28. "Historiography," 89.

29. For an excellent account of which, both consonant with Troeltsch, but more sophisticated in its treatment of the role of theory, representations, and concepts, and displaying careful, informed judgments about a variety of more recent historiography, see Mary Fulbrook, *Historical Theory* (London and New York: Routledge, 2002).

30. "Historical and Dogmatic Method," 15.

First, it brings a measure of uncertainty to the facts of history, because in a sense all facts about the past are always questionable. This degree of uncertainty means the connection between "original fact" and "present influence," that is, between an event that has been taken traditionally as the origin of a religious tradition, becomes somewhat obscure.[31] It is no longer straightforward to trace Christianity back to its origins, both because the facts about those origins are subject to judgments of probability always open to revision and because the intervening causal links are likewise subject to the same kinds of judgment. The import of this shift is to loosen the connection between religious faith and any particular fact such that the former cannot any longer be based on the latter. One might reply that absolute certainty is not required for Christian faith, based as it is on a contingent event.[32] Troeltsch's next point, however, is less contestable.

Second, historical inquiry correlates "original facts" and their links with religious faith with the much larger historical context out of which they arose and in relation to which they must be understood. This move does not deny the originality of any particular fact, for, as we have seen, historical method can admit a considerable degree of irreducible individuality in historical phenomena. It does mean, however, that the originality of any particular fact "is analogous to others emerging from the same common context and is neither more nor less mysterious than these."[33] This conclusion has clear consequences for core Christian doctrines, which Troeltsch goes on to draw out next.

The thrust of the third consequence is the relativization of the origins of the Christian religion with respect to their historical context. Historical method makes historical events relative "in the sense that every historical structure and moment can be understood only in relation to others and ultimately to the total context, and that standards of values cannot be derived from isolated events but only from an overview of the historical totality."[34] The events of Christian origins, or those of ancient Israel, cannot be isolated from a wider nexus of causality, nor can they be understood as absolute exceptions to wider patterns, nor, finally, can they provide a privileged basis for values.

Much more is at stake here than the plausibility of the miraculous. Troeltsch does indeed criticize what he calls naïve appeals to revelation and miracle, which rest on a claim to immediate divine causality, on the basis that these have been made impossible by the demonstration of the "thoroughgoing

---

31. "Historical and Dogmatic Method," 17.

32. So Rae, *History and Hermeneutics*, 11–12.

33. "Historical and Dogmatic Method," 7.

34. "Historical and Dogmatic Method," 18.

continuity of the causal process."[35] As Troeltsch argues in another essay, this enmeshment of Christianity in its religious and cultural context makes the notion of Christianity as the eternal absolute center of salvation for all humanity impossible or at least highly improbable.[36] Human beings have lived for hundreds of thousands of years on earth and may live for a similar period to come. Therefore it is "hard to imagine a single point of history along this line, and that the centre-point of our own religious history, as the sole centre of all humanity."[37] Thus there is, for Troeltsch, no way from historical inquiry to anything like a traditional doctrine of the incarnation, nor even the reconstructed doctrine formulated by Schleiermacher. Any account of Jesus Christ that excepts him or elevates him above the kinds of contingent, interconnected historical causality that pertains to exceptional events elsewhere in history cannot be sustained on the basis of historical criticism.

Instead of revelation, Troeltsch seeks a way to establish normative value on the basis of historical study: values must be drawn from reflection on the whole of history.[38] Historical inquiry, Troeltsch implies, involves making ethical judgments about the past. It is thus a critical enterprise in this respect also, but problematically so, as Troeltsch's discussion of the matter in his "Historiography" essay shows. For while the historian may intuit historical tendencies toward ethical ideals, a system of ethical ideals cannot be demonstrated from history.[39] Rather, we postulate the concept of ethical development, based on the actual occurrence of the aggregates of ethical life, and under this concept we see only partial developments, both progressive and regressive. There is no ideal available apart from history by which to judge, nor an overall progress by which to measure individual instances. Instead the ideal

---

35. Troeltsch, *The Absoluteness*, 53. The same point could also be made in terms of an issue of judgments of probability given present experience as well as of analogy with miracle stories in mythical literature, rather than *a priori* exclusion on metaphysical grounds, as Harvey also argues; see *The Historian and the Believer*, 86–88. One might object that some people *do* experience divine action and the miraculous today, warranting judgments of higher probability for miracles in the past and calling Troeltsch's exclusion of God from the causal web into question. See, for example, C. Stephen Evans, *The Historical Christ and the Jesus of Faith*, 197ff. Such warrants are not shared by everyone, but the deeper issue is how to relate divine action to the causal web examined by historians.

36. Troeltsch, "The Significance of the Historical Jesus for Faith," in *Ernst Troeltsch: Writings on Theology and Religion*, ed. Robert Morgan and Michael Pye (Louisville: Westminster John Knox, 1990), 189. See also his *The Absoluteness of Christianity*.

37. "The Significance of the Historical Jesus," 189.

38. For a fuller account of Troeltsch's constructive theology and ethics, see Chapman, *Ernst Troeltsch and Liberal Theology*.

39. Troeltsch, "Historiography," 95–97.

is partially realized in individual instances, which must be judged in terms of its approximation to the absolute, post-historical end they project, a transcendent force "that actuates our deepest strivings and is connected with the creative core of reality."[40] The criteria for judgments about instances of ethical progress in historical phenomena, however, must emerge from historical research, and Troeltsch frankly acknowledges that their ultimate basis is a matter of subjective inner conviction.[41] It is not clear, therefore, how the ideals those phenomena project would have truly normative force for us, nor how stable they would be, given the openness to revision that is characteristic of historical judgments. It seems very difficult to generate normative concepts on the basis of the observations of historical inquiry so construed. Nevertheless, the recognition of the relativity of ethical ideals involved in historiography is significant.

Historical criticism and the vision of history it uncovers and instantiates have clear consequences for the Christian doctrine of Scripture and the Christian practice of scriptural interpretation. When the Scriptures are examined in light of the vision of history that Troeltsch describes and using the procedures of historical method, the effect on the theological use of the Bible is considerable. First, there is the bifurcation of the history portrayed in the Bible from reconstructions of the history of Israel's religion and political life in the Ancient Near East. Next, since making absolute claims for particular events comes to seem inherently implausible to a modern historical sensibility, the theological witness of many biblical texts is put in tension with historical consciousness. It becomes impossible to reconcile the latter with a view of the world as governed by a God who intervenes in human affairs. Judged historically impossible or improbable by historical-critical criteria, the histories and theologies related in the Bible, one of Troeltsch's predecessors famously argued, are best understood as products of the primitive imaginative mentalities of the communities in which they arose, even when the form of narrative is apparently historical.[42]

For the same reason, historical consciousness also challenges any attempt to talk of God acting through Scripture or in respect of the formation or interpretation of Scripture and any attempt to view the modern world through

40. See also *The Absoluteness*, 91ff., 100. In this way, Troeltsch clearly distinguishes himself from Hegel's historical teleology. Troeltsch's key formula here is the claim that in the relative "we will find an indication of the unconditional." Ibid., 106.

41. *The Absoluteness*, 97ff.

42. See D. F. Strauss, *The Life of Jesus Critically Examined*, trans. George Eliot, ed. Peter C. Hodgson (London: SCM, 1973), Introduction. See especially §16. Strauss's notion of history here is broadly similar to Troeltsch's.

a scriptural lens. It will, moreover, be very difficult to ground normative concepts or values in the text, seen in its historical context, or in the events to which it bears witness. Indeed, the biblical text and the history to which it attests become subject to ethical evaluations based on revisable historical judgments about ethical developments across human history, with no privileged place for the history attested in the Bible.

At the bottom of all these problems, then, is the question posed to Christian theology by historical method: as Hans Frei put it, whether it is possible "to combine faith in an ultimate Creator and Redeemer, who limits space and time beyond all conceiving, with the 'open-ended' and in its way uniform historical universe which historical consciousness presents to us?"[43] Although other challenges have arisen besides historical consciousness, this question still seems as vital as ever, and as relevant in a culture still fascinated by the past and imbued with the basic pattern of thinking Troeltsch described and the historical relativism that often goes with it. It is this question as it impacts the theological interpretation of Scripture in the ways just described, that seems little discussed in recent literature in that field, as the following case studies indicate.

BREVARD CHILDS

The first of these is Brevard Childs's "canonical approach" to biblical theology, conceived as a bridging discipline between biblical exegesis and dogmatic theology. Here my focus will be on Childs's massive *Biblical Theology of the Old and New Testaments*, a programmatic summary of his position and an enormously erudite primer for the kind of biblical theology he advocated.[44] Childs advocates the hermeneutical significance of attending to the canonical shaping of the final form of the biblical text and canon in the service of discovering the divine will attested in and disclosed through Scripture. Yet, although Childs has something to say about divine action in the world and in respect of Scripture, his proposals are not very clear on the relationship between the all-encompassing action of God attested in Scripture and the world presented by historical consciousness. While he insists that the biblical texts attest divine action in space and time, on the one hand, and upholds

43. Hans Frei, "Niebuhr's Theological Background," in *Faith and Ethics: The Theology of H. Richard Niebuhr*, ed. Paul Ramsey (New York: Harper Torchbooks, 1957), 24.

44. Paul Noble notes that this work implements Childs's proposals to their fullest extent and that in it his work reaches a "natural completeness." See Noble, *The Canonical Approach: A Critical Reconstruction of the Hermeneutics of Brevard S. Childs* (Leiden/New York/Köln: E. J. Brill, 1995), 2.

some critical historical reconstructions on the other, he leaves the relationship between them ambiguous, suspended in an apparently irresolvable tension between two diverse perspectives.

For Childs, the biblical witnesses of both Testaments attest in different ways the one divine reality of Jesus Christ and are thus vehicles of the Spirit's testimony and the revelation of God's will. Their voice thus speaks to us today.[45] The task of biblical theology, therefore, is to understand the various voices within the whole Christian Bible as witnesses to the one Lord Jesus Christ, "the selfsame divine reality."[46] The canonical shaping of those witnesses, both at the level of the redaction of textual traditions and the composition of the canon, provides guidelines for apprehending its normative force.[47] These are traditions and texts passed on in such a way as to facilitate their religious function.[48] Thus the norm of communities who treasure the canon lies in the literature itself rather than reconstructed stages of its development.[49] To understand it means following the witnesses to the reality they attest-a theological reading in the mode of faith seeking understanding of Christ in the Spirit. This begins with hearing each Testament in its integrity, to grasp their partial grasp of reality, in order to understand the witness of each in light of the other and both in light of Christ himself.[50]

---

45. Childs, *Biblical Theology*; see e.g. pp. 8–9 (where he speaks of the Bible as the vehicle of God's will); for other uses of witness in this sense, see e.g. 20, 64, 74, 77–78, 83, 85, 91–93, 97, 105, 185, 215, 317, 226, 262ff., 333–34, 336, 344–45, 379–80, 520–21, 536, 551, 580, 721. See also 671 and 714, where he expresses approval of Barth's notion that "the Bible functions as the unique vehicle by which we're brought face-to-face with the person of God and the revelation of his will," and 87 on the role of the Spirit in knowledge of God. On the texts as speaking today, see 215 and 671. On Christ as subject matter of biblical witness, see 85 and 721.

46. *Biblical Theology*, 85.

47. *Biblical Theology*, 714.

48. *Biblical Theology*, 70–71. Childs instances the redaction of the parables in the Synoptics, the placing of Deuteronomy at the end of the Pentateuch as commentary on the rest of the Law, and the joining of the two Testaments with the prophets moved to the end of the Old to function as witnesses to the coming Christ (*Biblical Theology*, 343 and 71; on the joining of the Testaments, see 74–78).

49. *Biblical Theology*, 71. This claim is a key one for Childs's whole approach, yet it is not at all evident how Childs's broadly conceived doctrine of Scripture authorizes the normative status of canonical shaping as opposed to other features of the texts, including earlier levels of the textual traditions. Cf. Noble, *The Canonical Approach*, 48, speaking of Childs's *Introduction to the Old Testament as Scripture* (London: SCM, 1979): "it is far from clear why priority should still be accorded to the canonical form," especially when critical reconstruction uncovers the influence of factors like political infighting, poor historiographical method, misunderstandings of the material, or "sheer antiquarianism" in the formation of biblical traditions.

The subject of the biblical witnesses is, by and large, a history, but a history that evokes a responsive testimony in often nonhistoriographical terms. So Childs writes that it is compatible with the Old Testament's canonical structure to describe its witness to God's redemptive will in the context of the history of Israel, for Israel was the texts' original addressee and tradent. The witness of the Old Testament was made with constant reference to Israel's history, and a fundamental characteristic of that witness is the "once-for-all" quality of these historical events in chronological sequence, namely the revelatory events of creation, the call of Abraham, the exodus, the encounter with God at Sinai, the possession of the land, the monarchy, the destruction of Jerusalem, the exile and restoration.[51] Yet peculiar features of God's revelation in Israel's history resulted in a "far more complicated and intensified form of biblical response" in three respects.[52] First, the quality of happenings takes precedence over chronology; second, the beginning and end of human history are set within God's purposes; third, Israel's life is recorded also in terms of institutions, rules, and a cultic calendar. Furthermore, Israel's witness to these events was preserved in living traditions that were shaped and reshaped by subsequent generations of tradents, whereby some foundational happenings were reinterpreted with a view to the present or future and others consigned to unrepeatable occurrence in the past. Hence biblical theology must describe "the theological functions of the great revelatory events in Israel's history and their subsequent appropriation by the tradition."[53] In the same way, Childs asserts that it is compatible with canonical structure to describe the New Testament's witness as pointing to God's redemption through Jesus Christ in the context of the early church, specifically to Jesus Christ's life, death, and resurrection and the effect of this good news on the formation of the church.[54] This witness arose from a revolutionary encounter with the risen Lord. Hence the New Testament's witness is related to a particular history. It is "grounded in the historical concreteness of Jesus Christ at a particular time in Palestine."[55]

---

50. *Biblical Theology*, 75, compare 83 and 265. Childs comments that biblical language may "resonate in a new and creative fashion when read from the vantage point of a fuller understanding of Christian truth," provided the canonical restraints of the canonical shaping of the text and its historical voice are preserved (pp. 87, 334–36, and 379–80).

51. *Biblical Theology*, 91–92.

52. *Biblical Theology*, 92.

53. *Biblical Theology*, 92.

54. *Biblical Theology*, 93.

55. *Biblical Theology*, 93.

The Old Testament history that biblical theology examines, then, is Israel's "canonical history," its testimony to God's redemptive action.[56] This historical witness is distinguished by its perspective on historical reality, which is not a neutral, "objective" perspective, but a theological perspective, viewed from a confessional stance within a community of faith.[57] For Israel's history involves "both divine and human agency."[58] The Old Testament God "is continually described as an agent in history who speaks and acts, who directs and communicates his will."[59]

According to Childs, a "subtle relationship" obtains between this perspective and that of nonconfessional historiography of ancient Israel, with its impressive claims and sophisticated methodology. At times Israel's confessional witness overlaps fully with a common public testimony and a confirmation of events can be elicited from even foreign and hostile nations, for example, the destruction of Jerusalem in the sixth century. At other times, there is virtually no relation between Israel's witness and extrabiblical sources. The challenge for theology, he adds, is to exegete such passages without recourse to "the rationalistic assumption of a common reality behind all religious expression or the threat of super-naturalism which would deny in principle any relation between an outer and inner side of history."[60] It must also be recognized that the canonical history of Israel is aware of a genuine past, recognizes elements of historical contingency, and "has a clear grasp of growth and change in the history of one nature," but at the same time it oscillates between past, present, and future, introducing the writers and their audience into the history and aligning events typologically, or restructuring them by an eschatological perspective as manifestations of God's righteous rule.[61] Israel's canonical history is also selective in its treatment of material, not only in what it places in the foreground but also in what it omits, represses, or consigns to the margins or blurry background.

In this way, Childs seems to bring to the fore the kind of problems highlighted by reading Troeltsch and formulated by Frei: how faith in an ultimate Creator and Redeemer—the God attested as acting in history by Israel's traditions—may be combined with the world as historical consciousness presents it. Childs speaks of the "genuine dialectical tension" between the

---

56. *Biblical Theology*, 97.

57. *Biblical Theology*, 100.

58. *Biblical Theology*, 100.

59. *Biblical Theology*, 100.

60. *Biblical Theology*, 98.

61. *Biblical Theology*, 101.

two perspectives, although he also recognizes that the term "dialectical" is problematic, and may be a sign of the lack of a comprehensive philosophical or hermeneutical system to integrate the problems arising from the historical-critical method.[62] Indeed, it is not clear what kind of dialectic Childs finds between canonical history and the findings of historical-critical research on ancient Israel. It would be clearer simply to speak of a tension between them, one that Childs does not attempt to resolve. The tension is all the more strained because Childs relies on the findings of critical historical research on ancient Israel for a kind of investigation of the history of the textual traditions, the history that elucidates the decisions that produced the final form of the text, which Childs treats as hermeneutically significant. It is theologically illuminating, he holds, to understand why different groups responsible for the redaction of certain texts found earlier traditions normative and to grasp what was the effect of their preservation in later textual configurations. Such understanding is also hermeneutically important because to some extent the final form of the texts reflects qualities of earlier traditions in their original life.[63]

This tension between the history projected by the textual witness and the history of Israel as reconstructed through critical historiography is evident in Childs's treatment of particular biblical books, for example between the testimony of the earliest stage of tradition in the book of Joshua, together with the evidence of archaeology, and the witness of the Deuteronomistic redaction of Joshua.[64] To say, as Childs does with Gerhard von Rad, that faith has mastered the material so that it is seen from within and the late picture is shaped and supported by a zeal for the glory of Yahweh seems to clarify little.[65] Later he remarks that the shaping of the Pentateuch "resulted in a conscious theological construal of the giving and receiving of the law which often ran roughshod over the actual historical sequence of this process."[66]

Childs is unambiguous about his commitment to the historicity of certain elements of the biblical witness. He asserts that "[i]t is basic to Christian theology to reckon with an extra-biblical reality, namely with the resurrected Christ who evoked the New Testament witness."[67] Elsewhere in the book he claims that in Jesus Christ, "God himself entered our concrete history as God-with-us."[68] His position is to try to hold on to both the witness of the biblical

62. *Biblical Theology*, 101, 99.
63. *Biblical Theology*, 105.
64. See *Biblical Theology*, 143ff.
65. *Biblical Theology*, 146.
66. *Biblical Theology*, 535.
67. *Biblical Theology*, 20. He makes a similar point on 665.

texts to canonical history without denying plausible historical reconstructions, even when the two run counter to one another. Time and again he stresses the need to take the witnesses seriously as such by treating them theologically: they offer a different perspective that is lost when subjected to historical method. In the end, this stance only returns us to the problems raised by Troeltsch and to Frei's question.

The notion that the biblical witnesses offer a distinctive perspective needing theological analysis and evince a historical sensibility of their own suggests that they may have something to offer, even when at odds with historical reconstructions of the past, but Childs does not explore these possibilities (as Frei does).[69] In the end, Childs does not transcend the bifurcation of the history related by biblical texts and reconstructions of Israel's religious and political history in its Ancient Near Eastern context. Since he upholds both historical method and the scriptural witness to a sovereign God, he affirms both sides of the problem Frei summarizes, but without attempting to show how commitments to both might be combined—and the unresolved issue of the theological implications of historical consciousness must surely trouble his account of the text as the vehicle of divine revelation and its normativity for Christian communities.

Sandra Schneiders

In *The Revelatory Text*, Sandra Schneiders writes from the Roman Catholic tradition, with a view to the liberation of women readers of the New Testament.[70] Like Childs, she wishes to transcend a purely historical-critical approach to Scripture in this interest; like him she focuses on the final form of the canonical text. She wishes to give an account of interpretation that recovers the spiritual function of Scripture for marginalized and oppressed readers, feminists especially, while fully acknowledging the need for ideological criticism of its contents. The result is a sophisticated account that acknowledges historical consciousness and implicitly recognizes the issues it raises yet fails adequately to address them. These problems first come to light in her treatment of the metaphor "Word of God."

---

68. *Biblical Theology*, 520.

69. On the Bible's recognition of features of historical existence and the social structures of human life, see *Biblical Theology*, 101, 575–80.

70. *The Revelatory Text: Interpreting the New Testament as Sacred Scripture* (Collegeville, MN: Liturgical Press, 1999).

"Word of God," Schneiders explains, is a root metaphor by which we refer to the reality of divine self-revelation, God's accepted self-gift to human beings.[71] Personal revelation, she argues, is personal self-disclosure, inviting another into one's interiority, with the goal of a shared life characterized by irrevocable commitment. It is "mutual self-gift expressive of and terminating in love."[72] With human beings, this self-disclosure takes place through language, which, because it is symbolic, has the capacity to disclose being, even divine being. A symbol is a "mode of presence of something that cannot be encountered in any other way."[73] It participates directly in the presence and power of the reality it symbolizes, thus embodying and so expressing a reality it can never fully articulate, like a pinpoint of starlight shining out of a vast blackness. It is therefore ambiguous, needing interpretation yet never exhausted in any one interpretation, but inviting further engagement with the real. She stresses the mutual dependence of symbol and interpretation, casting human beings as those through whose interpretation of the symbolic force of nature and history the meaning of being is realized.

This account of self-disclosure and symbols introduces and informs Schneiders's account of divine revelation. God, she explains, is an infinitely meaningful reality, who is eternally self-expressive. In order to invite us into divine intimacy, God had to approach us symbolically. The metaphor "Word of God" embraces divine self-disclosure through symbol in nature, the life and history of Israel, and in Jesus Christ. All of human experience is meant to be revelatory in respect of God's desire for self-gift, but that desire is frustrated by human nonreceptiveness. Only in Jesus Christ "did the boundless divine desire to give encounter the fully adequate human response."[74] Hence, only in Jesus of Nazareth "do we see an entire human existence so fully actualized by the divine self-gift that we can affirm that he *is* Word of God (i.e., revelation) incarnate."[75] Jesus in his person, work, and paschal mystery is thus the paradigmatic instance of divine revelation. He is "symbolic revelation fully achieved."[76] The Scriptures belong to this economy of revelation; they bring to symbolic disclosure in written discourse "that which is primordially disclosed in Jesus Christ."[77]

71. *The Revelatory Text*, 34.
72. *The Revelatory Text*, 34.
73. *The Revelatory Text*, 35.
74. *The Revelatory Text*, 53.
75. *The Revelatory Text*, 45.
76. *The Revelatory Text*, 53.
77. *The Revelatory Text*, 53.

We should note that Schneiders is working with a weaker notion of scriptural authority and its formative power than Childs, since for her revelation and Scripture as its symbolic attestation depend on human interpretation for their realization. "Symbolic revelation is characteristic of a God who offers and invites but does not compel response," she claims.[78] Revelation has a disclosive, relative authority, like appeals of the beautiful to aesthetic response, of a suffering human being to compassion, of a parent to filial piety, of a loving rebuke from a true friend to a hearing, or even to a repentant response and conversion. Normativity, on this view, is "the ever-developing guiding influence on our thought and action of an ever-deepening familiarity with God in Jesus."[79] The semantic meaning of the text symbolically discloses what Paul Ricoeur calls new possible ways of seeing and being in the world for the reader to actualize.[80]

The meaning of a text, distanced from the original writer, audience, and context by being written, is a function of the dialectic between its semantic sense and its reference or truth-claim (which may be manifold and complex). That dialectic in itself constitutes, she argues, the ideal meaning of the text, which must be realized in any act of interpretation and so supplies a criterion for valid interpretation. To establish this ideal meaning is the function of exegesis and criticism—historical, literary (especially structuralist), and ideological criticism all help here.[81] The ideal meaning of the text norms and is realized in an endless variety of possible interpretations, like the numerous performances of a musical score or dramatic script. Like them, the Bible "creates a world with its own dynamics," into which the reader is drawn to find her identity.[82] Yet the text needs interpretation in order to find its voice in new circumstances. Interpretation is a dialectic between clarifying sense and reference and appropriating content as an expansion of one's being. Schneiders describes this act of appropriation as an experience of conversion through participation in the possible world projected by the text, in which one accepts the new self, the new way of seeing the world and acting in it, which the text discloses.[83] Such appropriation, she adds, involves a passage through the critical scrutiny of the text's relation to its subject matter, its structures, strategies, and relations

---

78. *The Revelatory Text*, 55.

79. *The Revelatory Text*, 58.

80. *The Revelatory Text*, 167–68. See also Ricoeur, *Interpretation Theory Discourse and the Surplus of Meaning* (Fort Worth: Texas Christian University Press, 1976), 87–88, 91–95.

81. *The Revelatory Text*, 143–47.

82. *The Revelatory Text*, 150.

83. *The Revelatory Text*, 167–68.

to power agendas, to protect the reader from premature appropriation of its harmful ideologies, to a "second naïveté," an aesthetic surrender to the world disclosed by the text beyond its ideological truth-claims.[84]

This account of interpretation seems to recognize the historicity of readers in allowing for multiple possible realizations of the text's ideal meaning. Yet the Christocentric character of Schneiders's account of revelation invites criticism in light of Troeltsch's account of historical consciousness and method. By making divine action here coextensive with human experience, Schneiders avoids the problems of reconciling a more interventionist account of divine action with historical consciousness. Nevertheless, she does not discuss how such an account of divine action might be consistent with a historical view of human beings. Furthermore, it is difficult to reconcile the exceptional status granted Jesus here in virtue of his unique receptivity to divine self-disclosure with the principles of historical method as articulated by Troeltsch. It seems unlikely that Jesus' unique capacity is really consistent with his historicity, his location in the same kind of causal web as the rest of us.[85]

Such a problem would have immediate consequences for a Christocentric theology of Scripture such as Schneiders has set forth. Her account of the symbolic character of Jesus' revelatory function seems to side-step such issues, moreover, in a problematic way. If Jesus is the full instantiation of symbolic revelation and if symbols work to disclose a greater depth *beyond* themselves, then Jesus' humanity will be merely a sign gesturing to something beyond itself, to which his historical particularity will be quite secondary.[86] This conclusion seems to be borne out by Schneiders's approach to the interpretation of the Gospels. She is able to acknowledge the historical origins of the Gospels, their relation to a particular time, context, and to certain cultural influences, and the historical character of much of their content, by which she means "that which takes place in space and time according to laws of cause and effect and is, at least in principle, publicly available."[87] The content of the Gospels, however,

---

84. *The Revelatory Text*, 169–77.

85. Troeltsch was concerned to rule out just this move: to grant Christianity or Jesus Christ a unique status in a suprahistorical way. See e.g. his "The Significance of the Existence of the Historical Jesus for Faith."

86. This implication seems to follow all the more clearly if Schneiders's account of symbol is read in light of that of Paul Ricoeur, on whose *Interpretation Theory* she draws for her account of meaning (as she acknowledges in *The Revelatory Text*, 15). For Ricoeur argues there that the symbol works in a similar way to metaphor: the literal level becomes the means of access to a deeper level, through our perception that the significance of the symbol is incongruous with identifying its meaning with its literal content (*Interpretation Theory*, 54–57).

87. *The Revelatory Text*, 101.

renders historical categories inadequate to their meaning. They express the early church's paschal imagination, which combines the historical Jesus of Nazareth and the transhistorical Jesus, the Christ, in tensive relation to one another.[88] These elements are inseparable so that the Gospels do not permit a purely historical analysis that would uncover the actual, earthly Jesus.[89] Rather, the historical character portrayed in the Gospels is only the medium for the disclosure of the actual Jesus, the symbolic self-disclosure of God. In fact, metaphor becomes more significant than historical writing as a vehicle for revelation. Metaphorical language, Schneiders explains, uses likeness and dissimilarity to "tease the mind into newness of thought . . . challenging the mind to exceed the bounds of the expressed and conceive what cannot be grasped in clear and distinct ideas."[90] By opening up toward the unsaid, language reveals to us more than we can know; it "bridges the gap between the infinite mystery of God and the finite human capacity for mystery."[91] Not only does this seem to claim too much for language if God is truly transcendent; the primacy given here to symbol and metaphor make the historical world rendered by the text of no intrinsic interest for theological interpretation.

The problem of reconciling exceptional human responsiveness to revelation with the historical situatedness of human beings recurs in Schneiders's account of the inspiration of Scripture. The claim that Scripture is inspired, she claims, is simply the acknowledgment that it discloses God in a unique way so as to ground a claim to special divine influence upon it.[92] Talk of special divine influence seems again to involve a claim to the kind of divine intervention Troeltsch finds implausible, but Schneiders is careful to distinguish this divine self-disclosure from the empirical phenomena through which it takes place: these can be adequately explained without reference to revelation; Scripture's disclosive power is not of that order. The mode of inspiration "refers to the way symbolic revelation occurs in and through human interaction with a text under the influence of the Spirit of God," in both the production and reception of the text.[93] What Schneiders seems to be suggesting is a realm of divine-human interaction discrete from the empirical world of historical causation, but this would seem to involve withdrawing human beings from full

88. *The Revelatory Text*, 101–2, 105.

89. *The Revelatory Text*, 105.

90. *The Revelatory Text*, 139. The metaphors Jesus uses for the reign of God are paramount examples here.

91. *The Revelatory Text*, 140.

92. *The Revelatory Text*, 50.

93. *The Revelatory Text*, 53.

immersion in history in a way that Troeltsch finds inconsistent with historical consciousness. She seems to reduce the problem by clarifying that the question of inspiration is not a question of divine operations but of "a phenomenology of the human experience of divine revelation mediated by the revelatory text of scripture."[94] Inspiration is about the human reception of divine influence, ascribed to the Holy Spirit, whose special degree is presumably related to an unusual human receptivity.[95] Yet it is still not clear how such divine influence here, and the unusual human receptivity for it, can be reconciled with a historical understanding of human psychology, where any human achievement, however exceptional, is intelligible in light of some degree of analogy with other actions and events.

In all these ways, then, Schneiders's position invites questioning from Troeltsch's account without appearing to offer any answers. She does, however, address issues of historical consciousness explicitly in her treatment of church tradition, which she formulates to flesh out her claim that the most adequate context for the emergence of the Bible's full meaning is the church.[96] The radical change in our understanding of history since the nineteenth century, she says, must affect our understanding of tradition. "We are never 'outside' history but always participating in it . . . as ever-changing historical entities."[97] This statement articulates something apparently very close to the historical consciousness Troeltsch articulated. On Schneiders's account, this immersion in history lends a historical, dynamic character to our engagement with the past. The experience we have of realizing that something first experienced as a tragedy was in fact a great grace supports the claim, she argues, that the past alters with its changing relationship to us and to "the wider historical macrosystem."[98] This apparently odd claim—that the past alters with our altering relationship to it—becomes more intelligible in light of Schneiders's claim that the past only exists insofar as it constitutes the present, that is, it exists only in its effects on us.[99]

---

94. *The Revelatory Text*, 53.

95. In a similar way, she claims that "only one whose spiritual sensibility has been formed and educated by life in the Christian community, whose intelligence has been enlightened by the faith of that community, whose affectivity is enlivened by the experience of God's love in Christ can hear integrally what the text *as scripture* is saying." *The Revelatory Text*, 60–61.

96. *The Revelatory Text*, 64.

97. *The Revelatory Text*, 65.

98. *The Revelatory Text*, 67–68.

99. For example, on the individual level, it is effective unconsciously, in memory, in healed or unhealed trauma, in habit, learned or acquired characteristics or knowledge, etc.

Tradition is one way in which the past is made actual and effective through a process of selection, whether conscious choice or spontaneous and episodic development, by which what is felt to be of value for present and future generations is passed on. Traditions are consciously appropriated, stabilized in form and meaning, so that they can be actualized again in the future, for example in the transmission of narratives or ritual. In this way, she claims, tradition is the primary form of historical consciousness, and so viewed may be reappropriated after a critical distancing from its products. In tradition, therefore, the effects of the past, like symbolic revelation, are contingent on present actualization, which can incorporate a critical moment.

While this account of the activity of transmitting traditions clearly assumes a sense of human beings immersed in their historical contexts like that which Troeltsch describes, the claim that tradition just is the "primary form of historical consciousness" seems to risk reducing the sensibility Troeltsch describes, which is contingent on particular modern developments, to something less critically aware of the causal interconnectedness of persons and events. It is perhaps that ambiguity that allows Schneiders to claim that tradition is "the Spirit of Jesus, that is, his active presence embodied in the Church."[100] For she notes that the shape and form of the Spirit's indwelling of disciples in John 14 and 16 is described in "specifically historical terms: the Spirit will ensure that the disciples *remember* all that Jesus has said to them (John 14:26) and will *lead* them into that fullness of truth that the first disciples were not yet able to bear (John 16:12-13)."[101] She concludes: the Spirit is "the ever-actual presence of Jesus bringing forward the past to enlighten and be enlightened by and present in terms of the future."[102] The content of the church's historical consciousness is thus "constituted by the interaction between the Spirit-animated Church and the existential situations in which the Church lives."[103]

It seems unlikely, however, that the historical consciousness Schneiders describes could be easily reconciled with that which Troeltsch describes. The past for Schneiders is something that exists in its present meaningfulness for those who appropriate it. Following Hans-Georg Gadamer, she sees understanding as a historical condition, in which we are shaped by the language, culture, and informal and formal education through which the effects of history are transmitted to us.[104] Such an account assumes the location of

100. *The Revelatory Text*, 73.
101. *The Revelatory Text*, 73.
102. *The Revelatory Text*, 73.
103. *The Revelatory Text*, 74.
104. *The Revelatory Text*, 159.

individuals in historical contexts, yet it avoids the full theological implications of Troeltsch's vision of the complex, contingent causal interactions of facts that throw up irreducibly individual realities in comparable ways.

Nevertheless, in one respect at least Schneiders does offer a way of responding to Troeltsch. One feature of Troeltsch's vision is the critical and ethical revaluation of the past to which historical consciousness leads. It is just this critical evaluation that leads to the situation Schneiders wishes to address. Schneiders's way of meeting this situation allows for critical scrutiny of biblical testimony in a way that takes account of the historical character of both the text's composition and its interpretation.

For her, the possibility of critically recovering revelatory meaning from ancient texts lies in the way texts are free from authorial intentions, original audiences, and ostensive reference through inscription.[105] What remains is the texts' ideal meaning, the product of the dialectic of propositional meaning and its claim to say it about something (sense and reference).[106] In the case of the Gospels, their ideal meaning seems to be different versions of the primitive church's image of the paschal mystery of Jesus Christ.[107] The reader's engagement with ideal meaning enables a new event of meaning that reactualizes the original experience of meaning that produced the text: the revelation of God in Jesus Christ.[108] The text, through its disclosure of the mystery of Christ, opens up to the reader "a world of possibility, a way of being, that the reader must assess and either accept or reject."[109]

The text is thus like a musical score or dramatic script, allowing for many different performances of its meaning, in which the performers discover their identity. This act of understanding is shaped by our involvement in the flow of history, by our historical consciousness in the sense we saw above: the shaping of the mind by the language and culture we participate in and the education we receive. In this way, the past is reconstituted through its own effective history, its impact upon our formation. Such understanding involves a renewed immediacy to the text, after the critical distancing of exegesis: a surrender to the world the text creates so as to encounter its existential truth-claims. It also makes possible critical questioning of the text's meaning, shaped by the reader's historical location, and realizations of it that transcend its limitations, so that,

---

105. *The Revelatory Text*, 143–44, following Paul Ricoeur's account in *Interpretation Theory*. Ostensive reference names "the capacity of language to refer directly to its subject matter as present."

106. *The Revelatory Text*, 15, 145–46.

107. *The Revelatory Text*, 105–7.

108. *The Revelatory Text*, 137.

109. *The Revelatory Text*, 148–49.

for example, modern readers may fulfill the liberatory agenda of Paul's writings beyond his affirmation of slavery and male domination.[110]

This attractive account complicates our assessment of Schneiders. The kind of reading she advocates is clearly capable of informing and transforming life in history.[111] She thus offers one way of accommodating the ethical criticism to which historical consciousness gives rise, on Troeltsch's account, and in such a way as to uphold a certain kind of textual authority on the part of Scripture. Yet it is not clear how such appropriations relate to the concrete, historical reality of Jesus of Nazareth. Nor does this account otherwise mitigate the challenge posed by the historical vision Troeltsch articulates to Schneiders's core theological claims: about divine revelation in Jesus Christ, and through the medium of biblical texts, the inspiration of the biblical texts and the Spirit's animating of the historical process of tradition. This challenge places in question the theological terms in which Schneiders articulates the authority of Scripture, its capacity to transform readers, or those in which Scripture affirms the full status of women before God.

KEVIN J. VANHOOZER

Kevin Vanhoozer's theology of Scripture offers a more promising way forward. His theology of divine authorship and divine communicative action furnishes a more developed account of divine action in respect of Scripture and history. Even so, Vanhoozer's account fails to do justice to the complex interrelationships that constitute historical existence. To examine that account I will focus primarily on Vanhoozer's *Remythologizing Theology*, for it is here that he spells out the doctrine of God implied by his treatment of Scripture and doctrine.[112] I will also draw on his *Is There a Meaning in This Text?* and *The Drama of Doctrine* to amplify his doctrine of Scripture where necessary.[113]

One of the chief merits of Vanhoozer's recent work, over the other two proposals we have considered so far, is that it takes seriously the need to flesh out an adequate account of divine agency that does justice to the agency of human creatures. His claim is that the best way to do so is to think of the

---

110. *The Revelatory Text*, 175–47.

111. Her own reading of John 4:1-42 further bears this out in chapter 7 of *The Revelatory Text*.

112. Vanhoozer, *Remythologizing Theology: Divine Action, Passion, and Authorship* (New York: Cambridge University Press, 2010).

113. Vanhoozer, *Is There a Meaning in This Text? The Bible, the Reader and the Morality of Literary Knowledge* (Leicester: Apollos, 1998); Vanhoozer, *The Drama of Doctrine: A Canonical Linguistic Approach to Christian Theology* (Louisville: Westminster John Knox, 2005).

God of Israel and Jesus Christ as an author or communicative agent, one "who speaks and acts."[114] Seeing God in this way immediately foregrounds history as "the medium through which God relates to his people" through his communicative actions, attested in Scripture, which together constitute the drama of redemption.[115] In making such a claim, Vanhoozer invites scrutiny as to the adequacy of his account of divine action in history.

Vanhoozer's notion of history is focused on dialogical interaction between God and human beings, conceived as personal communicative agents. God is the paradigmatic communicative agent, as his acts reveal: the Father who communicates himself in the activity of the Son and Spirit.[116] The dialogical interaction between Father and Son in the gospel narrative reveals that this agency is personal. Like God, human beings are analogously personal communicative agents; unlike God they are not self-authored or unconstrained nor the creator of all things.[117] The world is a stage set for the dialogical interaction of persons. For Vanhoozer, therefore, dialogic communicative agency, rather than the impersonal causal laws to which events are ascribed, is the primary category for thinking about causality in the history of salvation.[118] Yet history, seen from the perspective of historical method as Troeltsch articulates it, is much more complex than the dialogical interaction of persons. For those personal interactions, in virtue of the embodiment and insertion of human persons in society and cultures and particular geographies, are shaped, informed, interrupted, and stimulated by a variety of other forces interacting with them and one another. The problem of accounting for history so understood will return to challenge Vanhoozer's construal of divine action and providence.

Vanhoozer rightly grounds the whole of history in the communicative action of God, so making history *as a whole* properly contingent on divine action. This is an important step toward meeting the challenges Troeltsch identifies, for it makes it possible to begin thinking about the whole historical continuum as upheld by God rather than as a system closed to divine interference. Equally important, he in turn grounds God's communicative action in the inner life of God, thus securing its freedom, gratuity, and

---

114. *Remythologizing*, 182.

115. *Remythologizing*, 182. This "theo-dramatic" construal of salvation history is worked out in *The Drama of Doctrine*, 38–44.

116. Vanhoozer follows Barth's maxim that God is who God is in God's acts.

117. *Remythologizing*, 226–27. Other creatures merely communicate what they are by their normal operations; see 224–27.

118. *Remythologizing*, 227–28, 234, 239. Vanhoozer makes a similar claim in *The Drama of Doctrine*, 49.

difference from creaturely agency: key conditions for being able to talk about divine agency in a way that does not depict it as being in competition with creaturely agency and so as the kind of supernatural agency of which historical explanation has no need. God's communicative life is eternal, characterized at once by succession and simultaneity, and it is a willed enjoyment of communion: a life of love, "the eternal delight of the dialogical dance of call, response, acknowledgement, and affirmation."[119] The gospel is the temporal execution of God's decision to communicate that life to others and with it the capacity to communicate, to share one's being, with others. Jesus Christ is central as the embodiment of the Father's utterance. His speech and actions "communicate God's intra-trinitarian self-communication."[120] Through the Holy Spirit, God communicates a share in his life to those who participate in Christ's history, eventually even to our risen bodies.[121]

The historical medium of this communicative action raises the question of "how God acts in a world of nature and human freedom."[122] Vanhoozer is close here to recognizing the problems Troeltsch identified, but again lacks a sense of the thorough interconnectedness of human agency and psychology with other kinds of causation and events that historical research assumes. His answer to the problem as he conceives it rests on explicating the claim that "God's relation to the world is a function of his triune authorial action, the self-communicating of God the Father through the Word in the Spirit."[123] To do so, he draws upon Mikhail Bakhtin's notion of the outsideness of the author: "the asymmetrical, nonreciprocal boundary that distinguishes author and hero" (someone about whom a story could be told), whereby the former authors the whole of the hero's life and relates to that life as a whole, but the hero does neither for herself.[124] Because the author is "outside" the hero in this way and sees the whole of the hero's existence, authors can confer wholeness and so meaning on the lives of their heroes.[125] This concept provides a powerful analogy for the transcendence without distance that characterizes divine action in the biblical witness, but must be taken further for, Vanhoozer notes, God confers wholeness upon the whole of history.[126] This consummating

119. *Remythologizing*, 258–59.

120. *Remythologizing*, 260–61.

121. *Remythologizing*, 279, 282, 289, 267–68.

122. *Remythologizing*, 300.

123. *Remythologizing*, 302.

124. *Remythologizing*, 324–25.

125. *Remythologizing*, 325–26.

126. *Remythologizing*, 327.

communicative action is what eschatology describes, whereby human lives are consummated as our stories are taken up into the perfect life of Jesus Christ, the participation described above.[127]

Vanhoozer seeks to secure the freedom of heroes in relation to divine action by drawing on Bakhtin's analysis of voices in Dostoevsky's novels. Here, each voice is an embodied point of view with its own spatiotemporal location; the production of voices is the authoring of free characters who incarnate unfinished authorial ideas in dialogical relation to other embodied consciousnesses with alternative perspectives and locations.[128] These voices and perspectives cannot be abstracted from the persons who give them voice. What matters here is the hero's response to their situation, "his or her self-consciousness."[129]

This notion provides an apt analogy for reconciling the sovereignty of God with creaturely responsibility: "God authors/elects creatures to be dialogical agents in covenantal relation through whom his Word sounds."[130] The divine author engages his creatures as subjects of address, and puts them into specific situations in order that they might freely actualize the voice-idea for which they were created. The author is thus "an *involved* outsider, an interlocutor in a world that he himself has created."[131]

This actualizing of voice-ideas takes place through dialogue, as heroes answer in their speech and action the questions posed by various life situations, gradually disclosing a pattern, the "particular shape of answerability" that each of their lives represent.[132] The divine author discerns and names this pattern, so consummating each life—and the world at large.[133] God thus engages human beings "according to their rational, volitional, and emotional natures," by provoking, questioning, objecting, answering them, so drawing out the responses to situations that enact their selves.[134] As characters' voices are so created as to develop according to their own inner logic, distinct from the author's own voice, so we have self-determination in and through our dialogue with the divine Author who calls us into being and consummates our lives with meaning.[135]

127. *Remythologizing*, 328–29.

128. *Remythologizing*, 330.

129. *Remythologizing*, 330.

130. *Remythologizing*, 331.

131. *Remythologizing*, 332.

132. *Remythologizing*, 332.

133. *Remythologizing*, 332–33.

134. *Remythologizing*, 333.

This notion of divine authorship of human "voices" seems to picture divine agency in terms both transcendent of historical causality and yet most deeply involved with human beings in their individuality. We may wonder whether human lives manifest so clear a pattern as to constitute, for their subjects, a divine address calling for a lived response—or whether call and response could here be so neatly distinguished. Moreover, while this account relies upon divine authorial shaping of personal circumstances, the concept of voices does not lend itself well to illumining the manner of that shaping. Instead, that focus on the interaction of subjectivities and the ideas they express seems to make their interaction with their environment and circumstances become a means for the divine evocation of and medium for their self-realization and self-expression, rather than deeply constitutive of their identities. The risk is that history becomes merely the veil through which authorial and heroic consciousnesses engage one another.

Further problems attend Vanhoozer's account of divine and human agency in salvation. The human need for salvation is clear, for the freedom to reorient one's life toward God is one for which we must be liberated. To this end God's own voice took flesh, the Author emplotting himself in his own drama and in particular into the long history of God's covenantal discourse with Israel.[136] The notion of divine self-emplotment is not nearly so immediately intelligible as Bakhtin's notion of authorial "outsideness," for although it is quite easy to conceive of an author writing him or herself as a character into a story, it is much more difficult to think of that character as retaining authorial "outsideness." It appears to stretch the authorial analogy beyond its elasticity and to introduce a historical agent who is not subject to the constraints of history, an exception to the historical order established by the Author and to the sense of continuous interconnection presupposed by historical method, according to Troeltsch.

This challenge extends to Vanhoozer's account of the place of Scripture in God's providential governance of the world. Providence, for Vanhoozer, is primarily rhetorically enacted. God "convincingly persuades some of the [human chess] pieces freely to play of their own accord in a way that so corresponds to God's will that we can speak (albeit hesitantly) in terms of dual agency."[137] This authoring may happen as God elicits someone's realization of themselves in the withholding of his Spirit (as in the case of the hardening of Pharaoh's heart in the book of Exodus). Alternatively, God may act "*within*

---

135. *Remythologizing*, 334.
136. *Remythologizing*, 357–59.
137. *Remythologizing*, 367.

and *through* [persons] in such a way that . . . God brings them to their senses and makes them the creatures they were always meant to be."[138] This is God's effectual call: the Spirit's enabling of the hearer to understand the full force of what has been said so as to respond freely with faith, restoring and reorienting spiritual and cognitive capacities so as to apprehend and embrace the beautiful, good, and true gospel of Jesus Christ.[139]

Providence is the extension of this kind of action: an effectual prompt, whereby God directs the church in the drama of redemption.[140] Scripture is instrumental in this prompting. The Father rules "by speaking Christ through the Spirit into the minds and hearts of the faithful."[141] Here "Christ" denotes "what the law, prophets and other biblical writings say about the new thing God is doing in Christ."[142] As in the story of the word of the Lord in the book of Acts, so today, "God continues to act in the world by acting in his people, and God acts in his people through the Spirit's ministry of the written word."[143] In fact, God does through Scripture "as many things as there are speech genres in it."[144] This account gestures to two further ideas that Vanhoozer has explored in earlier works.

The first is that there is a sense in which God authors Scripture: that "Scripture is taken up in complex ways into God's triune self-communicative action," as God uses its human words to promise, exhort, command, warn, comfort, predict, lament, and plead.[145] Here Vanhoozer draws on speech-act theory to articulate an account of both human and divine textual communication.[146] At the human level, as written texts, scriptural writings embody the illocutionary enactments of the communicative intentions of their human authors through the use of linguistic conventions.[147] Any well-intentioned reader, following the rules of language and literature, can discover the illocutions of the biblical authors, especially if they embody interpretive

138. *Remythologizing*, 370. In presenting these two complementary alternative ways in which God elicits human responses that realize them, I am harmonizing Vanhoozer's account of Pharaoh with his predominate tendency to speak of divine action and providence in terms of conversion.

139. *Remythologizing*, 374–75.

140. *Remythologizing*, 376.

141. *Remythologizing*, 376.

142. *Remythologizing*, 376.

143. *Remythologizing*, 376–77.

144. *Remythologizing*, 377.

145. *The Drama of Doctrine*, 46–47.

146. Vanhoozer is not alone in using speech-act theory to explore the idea that God speaks through Scripture. See, for example, Nicholas Wolterstorff, *Divine Discourse: Philosophical Reflections on the Claim That God Speaks* (Cambridge: Cambridge University Press, 1995).

virtues: dispositions toward understanding enacted authorial intentions, to welcome the text as an extension of the communicative agent, which virtues literature cultivates in readers.[148]

Since authorial intention accounts for the unity of a written text, it is important to take account of conventions of genre as media for illocutionary enactment of authorial intention. Genres are historically contextual literary forms that embody complex patterns of communicative action according to certain conventions; their relative stability facilitates literary communicative action.[149] Each literary genre does something distinctive: each enables a distinct way of engaging reality and interacting with others.[150] Genre is especially important for literary texts intended for future, unknown contexts and readers, by providing in shared understanding of form a substitute for a shared communicative situation and additional rules for making and interpreting meaning, and signals the kind of thought the text expresses and the kind of life situation it belongs to.[151] Thinking about illocutionary action at the level of genre conventions raises the question of the illocutionary force of literary genres, like narrative. Narratives enable authors to display worlds and take up a stance toward it and invite the reader to see things the same way.[152] To learn from texts therefore requires indwelling them, to inhabit the perspective on the world that they embody.[153]

The diverse biblical writings, enacting diverse illocutions, are caught up in the agency of the triune God. God appropriates these human illocutions,

147. Where intentions are not to be confused with motives for writing; see *Is There a Meaning in This Text?*, 239. Vanhoozer talks of texts as embodied intentions on 253. Vanhoozer argues, plausibly, that written texts are only intelligible as discourse when ascribed to communicative agents, as the products of their communicative intentions. Authorial intention is "the originating and unifying power that puts a linguistic system . . . into motion in order to do something with words that the system alone cannot do" (249).

148. *Is There a Meaning in This Text?*, 315–16, 376–78, and 397–98. Such virtues include respect for those intentions, faith, hope, love, honesty with respect to one's commitments, and preunderstandings, openness, attention, and obedience.

149. *Is There a Meaning in This Text?*, 337–39.

150. "From Speech Acts to Scripture Acts," in Vanhoozer, *First Theology: God, Scripture and Hermeneutics* (Downers Grove, IL/Nottingham, UK: IVP Academic/Apollos, 2002), 191.

151. *Is There a Meaning in This Text?*, 339–40.

152. *Is There a Meaning in This Text?*, 227, 341. This kind of illocutionary force seems of a different order to the kind of illocutions Vanhoozer (with biblical warrant) usually ascribes to God in respect of the divine authorship of Scripture—promising, exhorting, comforting, warning, etc. (see e.g. *The Drama of Doctrine*, 47).

153. *Is There a Meaning in This Text?*, 349.

especially at the level of whole texts in their use of genre codes (God still uses the book of Jonah to satirize religious ethnocentrism, for example), but draws them into a larger, more complex order, the canon.[154] In virtue of this gathering, God may do new things with Jonah and other biblical texts, namely the canonical illocutions of testifying to Christ, instructing the church, making covenant. Indeed, for Vanhoozer, the biblical canon seems to be the preeminent expression of divine authorial intention.[155] The diverse genres of the Bible are thus divinely appropriated for a larger communicative purpose: one "of witness to . . . the revelatory and redemptive acts of God in the history of Israel, and, above all, in the history of Jesus Christ."[156] Scripture thus projects the voice and extends the action of Jesus Christ, God's Word.[157] It is in these ways that the Bible is "the Word of God," and Vanhoozer goes so far as to identify it as a divine act, or more properly, a result of God's work, which shares in the perfections and authority of that work without being divine.[158]

Second, Scripture has a particular function in salvation that Vanhoozer depicts in theo-dramatic terms. On this account, God here is playwright and principal actor, whose words and actions impel the drama.[159] Scripture is the divinely authored script for the Spirit-enabled faithful performance of the church on the world stage.[160] Through Scripture, expounded in the church, God summons and informs our participation in the theo-drama. Scripture is thus "the locus of God's ongoing communicative action in the church and in the world."[161] Genre is key here again, for different genres envisage specific kinds of social situation and demand a certain kind of social response; they provide fitting direction for participation in those situations.[162]

To understand the script most fully is to participate in the action it envisages: Scripture is to be performed under the direction of the Spirit and with dramaturgical guidance of right doctrine.[163] Faithful performance here is a matter of continuing the action fittingly, corresponding to the central

154. Vanhoozer, "From Speech Acts to Scripture Acts," 194.

155. "From Speech Acts to Scripture Acts," 194; *Is There a Meaning in This Text?*, 264.

156. *Is There a Meaning in This Text?*, 313, 349. Elsewhere Vanhoozer makes the related category of promise the overarching canonical illocution. See his "God's Mighty Speech Acts: The Doctrine of Scripture Today," in *First Theology*, 154.

157. *The Drama of Doctrine*, 48.

158. *The Drama of Doctrine*, 48, 63, 65.

159. *The Drama of Doctrine*, 64–65.

160. *The Drama of Doctrine*, 22, 31–32.

161. *The Drama of Doctrine*, 71. Here Vanhoozer tends to speak of Scripture as a divinely commissioned agent, on analogy with Son and Spirit. But a text is not an agent.

162. *The Drama of Doctrine*, 215–16.

performance of Jesus Christ as rendered by the canon, and allows for a variety of proper responses in new cultural situations.[164] The key is dramatic consistency: the embodiment of communicative actions that recapitulate the pattern of Jesus Christ's communicative action, of which the canon is the norm.[165] Grasping the divine illocutions of Scripture so as to follow their promptings is conditional on the illumination of the Holy Spirit.[166] By responding to the illocutions of Scripture that testify to Christ, we become covenantally related to Him, by the ministry of the Spirit, and empowered to bear witness to Him.[167]

There are problems inherent to both these rich ideas. First, it is far from self-evident *how* the canon should be read as a whole, even if one specifies it is to be read Christocentrically; and yet invoking the Spirit's illumination, by itself, does not give a thick enough description of canonical illocutions sufficient to inform theological exegesis.[168] Vanhoozer needs to specify further the way in which God may appropriate human illocutions in his own illocutionary action so that it is a distinct, intelligible illocution recognizable and followable by human interpreters in their respective contexts by the aid of the Spirit.[169] Second, this account does not clarify the divine illocutionary appropriation of

163. *The Drama of Doctrine*, 102. As he acknowledges, Vanhoozer is not the first to argue that scriptural interpretation is a matter of performing the text. See for example, Nicholas Lash, "Performing the Scriptures," in *Theology on the Way to Emmaus* (London: SCM, 1986), 37–46; Frances Young, *The Art of Performance: Towards a Theology of Holy Scripture* (London: Darton, Longman & Todd, 1990); N. T. Wright, *The New Testament and the People of God* (London: SPCK, 1992), 140–43; Stephen Barton, "New Testament Interpretation as Performance," *Scottish Journal of Theology* 52, no. 2 (1999), 179-208. Vanhoozer's reprisal of this theme is arguably distinctive in his attempt to combine it with an emphasis on authorial authority articulated by way of speech-act theory. For his fruitful notion of the theologian as dramaturge, see *Drama of Doctrine*, 244ff.

164. *The Drama of Doctrine*, 104–6, 255f.

165. *The Drama of Doctrine*, 106–10, 145–46. The emphasis on embodying Scripture and the virtues and practices needed to do so wisely is a significant theme in Stephen E. Fowl and L. Gregory Jones, *Reading in Communion: Scripture and Ethics in Christian Life* (London: SPCK, 1991) and Fowl, *Engaging Scripture: A Model for Scriptural Interpretation* (Oxford: Blackwell, 1998). Again, Vanhoozer's emphasis on authorial intention and authority is in marked contrast to Fowl's.

166. *Is There a Meaning in This Text?*, 316, 413, 421–22. At times Vanhoozer likens the Spirit to the perlocutionary effect of the speech act (for example, engendering faith might be the perlocutionary effect of making a promise), e.g. *Is There a Meaning in This Text?*, 410ff.; "God's Mighty Speech Acts," 155. It might be better to speak of the Spirit as the agent of the perlocutionary efficacy of divine illocutions in Scripture.

167. *The Drama of Doctrine*, 68, 72–73.

168. Vanhoozer provides a little more clarity in *The Drama of Doctrine*: one kind of canonical reading practice is to read the Old Testament figurally in light of Christ and following his example, as the early church did in Acts; see 119–20, 194–95, 220–23.

scriptural illocutions, canonical or otherwise. Nor, third, is it easy to reconcile the description of Scripture as a means by which God plays his part onstage with the analogy of a script, though that analogy has other strengths.[170]

Above all, it is not clear how God's speech-agency through Scripture in the theo-drama can be reconciled with the complex interactions of the historical world in which Scripture is read. Scripture too is a strand in the densely interwoven historical world, yet here is called to play an instrumental role far in excess of the instrumentality Vanhoozer attributes to other historical media of God's authorship, a role that seems to pick it out of the historical continuum in a way that they are not. Just as, therefore, the authorial analogy does not seem to account for the exceptional status, historically speaking, of Jesus Christ that Vanhoozer accords him, so it must also struggle to account for Scripture in Vanhoozer's account, since Scripture is conceived of as almost an extension of God's embodied self-communication in Jesus Christ.

Nor is the ecclesiocentrism of his account of Scripture and providence tenable in light of an awareness of the scope and complexity of history. Even if we concede a considerable influence to church communities and their members on human society, culture, and institutions in an ever-widening variety of historical contexts through time, the extent of this influence even at its widest does not seem sufficient to account for the governance of the whole world, even the whole human world. For, on the one hand, there are places where that influence remains relatively slight and, more importantly, that influence is historically conditioned by a whole host of other factors and dynamics and agencies. Finally, it is not clear how far Vanhoozer's account of scriptural authority would allow him to entertain moral evaluations of the biblical text, since it is so unequivocally invested with divine authority.

MURRAY RAE

Rae offers a more direct and sustained engagement with the problem of history as it bears on the theology and theological interpretation of Scripture. He

169. It does not suffice to argue that God *can* do so, just as God can become human in Christ (*Drama of Doctrine*, 47–48). Even in the case of God using Jonah to satirize religious ethnocentrism, such a divine illocution seems distinct from the book's own context-specific illocutionary act: How does this work, how do we recognize it when God uses it in respect of other contexts? For one answer to this difficulty, see Wolterstorff, *Divine Discourse*, chapters 11–13.

170. In particular, it illumines the claim that right understanding involves right action and allows for flexibility and freedom in the way the text is received in different contexts—for improvisation. The notion of the Spirit as prompt also provides an alternative to dictation theories of inspiration.

recognizes explicitly that Troeltsch poses a challenge to this project. On his account, Troeltsch excluded God's involvement from the closed causal nexus of history.[171] The problem with Troeltsch, he claims, is a faulty view of history that supposes that history cannot be the medium of divine self-disclosure.[172] That characterization, however, does not do justice to Troeltsch's appeal to the historical sensibility enshrined in the way historians actually work, or the specific force of his case with respect to the immersion of historical phenomena in complex, contingent causal interconnections. Rae's constructive response to this challenge has much to offer in terms of theological method, but fails to get to grips adequately with the full force of that challenge.

Rae's first move, taking clues from Martin Kähler, Karl Barth, and Hans Frei, is to prioritize revelation in our understanding of what history is. "We cannot presume that we know what history is in advance of the Lord of history disclosing its true nature to us."[173] This revelation is Christocentric and comes, he implies, by way of the biblical narratives, which tell "a story of history as the space and time in and through which God encounters his people and brings about his purpose."[174] The biblical narratives "demand a reconsideration of how reality is constituted and thus also of how history itself is to be construed."[175] Rae's explication of this reconsideration in relation to the doctrine of creation *ex nihilo* and the teleological character of history under God's direction does not go far enough, however.

Creation *ex nihilo* means that matter is created for a purpose and thus has a *telos*. History "is to be understood as the space and time opened up for the world to become what it is intended to be."[176] It also means that everything in history happens under God's will and purpose, has coherence in his care, is contingent (because not necessary to God), and has meaning in its own right. Within this context, human actions have significance: God "entrusts to the precarious stewardship of human beings a measure of responsibility for the way that history takes shape."[177] God elicits human participation in the working out of his purpose. The calling of Abraham in Genesis 12 shows that through particulars, "God invests the whole of history with its meaning and purpose."[178]

---

171. *History and Hermeneutics* (London: T. & T. Clark, 2005), 16.

172. *History and Hermeneutics*, 21.

173. *History and Hermeneutics*, 33.

174. *History and Hermeneutics*, 35.

175. *History and Hermeneutics*, 42.

176. *History and Hermeneutics*, 51.

177. *History and Hermeneutics*, 53.

178. *History and Hermeneutics*, 57.

Jesus Christ is the fulfillment of human participation in history and of God's use of human particulars—his election of them.

What happened to and through Jesus requires a transformation of what we suppose is possible in the world, so that the old paradigms of historical and scientific enquiry will be inadequate for the task of apprehending this reality (because history has been misconceived there as a causal series from which God is necessarily excluded).[179] In the first place, "historical" means "that which has taken place within the created order," which belongs to God and is in process of being redeemed and perfected by God.[180] Furthermore, the central place of Christ's whole career and his resurrection in God's redemptive work means that the resurrection is an eschatological event, whereby the eschatological reality of the created order is made present in history. This means that the resurrection bursts the bounds of the present order and of its historiography, so that it "cannot any longer be thought to exclude the transforming presence of God."[181] The creator is at work with the open-textured tapestry of space and time, weaving in the threads of new life.

Discerning this event requires Christ's self-disclosure, beyond the limits of historical-critical tools, on the occasion of the biblical witnesses.[182] This role of the texts in attesting this reality constitutes its meaning, which unfolds with the unfolding significance of that reality in God's economy, beyond the intentions of authors or redactors. Participation in that reality, as God addresses and justifies us, enables us to understand the subject matter of Scripture.[183] Hence the church has a certain privilege as an interpretive community in relation to these texts.[184] The church continues to use critical tools, but now incorporating theological categories and reshaping critical principles in light of the revelation of God in Christ, placing the burden of proof on skeptics of claims to divine action in history, making the Christ-likeness of witnesses a key criterion for assessing their competence, including divine action in the complex of correlated causes, and testing claims to divine action on analogy with what we learn of God's dealings with the world from elsewhere.[185]

Recasting our understanding of history in light of the reshaping of history in Jesus Christ is a move of significant promise, as we shall see when we turn to

179. *History and Hermeneutics*, 68.

180. *History and Hermeneutics*, 72.

181. *History and Hermeneutics*, 73.

182. *History and Hermeneutics*, 87, 93, 100–103.

183. *History and Hermeneutics*, 149–50.

184. *History and Hermeneutics*, 144.

185. *History and Hermeneutics*, 154–55.

Hans Frei. Such a move will also make adequate understanding of the character of history dependent on a kind of knowledge besides historical investigation. As C. Stephen Evans and Alvin Plantinga have argued in relation to this issue, the appeal involved to God's self-revealing action as the direct grounds for beliefs is epistemologically defensible.[186] It also makes sense to then rethink the witness of Scripture, its role in God's saving activity, where and how it is read in light of this rethinking of history, and to examine how the principles of historiography might be transformed accordingly. Such moves, however, are by themselves not sufficient to meet the challenge identified by Troeltsch. Although Rae rightly asserts that God acts in Christ in history so as to shape its very character, and draws us to participate in this action, the challenge Troeltsch leaves us with is how to reconcile divine action, even when so comprehensive in scope, with the immanent interrelated web of historical phenomena disclosed by historical research.

To that end we turn to Gregory of Nazianzus and Hans Frei, the former for a more detailed, premodern model of thinking about divine action shaping history and human lives through Jesus Christ and through Holy Scripture; the latter for an account of how Scripture discloses such an ordering of history in a way that transforms modern historical consciousness and informs discerning discipleship in the midst of history. Together they point us to the shape of an answer to the challenge of history for the theology and theological interpretation of Holy Scripture.

186. See Evans, *The Historical Christ and the Jesus of Faith*, and Plantinga, "Two (or More) Kinds of Scripture Scholarship," in *Behind the Text: History and Biblical Interpretation*, ed. C. Bartholomew, C. S. Evans, M. Healy, and M. Rae (Carlisle/Grand Rapids: Paternoster/Zondervan, 2003), 19–57.

2

God, Christ, and History in Gregory of Nazianzus

For Troeltsch, the closely interwoven web of immanent historical causes—natural, psychological, and personal—precludes recognition of divine intervention in history or the attribution of any particular historical event with absolute significance. Gregory of Nazianzus lived many centuries before the development of the modern historical consciousness that Troeltsch was concerned with. Nevertheless, his theology models several elements necessary to help frame a theology of Scripture adequate to Troeltsch's challenge, which critically complement and are complemented by Hans Frei's account. Gregory's accounts of God and creation, of the constitution of human beings at the heart of the created order, of salvation as divine pedagogy, all contribute to depict divine action as much more fundamental than an intervention, and one that is congruent with the character of the created order, yet acknowledges its immanent causalities and freedoms.

Gregory and Ancient Historiography

Gregory is not known as a historiographer or theorist of historical inquiry (ἱστορία) or historiography. He gives us neither genealogy, nor ethnography, nor horography, nor chronology.[1] Nor did he give us historiography in the sense of a verisimilitudinous *mimesis* of the warlike deeds of the great men of the past and the prehistory to those events, like Herodotus' *The Persian War*.[2] Nor did he follow Thucydides and leave us with a monograph on a contemporary war, nor a universal history like those of Ephorus, Polybius, or—nearer to his

---

1. These were the first historical disciplines, along with history proper, according to Charles W. Fornara, *The Nature of History in Ancient Greek and Rome* (Berkeley, Los Angeles, and London: University of California Press, 1983), 1–28.

2. Fornara, *The Nature of History*, 28–32.

own time—Ammianus.[3] He does not seem to have worked with documentary sources.[4] Nor does he attempt a comprehensive history of the church and its continuity through time, as Eusebius did, drawing on documentary evidence in church archives.[5] Yet Gregory seems to have had a good knowledge of classical historiography.[6] And in some of his poems he presents himself in the guise of a classical historiographer as he puts the record straight on great events in which he was involved, and especially on his own deeds, drawing critically on others' reports as well as his own memory and explaining events as an inspired writer, explanations that are theological as well as historical.[7] These poems also show that he shared with most ancient historians a concern with the rhetorical nature of writing about events and its pedagogical function. For Gregory, this concern reflected the pedagogical and rhetorical character of the divine intention that guided historical events.[8] It is with Gregory's theological conception of history that I am primarily concerned: the character and order of temporal events in their interconnections and relations to contexts and circumstances, and which can be found in more explicit form mainly in his orations.

God

One component of the problematic Troeltsch articulates for Christian theology is the difficulty of recognizing divine action as a component of or interruption in the closeknit weave of historical causality. When he criticizes traditional theology in this respect, Troeltsch seems to be attacking an understanding of God as an external agent, whose action might provide an alternative

3. Fornara, *The Nature of History*, 32–45.

4. Oral testimony was one of the main sources for early Greek historiography (along with the author's own memory); Roman historians, concerned primarily with Rome and with the resources of excellent archives of the city's oligarchy, introduced documentary research. See Fornara, *The Nature of History*.

5. See further, William Adler, "Early Christian Historians and Historiography," in *The Oxford Handbook of Early Christian Studies*, ed. Susan Ashbrook Harvey and David G. Hunter (New York: Oxford University Press, 2008), 584–602; and Glenn F. Chesnut, *The First Christian Histories: Eusebius, Socrates, Sozomen, Theodoret, and Evagrius* (Macon, GA: Mercer University Press, 1986).

6. He expresses the wish, in Or. 4.92, to write about Julian the Apostate with the erudition of Herodotus and Thucydides. I owe this reference to Suzanne Abrams Rebillard, "Historiography as Devotion," in *Re-reading Gregory of Nazianzus: Essays on History, Theology and Culture*, ed. C. Beeley (Washington, DC: Catholic University of America Press, 2012), 126.

7. See Suzanne Abrams Rebillard, "Historiography as Devotion." On ancient historians' reliance on their firsthand experience of events, see Fornara, *The Nature of History*, 47–56.

8. See Frances Young, *Biblical Interpretation and the Formation of Christian Culture* (Cambridge: Cambridge University Press, 1997), 166–67.

explanation for worldly events to those that the historian might offer. One step, therefore, toward a theological response to this problem that will help frame an adequate theology of Scripture, is to limn a doctrine of God that presents an alternative to that picture: a God whose involvement is more immanent and fundamental to, and yet not of the same order as, creaturely systems, processes, and actions. Gregory's understanding of God is fundamental to his theological vision of history, and offers us one model for how to offer an alternative to the theology Troeltsch rejected.[9]

In several of his Orations, before launching into the exposition of a theological theme, Gregory prefaces his teaching with some grammatical remarks about God and theological language. His concern, in each instance, is primarily to refute the whole intellectual ethos of the theology of Eunomius of Cyzicus, whose key premise was the possibility of defining God as "Father." In Gregory's so-called "Theological Orations," Oration 28 is largely devoted to this subject, it informs the argument of Oration 29, and recurs explicitly in Oration 30.

Oration 28 provides the most extended account, and frames it in the most striking terms. There Gregory pictures himself as Moses, climbing Mount Sinai in order to meet God, taking Exod. 33:7-22 as his intertext.[10] Having freed his mind as far as possible from material things that might distort his understanding of God and having collected himself, he looks out from the vantage point afforded by the Word made flesh, the one in whom God is made manifest to us, according to Gregory. (We should note therefore that in this narrative contemplative ascent is framed within and enabled by God's saving economy.) The Exodus narrative supplies the theological lesson Gregory wishes to impart. Moses had asked to see God's glory; God shows him not his face, but his back. The contemplative-as-Moses sees, in Gregory's words, "not the first and unmixed nature, known to itself—I mean to the Trinity—and as much as dwells within the first veil and is covered by the cherubim, but as much as finally reaches us."[11] God's back, Gregory explains, is "the majesty of God in creatures and the things produced and governed by God, or, as divine David calls it, God's 'magnificence.'"[12] For these, he continues, are the "'back parts of God,' that is, what we recognise of him after he passes by, like the images and shadows of the sun which indicate it to weak eyes" since the purity of its light is too much for us.[13]

9. I do not mean to suggest his is the only possible premodern model.

10. Or. 28.2–3.

11. Or. 28.3, *SC* 250, pp. 104, 106.

12. Or. 28.3, *SC* 250, p. 106.

Gregory thus draws on and interprets the Exodus text as an object lesson in the nature of the theologian's knowledge of God. Negatively, the theologian does not know God's nature as God knows it. Weaving in a second biblical image, Gregory tells us that the divine nature is shielded from us like the presence of God between the Cherubim within the Holy of Holies.[14] God's nature is seen in another fashion. The glory of God which the theologian may espy in Jesus Christ, like Moses in the cleft of the rock, is God's back. As Moses saw the back of God as he passed by, proclaiming his Name, so the theologian sees God's nature as reflected in the effects of his activity in creatures. This reflected image is his majesty or magnificence: terms closely connected with the wondrous works of God in several biblical texts.[15] The metaphor of the sun, its light, and its image in water implies that the theologian really sees God, for as Christopher Beeley argues, his use of similar imagery elsewhere indicates the continuity between the sun and its image in the water.[16] Indeed, Gregory's use of the imagery of sunlight, Beeley rightly argues, closely connects the believer's knowledge of God with the being of God itself: "God's transcendent being overflows, as it were, into our knowledge of him."[17] To integrate this insight into the reading of this passage so far, we may say that Gregory's use of this imagery here implies that God's activity in creatures is a manifestation of his nature, as sunlight communicates the image of the sun. But just as that image must be viewed safely in a reflection, so our knowledge of God is qualified: the manifestation of his being in action is seen reflected in creaturely things upon which we can safely gaze.

The issue here is not simply the purity and power of divine light overcoming sinful creatures. For "every heavenly being, even the supercelestial, however more exalted in nature than us and closer to God, is farther from

---

13. Or. 28.3, *SC* 250, p. 106.

14. In Or. 6.22, Gregory tells us explicitly that the Trinity alone possesses the Holy of Holies and excludes from it all creation, the heavenly and angelic world by the first veil, and the rest by the second.

15. Thus "majesty" (μεγαλειότης) in Luke 9:43 and 2 Peter 1:16, which may well be in Gregory's mind, and "magnificence" (μεγαλοπρέπεια) in Ps. 8:1 (LXX), which he explicitly alludes to here.

16. C. Beeley, *Gregory of Nazianzus on the Trinity and the Knowledge of God: In Your Light We See Light* (New York: Oxford University Press, 2008), 107, referring to Gregory's image of the sunbeam, its reflection on a wall, and refraction in water in Or. 31.3. This analogy between God and the sun is widespread in Gregory's theology. It derives from Plato's *Republic* 6, 508C, as Paul Gallay points out (*SC* 250, p. 168, n. 1). Gregory is quite aware that he is borrowing this figure from a non-Christian source, for, in Or. 28.30 he attributes it to "a non-Christian thinker" (literally, "one of the foreigners," *SC* 250, p. 169). That Gregory should find Plato's analogy congenial in no way negates the great difference between them in their accounts of God and our relation to him.

17. Beeley, *Gregory of Nazianzus*, 107, citing Or. 39.8–10 in support.

God and the perfect comprehension of God" than it is higher than us.[18] It is impossible for created beings, and certainly impossible for us, enveloped in our thick flesh, to comprehend God, though spiritual beings may enjoy fuller illumination.[19] What Gregory means here is not that we are condemned to ignorance of God, but that we cannot comprehend what God is: the manner of his being.[20]

Such an argument does not entail the remotion of God from creation. On the contrary, Gregory's argument is about the excessive quality of the divine reality active and manifest in the creation and governance of creatures. Its force is that not only the being but the agency of God (the two seem closely connected, as I have argued) are beyond our comprehension. In similar fashion, Gregory goes on to argue that divine incomprehensibility in no way subverts the argument for a first cause of all things from observation of the fixity, order, and yet mobility of visible things—an ever-mobile arrangement whose fragility argues its dependence on a transcendent source for both its motion and orderly subsistence.[21] Gregory's point here does not flesh out his account of how God relates to creation, but it implies a first cause who is the constant source of the movement and order that characterize visible creatures, a notion that suggests finely balanced systems whose preservation is contingent on their proper configuration, itself contingent on a higher source of order in a way that is not going to be fully explicable or amenable to clear conceptualization.

Gregory demonstrates the impossibility of reducing God's being and activity to clear, comprehensive concepts in the next step in his argument, thus making it more difficult to characterize God as an external agent to range alongside other historical agencies. God cannot be thought to be a body, since God is limitless, infinite, without form and invisible, he claims.[22] For, he reasons, what is circumscribed cannot be revered as God and what is bodily is also composite and composition is the origin of strife and strife of division, which is alien to God. Again, if God is circumscribed, how can God fill and penetrate all things, as Scripture teaches?[23] Either he will exclude everything else, or be a body among bodies, or be somehow mixed with them. To think of God as

---

18. Or. 28.3, *SC* 250, p. 106.

19. Or. 28.4.

20. Here I agree with both Jean Plagnieux Christopher Beeley that Gregory does not intend an absolute denial of knowledge of God's essence. See Beeley, *Gregory of Nazianzus*, pp. 93ff, and Plagnieux, *Saint Grégoire de Nazianze Théologien* (Paris: Éditions Franciscaines, 1951), 278ff.

21. Or. 28.4–6.

22. Or. 28.7.

23. Or. 28.8.

immaterial but limited fares no better, as though the Creator were also among the beings subject to movement: for in that case, what moves everything, and what moves it in turn, and so on?[24]

In Gregory's thinking, then, God, as first cause, must be a being the nature of whom does not lead to this kind of infinite regress and that is an unlimited and unconditioned being, subject to nothing else. Such a being, however, is not "external" to creation in the way bodies, however subtle or interpenetrating, are to one another. On the contrary, one of the consequences of God's limitlessness, besides simplicity and incorporeality, is that God cannot be said to be absent from anywhere. As Gregory goes on to argue, to think of God as located in respect of the cosmos, whether in part of it, or in the whole or above the whole, is to think of God as limited by some boundary.[25] God's limitlessness means we cannot think of God's presence everywhere, God's filling all things, as occupying spatial location. The force of this point is not to clarify the mode of God's presence in all things, but to rule out an inadequate way of conceiving it on analogy with the modes of presence familiar to us. And it brings Gregory to his underlying point, that God cannot be grasped by human thought because comprehension is also a form of circumscription.

In all these ways Gregory reasons through to a position he later summarizes with reference to the divine name that God disclosed to Moses in Exod. 3:14. God cannot be named, he claims in Oration 30. Just as no one can breathe in all the air there is, so no mind can contain the whole being of God nor any sound comprehend it[26]. Rather, we adumbrate his being from its environment—the effects of his actions in creatures, presumably—and assemble "an obscure and weak image from here and there."[27] Theology is a matter of imagining God on this basis, of assembling better and worse images or shadows of the truth.[28] The name that God discloses to Moses, Gregory continues, is the most appropriate of the divine names and the only truly proper name of the divine nature, because it indicates not what God is, but his limitlessness and aseity (the two concepts seem closely connected for Gregory, and necessary to the concept of creator of all things).[29] In Oration 38, Gregory parses the Septuagint's rendering of the Name, ἐγώ εἰμι ὁ Ὢν, as meaning that "God always was, and is and

24. Or. 28.8.

25. Or. 28.10.

26. Christopher Beeley has noted Gregory's tendency to use images of magnitude to express divine incomprehensibility (*Gregory of Nazianzus*, 96–97).

27. Or. 30.17, *SC* 250, p. 263.

28. See my "Divine Names and the Embodied Intellect: Imagination and Sanctification in Gregory of Nazianzus' Account of Theological Language," in *Studia Patristica* L (Leuven: Peeters, 2011), 217–31.

will be; or rather he always 'is.'" [30] Existence in the past and future tenses, he explains, "are fragments of our time and flowing nature."[31] Gregory here does not characterize eternity as timelessness, but in terms of a fullness and unity of existence lacking to temporal beings. In contrast to them, God "possesses existence whole, gathered in himself, neither beginning nor ending, like a sea of being, infinite and unlimited, wholly surpassing all conception of time and nature."[32] All we can comprehend of God is his incomprehensibility. As eternal and infinite, God thus far transcends creatures and creaturely understanding by way of plenitude and integrity of being, but it does not make God remote from them; rather, it means that the entirety of time is present to God and united by God, as Gregory explains in Carmen 1.4.

We have already begun to see the potential benefits of this kind of apophaticism in excluding ways of imagining and conceptualizing divine presence relative to spatial location, but the implications extend to all and every possible manner of thinking about or talking about God and divine action, including scriptural descriptions: not to exclude them, but to insist we shake ourselves loose of the many ways in which they may lead us to think of God as limited, as existing and operating in modes whose possibilities and dynamics we can analyze and from which we can draw secure, clear, and positive inferences. These implications make it much more difficult to characterize divine action as something that could be compared in any straightforward way with historical causes, as another putative cause of historical events that historical inquiry has rendered superfluous for explanatory purposes. To grasp the limits of our concepts and pictures of God is to see how problematic it is to cast God as an agent external to the historical order, whose acts simply interrupt its continuous causal web. It also makes it much more difficult to explain away talk of divine action as merely mythological. In effect, Gregory allows that theological conceptuality and language is mythological in the sense that it is an imaginative way of thinking, but he does not think it follows that such thinking necessarily fails of its object entirely. Instead, it pictures God in terms of the impression we gain of God in God's activity reflected in its effects, and must therefore be subject to careful analysis, to deny of God what such concepts

29. Or. 30.18, SC 250, p. 264: "But we seek a nature to which existence belongs by itself, without being bound to another, and this is truly and wholly proper to God, who is neither limited by something before him nor cut off by something after him, for he was not and will not be."

30. Or. 38.7, SC 358, p. 114.

31. Or. 38.7, SC 358, p. 114.

32. Or. 38.7, SC 358, pp. 114, 116.

would ordinarily denote when applied to creatures. Such analysis is evident in several places in the "Theological Orations."[33]

CREATION AND PROVIDENCE

A second step toward addressing Troeltsch's challenge would be to develop a positive account of divine action in respect of the causal web that constitutes the ordinary historical world, within the constraints of the quality of our knowledge of God's being and action. We have already reviewed some of Gregory's most basic cosmological principles. It is axiomatic for Gregory that composite things left to themselves tend to conflict and division, and that their unity therefore depends on something beyond themselves, ultimately on something not subject to composition or arrangement alongside other things. We have also seen that it is axiomatic for him that there must be some cause for the motion that characterizes the visible world, which is not itself subject to motion nor begun or curtailed by anything. "God" names that entity to which these two paths of observation and reasoning point. Gregory, however, has more to say about how God creates and sustains the cosmos.

For Gregory, the cosmos is twofold: there is a spiritual cosmos, populated by hierarchies of angelic beings, and there is a material cosmos, constituted by an ordered arrangement of material entities shaped by form; human beings inhabit both worlds simultaneously.[34] God created both the visible and invisible worlds, Gregory declares in several places, making actual the world always known to God.[35] The divine mind, fruitful with the forms of what would be, brought the universe into existence by his Word and Spirit.[36] The creation of these two worlds is not an act that God is compelled to undertake, but a willed expression of his creativity and goodness.[37] The act is effortless, in contrast to human beings, for "with God the act of will and its fulfilment are identical."[38]

In creation, God's Word or Logos actualizes the Father's conception of the cosmos, realizing its forms like a master-craftsman, having the Father's own knowledge of them.[39] He endows things with their forms (τὰς ἰδέας), and shapes (τὰ σχήματα), order (τάξις), and existence.[40] That the Logos binds things in ordered relation to one another is a vital condition for the subsistence

33. See Or. 28.15, Or. 29.2–8, Or. 31.7–8. For more on this procedure, see my "Divine Names and the Embodied Intellect."

34. See e.g. Or. 38.9–11 and Carmen 1.4 for the two worlds and the place of human beings; see Or. 28.31.

35. Carmen 1.4, 67–77.

36. Carmen 1.4, 67–77, and Or. 38.9.

of the cosmos.⁴¹ The gift of form and shape, we may suppose, denotes the configuring of things with particular properties. Elsewhere Gregory instances color and the molding of clay into pots and stone into sculpture as examples of the application of form to matter, which he attributes to God in respect of created things.⁴² In Oration 30 Gregory also attributes to the Logos as Wisdom "knowledge of things divine and human," including the *logoi* of the things he has made.⁴³ The association here of the *logos* of something with its making suggests taking *logos* here as the causal principle by which something is brought to be. If so, then Gregory may well, like Plotinus before him, be borrowing the Stoic notion of *logos* as a formative principle and explanatory reason of something—specifically, in Plotinus, causal principles of the organization and unity of things, and distinct from their forms.⁴⁴ This concept seems congruent with Gregory's concern for unity in creatures and in that light makes sense of his use of the term in Oration 30. In Carmen 1.5, Gregory speaks of the divine Mind bearing creation within himself while transcending it at the same time, and whipping it into motion like a spinning top with his unmoving *logoi*.⁴⁵ Nor is this creative action of God by his Word limited to initiating the universe and endowing it and its constituents with unity, order, and form; it is continual,

37. Carmen 1.4, 77; Or. 38.9. In the former passage Gregory speaks of God willing to create intellectual natures; in the latter he talks of God not being satisfied to move in self-contemplation, but as the Good needing to flow out and go forth. This expression would suggest emanation and a natural process, except that the logic of compulsion here is that of beneficence, as he explains: God, being goodness itself, must go forth in order to maximize the number of God's beneficiaries. This conclusion is supported by Carmen 1.4, and two further passages. In Or 29.2, Gregory specifically rules out the thought of God naturally overflowing with respect to the generation of Son and Spirit (Or. 29.2). Earlier in the same oration he also says that God's rule of the universe is founded in part on harmony of will between the divine hypostases (Or. 29.1).

38. Or. 20.9 in Martha Vinson's translation, *St. Gregory of Nazianzus* (Washington, DC: Catholic University of America Press, 2003), 113.

39. Or. 30.11. Here Gregory is speaking primarily of Christ's miracles but widens the scope of the Logos' action to the government, preservation, and creation of all things. See also Or. 38.9.

40. Or. 32.7.

41. Or. 6.14.

42. Carmen 1.4, 9–17. Here Gregory talks of εἶδος rather than ἰδέα or σχῆμα, but the sense seems to be the same.

43. Or. 30.20. This definition of wisdom goes back at least as far as Philo, who defines it as "the knowledge of things divine and human and the causes of those things" in *De congressu eruditionis gratia* 79, cited in Kenneth Schenck, *A Brief Guide to Philo* (Louisville: Westminster John Knox, 2005), 11.

44. See Kevin Corrigan "Essence and Existence in the *Enneads*," and Michael F. Wagner, "Plotinus on the Nature of Physical Reality," in *The Cambridge Companion to Plotinus*, ed. Lloyd Gerson (Cambridge: Cambridge University Press,1996).

and creatures are continually dependent upon God in this way. The Logos is called "Power," Gregory explains, as "the one who preserves created things, and supplies them with the power of cohesion."[46] Gregory has in general less to say about the work of the Spirit in creation. His role, according to Oration 38.9, is to perfect the creatures actualized by the Logos, and that role seems to be one of bringing rational beings into communion with God.[47]

Altogether, Gregory's use of these concepts indicates an understanding of divine action that establishes things in their particular organizational unities, with their characteristic forms, qualities, and attributes, and in their particular contexts within a wider order, thus bringing about, through a mode of action incomprehensible to us, the conditions for complex causal interactions in the balanced fluidity and stability we observe in the world. In all this, God is intimately involved without becoming an immanent cause as the source of the ideal causal forces that configure and lend coherence and cohesion to the cosmos.

We can fill out this picture in a little more detail, first with respect to spiritual beings. Here Gregory is explicitly cautious, aware of the limitations of human knowledge of this realm that inspired Scripture discloses.[48] God, Gregory implies in Oration 28, conserves "spiritual and heavenly nature" by the word by which he brought them into being.[49] This nature is incorporeal, and of it we know only that there are angels, archangels, thrones, powers, principalities, Dominions, Splendors, Ascensions, and spiritual powers. These are unmixed, pure natures that either cannot or only with difficulty turn toward evil, and they always move around the first cause, from which they derive

45. Carmen 1.5, 2–3. For Gregory, we may infer, motion depends on order. Indeed, he seems to think that form is kinetic when he claims that "Matter is more when mixed form in motion," Carmen 1.4, 19, in Moreschini, ed., *Poemata Arcana*, 16.

46. Or. 30.17, *SC* 250, p. 268.

47. Or. 38.9, Or. 41.11 and 14, where the Spirit is "co-creator" with the Son (*SC* 358, p. 344). See further on the work of the Spirit below.

48. On Gregory's caution, see Or. 28.31 and Carmen 1.6, 27ff. On Gregory's understanding of Scripture, see chapter 3. His reference to various kinds of spiritual being in Or. 28.31 alludes to a host of scriptural texts, at least some of which are helpfully identified by the *Sources Chrétiennes* editors, Paul Gallay and Maurice Jourjon: Rom. 8:38; Dan. 10:13 (LXX); Jude 9; 1 Thess. 4:16; Col. 1:16; Eph. 1:21; Rev. 4:5; Heb. 1:14.

49. Or. 28.31. Here Gregory discusses "spiritual nature" in order to show how little we understand of it. When discussing Ps. 103:4 (LXX) he ventures the possibility that "makes" here means only that God "conserves [them] by the word according to which he brought them into being." It would seem reasonable to infer that Gregory holds this view about the sustaining of angels; the uncertainty is as to whether it explains the meaning of the verse.

their purest splendor, which differs, Gregory speculates, in degree in proportion to their nature and rank.[50] He pictures an ordered world of beings whose characteristic quality—splendor—derives from God.[51] Indeed, on his account, it is the way they take form from their divine archetype that constitutes them the kind of creatures they are and enables them to pursue their characteristic actions: "So far are they shaped and formed by Beauty that they become other lights and are able to illumine others by showering and transmitting the light that comes from God."[52] Indeed, this constitution enables them, we may infer, to help order and unite the visible cosmos. They are "servants of the divine will, powers by natural and acquired strength, ranging over everything, present and ready to all everywhere, by the zeal of their service and the nimbleness of their nature." According to God's ordering and delimiting of their responsibilities, they serve in different parts of the cosmos, leading everything into unity "at the beck and call of the Creator of all things."[53] All the while, Gregory adds, they ceaselessly hymn the divine magnificence, in order that they should not cease to receive God's blessings: a claim that suggests that their well-being and effective service are contingent on their orientation to one from whom they derive their light, order, and function.

Elsewhere, Gregory likens the action of God in constituting these spiritual beings so that they can pursue their apportioned and characteristic activities to the action of sunlight in the atmosphere:

Even as a sunbeam, travelling through rain-heavy, calm air, encountering clouds in its refracted, revolving movements, produces the many-coloured rainbow curve; everywhere around, the upper air gleams brightly with many circles dissolving towards the edges; such

50. Gregory makes the same point about the difficulty with which angels turn to evil also in Or. 38.9 and Carmen 1.6.

51. Cf. Or. 32.8, where Gregory specifies that order maintains celestial things and that there is order in spiritual beings and in angels.

52. Or. 28.31, *SC* 250, p. 172. It does not necessarily follow that Gregory here has in mind a descending chain of emanation whereby the lower a being is in the chain the further from God. Indeed, as we shall see, his cosmology rules this out. Rather, his point is to emphasize the consequence of the intensity of formation the angels receive from God: so light-like do they become that they communicate to others the light they have received.

53. Or. 28.31, *SC* 250, p. 174, following Lionel Wickham's rendering of πρὸς μίαν σύννευσιν in *On God and Christ: St. Gregory of Nazianzus: The Five Theological Orations and Two Letters to Cledonius*, trans. L. Wickham and F. Williams (Crestwood, NY: St. Vladimir's Seminary Press, 2002), 65. Their own harmony, Gregory implies in Or. 6.12, derives from God.

is the nature of lights also, the highest light always shining brightly upon minds which are lesser beams.[54]

God is the source of lights, "a light inexpressible, eluding capture, fleeing the speed of a pursuing mind, whenever it approaches . . ."[55] After God there are second lights, "shining angels" who run swiftly through the air at God's command, some attending him, others overseeing men, cities, and nations.[56] Gregory's denial of the eternity of matter precludes us thinking of God acting on preexisting matter and ought to govern our reading of this imagery. What it does indicate is a conception of divine action, continuous with God's being, and producing effortlessly a glistening, harmonious society of spiritual beings, at once communicating existence, form, and beautiful order by its operation without change or alteration to itself.

Second, Gregory paints an even more detailed picture with regard to the earthly world. Here he does not introduce new theological concepts, but rather fills out his vision of the effects of the divine creative action we have already discussed on visible things. In Orations 6, he depicts in detail the manifold ways in which the visible creation exhibits the order that derives from God. Commending the virtues of peace and harmony to his father's recently divided congregation in Nazianzus, Gregory incites them to imitate God, in whom there is such concord that God is named Peace and Love.[57] The angels who did not fall are likewise characterized by peace because they participate in God's own unity by divine gift; those who show their attachment to peace are close to God and things divine.[58] In imitating God, the soul made in the image of God preserves its character and nobility. We are taught the same lesson, Gregory continues, by the visible creation.[59] God reveals himself in the silent proclamation of its peaceable order, "so long as that cosmos is tranquil and at peace with itself, remaining within the proper limits of its nature and none of its elements rises up against another, nor oversteps the bounds of kindness with which the craftsman-Logos bound the universe."[60]

These kindly bonds and this order are exhibited, Gregory argues first, in heaven's relations to the air, through light, and to the earth, through rain. In

54. Carmen 1.6, 1–7, in D. A. Sykes's translation in *St. Gregory of Nazianzus: Poemata Arcana*, ed. C. Moreschini (Oxford: Clarendon, 1997), 27.

55. Carmen 1.6, 8–9, in Sykes's translation in Moreschini, ed., *Poemata Arcana*, 27.

56. Carmen 1.6, 11–26, quoting from Sykes's translation in Moreschini, ed., *Poemata Arcana*, 27.

57. Or. 6.12–14.

58. Or. 6.13–14.

59. Gregory makes the same point to a similar end in Or. 32.8.

60. Or. 6.14, *SC* 405, p. 158.

turn, the earth and the air display the affection of parents toward their offspring in respect of living beings "by providing nutrition and favouring all living things with means to respire, thus preserving them in life."[61] The seasons too, "which mingle gently, and gradually make way for one another, and tame their extremes with the mean," also seem directed by peace.[62] The same goes for the regular alternation of day and night—the one disposing us to work, the other to rest, the sun, moon, and the orderly succession of the stars, the sea and land "in their gentle intermingling and useful give and take," feeding and richly furnishing human beings with supplies.[63] Gregory goes on to adduce rivers flowing through mountains and plains, spilling over only to benefit and not turning back to cover the earth, the mingling and fusion of the elements of the body, the proportions and agreements of limbs, the distinct foods, kinds and dwellings of animals, some ruling, others ruled, some domesticated, others free.[64] All these things are thus directed and governed "by the first causes of harmony."[65] In all these ways, we see in visible things the order bestowed upon it by the Logos.

Divine action, in this way, establishes and maintains a multitude of complex and fluid systems and organisms, not by constant micro-interventions but by supplying and constantly upholding their basic principles of operation, organization, and unity. To make this claim, however, is not to explain the inner workings of such entities. More than a decade after delivering Oration 6, Gregory offered his congregation in Constantinople another vivid pen-portrait of the visible world in its ordered ways, in a passage that frequently echoes God's interrogation of Job about the mysteries of nature in Job 38–40, and that serves to illustrate the limits of human understanding of that order and hence to argue *a fortiori* our epistemic constraints in understanding the divine nature. What, he begins, is the mixture that is a human being?

> What is its motion? How is the immortal mingled with the mortal? How does it both flow below and is borne about above? How does the soul circulate, giving life and participating in the passions?

---

61. Or. 6.14, *SC* 405, p. 158.

62. Or. 6.15, *SC* 405, pp. 158, 160.

63. Or. 6.15, *SC* 405, p. 160.

64. I take the elements (στοιχεῖα) Gregory mentions here to be those of the body given the mention of limbs that follows and the parallels with Or. 32.8, where in a similar list Gregory specifies "the order among the elements which compose the body" as an illustration of how order constitutes the universe, *SC* 318, p. 100.

65. Or. 6.15, *SC* 405, p. 160.

> How is the mind circumscribed and unlimited, remaining in us and
> flowing forth into all things with rapid motion? How is it partaken
> of through speech, moving through the air and entering into the
> realities? How does it commune with sense and withdraw from the
> senses?[66]

Just as puzzling, Gregory points out, is the formation of such beings, their
construction in nature's workshop and their induction into ways of sustaining
life. Equally in need of explanation are various features of human sociality
and behavior: the disposition toward mutual relations of parents and offspring
so that they hold together in affection. More generally, he wonders at the
distinct characteristics of different races, the mortality and immortality through
reproduction of the same (human) animals, the harmonious, beautiful, and
practically advantageous arrangement of limbs and body-parts, the production
of voice and its reception by way of the beating and shaping of the air in
between, the workings of sight and other senses, of sleep, dreams, memory,
reason, anger, and desire.

Gregory goes on to raise a host of questions about other animals and
their differences from us and one another in respect of their natures, how they
produce and raise their young, their habitats, habits, and self-governance; the
ways they are organized (in herds, as solitaries), the ways they feed (herbivores
and carnivores), their temperaments (fierce, gentle), their relations with human
beings, their different levels of intelligence and teachability, sensory awareness,
mobility, size, beauty, strength, ability to protect themselves, their industry,
stature, their relation to their habitat, their ornamentation, conjugality or lack
of it, and so on. Then he inquires more particularly about the habits of fish,
birds, bestial intelligence, and the characteristics of various plants before turning
to examine diverse features of sea and landscape, the air and the heavens. As
his general questions about animals had already indicated, these closer inquiries
evince close attention to the characteristics of natural phenomena, as his
discussion of fish shows:

> Examine for my sake things that swim, which slip through the
> waters, and fly, as it were, upon the fluid element, and suck from
> it their own air, even though they are endangered by ours, as we
> are in water; examine their habits and passions, their minglings
> and offspring and greatness and beauty, their love of their habitat
> and their wanderings, assemblings and dispersions, the properties in

66. Or. 28.22, *SC* 250, pp. 144, 146.

which they nearly resemble things that live on land, the things they have in common and those which are opposed in form and name.[67]

As in Oration 6, Gregory here is keenly observant of diverse, richly complex organisms, whose fluid order, form, qualities, and existence, from moment to moment, he would ascribe to the Logos. [68]Yet here he emphasizes the mysteriousness of these forms of order and puzzling regularity. That they can be described suggests they can be further investigated, and so that Gregory's theological explanation of this wealth of evidence of order and form does not at all preclude partial and successful explanations of the workings of the things he marvels at, only that to account for their having order and unity at all is ultimately a theological question that cannot be solved in clear, comprehensive explanations. This conclusion takes us a little further, for it suggests that in Gregory's thought one could coherently hold together the activity of God in configuring, ordering, upholding, and uniting the complex systems and organisms of the universe with the complex, interconnected causal operations those systems and organisms involve, and the investigation of those systems and organisms in their own terms and in relation to their environments and contexts without need to invoke theological explanations until one reaches a fundamental level of inquiry.

All this verges upon an account of God's providential governance of the cosmos as well as of its continual creation. In Carmen 1.5, Gregory declares that it is not the stars but God who "governs [or 'steers'] all things, as the Word guides here and there what he placed by his purposes above and below."[69] The language of governing here is taken from the nautical world. It could be rendered, as Sykes does, "God steers." Together with the language of guidance, it suggests that providence involves a directing of the whole complex, finely balanced order and its many component systems. Rather than an absolute determination of every individual event, God's governance is usually effected through the normal operation of systems and organisms. However, Gregory does not exclude God from disrupting those operations in accordance with his purpose. In Oration 6, he argues that we realize how good is peace when

[m]atter is at odds with itself and becomes hard to manage, whether because it seeks dissolution through conflict, or because God casts loose something from the harmonious order in order to frighten and

---

67. Or. 6.16 *SC* 405, p. 160.

68. In *St. Gregory of Nazianzus: Poemata Arcana*, 25.

69. Carmen 1.5, 34–36.

> punish sinners—the sea assaults or the earth shakes, or strange rains
> fall, or the sun is eclipsed, or the season is too long, or fire spreads . . .

Such disasters, then, may be due to the inherent propensity of matter to dissipate, or to God disrupting the order he upholds things in. That God might for good reason loose some part of a harmoniously configured whole seems consistent with Gregory's view that it is God who, by his Word, is the source and upholder of that order in the first place. Because the order of complex causal systems always already derives from God as the fount of its unity, such an action is not an external intervention but a withdrawal of a measure of the ordering power that makes the system possible from moment to moment. In any case, Gregory can also entertain the possibility that such disasters may even be part of an ordered universe under God's guidance, for the correction of sinners.[70] He seems to be able to conceive that the operations of creaturely processes and systems may be directed without interruption in such a way as to enact God's purposes toward particular human beings, rather like instruments. Indeed, such instrumental use of creaturely causes seems implied by the metaphor of steering all things.

HUMAN BEINGS

One of Troeltsch's concerns, in his understanding of history, is to uphold the free action of human agents within the wider nexus of historical causes, and to relate their highest moral accomplishments to a postulated suprahistorical goal. Gregory's theological anthropology relates them to God as the source and goal of their subjectivity but locates the realization of their freedom in pursuit of that end in the context of the temporal, material cosmos. This understanding frames human actions as purposeful and responsive in and through their context in time and configured creaturely interactions. It establishes the possibility of a meaningful pattern to their actions in those circumstances, and indicates the way in which Gregory understands God's ordering of those circumstances with a view to human response, namely in terms of pedagogy.[71]

In Oration 38, Gregory sets the creation of human beings in the context of God's benevolent creative action. The basic plot of his narrative, which seems to

70. Or. 16.5.

71. Gregory thus invoked a long tradition of thinking about God's saving action in pedagogical terms, stretching back to Clement, Irenaeus, and Origen, and drawing on traditions in Hellenic philosophy. See F. X. Portmann, *Die göttliche Paidagogia bei Gregor von Nazianz. Eine dogmengeschichtliche Studie* (St. Ottilien, Deutschland: Eos Verlag der Erzabtei St. Ottilien, 1954).

amount to a gloss on the Genesis creation stories, is the goodness of God and the wondrous expansion of divine benefaction in creation and redemption. Thus the intrinsic desire of Goodness to multiply its beneficiaries led God to create the spiritual realm.[72] And since he saw that that world was good, "he conceived a second, material and visible cosmos, that which is composed of heaven and earth and the things in between them."[73] This world too was laudable because of the harmonious arrangement of everything in it, "one thing finely adjusted to another and everything toward everything else."[74] Finally, the Word created a being in whom all the wealth and wisdom of God's goodness could be made known, and hence the Word formed a living being from both visible and invisible natures: the human being, "taking his body from pre-existing matter and breathing into it his own breath, which is . . . the intellectual soul and image of God."[75] In this way, the human is a microcosm partaking of both the spiritual and visible worlds.[76] This dual constitution serves a divine, pedagogical purpose. Human beings are spirit and flesh: the one because of grace, that human beings might endure and praise their benefactor; the other on account of human pride, so that by through suffering the constraints of the flesh we might be recalled (to our spiritual vocation) "and be trained when ambitious for greatness."[77] Humans are immortal as spiritual beings yet mortal because of their materiality, and that materiality constrains them in their participation in the spiritual realm, which limitation is intended to curb their pride and ambition and so to train them. Some greater future for them is clearly implied, but one that will be reached through a process of education.

Gregory has already said that human beings are initiates of the spiritual world, and he now adds that the height of the initiating event, the mystery, of their created constitution is that they are "being deified by their inclination to God."[78] For, he explains, the measure of light of truth we receive here bears me toward this goal: "to see and experience the splendour of God."[79] Human beings, in Gregory's understanding, are rational animals. Like angels, they have

72. Or. 38.9.

73. Or. 38.10, *SC* 358, p. 122.

74. Or. 38.10, *SC* 358, p. 122.

75. Or. 38.11, *SC* 358, p. 124.

76. For an extended study of this duality in Gregory's anthropology, see Anna-Stina Ellveston, *The Dual Nature of Man. A Study in the Theological Anthropology of Gregory of Nazianzus* (Uppsala: Uppsala University, 1981).

77. Or. 38.11, *SC* 358, p. 126.

78. Or. 38.11, *SC* 358, p. 126.

79. Or. 38.11, *SC* 358, p. 126.

rationality through participation in God's own light, which constitutes them as lights of a lower order. Gregory tells us in Oration 40 that "God is the highest and unapproachable and ineffable light . . . the illuminator of rational nature."[80] The first such nature after God is the angelic: "an outflow or participation in the first light." We may conclude that the angels partake in God's light by way of divine illumination, God's intellectual action of bestowing such participation. Since man is "a third light," it follows that we enjoy rationality on the same terms (if not to the same degree). We may also conclude that to be spiritual, to be πνεῦμα, is to receive (and be constituted by reception of) that illumination. It is for this reason that Gregory says in Oration 38 that humans are πνεῦμα "because of grace" and that they might be recalled to their vocation. For, as he explains in Oration 21, God is the one to whom human beings are returned "through the illumination innate in them."[81]

Because humans are embodied, they receive only a small ray of illumination in this life, which limits the degree and quality of their apprehension of God and the spiritual world. Yet that light excites in them a desire for God. For God, moreover, not only sustains but is also the supremely desirable object of our intellectual gaze. As the sun enables vision and visibility but is also the most beautiful of the things we can see, so God "who bestows the power to understand or be understood is himself the highest of intellectual realities, to whom all tend and beyond whom none are borne."[82] As Gregory says in Oration 28, "All rational nature desires God and the first cause."[83] In God is thus (according to Oration 21.1) "the end of our desires and for those who attain to him, the repose of all contemplation."[84] Gregory implies in these passages that this goal is reached in knowledge of God. As he says in Oration 20, "the perfection of beings [is] the knowledge of God."[85] Here rationality is, from the start, linked to God as its source and ordered to him, and thus inseparable from rational desire (as distinct from irrational passions). Knowledge of God is much more than justified true belief; it is the apprehension of, and (he implies) delight in, the ultimate and ultimately beautiful reality that transcends our minds. It is our small enjoyment of that light which excites our desire for more.

---

80. Or. 40.5, *SC* 358, p. 204.
81. Or. 21.1, *SC* 270, p. 110.
82. Or. 21.1, *SC* 270, p. 112.
83. Or. 28.13, *SC* 250, p. 128.
84. Or. 21.1, *SC* 270, p. 112.
85. Or. 20.12, *SC* 270, p. 82.

Gregory amplifies this notion in terms of divine pedagogy in Oration 28 and earlier in Oration 38. In Oration 28, Gregory speculates as to why God is so difficult for human beings to apprehend. It is perhaps, he ventures, "lest ease of acquisition should make casting away the acquired easy also."[86] what we acquire with difficulty we tend to preserve, whereas what we acquire easily we swiftly spurn, thinking we can recover it again. It is perhaps also to avoid the fate of Lucifer, who received full illumination and rebelled against God. Hence God "placed the darkness of our bodies between us and him, like the cloud of old between the Egyptians and the Israelites."[87] The body is, he suggests, the darkness in which God hides from us, "through which a few espy only a little."[88] This constraint upon our spiritual vision is intended, again, to train us to value the vision of God and to prevent us, perhaps in our immaturity, from letting full enjoyment of God give rise to proud conceit and defiance.

In Oration 38, the pedagogical theme has a more positive content. Having discussed God's infinitude and the difficulty of contemplating God, Gregory explains the reason for this difficulty. It seems, he explains, that God wishes

> by what we can grasp, to draw us to himself—for he is finally ungraspable, beyond our hope and reach—and by being ungraspable to excite our wonder, and being wondered at, might be the more desired, and being desired, might purify, and purifying might make us God-like, and with those who become so, as with his kindred, to dwell with them—I dare to speak boldly—as God is united with gods and known, perhaps even as much as he already knows them.[89]

What we see of God, by the little illumination we enjoy now, draws us toward him as our wonder at what lies beyond excites our desire and so motivates us to undergo the purification that will assimilate us to God and so prepare us for union and intimacy with God. In Oration 32, Gregory spells out this connection between purification and assimilation as different terms for what prepares us to see God more explicitly. God is Light, says Gregory, but hides himself from us so that "Light may converse with light, always drawing [us] to the height through our desire, and so that the mind may approach the most Pure through purification, and he may appear in part now, in part later, as the reward for our inclination or assimilation to him now."[90] In Oration 2, Gregory

86. Or. 28.12, SC 250, p. 124.

87. Or. 28.12, *SC* 250, p. 124.

88. Or. 28.12, *SC* 250, p. 124.

89. Or. 38.8, *SC* 250, p. 116.

presents the same idea in more explicitly erotic terms. God, the purest light, "illumines the intellect and escapes its swiftness and elevation, which always retires as much as it is comprehended and leads his lover to the heavens, by fleeing and hiding as though he were being laid hold of."[91]

Altogether, these passages understand human beings as constituted in view of a project, namely, to attain to union with God, intimacy with God, the unimpeded vision of God.[92] This is the goal God sets before them, and to which they are constitutionally ordered by being spiritual beings. It is, however, a goal they will have to reach over time and through a process of transformation, because they are embodied.[93] This process precludes their attaining their goal with an ease and rapidity that might precipitate pride, rebellion, and the rejection of God. Instead God seeks to educate human beings, drawing them after himself, motivating their participation in a process of transformation that will prepare them to enjoy the end for which they are created. So constituted, human beings are created as beings who are to undergo a history. They are to grow in likeness to God, progressively over time, as embodied beings in the midst of the complex systems of organisms and processes, which Gregory calls in Carmen 1.4 "a royal palace to house God's image."[94]

Implicit in this account so far is the idea that human beings as rationally desirous creatures are also possessed of free will.[95] Gregory makes this idea explicit when he goes on to discuss the story of the first humans in the Garden in Genesis 2–3. God placed this mixed being who longs for God in paradise,

90. Or. 32.15, SC 318, p. 116. Cf. Or. 40.5, 4–5: "as much as we are purified, [God] appears [to us]," SC 358, p. 204.

91. Or. 2.76, SC 247, pp. 188, 190.

92. I take deification, for Gregory, to be a process of human beings' assimilation to and increasing participation in God culminating in graced union with God. There is not space here to discuss this issue further. For a range of views see Beeley, Gregory of Nazianzus, 116–17; Ellverson, The Dual Nature of Man, 25; Donald F. Winslow, The Dynamics of Salvation. A Study in Gregory of Nazianzus (Cambridge, MA: The Philadelphia Patristic Foundation, 1979) and Norman Russell, The Doctrine of Deification in the Greek Patristic Tradition (Oxford: Oxford University Press, 2004), 213–24. Of these views mine is closest to Beeley's.

93. Here I agree with both Donald Winslow and Christopher Beeley that for Gregory human beings were created to grow toward God in a process of divinisation. See Winslow, The Dynamics of Salvation, 58–60; Beeley, Gregory of Nazianzus, 116–18.

94. Carmen 1.4, 99, in Sykes's translation, in Moreschini, ed., Poemata Arcana, 23.

95. For Gregory, free will would seem to be more an attribute of a rational nature than a distinct faculty. For he describes willing or intention (βούλησις) as the inclination (or turning,' ροπή) of the intellect and the concurrence (συνδρομή) [with the intellect in that orientation] of the things within us," Carmen 1.2, 34, 35–36 (PG 37 948A).

whatever it was, and honored him with free will (αὐτεξουσία), "so that the good might belong to the one who chooses it no less than to him who provided the seed."[96] Human choices, then, will be central to the history to unfold, in order that human beings may truly enjoy the good for which they are ordered, as something they have embraced for themselves, suggesting that, since human beings are embodied from the beginning in this account, human actions will be central too.

Gregory's description of the original condition of human beings returns us to the theme of divine pedagogy. God gave human beings a law "as material for their free will."[97] Gregory understands the tree of knowledge that they were not to touch as a symbol of contemplation, which is only safe to attain for the more perfect in disposition. For those less developed in character and still greedy or curious in their desire, however, it is not good. Gregory thus suggests an immaturity to human beings as created in respect of the desire they have for God, and hence a need of moral formation and an element of drama in the history they are involved in.[98] That potential for drama is quickly realized when Adam and Eve succumb to temptation, and, banished from paradise, undergo a deleterious change in their condition. They make for themselves garments of skin, which Gregory interprets as "the thicker flesh, mortal and stubborn"; they also become mortal, in order that God may set a limit to their sin: a form of divine compassion for them.[99] This is the condition Gregory often laments in his writings: the warring passions, tossing us up and down like waves, the dizzying impact of the senses and the way we are carried hither and thither by our desires, the confusion and ignorance "like a night-battle."[100] At the heart of this problem is the soul's disordered orientation to matter instead of God, an orientation that entails bondage, preventing it from turning to God's light.[101] In this condition the soul, created in God's image as a mirror of divine things, becomes marred and tarnished.[102] For Gregory, human and cosmic history takes its shape from God's compassionate antidote to this plight.

96. Or. 38.12, *SC* 358, pp. 126, 128.

97. Or. 38.12, *SC* 358, p. 128.

98. As Winslow points out, on Gregory's understanding the potential for failure attends the potential for growth in humanity's created constitution (*The Dynamics of Salvation*, 60–61).

99. Or. 38.12, *SC* 358, p. 130.

100. E.g. Or. 2.91; Or. 7.17, *SC* 405, p. 222, from which the quoted phrase is taken; Or. 7.21 and Or. 8.23.

101. As Gregory implies, for example, in Or. 8.19, Or. 20.1, and Or. 21.2.

102. As Gregory implies in Or. 20.1.

The Divine Economy

Gregory's understanding of history is structured by the salient moments of God's pedagogical saving action: the period of the Law, the incarnation, the gift of the Spirit, and the consummation of the Kingdom. In this way, Father, Son, and Spirit educate the human race, and manifest themselves to us. That education and explication give to history the shape of salvation.

This shape Gregory explicates most fully in Oration 31. In the course of an argument about whether calling the Holy Spirit "God" is scriptural, to which I will return in the next chapter, Gregory describes the shifts in history brought about by God's saving activity. He speaks there of two transitions in human affairs, which Scripture calls Testaments and shakings of the earth (an allusion to Heb. 12:26). "The first was the change from idols to the law, and the second from the law to the Gospel."[103] Scripture announces a third shaking, the transition from here below to the things "there," to the eschatological condition, we may infer, where things may no longer be shaken. None of these changes were sudden, "so that we might not be coerced, but persuaded."[104] For what is not done voluntarily, Gregory reasons, does not endure, whereas what is voluntarily done also lasts longer and is more secure, since it depends not on the coercer, but on ourselves. The latter, he maintains, is proper to God's goodness, the former to tyranny. Thus God, "like a teacher and like a doctor, removes one custom, but concedes another, permitting a little for pleasure."[105] For, he adds, "it is not easy to change things honoured by custom and the long passage of time."[106] Hence the first change—from idols to the law—"allowed sacrifices while abolishing idols, and the second abolished sacrifices, but did not check circumcision."[107] The removal of one thing is accepted for the sake of what is permitted. In this way Gentiles became Jews and Jews, Christians, drawn toward the gospel by gradual changes. The gospel, we should note, here denotes not merely a message but a form of human life comparable to life before and life under the Law. Gregory thus fills out a grand vision of divine pedagogy at the level of the whole human race, whose rationale accords with that given for the gift of free will to human beings; just as they must be able to choose in order truly to enjoy God's good gifts, so they must be willing participants in their own reformation once they go astray.

---

103. Or. 31.25, *SC* 250, p. 322.
104. Or. 31.25, *SC* 250, p. 324.
105. Or. 31.25, *SC* 250, p. 324.
106. Or. 31.25, *SC* 250, p. 324.
107. Or. 31.25, *SC* 250, p. 324.

Gregory gives a similar account of the first of these shifts in Oration 45, when explaining the origins of the feast of Pascha. When God wished, in his mercy, to recall us to our original condition, Gregory tells us, no violence could be deployed, since such a cure "would not persuade us" and might indeed aggravate our condition by affronting our chronic pride.[108] For "a slanting sapling cannot bear to be bent the other way all at once, and straightened by force of hand, it will be sooner broken than corrected; nor will a spirited horse over a certain age [bear] the tyranny of the whip without coaxing and encouragement."[109] We cannot be recalled to wholeness by coercion, only through persuasion. Therefore God

> gave us the law as an aid, like the wall around a fortified place, standing between God and idols, and drawing us away from the latter and towards the former.[110] He concedes a little at the beginning, in order to take a greater part. He concedes sacrifices for a time, in order to establish God in us. Then, at the right time, he destroys sacrifices, wisely delivering us by gradual removals, and drawing us over to the Gospel when we were already trained in obedience.[111]

"Thus and for this reason," Gregory concludes, "the written law came in, gathering us into Christ."[112] It was a means of preparing us for the gospel. Like a citadel wall, then, the Law was intended to enable us to pass out of danger and idolatry and into a place where God is worshipped, and facilitates our entry, and the establishment of right worship among us, by permitting sacrifices until such time as we are trained in obedience to God. God, for Gregory, is characterized by mercy—an idea well attested in the Bible—whose response to human failure is not punishment as such but to work patiently for our restoration by a process of reeducation, step by step. To the notion in Oration 31 of the removal of customs being facilitated by the concession of others, this passage adds the thought of law as a kind of training or formation in obedience, conducive to the reception of further transformation.

108. Or. 45.12 (PG 36 640A).

109. Or. 45.12 (PG 36 640A–B). "Coaxing and encouragement" is Browne and Swallow's translation of τινὸς κολακείας καὶ ποππυσμάτων (Nicene and Post-Nicene Fathers VII, 427).

110. Gregory must have in mind what a citadel represented to those dwelling in its hinterland: a place of refuge toward which one was drawn in time of danger. Perhaps he was thinking particularly of Jerusalem, the city where God's presence dwelt.

111. Or. 45.12 (PG 36 640B).

112. Or. 45.13 (PG 36 640C).

Here and elsewhere Gregory seems to treat the history of Israel as representative of God's dealings with all of humanity. One finds a similar treatment of Israel as standing for all of humanity in Oration 38, where Gregory tells us that after human beings disobeyed in Paradise, they were at first corrected (παιδευθεὶς) in many ways to counter many kinds of sin, "which the root of wickedness brought forth according to different causes and at different times."[113] Nazianzen then lists these different kinds of pedagogical discipline, encouragements, and training: "by word, law, prophecies, benevolent acts, threats and promises, calamities, floods, conflagrations, wars, victories, losses, signs in heaven, signs in the air, from the earth, from the sea, un-hoped for changes in men, cities, and peoples."[114] The list alludes in general terms to events to which the Old Testament bears witness: it is largely Israel's history, taken to stand for that of all humanity before Christ. The list also indicates the pluriform character of God's saving pedagogy; that God finesses this education and correction to times and circumstances.

In Carmen 1.8, however, Gregory attends more closely to the particularity of Israel in God's purposes. He tells us that divine law was given for the Hebrews, "who were the first to perceive the God who rules on high," and later law was extended to the ends of the earth.[115] The reason for this order of things lies in God's loving succor, Gregory explains. The enemy of humankind, having driven Adam from Paradise, sought to mislead his descendants into evil and death by turning their eyes to the stars and to idolatry in respect of legendary figures from the past. The "race of holy Hebrews" also came to grief, he continues.[116] For "they did not yield to the prophets who lamented their condition, who pleaded with them, and always proclaimed the wrath of their Lord—instead, they killed them."[117] Most of Israel's kings were wicked and idolatrous, and hence Israel "drew the jealous anger of the great God, and were scattered."[118] The Gentiles

> entered upon the road in their place so that, by drawing them to
> jealousy, God might guide them back again to be led into pious faith

113. Or. 38.13, SC 358, p. 130.

114. I have translated apeilais as "threats and promises," for the word can bear both meanings in extension of the basic notion of "something held out before somebody." The context is open to both and both are in fact found in biblical narrative, law, and prophecy.

115. Carmen 1.8, 2–4, in Moreschini, ed., Poemata Arcana, 40.

116. Carmen 1.8, in Moreschini, ed., Poemata Arcana, 42.

117. Carmen 1.8, in Moreschini, ed., Poemata Arcana, 42.

118. Carmen 1.8, in Moreschini, ed., Poemata Arcana, 42.

in Christ, changing course late in the day, when they are full up with sorrow, through envy of a newly come people.[119]

This hope, Gregory adds, is for a later time. In the meantime, where the Hebrews have dishonored their Law, the whole world has at last come to enjoy a share in the honor of divine Law, through the actions of the incarnate Son. This account of the Jewish people credits them with perception of God's rule, and Gregory frequently makes appeal in his orations to Old Testament saints as examples of theologians and holiness. At the same time, his is an account dominated by their failure to keep the Law, deeply colored by the criticisms of Israel voiced in the prophetic literature of the Old Testament. Israel's history as a nation often has a monitory value in Gregory's rhetoric.[120] While aware of their privilege in God's purposes, he lacks any developed sense of God's abiding bond with his people, of their election in the divine purposes (an omission that does not help Gregory acknowledge or make sense of Jesus Christ's identity as a member of the "holy race of Hebrews").

Nevertheless, Gregory shows here both a reverence for Israel's past and a hope for Israel's future that is characteristic of his work and rare in the early church.[121] Moreover, he clearly thinks that the Jewish people continue to feature prominently in God's plans, to the extent that, somewhat as in Paul's argument in Romans 11, the entrance of Gentiles in their place is a means whereby to provoke their return. At the same time, in all these passages, Gregory thinks of human existence as immersed in time and change, but a time and changefulness through which God works. God's saving work is calibrated to the particularities of our needs at different stages in time, each change preparing for future transformation. Equally, Gregory stresses the pedagogical character of God's work: the persuasion, training, and correction of human beings. All these ways somehow lead up to Jesus Christ and the gospel, which in turn prepares for a third, presumably eschatological transformation.

119. Carmen 1.8, in Moreschini, ed., *Poemata Arcana*, 42.

120. See e.g. Or. 6.17–18, where Israel's divisions, dispersions, and sufferings are for Gregory a cause for lament and sorrow, but also an object lesson for the congregation in Nazianzus.

121. Gregory also shows respect for some contemporary Jews when he quotes them as sources for their past, which he venerates. See his approval of "an ancient Hebrew custom" regarding Scripture related by the "wiser Hebrews" in Or. 2.49, his commendation of the Maccabean martyrs for their devotion to the Law in Or. 15, and his appeal to their refusal to use the Tetragrammaton in speech in Or. 30.17. At the same time, however, "Jewish" was also for him a term of abuse to apply to those who denied the divinity of Son and Spirit (e.g. Or. 2.37), or to insist the latter be literally enunciated in Scripture (Or. 31.24), and he often contrasted the literal keeping of festivals by the Jews with their spiritual celebration among Christians (Or. 11.6; Or. 41.1).

In Oration 31, Gregory contrasts this pattern of progress through gradual suppressions with a second, of "perfection through additions."[122] Thus:

> The Old Testament proclaimed the Father clearly and the Son more obscurely. The New revealed the Son, and indicated the divinity of the Spirit. Now the Spirit dwells amongst us, and provides us with a clearer disclosure of himself. For it was not safe to proclaim clearly the divinity of the Son when that of the Father was not yet confessed, nor when the Son's divinity was not yet accepted, to add the burden of the Spirit's divinity as well.[123]

Otherwise the risk is that human beings would be overcome by the weight of divine glory, whereas by gradual additions and progressions "'from glory to glory,' the light of the Trinity shines forth with greater splendours."[124] Thus just as God gradually trains human beings to greater obedience and weans them from their ancestral customs to the form of life of the gospel, so the Trinity is made manifest to human beings step by step. In each case, the principle is broadly the same: to accommodate human beings' free will and finite capacity by gradual changes. In both cases, this strategy configures human history into a sequence of eras ordered to the goal of human beings dwelling with God.

Conclusion

Gregory's understanding of God's lack of creaturely limitations and his ordering of creaturely systems and causes makes it conceivable that God might order human history pedagogically in respect of natural events. Gregory's notion of the participation of rational creatures in God makes it conceivable that God might influence human thinking in a particular direction, so long as such influence did not negate human freedom, in such a way as to order human events pedagogically in their interrelations with natural events. Furthermore, this same idea makes it conceivable that God might enable human beings to understand their history in these terms, and respond appropriately. It is in such terms that Gregory seems to think about prophetic inspiration, to which we shall turn in connection with the work of the Spirit.

If we may line up Gregory's two schemas of God's pedagogical ordering of history, we can produce a sort of composite account. After the fall, that history

122. Or. 31.26, *SC* 250, p. 326.
123. Or. 31.26, *SC* 250, p. 326.
124. Or. 31.26, *SC* 250, p. 326.

really gets going with God's relationship with Israel, wherein human beings are drawn over from idolatry to the worship of God and in which God as the one who rules the world and the Father of human beings is made manifest. In many ways God seeks to combat human sinfulness providentially and through the prophets, teaching and training them, but such is human weakness that Israel tends to refuse this tutelage. Jesus Christ is at the heart of the economy, making the Son manifest and teaching the way of life that is the gospel. With the coming of the Spirit, God dwells among human beings, so that the Spirit's divinity is made clear in the church, and (we may suppose) human beings are enabled to live out the way of life ordered by the gospel, in expectation of the eschaton and a fuller communion with God. In these schemas we have the outline of a theological view of human history, ordered by God's action in creation and salvation, in such a way as not to negate human freedom but to draw human beings to God in the midst of their creaturely contexts and over time.

In light of Gregory's account of God, creation, and humanity, this account thus begins to disclose a suggestive model for thinking theologically about history, in order to be able to think theologically about Scripture. On this model, God is understood to uphold the complexly ordered causal interactions of creatures and to act in a way that transcends all of them; where human beings are constituted as embodied, free rational agents, immersed in the creaturely order yet with desire for God; and where human history configured by divine action becomes a field wherein in and through their temporal, embodied condition fallen human beings may be drawn back to God and readied for deeper encounter with God.

We cannot simply borrow Gregory's account to address the issues Troeltsch raises for us, since his understanding of the interrelationship of events, benefiting as it does from a wealth of modern research, is far more complex and expansive than Gregory's. Nevertheless, these features of Gregory's account are suggestive for lines of a response to Troeltsch whereby God so transcends creation as to be intimately and immanently involved in such a way as to uphold the very contingent systems and interactions that constitute historical reality, where human agency has significance and meaning, and where human desire is somehow ordered to that active divine presence. In order to further this account of how Gregory sketches lines for a response to Troeltsch, we need to investigate further what he has to say about two key moments of this history, in which God dwells as and with human beings, the incarnation and the descent of the Spirit, and about how human beings partake of those realities.

3

The Reshaping of History
Jesus Christ and the Baptized Life in Gregory of Nazianzus

In the previous chapter, we saw how Gregory's account of God, creation, humanity, and the divine economy begins to sketch a premodern model that helps us think about how to respond to Troeltsch. However, central to that account are two events that seem to run directly counter to the intuitions of historical consciousness and their implications for theology, as Troeltsch understands them. For in the incarnation of the Word and the descent of the Holy Spirit upon humanity, Gregory would seem to ascribe absolute value to historical phenomena, thus excepting them from their context and historical contingency; such divine interventions seem also to offend against the continuous character of reality in history. Any response to Troeltsch has to begin by thinking, as he does, of history in its totality, but thinking it theologically. Gregory limns some basic lines for this rethinking, for on his account, Jesus Christ is a historical event of an unprecedented order—a new creation—whose effects ramify across the whole, backward and forward. For in Christ, the divine Word makes a human life in time and space his own, and in the midst of contingent forces shapes a pattern of life that breaks free of and reverses the effects of the fall and fulfills the human vocation; a pattern in which others may participate in their own times and places.

JESUS CHRIST

When Gregory talks about Jesus Christ, he tends to think in terms of the Word's assumption of human nature, extending through Christ's whole career and on into his heavenly session, and its salvific purpose. The event of incarnation, therefore, as an extended event, bears the emphasis, where important actions and sufferings of Christ, like the cross and resurrection, are key moments within that larger "economy" and integral to it. Gregory's Christology explains the reason for the incarnation in terms of the salvific intent of the Word. This Word Gregory identifies as fully divine, the subject of the incarnation, who assumes full humanity for us in a union so strong that God assumes creaturely attributes and becomes subject—without changing—to the conditions of historical life.

Everywhere in Gregory's writings, the motive for the Word's assumption of human nature is compassionate and salvific. For example, in Oration 1, Gregory tells us that the Word became human for our sake.

> He assumed what was worse, in order to give us what was better;
> he went begging, in order that we might be enriched by his beggary;
> he took the form of a slave in order that we might receive freedom;
> he came down in order that we might be raised up;
> he was tested, in order that we might conquer;
> he was dishonoured, in order that he might glorify us;
> he died, in order to save us;
> he ascended, in order to draw us to himself who were laid
> low in the fall of sin.[1]

Gregory thus has in view the entire course of Christ's existence, not only his becoming human but all that this entailed, signaled by the inclusion of his temptation, passion, death, and ascension. In all its aspects, the Word's human existence secures our salvation from sin, the defeat of Satan, and our return to God. Elsewhere Gregory adds the resurrection of the flesh, the rescue of the soul made in the image of God, the deification of the soul, and the re-creation of humanity, united in Christ.[2] That goal is secured through the Word's assumption of our condition, effecting an exchange of conditions: he becomes like us in order that we become like him. This formula, which goes back to Pauline writings and was taken up by Irenaeus and Athanasius before Gregory, can be found in many places in Nazianzen's writings.[3] The Word assumed human spirit and flesh, Gregory says in Oration 29, "in order that I might become as much God as he became human."[4] The goal of the incarnation is that union with God for which human beings were originally created and ordered as rational creatures.[5]

1. Or. 1.5, *SC* 247, p. 78.

2. See Or. 2.22–23, Or. 7.23, Or. 29.18–19.

3. See Irenaeus, *Against Heresies* Book 3.19.1; Book 5, pref.; Athanasius, *On the Incarnation* 54.3.

4. Or. 29.19, *SC* 250, p. 218.

Gregory emphasizes the full divinity of the Word. In Oration 38 he describes the subject of the incarnation as

> the Word of God himself, who was before the ages, the invisible, incomprehensible, incorporeal, the beginning from the beginning, light from light, the source of life and immortality, the beautiful impression of the archetype, the unmoved seal, the exact image, the definition and explication of the Father.[6]

The Word is thus ascribed first a series of negative attributes indicating divine transcendence of creaturely conditions and comprehension, followed by several phrases that identify him in terms of his unique relation to the Father, a relation whereby he shares the Father's nature and role with respect to the cosmos and thus perfectly represents the Father. Gregory leaves us in no doubt that the one who comes to us in Christ is God, one who presents the reality of the Father to us in himself, in his very being. And this description thus helps to amplify the claim Gregory makes earlier in the same Oration, that in Christ's nativity "God appears to human beings through birth."[7] The full divinity of the Word is logically required, moreover, if the incarnation of this Word is to be the means for the deification of human beings.

The advent of the Word involves the assumption of full humanity. The Word, Gregory tells us, comes to his own image.[8] The intellectual soul, we may infer, is made in the image of the divine Image, the Word, for Gregory as it is for Origen, and in this sense Gregory refers to the soul as made according to the image of God (κατ'εἰκόνα).[9] The Word is mixed with the human soul and purifies it. Through the medium of that soul, the Word also assumes human flesh—Gregory is careful to use the Pauline term with all its freight. The Word assumes and thus heals human nature in its fallen condition, and so becomes human in every way except for sin, including the assumption of a human mind. For, as Gregory argues in his first letter to Cledonius, "what is not assumed is

---

5. As Donald Winslow and Christopher Beeley have both noted. See Winslow, *The Dynamics of Salvation. A Study in Gregory of Nazianzus* (Cambridge, MA: The Philadelphia Patristic Foundation, 1979), 86; and Beeley, *Gregory of Nazianzus on the Trinity and the Knowledge of God: In Your Light We See Light* (New York: Oxford University Press, 2008), 119.

6. Or. 38.13, *SC* 358, p. 132.

7. Or. 38.3, *SC* 358, p. 108.

8. Or. 38.13, *SC* 358, p. 132.

9. Or. 6.14, *SC* 405, p. 156; Or. 2.22, *SC* 247, p. 118. Henri Crouzel's description of Origen's position is also apt for Gregory: "man is created after the Image of God who is the Word, at once agent and model for the creation of man." in *Origen*, trans. A. S. Worrall. (Edinburgh: T. & T. Clark, 1989), 93.

not healed, but what is united to God is saved."[10] It was the whole Adam who fell and needs to be assumed, therefore.[11] And only with a human intellect is Christ truly human.[12] There is no difficulty with the notion of such a union, Nazianzen explains, once we remember that spiritual things are incorporeal and nondimensive.[13] They may mix with one another and with bodies without competition, just as many sounds may be heard together, the appearance of many objects may be captured in one view or their smells in one olfaction; the greater overshadows but does not exclude the lesser, any more than the presence of full sunlight in a room drives out a single beam.[14] The human intellect, while sovereign with respect to the soul and body, is not absolutely so, not in respect of God, whose servant it is.[15]

The clear implication of Gregory's argument and imagery is that in the union of the Word with the human intellect, the human mind remains but is thoroughly shot through with the light of the Word, which governs that mind without impairing its normal operation with respect to the soul and body. The imagery of light here, in particular, recalls Gregory's discussion of the overpowering and unlimited light of God in Oration 28, which creaturely minds cannot comprehend. This connection should caution us against thinking of the union of the Word and Christ's human mind on analogy with any relationship we might conceive between two human minds; the logic of Gregory's images is that there is almost no comparison and certainly no competition between the human νοῦς and the divine Word, but their mingling would seem to entail the comprehensive conditioning of the former by the latter. In this union, Gregory's argument also seems to imply, the Word is unchanged. As he affirms elsewhere, "what he was, he remained, what he was not, he assumed."[16]

The force of this account of the Word's sovereign assumption of human nature leads to a strong formulation of the unity of Jesus Christ. Thus in Oration 38, having described the Word's assumption of an intellectual soul and human flesh, Gregory continues, alluding to Christ's birth: "God comes forth with what he assumed, one from two opposites, flesh and Spirit, the one divinising, the other divinised. O new mixture, O wondrous blending!"[17] God

10. Epistle 101.32, *SC* 208, p. 50.
11. Epistle 101.33, *SC* 208, p. 50.
12. Epistle 101.34, *SC* 208, p. 50.
13. Epistle 101.37–38, *SC* 208, p. 52.
14. Epistle 101.39–40, *SC* 208, pp. 52, 54.
15. Epistle 101.43, *SC* 208, p. 54.
16. Or. 29.19, *SC* 250, p. 216; so also Or. 39.13.

remains the subject of the verbs in Gregory's formulation, but the consequence of God's assuming humanity is a Christ who is one by the divinizing of his humanity, a phrase that implies the continuing distinction of Christ's humanity from the divine Word to which it is so intensely united. Gregory makes the same point in Oration 29, adding that God and his humanity "became one, by the greater prevailing": this unity is forged and defined by the Word's act of assuming human nature. Again in Oration 37, Gregory stresses the unity of Christ. The Word, he says, "did not become two, but endured to become one from two."[18] The two natures "concurred into one not two sons; lest the mixture (σύγκρασις) be belied."[19] Gregory's usage of the term σύγκρασις, and of similar terms in Oration 38 (μίγνυμαι, μῖξις, κρᾶσις), in the wider context of his Christology as outlined above indicates not an abolition of the distinction between the natures, but "the close unification of elements that still remain naturally or numerically *different*," as Brian Daley says of Gregory of Nyssa's usage of the same terminology.[20]

So strong is this unity, Gregory holds, that the divine Word acquires in respect of the humanity he assumes creaturely attributes, and all to salvific effect for us. Gregory revels in the paradoxes that ensue in Oration 38: "The one who Is becomes and the uncreated is created and the uncontainable is contained, through the medium of an intellectual soul mediating between divinity and the coarseness of flesh."[21] The purpose of God in taking on human finitude in this way is, of course, for our benefit, and amplifies the formulas of exchange mentioned above: "He who is rich becomes poor; for he impoverishes himself in respect of my flesh in order that I may be rich with his divinity."[22] The Word participates in our flesh, Gregory says, "in order to save the image and immortalise the flesh."[23] He thus institutes a second communion between God

17. Or. 38.13, *SC* 358, pp. 132, 134.

18. Or. 37.2, *SC* 318, p. 274. See also Epistle 101.13–14, *SC* 208, pp. 40, 42: "For we do not separate the man from the divinity, but teach one and the same, first not man, but God and only Son before all ages . . . who at last was also man, assumed for our salvation . . ."

19. Or. 37.2, *SC* 318, p. 274. Gregory thus avoids the dualism of "two sons" with which Apollinarians charged those who asserted the full humanity of Christ, including a human mind, as Brian Daley explains with reference to Gregory of Nyssa in his "Divine Transcendence and Human Transformation: Gregory of Nyssa's Anti-Apollinarian Christology," *Modern Theology* 18, no. 4 (2002): 498.

20. Daley, "Divine Transcendence," 501–2. The emphasis on the oneness of Christ is marked in Gregory's Christology, as Christopher Beeley has argued. See his "Cyril of Alexandria and Gregory Nazianzen: Tradition and Complexity in Patristic Christology," *Journal of Early Christian Studies* 17, no. 3 (Fall 2009): 388–94.

21. Or. 38.13, *SC* 358, p. 134.

22. Or. 38.13, *SC* 358, p. 134.

and humanity more marvelous than that which pertained with Adam, for now God lives a human life. The Word's assumption of human life and its finitude, within history, in itself not only heals the human soul, but somehow makes possible the deification of human beings and their communion with God by realizing deification in the person of Christ—even in respect of his body.[24] Already we can see that for Gregory there is universal significance in this extraordinary historical particular, Jesus Christ.

In a similar vein, in Oration 39, Gregory finds further salvific purpose in the divine Word's assumption of human finitude: the Son of God becomes Son of Man by assuming our humanity, "in order that the uncontainable might be contained, conversing with us through the medium of the flesh, like one who is veiled, since his pure divinity cannot be borne by what is subject to generation and corruption."[25] We might gloss Gregory's point by saying that the Word's humanity is, as it were, translucent to the light of his divinity, and allows us to bear the manifestation of that divinity. It is this assumption of humanity in order to communicate his divinity to us that is the content of the Word's kenosis. As Gregory elsewhere explains: "I call 'emptying' (κένωσις) this diminution and abatement of his glory, by which he becomes graspable."[26] As in Oration 38, so in more detail in Orations 37 and 39, the Word made flesh makes manifest the Father's divinity, to recall us to the light of God.

The incarnation, therefore, involves the divine Word assuming the conditions of historical life. In order to communicate with us, Gregory says in Oration 39, God was mixed with becoming, the atemporal with time, the impassible with suffering, and the immortal with corruption.[27] The Word assumes a form of existence that belongs to the complexly ordered and temporally fluid reality that he himself sustains in existence and order. Indeed, in Oration 39, Gregory takes this thought a little further when commenting on Christ's age at the time of his baptism in the Jordan. Christ had to undergo the passion in order to save the world and so had to go through all that leads up to the passion: his baptism, the Spirit's testimony, the preaching, the crowds following, the wonders.[28] For, Gregory explains, the baptism and preaching

---

23. Or. 38.13, *SC* 358, p. 134.

24. As Gregory says in Or. 39.16: this is why the Spirit descends on Christ's *body* in the form of a dove, attesting that it too is God by divinization. Here again I agree with Winslow, *The Dynamics of Salvation*, 87–88, and Beeley, *Gregory of Nazianzus*, 121.

25. Or. 39.13, *SC* 358, p. 176.

26. Or. 37.3, *SC* 318, p. 276.

27. Or. 39.13, *SC* 358, p. 176. There is not space here to explore Gregory's account of the cross and resurrection. See especially Winslow, *The Dynamics of Salvation*, 97–112.

attracted the crowds, which in turn led to the signs and miracles designed to draw them to the gospel, and these provoked the envy of Jesus' enemies, which led to hatred, leading to plots and betrayal, which led to the cross.[29] Thus, in great brevity, Gregory places Jesus' baptism at the beginning of a sequence of events in which his actions will be interrelated with other human agencies and forces in a causal sequence that will lead to his death. It is a sequence that locates Jesus' agency in relation to wider historical agencies—the crowds, the religious factions that opposed Jesus, and implicitly the Romans—even while these help him to accomplish his salvific purpose (something about which Hans Frei had more to say, as we shall see).

At this point, Gregory's Christology appears to offend grossly against Troeltsch's strictures about the appearance of the absolute in history while also maintaining a view of embodied creaturely existence that bears some analogy with historical consciousness as Troeltsch presents it. Gregory does not attempt to explain the conditions of possibility of the incarnation. What is possible for God is not something that finite minds are capable of grasping, as we have seen, and so different is God from creatures that time and space cannot be considered obstacles to his action or involvement, even to this degree. Rather, the underlying objection Gregory is countering in the passages we have been examining has to do more with God's dignity, which is why Gregory emphasizes the Word's compassionate humility so much. To what extent, however, might Gregory's thought sketch a strategy for responding to Troeltsch's objection?

We have already seen that Gregory sees universal import for human beings in the incarnation, and we can extend this point with respect to the whole of Jesus' existence. For Gregory's Christology involves the Word becoming the subject of historical human acts and experiences. In response to objections to the Word's full divinity that cite biblical verses denoting Christ's human acts, sufferings, and weaknesses, Gregory regularly ascribes these to the Word as incarnate, in respect of his humanity.[30] Nazianzen explains his basic principle in respect of such verses in Oration 29: they are to be attributed to "the composite one, and him who was emptied and made flesh for you and . . . made human and then was exalted," that is, the en-humaned Word (and not, as is sometimes alleged, the humanity of Christ), in virtue of his assumption of our humanity.[31]

---

28. Or. 40.29, *SC* 358, p. 264.

29. Or. 40.29, *SC* 358, pp. 264, 266.

30. These are not the only kinds of verse Gregory deals with in such passages. He also has to deal with verses that suggest that the Word in himself is inferior to the Father.

In the passage that follows, Gregory pairs opposing divine and human actions and experiences ascribed to Christ in Scripture. The most significant of these come toward the end of the passage:

> He was carried in his mother's womb, but was recognised by a prophet who was himself in the womb and who leaps in the presence of the Word through whom he was made.
> He was wrapped in swaddling bands, but cast off the grave wrappings in his resurrection.
>
> He was placed in a manger, but was glorified by angels, and indicated by a star, and worshipped by magi.[32]

By alluding thus to the gospel stories, Gregory's pairs draw out the conjunction in Jesus Christ of properly human experiences—gestation, birth, neonatal dependency, poverty, and death—with experiences that signal the presence of something more than creaturely in the one who is carried, born, cared for in poverty, and dies. The exceptional oddness of attributing such a set of episodes to a historical person does not, for Gregory, mark a sheer irruption of the historical order. Rather, from what we have seen of his Christology so far, we must say that it belongs to a wider pattern characteristic of human history in theological perspective: the spontaneously generous, pedagogical action of the God who sustains and orders the world and what unfolds in it, the high vocation this God has given to human creatures, the identity of the Word as the one who re-presents this God in himself, and the purpose of this same Word to realize the salvation of human beings, which requires that he becomes human himself.

The next passage in the Oration takes us a little further. Here we have a second set of linked contrasts. Some function in the same way as those in the previous passage: Christ "was heavy with sleep, but is light upon the sea, and commands the winds, and makes Peter light when he was drowning."[33] He

---

31. Or. 29.19, SC 250, p. 216. In Or. 30.15, Gregory extends this principle even to Christ's ignorance: the Word cannot be ignorant in himself, but this same Word is ignorant "as a human being," SC 250, p. 258. To take this line of thought further would require further reflection on the relation between the Word and his human mind, which presumably remains finite despite, according to Gregory, being encompassed by the Word and therefore may not enjoy the omniscience of the Word. In Or. 30.16, Gregory offers a Trinitarian alternative—that in passages like Mark 13:32, Christ refers his knowledge to its cause, the Father, whereby he also knows what the Father knows. This solution seems to strain the biblical text.

32. Or. 29.19, SC 250, p. 218.

pays tax, but takes it from a fish, and is the king of those who tax him. Other contrasts indicate the ways in which Christ's deified humanity changes the circumstances of those around him: "He prays, but he answers prayer."[34] Some of Gregory's contrasts combine this kind of contrast with a wider significance: Christ "hungered, but nourished thousands, and is the living and heavenly bread."[35] He is sold, very cheaply, "but redeems the world, and at great cost, his own blood."[36]

More extended accounts of how Christ's actions have wider significance can be found elsewhere in Gregory's orations. In Oration 2, for example, Gregory explains that the deification of human beings explains the incarnation of the Word, salvation through his passion, and "[why] for each element of our condition something of the one who is above us was exchanged and became a new mystery, the economy of love for humanity who fell through disobedience."[37] Nazianzen then goes on to explicate this pattern of exchange with reference to the events of Christ's life as related in the Gospels. In a manner reminiscent of Irenaeus, Gregory finds correspondences in contrasting events between the circumstances of Christ's birth and the origins of the human plight: "His birth was for the sake of the creation of human beings, the virgin for the sake of the [first] woman, Bethlehem for the sake of Eden, the manger for paradise."[38] All these small, visible events were for the sake of hidden and great causes, Gregory adds. A little later Gregory finds a similar set of fitting contrasts between the phenomena of the passion and the events the passion undoes. For example, the wood of the cross is for the wood of the tree of the knowledge of good and evil; the generosity of Christ's hands extended and nailed on the cross oppose the hands that took covetously from that tree; the elevation of the cross opposes the fall; the gall opposes the taste of the fruit, and so on. The force of this comparison is to communicate the sense that in his own actions, sufferings, and circumstances, Jesus Christ forges a new, alternative origin for human beings, over against the beginning they have in Adam.[39]

33. Or. 29.20, *SC* 250, p. 220.

34. Or. 29.20, *SC* 250, p. 220.

35. Or. 29.20, *SC* 250, p. 220.

36. Or. 29.20, *SC* 250, p. 220.

37. Or. 2.24, *SC* 247, p. 120.

38. Or. 2.24, *SC* 247, pp. 120, 122.

39. In this way, as Winslow points out, Gregory takes up the theme of recapitulation, for which Irenaeus is celebrated. See Winslow, *The Dynamics of Salvation*, 96–97, cf. Beeley, *Gregory of Nazianzus*, 147.

Gregory makes similar points in his Orations on festivals of the Christian year. Thus, in Oration 38, Christ's birth is a second creation of the light, a new punishment of Egypt with darkness while Israel is illumined by a pillar of light, the light of knowledge that shines on those who walk in darkness.[40] The appearance of God in Christ's flesh is cast here as an event of universal significance: God appears "to human beings" in birth, not merely those who saw the infant Jesus with their own eyes.[41] Gregory's term for this event and others like it in Christ's life is μυστήριον. Christ's baptism, Gregory tells us in Oration 39 with a backward glance to the celebration of Christ's birth, is "another action of Christ and another mystery."[42] Later in Oration 38, Gregory briefly expounds other events in Christ's life and ministry in the same vein: his baptism for our sanctification, his temptation in which he overcomes the tempter, his healings, resurrections, exorcisms, and miracles, his betrayal in which as priest he offers himself as lamb of God, his crucifixion bearing our sins, his resurrection as God, his ascension and his coming in glory.[43] These are all mysteries of Christ, which have one purpose, "my perfection and re-creation and return to the first Adam," an explanation that also illumines Gregory's use of μυστήριον in this context.[44] A "mystery" here is an action (or suffering) of Christ that furthers the goal of re-creating human beings, perfecting them and reversing the effects of the fall. It is a concept, therefore, whose use in respect of Christ's actions and sufferings bears universal significance for human beings in respect of the goal for which they were first created. That significance is equally evident when Gregory speaks of Christ's crucifixion and resurrection: the cross, by which humanity is purified and drawn into unity (we will see how later), and the crucifixion-resurrection sequence by which the incarnate Word assumes our death and defeats it, freeing us also from the tyranny of Satan.[45]

To attribute such significance to Jesus Christ's existence, actions, sufferings, and resurrection, however, risks magnifying the problem from Troeltsch's perspective. What makes Gregory's account of God's saving economy, centered on the incarnation of the Word, so suggestive in respect of the challenge Troeltsch poses is the way that Gregory sees the incarnation affecting everyday lives lived in the world. The clue to understanding this impact lies in Gregory's account of baptism in Orations 39 and 40 and his

40. Or. 38.2.
41. Or. 38.3, *SC* 358, p. 108.
42. Or. 39.1, *SC* 358, p. 150.
43. Or. 38.16.
44. Or. 38.16, *SC* 358, p. 142.
45. See Or. 45.13, 22, and 29; Carmen 1.1.33.

pneumatology, especially in Orations 41 and 31, especially when linked to themes in his ascetical theology.

Christ, Baptism, and the Holy Spirit

Orations 39 and 40 were preached on successive days, the first for the Feast of Lights, celebrating Jesus' baptism, the second before the baptism of candidates. Across those two sermons Gregory elaborates a theology of baptism that sheds light on his understanding of how what is achieved by the Word in the person of Jesus Christ comes to be effective for other human beings. On the one hand, Jesus' baptism seems to model an action whereby human beings may participate in him and the saving work he achieves in himself by imitation, thus initiating a pattern they are to follow for their entire lives. On the other, Jesus baptizes with the Holy Spirit, who deifies human beings and draws them into participation in the Word's divine light that shines through Christ. The first of these points indicates what other Orations also imply, namely that the economy of Jesus Christ is somehow present and available to human beings to partake in their own time; the second point goes some way to making sense of the conditions of possibility of that participation.

In Oration 39, Gregory tells us that Jesus' baptism is the ἀρχή, the beginning, the source, of the Holy Day of Lights.[46] The way he talks in that Oration about that festival and its celebration in baptismal terms, and the way he draws lessons in respect of Christian baptism and its candidates both imply that Gregory takes the celebration of baptism, which seems to have taken place on the next day, to be part of the festival.[47] Therefore we may infer that Jesus' baptism is, for him, the origin and source of Christian baptism, as it was for other early Christian theologians. Indeed, in Oration 40, Gregory tells us not only that Christ honored baptism "by his enfleshment and the baptism with

---

46. Or. 39.1, *SC* 358, p. 150.

47. Gregory tells us that the Day of Lights "effects my cleansing and strengthens the light which we received from him from above at the beginning, which we darkened and oppressed through sin," Or. 39.1, *SC* 358, p. 150. He exhorts the congregation to approach Christ and be illumined, reborn, recreated, and to recover the first Adam (Or. 39.2). Again, in Or. 39.14, he exhorts them to shine with Christ and go down with Christ in his baptism in order to rise with him; in Or. 39.20 he instructs them to celebrate the feast by washing and becoming pure as they are illumined by the Trinity. These terms are all specifically characteristic of the way Gregory describes baptism in Or. 40.3–8. Gregory draws lessons about baptism from Christ's baptism in Or. 39.14. Or. 40.1 indicates that in talking about baptism there, Gregory is continuing the subject of the previous day's discourse. A little later in the same Oration he says that baptism gives its name to the Day of Lights, which is his subject (Or. 40.3).

which he was baptised," but also that Christ's actions in his baptism were handed on to us to be a sketch or model (τύπος) for ours.[48] He thus suggests both that Christian baptism is somehow connected to Christ's incarnation and passion ("the baptism with which he was baptised," cf. Mark 10:38/Matt. 20:22/Luke 12:50), and that Christ's baptism is the clue to ours.

If we take these conclusions back to Gregory's exposition of Christ's baptism in Oration 39, the connections between Christ's passion, his baptism, and Christian baptism are reinforced and clarified further. To begin with, after exhorting his listeners to approach Christ and be illumined, reborn, and re-created, becoming what we once were in Adam, Gregory cites John 1:5: "the light shines in the darkness," explaining that it shines in the darkness of this life and flesh, is persecuted by the enemy who rashly assaulted the visible Adam but fell upon God and was vanquished in order that we might turn from darkness, approach the light, and become perfect light ourselves. "Do you see the grace of the day? Do you see the power of the mystery?" he asks. The clear implication is that in baptism we receive the liberation Christ effected in his cross and resurrection, the light that was not overcome by the darkness, and we are thereby transfigured, reborn, and re-created, recovering our original condition in Adam (and more).

Gregory's account of Jesus' baptism in the same Oration suggests further connections of this sort. He tells us that Jesus comes to John for baptism not only to sanctify John but also "to bury the old Adam in the water."[49] Again, Jesus rises up out of the water, bearing with him the world, and sees the heavens opening, which Adam had closed to himself.[50] These two comments seem to suggest that Christ's baptism effects human salvation, but in light of Gregory's understanding of Christ's cross and resurrection, it makes more sense to say that for Gregory Christ's baptism foreshadows his cross and resurrection and, as the origin of Christian baptism, connects Christian baptism to them. Baptism certainly symbolizes and seems somehow to be connected to Christ's burying of "the old Adam" (of humanity as subject to the passions and to Satan) in death and to his raising human beings to new life and to communion with God. It is in this way, we may infer, that Christ defeats Satan and liberates human beings from his reign through the passions and death. In light of Gregory's implication earlier that the power of that liberation is present in baptism, we may conclude that baptism is for Gregory a way of dying and rising with Christ that entails these liberating effects.[51] Hence in Oration 40, Gregory can describe baptism

48. Or. 40.2, *SC* 358, p. 200; Or. 40.30, *SC* 358, p. 266.
49. Or. 39.15, *SC* 358, p. 182.
50. Or. 39.16.

as "the deluge of sin . . . the removal of slavery, the dissolution of bonds," and hence in Oration 39 Gregory enjoins his listeners to go down with Christ in his baptism in order to rise with him—not merely, we may infer, out of the water, but from death to life with God.[52]

The effects of baptism, however, seem also to be closely linked to the gift and work of the Holy Spirit. Gregory tells us that Jesus came to John to be baptized above all to sanctify the Jordan, because Christ perfects (or initiates: τελειῶν) by Spirit and water.[53] A little later Gregory distinguishes the baptism Jesus administers from those of Moses and John because Jesus baptizes "in the Spirit," which is perfection.[54] And how, he adds, is the Spirit not God, "if from him you become God?"[55] Gregory thus briefly repeats an argument made elsewhere for the full divinity of the Spirit, most notably in Oration 31.[56] Initiation, union with God or deification and, in Oration 31.28, regeneration are all the work of the Spirit in baptism, according to Gregory, but the master metaphor that unites these other concepts and links the work of the Spirit to Jesus Christ in baptism is illumination.[57]

As we have seen, in Oration 38, Christ's birth by which God is made manifest to human beings is described with a string of biblical epithets as a second creation of light, a second pillar of fire to deliver Israel from darkened Egypt, the light of the knowledge (of God, we may infer) illuminating the people who have dwelt in darkness, at which the shadows of the Old Testament withdraw.[58] In Oration 39, as we have also seen, Gregory speaks of the baptism of Christ who is the true light illuminating everyone who comes into the world and enjoins his listeners to approach this light and be illumined and signed with the true light. Christ, he says, is the light shining in the darkness of the flesh, the light that the darkness has not overcome, the light we are to approach in becoming perfect sons of light. For Gregory, then, Jesus Christ is luminous with divine light, and it is as Light that he goes to the cross and

51. As Donald Winslow also argues (*Dynamics of Salvation*, 131).

52. Or. 40.3, *SC* 358, p. 202; Or. 39.14.

53. Or. 39.15, *SC* 358, p. 182.

54. Or. 39.17, *SC* 358, p. 186.

55. Or. 39.17, *SC* 358, p. 186.

56. Or. 31.4 and 28.

57. Cf. Susanna Elm, who argues that for Gregory baptism as illumination actualizes for individuals the fusion of God's essence with matter that took place in the Incarnation. See her "Inscriptions and Conversions. Gregory of Nazianzus on Baptism (*Or.* 38-40)", in *Conversion in Late Antiquity and the Early Middle Ages. Seeing and Believing*, eds. K. Mills and A. Grafton (Rochester, NY: University of Rochester Press, 2003), 6.

58. Or. 38.2, *SC* 358, pp. 104, 106.

rises again: the theme of light encompasses not only Christ's birth but also his cross and resurrection. And Gregory connects it to baptism, where Christ illumines those who approach him, such that they become luminous themselves. Illumination, then, seems to be an action of Christ by which others are caught up into his saving existence and in him encounter God and are transfigured and transformed.

It is in view of this connection that we need to read Gregory's statement of his theme in Oration 31. Here he boldly begins his "theology" of the Spirit by applying John 1:9—"he was the true light who illumines every man coming into the world"—to Father, Son, and Spirit, concluding, "'was' and 'was' and 'was,' but one 'was'; 'Light,' and 'light' and 'light,' but one 'light,' and one God."[59] Father, Son, and Spirit: each is the light that illumines every human being, yet their light and divinity are one. Nazianzen then claims that this single threefold illumination of the Trinity is what the psalmist experienced and attested when he said "In your light we shall see light" (Ps. 36:9; 35:9 LXX) and that his own theology proceeds from this same vision: "And now *we* have seen and proclaim, grasping Light—the Son, from Light—the Father, in Light—the Spirit, a brief and simple theology of the Trinity."[60] Gregory is describing one event of illumination in which Father, Son, and Spirit are simultaneously active and experienced in differentiated unity, and here it is "in" the Spirit that one sees the Father in the Son. As he says elsewhere, with reference to baptism and alluding to the same verse in the Psalm, "be illumined with the Son in the Spirit."[61]

In view of Gregory's understanding of Jesus Christ, we may reasonably suppose that he means that we see the Father in Jesus Christ and that we do so when we are "in the Spirit," caught up by his rays into the vision of God in Christ. Given the importance of the argument for the Spirit's divinity from his deifying work in baptism in Oration 31, and his description of baptism in terms of illumination in Oration 39, it would also seem reasonable to suppose that Gregory would see baptism as a primary instance in which we are caught up in Christ's luminosity by being "in the Spirit." This conclusion thus enables us to link together the sense of participating in Christ's light, death, and resurrection, and Gregory's claim that in baptism Christ perfects or initiates by the Spirit. The gift of the Spirit imparted to the baptismal candidate involves

59. Or. 31.3, SC 250, p. 280. Gregory is self-consciously not exegeting the verse but using it to make a statement about the Trinity, as T. A. Noble points out in "Gregory Nazianzen's Use of Scripture in Defence of the Deity of the Spirit," *Tyndale Bulletin* 39 (1988): 108–9.

60. Or. 31.3, SC 250, p. 280.

61. Or. 40.34, SC 358, p. 276.

them, incorporates them (in Sarah Coakley's language) into the incarnate Son's luminosity and his vanquishing of the darkness through death and resurrection.[62]

The Spirit, then, is the one by whose agency Christ baptizes, incorporating human beings into the luminosity of his incarnate existence, and it is this agency that accounts for the efficacy of baptism.[63] Hence Gregory says in Oration 40 that baptism, like human beings, is double. Because we are both flesh and spirit, so we are cleansed by water and Spirit, visibly and invisibly, the former the figure of the latter, presumably to figure it forth to those whose grasp of invisible things is always by way of the visible.[64]

Oration 40 also helps make sense of the full significance of illumination as a comprehensive theme for the saving efficacy of baptism. Illumination is the predominant name for baptism in this Oration also. Baptism gives its name to the Day of Lights, he tells us, and thereafter uses "illumination" (τὸ φώτισμα) to name baptism in a series of descriptions, which together suggest that the concept of illumination gathers together a wealth of aspects of the efficacy of baptism.[65] This illumination, Gregory declares,

> is the splendour of souls, the changing of life, the answer of the Godward conscience; this illumination is the help for our weakness and the putting off the flesh, the following of the Spirit, fellowship with the Word, the rectification of the creature, the deluge of sin, participation in light, the destruction of darkness. It is the chariot that takes us to God, the departure with Christ, the mainstay of faith, the perfection of the mind, the key to the kingdom of heaven, the changing of one's life, the removal of slavery, the dissolution of bonds, the transformation of composition. . . . It is the most beautiful and magnificent of the gifts of God.[66]

---

62. See Coakley, "Why Three? Some Further Reflections on the Origins of the Doctrine of the Trinity," in *The Making and Remaking of Christian Doctrine*, ed. Sarah Coakley and D. A. Pailin (Oxford: Clarendon, 1993), 36.

63. The incorporative dimension here clarifies further Donald Winslow's claim that for Gregory the Spirit enables us to appropriate the redemption accomplished in Jesus Christ and that "what Christ has accomplished universally, the Spirit perfects particularly" (*Dynamics of Salvation*, 129). Christopher Beeley makes the same point but emphasizes the ecclesial locus of this application (*Gregory of Nazianzus*, 177––78).

64. Or. 40.8; Or. 28.12–13.

65. Gregory says that it is because baptism's benefit has many aspects (πολυειδής) that it has many names. Or 40.4, *SC* 358, p. 202.

66. Or. 40.3, *SC* 358, pp. 200, 202.

In view of Gregory's understanding of Christ as the one who illumines candidates in baptism, it seems reasonable to infer that illumination names baptism in respect of the action of Christ and the Spirit and that the efficacy of this action is multivalent and comprehensive. He goes on to expound its other names, which convey a similar wealth of content: gift, because given unconditionally; grace, as given to debtors; baptism, as burying sin in water; chrism, as sacred and royal; illumination, because of its splendor; clothing, because it covers shame; bath, because it washes; seal, because it preserves and is the mark of the Master. It is, he adds, akin to the magnificence of the angels and the image of heavenly beatitude. The illuminating action of the Spirit which Christ bestows, catching us up into his luminosity, then, transforms human beings in respect of the things that distorted them and restores them to a greater measure of that participation in God's light and communion with God in which they find fulfillment as rational creatures, in anticipation of its fulfillment in heaven and eschatologically.

Gregory's exposition of the theme of light a little later in Oration 40 amplifies this conclusion and the connection between the notion of divine illumination in Oration 31 and baptism. There Gregory names God as the supreme light, unapproachable and ineffable, illuminating all rational nature, and appearing to us to the degree that we are purified and being loved accordingly.[67] This light, Gregory adds, is the light contemplated in Father, Son, and Holy Spirit, "whose wealth is the harmony and single outleaping of their splendour."[68] Angels are a secondary participation in this light, and human beings, he implies, participate also in lesser degree. Gregory goes on to recapitulate the history of salvation in terms of illumination, only to arrive at baptism, which is more properly illumination, and contains a "great and wonderful mystery of our salvation."[69] In baptism, we may conclude, gathering the threads together, Jesus Christ bestows the Spirit in whom Christ's luminosity is communicated, which includes all the saving efficacy of his incarnate existence. This communication of Christ's luminosity in the Spirit reforms, re-creates, regenerates human beings, undoing the enslavement to the passions entailed by the fall and restoring human beings' proper orientation to God and enjoyment of the divine light, in anticipation of its fulfillment in beatitude. This light is the light by which God draws us back to himself.[70] It is in this sense that Gregory speaks of baptism as illumination, in Oration 39, as

67. Or. 40.5.
68. Or. 40.5, *SC* 358, p. 204.
69. Or. 40.6, *SC* 358, p. 208.
70. Or. 21.1, *SC* 270, pp. 110, 112.

effecting our purification and helping the light we received from the Word in the beginning, but obscured through sin: it heals us as rational beings.[71]

Such an account of baptism presupposes the availability of Jesus Christ's luminosity to human beings in time, and the gathering up of the saving events of his life, death, and resurrection in him. Gregory seems to allude to that gathering up in Oration 40, when he says that since Christ had to suffer his passion to save the world, he had to unite in view of his passion everything that pertains to his passion—his manifestation, baptism, the heavenly testimony, the preaching, the following crowds, the wonders, "like one body, neither dispersed nor fragmented by temporal intervals."[72] For Gregory, as we have seen, the eternal Word unites creatures, and here we have an indication that in a similar way he holds together the several moments and events of his life. If so, then it does not seem to present any additional difficulty to suppose that, for Gregory, the risen and ascended Christ continues to hold together the temporal constituents of his creaturely existence.

That he also makes them available to human beings seems to be the condition of possibility of the realization of his saving work in individual human beings, especially in baptism. It also seems to be presupposed by Gregory's rhetoric in those Orations that concern liturgical festivals. Thus Gregory supposes that availability when he speaks of Christ's saving actions in the present tense and pairs them with imperatives calling upon his congregation to participate or respond appropriately to the event, whether when Gregory says "Christ is born, glorify him" in Oration 38 or "Christ is risen from the dead; rise with him" in Oration 45.[73] Gregory, as we have seen, holds that we participate in Christ by the Spirit. He sheds no further light on Christ's availability, but we may infer that the Spirit's descent on particular human beings in baptism incorporates them in time into Christ's particular, ascended luminous humanity, located in heaven—for Christ retains his flesh after his ascension, according to Gregory, and his body is with the Word who assumed it.[74]

---

71. Or. 39.1.

72. Or. 40.29, *SC* 358, p. 264.

73. Or. 38.1, *SC* 358, 104; Or. 45.1 (*PG* 36 624B).

74. On Christ's retention of his humanity, see Epistle 101.25. On its location with the Word, see Epistle 101.26, *SC* 208, p. 46: "where is his body now, unless with him who assumed it?"

Baptism and the Ascetic Life

The significance of this account for a theological response to Troeltsch has to do with this availability to human beings in their own times and the temporal way in which human beings partake of Christ. Baptism is illustrative in this regard, but is only a moment in a larger process. In Oration 40, Gregory describes God's re-creation of us in baptism as a seal for those beginning life and a restoration of the image for those more advanced in years, "lest we should become worse through despair" and deteriorate under its effects, falling from virtue and the good and ending up despising them.[75] Rather, "like travellers on a long journey who pause a while from their efforts in an inn, we shall finish the journey renewed and enthusiastic."[76] Gregory's image implies that baptism, whether at the beginning or along the way, enables the baptized to pursue a long and arduous journey, and so connects the grace of baptism to a life lived out over time.[77] For, as Gregory goes on to say, baptism is "like a compact (συνθήκη) with God for a purer life and conduct."[78] It entails a certain way of life, and Gregory is eager to counsel the candidates on how to lead it. First, he advises them to vanquish the devil by appealing to their baptism, and the bold words he gives them to respond to the temptation to worship Satan underline the sense in which baptism inaugurates a life in which the baptized are closely united with Christ: "I have been clothed with Christ, I have laid claim to Christ by baptism; you should reverence me."[79] Gregory's advice conveys the sense that the baptized life is a dramatic one in which the baptized, united with Christ, live out in daily spiritual combat the victory achieved by their Lord, thus investing that time with significance. "Let us be baptised then, that we may vanquish!"[80] Gregory conveys the same sense of the freighted character of time in the Christian life when he calls baptism an alliance with God by which one prevails against the spiritual Goliath.[81]

75. Or. 40.7, SC 358, p. 210.

76. Or. 40.7, SC 358, p. 210.

77. As Winslow (Dynamics of Salvation, 144) and Beeley (Gregory of Nazianzus, 87 and 177) have noted.

78. Or. 40.8, SC 358, p. 212.

79. Or. 40.10, SC 358, p. 218.

80. Or. 40.11, SC 358, p. 218. At this point Gregory is returning to an argument against delaying baptism until death that began in section 9. He urges them, in section 16, to appropriate the aid that baptism affords against Satan's attacks: you are safer baptized, in time of persecution, than as a catechumen, he urges. Gregory, we should also remember, believed in penance for post-baptismal sins (Or. 39.18).

81. Or. 40.17.

We find this sense of the efficacy of baptism extending into daily life when Gregory urges virgins to be baptized, that the power of baptism "may order your life and speech, all your members, movements and every sense."[82] This argument suggests that dying and rising with Christ, being illumined and gathered into his luminosity, conditions the entirety of embodied human agency and interaction with the world. The practical implications of this conditioning are suggested by Gregory's argument that baptism also helps the married preserve their chastity (σωφροσύνη), and calls the married to give to baptism times of abstinence during the time set aside for prayer, by mutual consent.[83] Later Gregory urges those who have been persuaded by his arguments to prepare for baptism and to guard its grace with "watches, fasts, sleeping on the ground, prayers, tears, compassion for those in need, sharing."[84] The list suggests that regular actions throughout the hours of daily life are a way of living out the power of baptism, as well as preparing for its fruitful reception.

The blessing the baptized have received is to remind them of the commandments, in effect transforming their perception of daily encounters in light of their participation in Christ:

A poor person comes to you? Remember how poor you were and how much you have been enriched. If they need bread or something to drink, then perhaps another Lazarus is cast at your gates? Revere the mystical table which you approach, the bread, which you have shared in, the cup which you have partaken of, being initiated into the sufferings of Christ. If a stranger falls before you, without lodging or somewhere to stay, receive through him the one who for your sake lived as a stranger even amongst his own and dwells in you by grace, and has drawn you toward his heavenly abode. Become Zacchaeus, yesterday's collector of taxes, and today's magnanimous man; offer everything for the entrance of Christ and you will appear great, even if you are small in bodily size, as you look finely upon Christ. If a sick person lies injured, respect your health and the wounds from which Christ freed you. "If you see someone naked, clothe them," and so honour your clothing of incorruption. This is Christ, "since as many of you are baptised into Christ, have put on Christ." If you receive a debtor who falls before you, tear up every unjust or even just bond. Remember the numberless talents which

82. Or. 40.18, *SC* 358, p. 234.
83. Or. 40.18, *SC* 358, p. 236.
84. Or. 40.31, *SC* 358, p. 268.

Christ forgave you. Do not be a miserly debt-collector of a lesser debt. And from whom? From your fellow slaves, you whom the Master has forgiven a greater debt. And do not undergo trial of the justice of his philanthropy, which you do not imitate despite having received his example.[85]

The memory of the benefit the baptized enjoy as those who receive Christ's saving effects in union with him urges their compassion, kindness, and generosity toward others they encounter who are in need of their help. In this way, the active presence of the power of Christ's saving reality, first experienced in baptism, is worked out through imitation of Christ in the midst of the weave of the interpersonal interactions that help compose the web of history.[86] For this is how, Gregory claims, baptism comes to be a bath not only for the body but also for the image, not only a washing of sins but a correction of one's way of life.[87] Purification must imbue you; it must be total and deep, showing through in your actions.[88] Gregory's comments on hospitality to the stranger and becoming generous like Zacchaeus go further still, for there is the sense here that Christ is encountered and welcomed in the welcoming stranger and in acts of generosity to others, in and through our embodied interactions with others.[89] It is as if Jesus Christ, by the Spirit, is now present to us through our historical circumstances and transforms us in and through them without prejudice to their contingent character or our freedom.

A little later Gregory exhorts the candidates, with respect to the distinction between the true light of God and false, Satanic light: "let us illumine ourselves with the light of knowledge; and this comes from sowing unto righteousness, and harvesting the fruit of life—for action introduces contemplation—in order that we may learn . . . what is the true light and what is the false."[90] This exhortation introduces a new point. If baptism is illumination, restoring communion with God, then it initiates into a life of seeking God contemplatively, for which just action is the way in. In this way, Gregory adds, we are to become light in the sense that Christ attributed to his disciples: "a

---

85. Or. 40.31, *SC* 358, pp. 268, 270.

86. Thus for Gregory divine grace underlies the human effort through which salvation is worked out, as Winslow and Beeley both argue. See Winslow, *Dynamics of Salvation*, 158–63, where the problem is treated at length, and Beeley, *Gregory of Nazianzus*, 85.

87. Or. 40.32.

88. Or. 40.32, *SC* 358, p. 272. I have drawn the inference that for Gregory, being imbued with purity means acting in the way he has described, from the sequence of his argument in sections 31–32.

89. Gregory says something similar in Or. 14.18 and 40 and Or. 16.18.

90. Or. 40.37, *SC* 358, p. 284.

living power for others" (cf. Matt. 5:14).[91] In this way we are to lay hold of God, by marching toward his light without stumbling over dark and hostile mountains. The contemplative fruit of baptism, of being illumined, is borne through righteous action, by which Gregory presumably means the kinds of compassionate acts he has earlier commended.

Gregory goes on to give a compelling picture of the thoroughness and totality of the transformation to which baptism should lead. We are, he says, to purify every member and sanctify every sense, leaving nothing unillumined.[92] Every sense, organ, and limb is to be purified. For example, the eyes must be cleansed to avoid idolatry, the ears and mouth to hear the speech of God and speak his wisdom, the sense of smell to delight in sharing in the spiritual odor spread through us as we are so transformed by Christ that he smells our pleasant scent; touch and taste to seek the risen Lord and taste his goodness. Even the loins and kidneys are to be purified, for "no-one escapes Egypt purely or flees the destroyer without this training."[93] The loins "are to be transformed with a beautiful transformation by transferring their faculty of desire entirely toward God," so that we become a man of the desires of the Spirit.[94] Finally, the foundation for this whole pursuit is the retention of good doctrine—the confession of faith in the Trinity as a companion and guardian for life, a secure habitation or vessel, which Gregory undertakes to inscribe upon the candidates' souls, like a fundamental disposition: the law engraved on the heart.[95] These various metaphors all denote something stronger than mere assent and more fundamental than cognition, which serves to orient human life safely in view of its goal in God. This is a picture of the complete orientation of the human agent toward God and the training of our every faculty to attend to God over idolatrous alternatives.

Gregory's account of the baptized life is thus an ascetic one, and it accords with other statements he makes about the ascetic life that help us fill out that account. A key theme in the latter sections of Oration 40 is that baptism should cleanse the image of God in us and that we should preserve and further that purification. In just this way, it suggests how the salvific achievement of Jesus Christ, the incarnate Word, impacts human lives in a temporally extended way, indeed so as to shape and transform embodied human action and interaction

91. Or. 40.37, SC 358, p. 284.
92. Or. 40.38.
93. Or. 40.40, SC 358, p. 290.
94. Or. 40.40, SC 358, p. 290.
95. Or. 40.41–45.

over time—crucial components of history, according to Troeltsch. To this account we may add four further points.

First, Gregory elsewhere amplifies this theme of participating in Jesus Christ through action in terms of the conformity of the image of God in us to Christ as the image, drawing on the notion of the virtues. In his panegyric on his sister, Gorgonia, Gregory praises her as one whose true city was the heavenly Jerusalem, where nobility is "the keeping of the image and the assimilation to the archetype, which reason, virtue and pure desire effect."[96] As I argued above, the Word is the archetypal image in whose image we are created, hence in this passage Gregory speaks of nobility as assimilation to the archetype, just after having described Christ as the citizen of heaven and founder of the heavenly city. Thus heavenly nobility is about conforming to Jesus Christ.

Three forces promote this assimilation. Desire for God is, as we saw in the previous chapter, fundamental to the human condition and motivates our participation in our own purification. Reason is the faculty through which the Word, the divine Reason, crafts both the married and the celibate to virtue, Gregory argues in the same Oration: it presides in the virtuous person.[97] Elsewhere Gregory tells us that reason (or Reason, λόγος) "anticipates all things and brings man, made in God's image, into step with him," so that everything is spiritual: action, movement, will, speech, even how we walk and what we wear.[98] Here is a picture like that presented of the sanctification of the limbs and senses in Oration 40, but now prioritizing the human being as a dynamic agent thoroughly conformed to God by the concordance of our reason with the Word.

Virtue is the concept that helps explain how this conformity takes seat in human beings.[99] Virtue, for Gregory as for Aristotle, is a firm disposition of the soul toward what is good, which forms a person so that goodness becomes natural and hard to change.[100] The virtues are opposed to vices: justice and charity, for example, are "praiseworthy dispositions, the one opposed to injustice, the other to hatred."[101] Gregory also describes the virtuous life as the

96. Or. 8.6, SC 405, p. 296.

97. Or. 8.8, SC 405, p. 260.

98. Or. 11.6, SC 405, p. 342.

99. In what follows I am indebted to Thomas Špidlík's discussion of the virtues in Gregory in his *Grégoire de Nazianze: Introduction à l'étude de sa doctrine spirituelle* (Rome: Pont. Institutum Studiorum Orientalium, 1971), 57ff.

100. "Consider with me that virtue is a disposition toward good things." Carmen I, II, 24, v. 49 (PG 37 949), quoted in Špidlík (*Grégoire de Nazianze*, 65); on the firmness of such dispositions, see Or. 23.1, SC 270, pp. 280, 282. Cf. Aristotle Nic. Eth. 2.iv, 1105b, 2.iv 1106b.

royal and middle road, clothing Aristotle's notion of virtue as the mean between extremes in more biblical language.[102]

To possess the virtues is to imitate God. For in the first place, God is supremely virtuous and the source of virtue.[103] Hence Gregory can ascribe to his parents the view that happiness is "virtue and kinship with the Greater good," describing the same idea in two different ways: virtue *is* kinship with the Good, with God, as the passage examined above from Oration 8 also implied.[104]

The model for our imitation is the Word, the Logos. Human beings, Gregory tells us in Oration 28, will discover God's nature—if ever they do—when our godlike intellect "is mixed with its kin, and the image ascends to the archetype, to which now it tends."[105] The ascension of image to archetype implies the assimilation of the former to the latter: like Origen, Gregory here pictures the human intellect made in the image of the Image as "a dynamic reality," tending back to its model.[106] Hence assimilation to God is also by way of assimilation to his Image, the Logos, who is the pattern for human fulfillment and transformation and the one who seeks to bring that fulfillment about in us. Given Gregory's soteriology, we are entitled to infer that he is thinking of the Logos as Jesus Christ and that, as Crouzel says in respect of Origen's doctrine, Christ "is virtue entire, animated and alive . . . virtue in general and each virtue in particular are the divine person of the Son."[107] On that account, he adds, "the practice of virtue . . . is a participation in Christ."[108] Gregory ascribes the virtues to Christ in Oration 30, and by postulating such an account on Gregory's part, we can also explain his talk of the "introduction of Christ into the heart by the Spirit" (an allusion and amplification of Gal. 4:19), which Gregory juxtaposes with the salvation of the image in us as component concepts of the deification of

101. Or. 28.13, *SC* 250, p. 126.

102. See Or. 2.34, *SC* 247, p. 132 and Or. 42.16, *SC* 384, pp. 82, 84. For the Aristotelian echoes see Aristotle, *Nic. Eth.* 2.iv 1106b. Gregory also alludes here to Num. 20:17 and Prov. 4:27, as Bernardi points out in the notes (cf. also Deut. 2:27 and 28:14).

103. Hence Gregory says that God presents himself to us as Peace and Love "so that we might lay claim to the virtues that are God's" (Or. 6.12, *SC* 405, p. 154), and describes God as the source of virtue in Or. 21.1, *SC* 270, p. 110.

104. Or. 7.4, *SC* 405, p. 188. Many scholars have pointed out the connection to Plato's *Theaetetus* 176a–b. Gregory's God is, of course, the Trinity, a doctrine foreign to Plato.

105. Or. 28.17, *SC* 250, p. 134.

106. Crouzel, *Origen*, 97.

107. Crouzel, *Origen*, 98.

108. Crouzel, *Origen*, 98. Gregory attends to those titles that names virtues, among others, in Or. 30.20, where he prefaces his exposition by speaking, among other things, about God being named in terms of the virtues: "the names of the virtues dispose [us] to practice" (Or. 31.19, *SC* 250, p. 266.

human beings in Oration 2.[109] The reference to the Spirit is significant here also, and if we may link these passages together in the way I have, we may conclude that as the Spirit incorporates the baptized into Christ, so also the baptized, through their ascetic acquisition of the virtues, are conformed to Christ in their dispositions by the Spirit and so conformed to God, and that this conformity is a kind of indwelling of Christ in the Christian, by the Spirit.

In the acquisition of the virtues, moreover, God offers us, as Gregory says, a way, a path by which we may conform to Christ over time. It is, furthermore, a way accommodated to the variety of human proclivities, psychological constitutions and occupations. For while, we may assume, virtue must be one in God, it is manifold in us. For Gregory the virtues in their variety offer us many paths by which to travel Godward. Each virtue, he says in Oration 14, is "one road of salvation, bearing towards one of the eternal and blessed abodes."[110] For "just as there are many different modes of life, so also there are many abodes with God, distinguished and distributed according to the worth of each."[111] What lies in some sense with us is the intensity with which we pursue the journey. The greatest saints possess all the virtues, uniting them in themselves, in imitation, surely, of God's simplicity of Goodness.[112] Nevertheless, he allows that "it is a great thing to follow one [road of virtue] eminently."[113] Virtues are acquired and exercised in the course of daily action and interaction, over time. The practice of the virtues, therefore, would seem to be a properly historical way in which we continue to appropriate, after baptism, the universal salvific achievement instantiated in Jesus Christ.

Second, participation in Christ takes a particular social form for Gregory. The Word became human in Jesus Christ, he tells us in Oration 7, in order that we might all become one in Christ "in order that we might no longer be male or female, barbarian or Scythian, slave or free, the distinctions of the flesh, but might only bear in ourselves the divine character, by and in which we are born, being so formed and impressed by it as to be recognised from it alone."[114] The purpose of the Word's incarnation is a humanity entirely characterized by its resemblance to God, where human distinctions of gender, ethnicity, or

109. Or. 30.20. On the formation of Christ in the heart, see Or. 2.22, SC 247, p. 118.

110. Or. 14.5 (PG 35 864A–B).

111. Or. 14.5 (PG 35 864A–B).

112. Athanasius, he says, by imitating the saints, "took from each what was beautiful uniting them in his own soul, like those who draw certain forms in excess, he clarified out of them all one perfect form of virtue," Or. 21.4, SC 270, p. 116.

113. Or. 27.8, SC 250, p. 90.

114. Or. 7.23, SC 405, p. 240.

political status have been replaced by the marks that distinguish us as God's. Such differences are transitory and in process of being eroded by the pursuit of virtue. The church as a social body imitates God not in these vestigial degrees of conformity to the flesh, but in the love, peace, and order it evinces, or is called to evince. Hence Gregory lauds the beauty of a harmonious, peaceful church congregation, whose order and cohesion, like that of creation, derive from and imitate the unity of the Trinity.[115] For the same reason, Gregory laments the scandal of a divided church.[116] The harmony Gregory celebrates consists in part in the mutual care of the members of the church for one another, and in part in its proper order, according to the Spirit's distribution of spiritual gifts and illumination.[117] Gregory thus sees in the temporal realization of Christ's salvation in human beings an intrinsically social character that further reinforces its historical character while at the same time setting up, at least in principle, a tension between the church and any existing social order based on wealth, class, gender, and racial status.

Third, church communities remain enmeshed in time and history. They are vulnerable both to the vagaries of the favor or disfavor of emperors and their officials, and to the threat of natural disasters. In both, consistent with his theology of providence, Gregory sees God active, pedagogically, to train and reform God's people, as he did before Christ. In Orations 16, Gregory maintains that in the devastation and horror of the loss of cattle and crops, which the people of Nazianzus had suffered in 373 CE, God intends to chastise and correct them for their oppression of the poor and their forgetting of God. Even when God's purpose in the tumult and apparent randomness of changing events is difficult to discern, the very darkness that hides God from us destroys our delusions of wisdom and teaches us to seek him beyond the vicissitudes of this world, Gregory argues in Oration 17.[118] In Oration 14, he even suggests that this very difficulty in comprehending how God directs our affairs whets our desire for God.[119] Thus Gregory locates the pursuit of virtue in ecclesial community within the ever-changing currents of contingent temporal events, which are divinely directed, albeit often in ways that defy our comprehension yet always with a pedagogical purpose.

---

115. On peace and harmony as beautifying the church, see Or. 6.7 and Or. 22.2. On the Trinity as the source and archetype of ecclesial peace and harmony (as well as that of angels and human bodies), see Or. 6.4 and Or. 22.14. On the church's imitation of the Trinity through its peace, see Or. 6.13.

116. E.g. in Or. 32.4–5.

117. See Or. 6.8 and Or. 32.10–12. In both cases, Gregory draws analogies with the natural order.

118. Or. 17.5 (*PG* 35 970B–972A).

119. Or. 14.33 (*PG* 35 904A).

Fourth, this pursuit of the journey begun or renewed in baptism through action and contemplation, in interaction with others and oriented by sound doctrine, looks toward a goal, and Gregory briefly sketches that goal at the end of Oration 40. The candidates, once baptized, will stand before the raised space (the βῆμα) in an attitude that prefigures heavenly or eschatological glory; the psalmody with which they will be greeted will be a prelude to the heavenly hymnody; the lamps they will light signify the guiding lights of faith with which virgin souls will greet the bridegroom.[120] In a similar way, toward the end of Oration 45 Gregory tells us that the celebration of *Pascha*, of Easter, prefigures a heavenly and eschatological feast.[121] In part, this is a hope of an enjoyment of God realized after death, when the soul can gaze fully on God, exposed entirely to divine illumination in a condition of complete purity. However, it is also an eschatological hope insofar as God intends also to reunite soul and body in the resurrection, under a new kind of bond that transforms what it is to be embodied so that matter itself may partake of deification. This dual hope clarifies the teleology and sense of anticipation and longing to the experience of living in time already present in Gregory's account in the metaphor of the journey. Indeed, Gregory's account of baptism as illumination and of the knowledge of God indicates that this is not simply a journey toward a remote end, but a journey in which the end, God, is already partially present, drawing us onward toward God by what we now enjoy and what remains to be grasped.[122]

CONCLUSION

Gregory's account of Jesus Christ and our participation in him by his Spirit deepens the model we began to sketch from Gregory in the previous chapter. While we cannot simply repristinate Gregory's theology of history, given the greater density and complexity of immanent historical reality as we now know it, nevertheless Gregory's thought suggests central lines for a response to Troeltsch within which to situate a theology of Scripture.

In particular, it indicates that it will be key to understand the incarnate Word as a particular person who comes to condition the whole historical continuum and the possibilities inherent in it, in anticipation of a more fundamental transformation yet to come. These possibilities human beings may

---

120. Or. 40.46, *SC* 358, p. 308.

121. Or. 45.23.

122. Cf. Or. 38.7, as explicated above.

enjoy and realize in themselves by the work of the Spirit, at once individually and socially, in and through historical interactions with one another and with the contingent causal systems of their environment. It is within such a vision of the basic operating conditions of history in God's pedagogical providence and in virtue of God's saving economy by Word and Spirit, that Gregory situates his theology of Scripture, the reading of Scripture, and the formation and ministry of those who unfold its teachings to others. By the incorporating work of the Spirit, human time and action, in contingent circumstances, are opened up and altered into a path of participation in Jesus Christ, thus reconfiguring historical existence.

4

Distributing the Word

Holy Scripture and the Preacher in Gregory of Nazianzus

Gregory's account of divine action in history allows him to understand Scripture theologically as the product of God's saving activity and its instrument, serving as the medium of Christ's pedagogical presence, without abstracting it from the historical continuum. Because the presence of Jesus Christ as teacher and divine wisdom is by the Spirit's inspiration at the heart of Scripture, in Gregory's understanding, and Christ is at the heart of history, there is for Gregory no tension between the teaching of Scripture and the world of the reader, nor is that teaching simply of only relative worth amidst the historical breadth of human culture. Rather, Christ's scriptural pedagogy enables Spirit-illumined readers to realize the universal saving force of the incarnation in their own lives and shapes their understanding and action. It is this sanctifying pedagogy that Christian pastors are called to serve in their exposition of Scripture, as the Spirit enables them and their listeners. In these ways, Gregory sketches premodern lines that can inform our response to the challenges presented by historical consciousness to the theology of Scripture.

Distributing the Word: Scripture and the Interpreter in the Economy

We can get a first glimpse of how Gregory locates Scripture, and its interpretation within his understanding of history configured around Jesus Christ, from his account of pastoral ministry and its demands in Oration 2. That account is central to his apology for having fled that ministry after his priestly ordination. For Gregory, the exposition of Scripture is one of the chief tasks of the Christian pastor, and his argument both contextualizes that task within the divine economy of salvation and begins to reveal his understanding of the nature and function of the sacred text.

Gregory's basic argument in Oration 2 is that the pastoral art is so difficult and so weighty in its responsibilities that no one should undertake it before they have acquired sufficient spiritual formation, and hence he may be forgiven for having recoiled from that task in order to prepare himself for it. One way in which Gregory makes that argument is by a comparison of two kinds of medicine: the care of human bodies and the spiritual care of human beings, in order to show just how much more difficult is the latter than the former. The climax to that piece of argumentation comes when Gregory contrasts the scope of the physician's art, which seeks the preservation of the flesh, with that of the pastoral art, which aims at the rescue, restoration, and deification of the human soul made in the image of God.[1] For, he explains, this work was the purpose of God's saving action, especially in the incarnation. For this reason, the Word assumed every aspect of our condition, as Gregory explains: "For each of our things, one thing of him who was above us was given in exchange and he became a new mystery, the economy of philanthropy for the one who fell through disobedience."[2] This exchange, according to Gregory, explains every feature of Christ's life, ministry, death, and resurrection. All these were a divine pedagogy and therapy for our weakness, Gregory explains, "leading the old Adam back to whence he fell and conducting us to the tree of life, from which the tree of knowledge estranged us when partaken of unseasonably and improperly."[3]

Of this therapy, he continues, those who are placed over others to lead in the church are "servants and fellow-workers . . . for whom it is already a great thing to know and heal our own passion and deficiencies."[4] And those who exercise this enormous responsibility have a very difficult task because of the great variety among those for whom they care. For motivations and impulses are not the same, he points out, "for women as for men, nor for old as for young, nor the poor as for the rich, or leaders and the led, wise and unlearned, cowards and courageous, angry and gentle, those who succeed and those who fail."[5] Similarly, he adds, there are great differences in desires and passions and

---

1. Or. 2.22. For a fuller account of Gregory on the pastoral art, see Christopher Beeley, *Gregory of Nazianzus on the Trinity and the Knowledge of God: In Your Light We See Light* (New York: Oxford University Press, 2008), 235ff.

2. Or. 2.24, *SC* 247, p. 120.

3. Or. 2.25, *SC* 247, pp. 122, 124.

4. Or. 2.26, *SC* 247, p. 124.

5. Or. 2.28, *SC* 247, p. 126.

internal composition between the married and the unmarried and of the latter between hermits and ascetics who live in community; between those advanced in contemplation and those "who can barely hold a straight course," between townsfolk and countryfolk, the simple and the scheming, business people and people of leisure, the misfortunate and the prosperous who may be ignorant of misfortune.[6] Some require doctrines to lead them, others are ordered by examples; some need spurring on, others curbing; some benefit from praise, others from censure; some need encouragement, others rebuke—some publicly and others privately.[7]

It is in the context of this psychologically astute account of pastoral ministry understood as an instrument of the application of the salvific force of Jesus Christ's therapeutic and pedagogical assumption of our human condition that Gregory introduces the subject of the exposition of Scripture. He raises the question of "the distribution of the *logos* . . . that divine and exalted *logos* which all now study."[8] It requires, he thinks, not a little of the Spirit to give to each in a timely manner their "daily portion and steward with judgment the truth of our doctrines" on a variety of subjects from matter, soul, and intellect through to God's saving action and triune identity [9] The *logos* Gregory speaks of here is Jesus Christ the incarnate Word, as he implies by the Christological allusions in his praise of Basil, in Oration 43, as steward of this same *logos* which is the bread of angels "wherewith souls are fed and given to drink, who are hungry for God, and seek for a food which does not pass away or fail, but abides forever."[10] This same *logos* is present in Scripture, as Gregory clearly implies in Oration 4 when speaking of the Christian *logos* "existing in doctrines and in testimonies from above, both ancient and new, ancient in the predictions and illuminating movements of the divine nature, new in the latest theophany and in the wonders from it and concerning it."[11]

6. Or. 2.29, *SC* 247, pp. 126, 128.

7. Or. 2.30–31, *SC* 247, pp. 128–30.

8. Or. 2.35, *SC* 247, p. 134.

9. Or. 2.35, SC 247, p. 134.

10. Or. 43.36, *SC* 384, p. 204. Gregory here alludes to a string of passages: the bread of angels in Ps. 78:25, the famine of hearing the words of the lord in Amos 8:11, and the food from heaven which the Son of Man gives and which endures for eternal life in John 6:27, which Jesus seems to equate with the true bread from heaven given by his Father, which bread, he also seems to say, is himself: "I am the bread of life."

11. Or. 4.110. Brian Daley identifies this *logos* in Or. 2.35 with Scripture in his "Walking Through the Word: Gregory of Nazianzus as a Biblical Interpreter," in *The Word Leaps the Gap*, ed. J. Ross Wagner et al. (Grand Rapids: Eerdmans, 2008), 514–31.

The implication of Gregory's descriptions is that the Word incarnate in some sense encapsulates the entirety of the divine pedagogy—the doctrines and testimonies from above both prior to and included in the incarnation—which is the truth of Christian teachings; that this truth is somehow spiritually edifying and nourishing; and that it is the task of the pastor to "distribute it" to each according to their need and circumstances ("in a timely manner"). Such distribution of this *logos* thus belongs to the wider pastoral art, contributes to its overall goal of applying the salvific force of the incarnation, and partakes of its challenging conditions with respect to the variety of temperaments, circumstances, and constitutions of human beings. Scripture thus seems to offer a Christocentric concentration of divine pedagogy and a crucial medium for its dispensation through the ministry of Christian pastors. The function of Scripture is thus in large part tied up with the pastoral art, and it and the expository task of the pastor are both situated within Gregory's understanding of salvation, which as we have seen, has a deeply historical cast, to which Gregory here adds considerable psychological realism. Thus Scripture and scriptural interpretation are to be understood in relation to the account of God's action in the world, centered in Jesus Christ, as we discussed in the previous two chapters. From Jesus Christ's central place in history Scripture derives its own secondary centrality and significance.

THE WORD TEXTUALLY INCARNATE

At the heart of that centrality and meaning is the connection Gregory makes between Jesus Christ and Holy Scripture. That connection sheds light on another passage, in Oration 45, which helps us understand Gregory's theology of Scripture more fully.

In Oration 45, Gregory expounds the meaning of Passover, and of the institution of the festival from Exodus 12. The historical Passover, he teaches, corresponds to "our spiritual progress and ascent from things below to things above and to the Land of Promise."[12] That passage, he also implies, is connected with Christ's passion and resurrection, the chief subject of the Christian festival. It is a transition still in progress, for the Sacred Night of the first Passover is "the match for the confused night of our present life" when we flee Egypt and Pharaoh for the world above.[13] Likewise the seven days for which the old leaven

---

12. Or. 45.10 (*PG* 36 636B), in Browne and Swallow's translation (Nicene and Post-Nicene Fathers VII, 426).

13. Or. 45.15 (*PG* 36 644A–B).

must be removed "corresponds to this present world": a further alignment of the process of liberation and the present time in which Christians now live. It is in that context that Christians keep Passover, and to which Gregory's exposition of the stipulations concerning the choice, preparation, and consumption of the Passover lamb in Exodus 12 belongs.

Gregory interprets the required qualities of the lamb in terms of its connection to Christ. "That great Victim . . . was mixed with the sacrifices of the Law, and was a purification, not for a small part of the world nor for a short time, but for the whole world throughout the ages."[14] It is this mingling that explains the choice of a lamb: "for this reason, a lamb is taken, on account of its innocence." The great Victim in question is, of course, Christ, and since his being mingled with the sacrifices explains the choice of the lamb, we must conclude that the lamb symbolizes him by its connotation of innocence. The timing of the meal, Gregory continues, signifies the timing of Christ's passion and the hour in which he instructed his disciples concerning the mystery of his passion (by instituting the Eucharist).[15]

This lamb must not be boiled but roasted, Gregory continues, "in order that for us the *logos* may have in it nothing that is not contemplated or that is watery, nor easily broken up, but be firmly whole and solid, tried by purifying fire, and free of everything material and vain."[16] If the lamb signifies Christ and "the *logos*," the most obvious way to reconcile what appear to be two meanings is to see them as one: for Christ, on Gregory's account, is the divine Logos incarnate. Therefore it seems that the Christian Passover, celebrated on the passage from sin and darkness to heaven, is kept by receiving the Logos himself, a reception by intellectual apprehension or contemplation, as Gregory says: for us the Logos is to have nothing not contemplated in it.[17] Roasting, then, signifies our contemplation of the Logos. The coals, Gregory also implies, signify aids to such understanding. He then continues:

> As much of the Logos as is fleshy and nourishing shall be eaten and consumed with the inner and hidden parts, and given up to

14. Or. 45.13 (*PG* 36 640C).

15. Or. 45.16 (*PG* 36 644C). Gregory says that Christ "communicated" the mystery to his disciples. Later in the Oration, this verb is used as a synonym for "to teach" (see below). The institution narrative is, of course, an explanation of Christ's passion, and it is that mystery, the mystery which is the subject of the festival that occasions the Oration, which I take Gregory to mean here, not the Eucharist.

16. Or. 45.16 (*PG* 36 645A).

17. θεωρία, contemplation, Gregory defines in Carmen 1.2 as "a consideration (σκέψις) of intellectual realities," Poem 1.2, 34 v. 130 (*PG* 37 955), cited in T. Špidlík, *Grégoire de Nazianze: Introduction à l'étude de sa doctrine spirituelle* (Rome: Pont. Institutum Studiorum Orientalium, 1971), 115.

spiritual digestion, even as far as the head and feet, the first insight concerning the divine nature and the last on the incarnation. Nor let us take it outside nor leave any till morning, because neither do we take the majority of our mysteries outside, nor is there any purification beyond this night and delay is not praiseworthy for those who partake of the Logos.[18]

Lambs, we know, are made of flesh and bone, skin and innards, various organs and vessels. Exod. 12:7 requires the head, legs, and inner organs all to be roasted with the rest of the lamb. Gregory interprets this command as an injunction to consume a whole range of "insights," from those concerning God's nature (the "head") to those about the incarnation (the "feet"), which the parts of the lamb signify.[19] "Spiritual" digestion, here, is digestion by the mind and is a manner of participation in the Logos. The Logos, then, is to be consumed not all at once but partaken of by way of a number of contemplations of aspects of him; aspects that amount to perspectives upon him that are the truth about different realities.

These insights, the θεωρήματα, appear to be discrete aspects in which the Logos presents himself, and that we are capable of receiving and being nourished by. Because these perspectives and subjects are relatively discrete, we can "consume" them one at a time. This presentation we may term teaching, for, as Gregory says later in the Oration with respect to the future mode of our participation in the Logos, "teaching is food."[20]

Gregory seems here to have a similar notion to Origen's of the unity of objects of contemplation in the Logos.[21] The multitudinous insights we may glean of God and God's works, creative and salvific, all inhere in the Word. This notion also coheres with Gregory's ideas, examined above, that the divine nature is made manifest in the Word incarnate, that a multitude of creaturely λόγοι likewise inhere in the Word, and that the Word incarnate unites in himself the several mysteries of his incarnate existence. It follows then that the way in which the Logos makes himself available for our contemplation and participation mirrors the way in which he works in creation and salvation to form a multiplicity of beings and a manifold salvation. Indeed, what are

18. Or. 45.16 (PG 36 644C–645B). From now on I shall use Logos instead of *logos* to transcribe the Greek, reflecting the interpretation of this passage advanced here and for the sake of clarity.

19. The word I have translated as "insights" is θεώρημά. This term derives from θεωρία, and in the present context denotes an intellectual vision of an intellectual reality. Gregory's use of this term in what we shall see to be a hermeneutical context has significance for standard characterizations of the difference between Alexandrian and Antiochene approaches to exegesis.

20. Or. 45.23 (PG 36 656A).

21. See Henri Crouzel, *Origen*, trans. A. S. Worrall. (Edinburgh: T. & T. Clark, 1989), 102.

presented for our intellectual contemplation are the realities by which the Word created and formed the cosmos and reformed human nature: the same divine power to shape is present to our minds, we may infer, in contemplation. In this way, the Word makes himself at once the compelling substance of our intellectual life and the nutrition for our spiritual growth. This approach a strategy of accommodation suited to the way in which we know God in this life, as we saw in Chapter 2: partially, obscurely, by way of the divine glory in the effects of God's activity[22] The Logos thus makes a way for God's truth into human minds, and a route for human minds to partake of God's own knowledge, albeit imperfectly: an imperfection by which, we may infer from his comments elsewhere, he draws us into deeper longing and purification, and so into fuller participation.

Furthermore, for Gregory God not only makes a way for himself into our sphere and a way for us into his knowledge, but also enables us to partake of this opportunity and secures the effectiveness of his self-disclosure. He does so by the work of the Spirit, to which Gregory clearly refers in our passage. The "bony," difficult parts of the Logos, for example, are to be "consumed with the fire with which the burnt offerings [are consumed], being threshed and preserved by the Spirit who searches and knows all things." The implied thought here is that, as Gregory says in Oration 2, it is the Spirit "by whom alone God is understood."[23] This work of the Spirit—to complete God's self-disclosure to us—reflects what Gregory holds to be his wider role in respect of creation, which is to perfect creatures.[24] This action in turn expresses what Gregory takes to be the Spirit's "role" in God, to whom he brings perfection or completion.[25]

Gregory's notion of the Logos and human knowledge of God is hermeneutically significant because of the idea he alludes to in this passage, namely that the incarnate Logos—who, after all, is now risen and ascended—and his θεωρήματὰ are mediated to us in Scripture, in which "flesh" Christ is, as it were, textually incarnate. Frederick Norris has noted the allusion to Scripture in Gregory's talk of the Logos here and the language of consumption of the text.[26] The interpretation of Oration 4 advanced above supports this view. The assertion made there that the Logos who nourishes us is found in the Old and New Testaments indicates to us that when Gregory speaks in Oration 45 of

22. Or. 45.15 (PG 36 645).

23. Or. 2.39, SC 247, p. 140.

24. In Or. 38.9, SC 358, p. 120, we learn that creation is a work carried out by the Word and "perfected by the Spirit."

25. In Or. 31.4, Gregory says that without the Spirit, God is incomplete (SC 250, p. 282).

the "embodied" Logos here he is speaking about Scripture, an idea Origen had earlier advanced in his very similar treatment of the same text and on the same subject when he asks "If the Lamb is Christ and Christ is the Logos, what is the flesh of the divine words if not the divine Scriptures?"[27] If Gregory does not make the same idea explicit, it is because it is so familiar to his audience and readership. What has yet to be noted is that Gregory not only alludes to Scripture thereby but also to a whole theology of Scripture. As Crouzel explains with regard to Origen, it is the Word already incarnate in human flesh whom the text announces and expresses.[28]

For Gregory, then, the text of Scripture is at once the route by which the incarnate Word makes his way into our condition and need as readers, and the way he makes for us into his own knowledge. By this means he provides for the fulfillment of our reason and its yearning, little by little, as it is nourished with the consumption of each object of contemplation. Like Origen before him, Gregory thus presents Scripture as a truly theo-logical text, embodying textually the incarnate Word of God, and which therefore demands to be taken with utmost seriousness and approached with utmost care; whoever reads it should purify the mind and seek divine aid in order to understand. Scripture is thus a text defined by the presence of the one who is central to God's shaping of history, and that presence is so ordered as to facilitate the appropriation of the saving efficacy of that manifestation of the Word in history by finite, timebound human beings.

The Body of Scripture: The Pedagogy of the Commandments

We may expand this claim about the configuration of Christ's scriptural presence for the appropriation of his saving import for human beings in history by turning to Gregory's account of the surface of Scripture and the pedagogical function of the commandments and exempla of holy lives. In several passages, Gregory contrasts the surface and depth or the clothing with the body of the sacred text. One example can be found in Oration 4, in the course of an

26. Frederick W. Norris, "Gregory Nazianzen Constructing and Constructed by Scripture," in *The Bible in Greek Antiquity*, ed. P. M. Blowers (Notre Dame: University of Notre Dame Press, 1997), 159–60.

27. Robert J. Daly, SJ, ed., "Treatise on the Passover" 26, in *Treatise on the Passover* (New York: Paulist, 1992), 41–42.

28. Crouzel, *Origen*, 70. Compare also Origen, *Homily on Leviticus* I.i, which describes the letter of Scripture as, as it were, the Word's flesh or clothing, as in his incarnation. One could read both passages as denoting the relationship of the Logos to the text, as distinct from the incarnate Christ.

argument for the superiority of Christian *paideia* or formation to that offered by a pagan Hellenism, as propounded by the Emperor Julian, which Gregory formulated in response to the imperial ban on Christians teaching Greek "letters."[29]

Here Gregory has his opponents defend their theological interpretation of Homer, Hesiod, and the Orphic hymns by arguing that such stories, for all their apparent immorality, conceal deeper, profounder meanings, the surface serving only to allure the reader and sweeten the message.[30] He has to concede an apparent parallel in Christian Scripture and its exegesis: "there are amongst us some stories which conceal; I do not deny it."[31] In other words, Christian Scripture also has, in places, both a manifest meaning and a latent, hidden theological or ethical sense (the parallel is between Christian Scripture and what the pagans call volumes of "theology or ethics," like Hesiod's *Theogony*).[32] But what, he asks, "is the manner of their doubleness, and what is their force?"[33] It does not follow, Gregory argues, that surface and depth in Christian Scripture are like their pagan counterparts. In the case of Christian Scripture, "the appearance is not unfitting, and what is hidden is wonderful and exalted and exceedingly bright to those who enter into the depth, and, like a beautiful and unapproachable body, it is veiled in clothing that is not mean."[34] For "in respect of divine things, the indications and appearances should not be unfitting or unworthy of what they signify."[35] In Christian Scripture, then, the surface content befits the deeper, theological, or ethical sense, a sense whose luminous beauty is in sharp contrast to that discovered by pagan exegetes, which "is not worthy of belief."[36]

29. The edict, *Edictum de Professoribus*, which McGuckin thinks was probably given on June 17, 362, banned any professor who does not believe in the gods from expounding the ancient writers, because "it is dishonest to think one thing and teach another," John McGuckin, *Saint Gregory of Nazianzus: An Intellectual Biography* (Crestwood, NY: St. Vladimir's Seminary Press, 2001), 117, n. 98.

30. Indeed, the practice of interpreting Homer as a theologian in ancient Greek philosophy had a long and ancient pedigree, though Gregory hardly does justice to that exegetical tradition. See for example Robert Lamberton, *Homer the Theologian: Neoplatonist Allegorical Reading and the Growth of the Epic Tradition* (Berkeley/Los Angeles/London: University of California Press, 1986), and Peter Struck, *Birth of the Symbol: Ancient Readers at the Limits of Their Texts* (Princeton: Princeton University Press, 2004).

31. Or. 4.118, *SC* 309, p. 282.

32. Cf. Or. 4.115, *SC* 309, p. 272: "You will present to them your diviners of the God-bearing oracles, as you call them, and unfold theological and ethical volumes. What are these, tell me, and by whom? The noble Theogony of Hesiod will be declaimed to them . . ."

33. Or. 4.118, *SC* 309, p. 282.

34. Or. 4.118, *SC* 309, p. 282.

35. Or. 4.118, *SC* 309, p. 284.

In light of my reading of Oration 45, it makes sense to understand Gregory's talk of the deeper sense of Christian Scripture to be a reference to the Logos "incarnate," for the mysteries he holds in himself would constitute just such a deeper sense of truly theological and ethical import, in contrast to the wild speculations of the pagan exegesis of myths. A similar passage in Oration 2 reinforces this conclusion, for there the hidden meaning is described as mystical, which description recalls the mysteries of Christ.[37] In Scripture, then, this depth of beautiful and luminous theological and ethical truth is Jesus Christ the Word incarnate in all his luminosity, presented in his manifold aspects, and to which brightness the reader must penetrate. However, Gregory does not think the surface of the text is merely a vehicle for this deeper meaning, but itself offers a diverse training in virtue.

Besides the nullity of their theology, Gregory's main critique of the pagan myths is that "the exterior is destructive."[38] Here he continues a long line of criticism that begins with Plato's condemnation of the stories of Hesiod and Homer in the *Republic* as unsuitable for the education of the young because of the immoral behavior they displayed.[39] Gregory asks, rhetorically, "what arguments can they use to form others in virtue and make the greatest number worthy by their recommendations?" He goes on to cite numerous examples of the vices displayed by Greek gods. He continues:

> In what way are these things similar to our [principles], for whom the limit of the love of each for himself is also that of [the love they have] in respect of others to desire for their neighbour what

36. Or. 4.119, *SC* 309, p. 284.

37. Or. 2.48, *SC* 247, p. 152. Kristoffel Demoen in *Pagan and Biblical Exempla in Gregory Nazianzen: A Study in Rhetoric and Hermeneutics* (Turnhout, Belgium: Brepols, 1996), 265, has seen a contradiction between this text and that in Oration 4, for in the former Gregory speaks of parts of Scripture "whose depth might do the greatest damage to the greatest number by their appearance," namely those clothed with a mean garment. Demoen comments, "this was exactly what Gregory reproached the pagan myths for: the allegorical explanation serves as an extenuation of the scandalous cloak. It seems rather inconsistent, then, to make use of the allegorical method to interpret the Bible" (cf. also Jean Pépin, *Mythe et allégorie: Les origins grecques et les contestations judeo-chrétiennes* [Paris: Études Augustiniennes, 1976], 474). The appearance of contradiction is mitigated when we consider both passages in context. Oration 4 concerns a contrast with the immoral stories of Greek gods, whereas Oration 2 alludes to a Jewish custom that Origen recounts in the Prologue to his Commentary on the Song of Songs, where the texts in question are the beginning of Exodus, the first chapters of Ezekiel, the end of the same book, and the Song itself. The difficulty of these texts is not of the same order as the immortality for which Gregory censures the Greek classics in Oration 4.

38. Or. 4.119, *SC* 309, p. 284.

39. See Lamberton, *Homer the Theologian*, 16–19.

they desire for themselves, and the charge is not only to do what is wicked, but also to be almost about to, since the desire is punished like the action: for chastity is treated so seriously that even the eye is restrained, and the murderous hand is kept so far away that even anger is moderated, and perjury is considered to be so terrible and excessive that for us alone swearing oaths happens to be foresworn?[40]

The significance of this passage derives from the fact that when Gregory discusses Christian *paideia* he alludes to Jesus' teaching in the Sermon on the Mount to exemplify its contents.[41] Given the context of Gregory's contrast between Greek myth and Christian Scripture in terms of the fittingness of the exterior to the interior sense, and the preceding critique of the example offered by the surface meaning of Greek myths, we must infer that Gregory means these dominical commands to illustrate the kind of formation offered by the surface meaning of Christian Scripture, what earlier and elsewhere he calls its appearance, exterior, clothing, or body.[42]

This inference is likewise supported and amplified when Gregory says that "even if we suppose that the counsels in their fiction chastise vice, how can they outstrip the measure of our virtue and formation?"[43] In fact, "the commandments" is a term Gregory frequently uses to summarize the biblical bases for the Christian way of life (especially as practiced by ascetics) that prepares us for contemplation.[44] This connection suggests that the formation offered by the commandments of Scripture prepares us for the contemplation of the mysteries and *logoi* in the depths of the same sacred text. We may therefore infer the suggestion in Gregory of an idea of Scripture as offering a comprehensive formation of habit and mind, the latter on the basis of the former, which is now in view.

40. Or. 4.123, SC 309, p. 290. I have translated γενέσθαι κακόν as "to do something wicked" since in English "being wicked" does not capture the force of Gregory's contrast between being wicked in actuality and being about to be wicked.

41. He alludes specifically to Matt. 7:12 ("do to others as you would have them do to you"), 5:28 ("everyone who looks at a woman with lust has already committed adultery with her in his heart"), 5:22 (where do not murder is extended by a ban on anger), and 5:34 ("But I say to you, do not swear at all").

42. Cf. Origen, *Peri Archōn* IV.2.2–8.

43. Or. 4.124, SC 309, p. 292.

44. So Or. 39.8, SC 358, p. 164: "where there is fear there is keeping of the commandment, and where the commandments are kept, there is purification of the flesh." Cf. Or. 20.12, SC 270, p. 82: "Do you wish to be a theologian one day and worthy of the divine nature? Guard the commandments, progress through the precepts; for practice is the stepping stone to contemplation."

Two further aspects of the mode of formation in view here deserve comment. The first is from the same passage. Gregory tells us that "what is most beautiful, is that whereas others penalise the results [of behavior] according to their laws, we chastise the causes."[45] In other words, the Christian formation set forth in the commandments is not really concerned with restoring order once vicious behavior has taken its course but with forming the self so as to root out vice at its source by inducing an internal discipline. He points, in effect, to the breaking of bad habits and the formation of good ones as the heart of what the commandments are intended to get us to do. Gregory indicates such an understanding more clearly when, in conclusion, he illustrates the superiority of Christian formation by saying that when "we have accomplished one virtue we take hold of another and long after a third."[46] By implication, it is virtues that Christian *paideia* forms in us through the commandments of Scripture.

As we have seen in the previous chapter, the virtues present a diversity of routes by which we may grow in likeness to and intimacy with God as we conform to Jesus Christ, the Logos incarnate and our archetype, the one who is virtue itself and the unity of all the virtues. The virtues are like the diverse aspects by which the Logos presents himself; they are another way by which Jesus Christ enters into the varied forms of our life to meet our need appropriately and to furnish us with a path of transformation. The function of the commandments, therefore, is to stimulate and facilitate our acquisition of the virtues: they are a key medium of this divine accommodation. And not only the commandments: in Oration 14, Gregory reinforces his praise of each of the Christian virtues by appeal to biblical exempla. "Faith, hope, love, these three are beautiful; of faith, Abraham witnesses, who was justified by faith; of hope, Enoch, who first hoped to call on the Lord . . . of love, the divine Apostle, who for Israel will dare to cry out against himself."[47] The force of this instruction is the display of the beauty of each virtue. It is a form of persuasion, as Gregory indicates. "Beautiful is prayer and vigil: let God persuade you who kept vigil before his passion, and prayed."[48] It is instruction nonetheless: "solitude and silence are beautiful, as Elijah's Carmel teaches me or John's desert, or Jesus' mountain, to which he seems often to have retreated and kept silence with himself."[49] The terms are varied, deliberately, from one unit of discourse to the next, but together they flesh out a rich notion of a teaching that persuades us

45. Or. 4.123, *SC* 309, p. 292.
46. Or. 4.124, *SC* 309, p. 292.
47. Or. 14.2 (*PG* 35 860B).
48. Or. 14.3 (*PG* 35 861).
49. Or. 14.4 (*PG* 35 861).

of the fineness of a given disposition on the occasion of its instantiation in the life and activity of God, Christ, or one of the saints set forth in the Bible. By its nature, such an approach to formation recognizes our free will and rationality and works through them.

Thus in respect of Scripture's surface, in the form of commandments and exemplary stories, Christ's teaching is ordered to engendering the acquisition of the virtues. Given the role of the virtues as a way in which human beings may embody and realize the saving efficacy of Jesus Christ for their own historical existence, in the commandments and exempla of its surface, Scripture offers another way by which the salvific import of Jesus Christ for all people in history may be appropriated by individuals over time in their social and historical contexts. In this way also, Scripture derives a historical central function and significance from that of Jesus Christ and is instrumental to the historical realization of his significance in the lives of others.

Scripture and the Transformation of the Exegete

Gregory's account of the transformative and sanctifying function of Christ's pedagogy in and through Scripture also serves his argument in Oration 2 about the formation required of the one who would teach Scripture to others, and this argument further reinforces and amplifies the account of Christ's pedagogy in Scripture examined thus far.

After explaining the difficulties of distributing the *logos* and the truth of Christian doctrines, with particular reference to the doctrine of the Trinity, Gregory explains that given all these difficulties he had decided that he needed to learn the pastoral art from more experienced pastors before practicing it himself.[50] In support of this principle, he appeals to an ancient Jewish custom, which did not entrust the whole of Scripture to every age group on the grounds that not every part is readily graspable to all, and those parts of Scripture with the greatest depths were capable of doing the most damage to many by their appearance.[51] Those that are accessible to most from the beginning of their scriptural studies, he adds, are those whose body is not unseemly. The rest, entrusted to those aged over twenty-five, are those that cloak their mystical beauty beneath a mean garment. That beauty, he continues, is the reward for hard labor and a shining life; it only shows itself to and shines upon

---

50. Or. 2.47.
51. Or. 2.48.

those purified in mind. Only those of such an age are capable, scarcely, of transcending the body and ascending to the letter from the spirit, he concludes.

Defending his decision to flee to monastic retreat before actively pursuing his priestly ministry, Gregory asks:

> Who [would take on himself the dress and name of a priest], whilst his heart has neither burnt with the holy and purified *logoi* of God when the Scriptures were explained to him, nor yet been inscribed these threefold on the tables of his heart so as to have the mind of Christ, nor gone inside the invisible and dark treasures hidden from the multitude so as to espy the wealth in them and be able to enrich others, explaining spiritual things to those who are spiritual?[52]

I take Gregory to understand the intellect by the biblical term "heart," for he says that by its inscription we come to have the mind of Christ. Here, then, he requires the mind of the priest to have been seared with the words of God, through the explication of Scripture, in which by implication those *logoi* are enfolded. When they are exposed to him in the sacred text as he reads, he is to internalize them (inscribing them on himself), which suggests a transformation of the reader.[53]

Another translation of the word rendered "to explain" (διανοιγῆναι) is "to open up." This choice of verb appears to be a deliberate allusion to Luke 24:32, where the disciples, who have met Jesus on the Emmaus road and have just recognized him, exclaim after he disappears, "Were not our hearts burning within us while he spoke with us on the road, while he explained (διήνοιγεν) the Scriptures to us?" It appears that for Gregory Christ is, in effect, the teacher who explicates the sacred text to the reader, such that when he does so the "divine *logoi*" are made manifest for the reader to accept them, and for them to burn the heart.

This notion makes sense in light of Gregory's belief that Christ, the Logos incarnate, indwells the Scriptures, and that he also illumines our minds and sanctifies us in conformity to God.[54] In light of these ideas, it seems reasonable

---

52. Or. 2.96, *SC* 247, pp. 214, 216. The content of the conditional clause at the beginning of the period must be supplied from the preceding *kolon*, which begins, "Or how could I take on the dress and name of a priest, before consecrating my hands with pious works?" Or. 2.95, *SC* 247, p. 214.

53. For similar (indeed bolder) conclusions about the salvific efficacy of the study of the Scripture for the preacher, see Beeley, *Gregory of Nazianzus*, 261.

54. See Or. 6.5, *SC* 405, p. 134, where he says that he seeks "the gifts of wisdom and of the Logos, who illumines our ruling faculty and enlightens our steps according to God."

to identify the *logoi* in our present passage with the teachings of Christ in a broad sense (including the θεωρήματά), and to take Gregory as intimating here that Christ is the inner teacher who enables us to identify and understand his teaching, so that we, receiving them, may be transformed by them.

Gregory has in mind here a stepwise transformation imparted by three levels of instruction. His reference to the threefold inscription of the *logoi* on the heart is both an allusion to Prov. 22:20-22 (LXX) but also thereby to Origen's distinctive interpretation of these very verses in respect of the interpretation of Scripture in *On First Principles*, as Kristoffel Demoen rightly observes.[55] It means, Origen tells us, that "one should inscribe on one's soul the intentions of the holy literature in a threefold manner."[56] He distinguishes three parts to Scripture, offering three kinds of teaching to readers—three degrees of spiritual maturity.

> The simpler person might be edified by the flesh of Scripture, as it were (flesh is our designation for the obvious understanding), the slightly more advanced by its soul, as it were; but the person who is perfect . . . by the spiritual law which contains "a shadow of the good things to come." For just as the human being consists of body, soul, and spirit, so does Scripture which God has arranged to be given for the salvation of humankind.[57]

According to Karen Jo Torjesen, Origen addresses the teacher "who must interpret Scripture for the congregation."[58] He alerts the exegete to an order in the doctrines contained in Scripture, one that "corresponds to the differentiated needs of the congregation."[59] He has organized the congregation into three groups, which "represent the three distinct phases through which the soul passes on its way to perfection."[60] There is a level of doctrine to fit the spiritual capacities of each group. Origen's point is that "contained in Scripture is an order of doctrines which corresponds to the progressive steps of the Christian's movement toward perfection," each stage preparing for the next and dependent on the one preceding it.[61]

---

55. Demoen, *Pagan and Biblical Exempla*, 264–65.

56. *Peri Archōn* IV.2.4 in Karlfried Froehlich's translation, *Biblical Interpretation in the Early Church* (Philadelphia: Fortress Press, 1984), 57.

57. *Peri Archōn* IV.2.4, 57.

58. Torjesen, *Hermeneutical Procedure and Theological Method in Origen's Exegesis* (Berlin and New York: Walter de Gruyter, 1986), 40.

59. Ibid.

60. Ibid.

Elsewhere Gregory also distinguishes between fleshy, soulful, and spiritual man as degrees of progress.[62] This fact reinforces the likelihood that when he cites this passage in Proverbs and speaks of a threefold inscription of God's words on the heart, he is consciously alluding to Origen's interpretation of that text in terms of a very similar threefold distinction in the spiritual progress of those taught, and thus also in the text from which the teaching is taken, and in the sanctifying power of that teaching. We may reasonably suppose, therefore, that Gregory takes from Origen his view of Scripture as containing, in Torjesen's words, "an order of doctrines which corresponds to the progressive steps of the Christian's movement toward perfection."[63] The priest, Gregory says, is to have inscribed on his heart, meaning his soul, all three different levels of instruction, which are perceptible to, and edifying for, those of differing grades of spiritual maturity. He is, therefore, one who has traversed all three grades in his own spiritual growth, by means of his reception of those teachings. Only then can he minister to others.[64]

The result of such transformation is that the reader should have "the mind of Christ," an expression from 1 Cor. 2:16 that for Gregory signifies the purification of the intellect by the imitation of, and by conforming to, Christ's mind, as he explains in Epistle 102.[65] In other words, the consequence is assimilation to Christ, who is the model for our creation and pattern for our transformation and ascent to God. As we have seen already, such growth in likeness to Christ is how we draw closer to God so as to know him more deeply. It is this transformation—the purification and conforming of the mind to Christ's—that the internalizing, or "inscription," of Scripture's threefold teaching brings about. This passage, then, brings into relief the transformative function of Scripture in God's saving activity toward us already implied in earlier analysis, and strengthens the case for seeing Scripture, in Gregory's thought, as a means by which Christ's saving efficacy, his reshaping of historical possibilities, is mediated to individuals and realized in their lives.

61. Torjesen, *Hermeneutical Procedure*, 41. See also Elizabeth Dively Lauro, *The Soul and Spirit of Scripture Within Origen's Exegesis* (Leiden: Brill, 2005), who argues, *contra* Torjesen, that these denote three levels of meaning that Origen holds to be found in every scriptural text.

62. "The soulful man is not yet good; / the fleshy man is really the lover of passions; / the spiritual man is not far from the Spirit" Carmen 1.2.34 (*PG* 37 963A). The qualifiers "not yet" and "not far" indicate that those in the soulful and spiritual states are moving toward greater maturity.

63. Torjesen, *Hermeneutical Procedure*, 41.

64. I return to the implications of these ideas for the formation of exegetes below.

65. "And not what we say, who maintain that those who have purified their mind by the imitation of his mind, which the Saviour assumed for us, and by conforming to it, as much as they can—these people are said to have the mind of Christ." Epistle 102.10, *SC* 250, p. 74.

Exposition as the Medium of Christ's Scriptural Pedagogy

Closely related to Gregory's idea of the function of Scripture in the passage just examined, finally, is the function of the exposition of Scripture in relation to it. Gregory requires that a candidate for priesthood should have gone "inside the invisible and dark treasures hidden from the multitude" to espy the wealth in them.[66] In context, the invisible and dark treasures must be those hidden within Scripture. Scripture has hidden treasures, which most cannot find, and entry into its interior and access to its wealth is a condition for being a priest. For such a one is "able to enrich others, explaining spiritual things to those who are spiritual."[67] One who is able to enter the depths of the sacred text can bring forth from them riches with which to endow those capable of receiving them ("the spiritual").

Here the force of the whole passage is made clear and confirmed: the priest must be capable of expounding Scripture, that is, of teaching its contents. Gregory presses the question of the fitness of the priest in respect of his greatest challenge as expositor of the Scriptures. The notion of exposition here is one in which the expositor mediates the transformative, sanctifying teaching of Christ embodied in Scripture: he is to enrich those capable of receiving the treasures hidden in the text. The example of mediating the wealth of Scripture to the spiritual does not exclude the mediation of the bodily and psychical teachings also. Karen Jo Torjesen's conclusion about the role of the exegete in Origen applies equally to Gregory: "The task of exegesis is to draw out of Scripture those teachings of Christ through which the souls, to which the teacher addresses his exegesis, can be advanced towards perfection."[68]

This view of the priest's exposition of Scripture is also reflected in Gregory's praise of Basil of Caesarea as an exegete, in his panegyric on his friend in Oration 43, delivered toward the end of his own career in 382.[69] According to Gregory, "Basil's writings are his greatest achievement and legacy, especially his exegesis of Scripture ('the divine oracles'), which alone suffice for one's formation."[70] Gregory supports his claim from his own experience of reading Basil's works: "When I handle his *Hexaemeron* and take it on my lips, I come

---

66. Or. 2.96, *SC* 247, p. 214.

67. Or. 2.96, *SC* 247, p. 216.

68. Torjesen, *Hermeneutical Procedure*, 43.

69. I follow McGuckin's dating of the Orations, in *Saint Gregory of Nazianzus*, vii–xi.

70. Or. 43.66, *SC* 384, pp. 270, 272.

to be with the Creator and know the *logoi* of creation and I admire the Creator more than before, when I use my teacher as my only means of sight."[71] Gregory says that in reading Basil's exegetical homilies on the Six Days of Creation aloud, he encounters the Creator in and as Basil's exposition brings him to apprehend signified in the text the *logoi* or mysteries of creation. If Gregory portrays the *Hexaemeron* as intended for more mature believers, he also tells us that Basil explicates his "other exegetical writings . . . for those who see only a little way."[72] By them Gregory confesses to be "persuaded not to rest with the letter nor look only to things above, but to advance further and proceed further still from depth to depth, deep calling out to deep and finding light in light until I attain the summit."[73] Here again Basil's exposition of Scripture is instrumental to progress in spiritual insight and advance in maturity, as the trope of ascent to the summit indicates.[74] As in Oration 2, Basil's exegesis is grounded in his own experience with the text: he expounds "having inscribed them threefold on the tables of his heart."[75] The allusion, again, is to Origen's account of the threefold order of transforming doctrines in Scripture. The implication is that Basil, having progressed through them, dispenses them to others in these works, so mediating those teachings that the readers who follow them may progress from degree to degree of spiritual growth. The exposition of Scripture for Gregory, therefore, serves the transformative purpose and function of God in Scripture, and partakes in the teaching and forming activity of Christ in the text. This function lends to the exposition of Scripture a central place not only in the pastoral art but also in history, theologically understood, for by God's aid they serve and share in the administration in history of the history-shaping luminosity of Jesus Christ.

CHRIST IN THE OLD TESTAMENT

This account immediately raises the question of in what sense Christ as teacher can be said to be present in the Old Testament, either in respect of the manifestation of saving divine truth or the formation of life. In the latter case, we have already seen something suggestive of part of the answer with respect

71. Or. 43.67, *SC* 384, p. 272. It is immaterial for my purposes whether all of what has come down to us purporting to be Basil's *Hexaemeron* is actually authored by him; what matters is what Gregory says about Basil's exegesis.

72. Or. 43.67, *SC* 384, p. 274.

73. Or. 43.67, *SC* 384, p. 274.

74. Bernardi in *SC* 384, p. 274, n. 2.

75. Or. 43.67, SC 384, p. 274.

to the lives of holy people recorded in Old Testament narrative, and the way Gregory prefaces his appeal to another Old Testament exemplum will enable us to develop the point.

Toward the end of Oration 2, Gregory explains how he turned to "one of the stories of old" for counsel when trying to decide whether to return to Nazianzus and resume the priestly ministry to which he had been ordained against his own inclination, and from which he had fled north to his friend Basil's monastic community at Annesoi in Pontus.[76] Unlike the Greeks and their myths, Christians believe such stories have a serious purpose, he insists. He explains:

> We, who draw out the Spirit's acute care to the merest jot or letter, will never admit—for it is not devout to do so—that the least actions have been treated by redactors and preserved by memory till the present without plan or purpose, but that we might have memoranda and lessons drawn from similar matters, if ever the opportune time should come to pass.[77]

The Spirit's minute care over the biblical text includes the writing down of what happened in particular instances and the preservation of those stories, so as to provide instructive examples for posterity. As Gregory explains elsewhere, an ἱστορία "is a source of instruction and pleasure for posterity."[78] Thus Athanasius legislated for the monastic life by writing the life of Anthony "in the form of a narrative."[79] Given Gregory's belief in the Spirit's inspiration of such stories for such a purpose, and given the way he tends to link closely the activity of Word and Spirit in creation and salvation, we may suppose that the pedagogy of the preexistent Word is expressed in such stories and that analogies may be drawn from them on the assumption of sufficient continuity in God's dealings with human beings before and after the coming of Jesus Christ. Indeed, in Oration 15 Gregory goes further and tells us explicitly that "none of those who were perfected before the coming of Christ encountered perfection apart from Christ."[80] For, he explains, "although the Logos was later openly proclaimed in his own time, he was known before to those pure in understanding, as is clear from the many honoured before him."[81] How Christ was known before his

---

76. Or. 2.104, *SC* 247, p. 224.

77. Or. 2.105, *SC* 247, p. 224.

78. Or. 21.5, *SC* 270, p. 118.

79. Or. 21.5, *SC* 270, p. 118.

80. Or. 15.1 (*PG* 35 912A–B).

advent is indicated by Gregory's account of the Law and his concept of figures or types.

In Oration 6, Gregory speaks of the Mosaic Law as the "double legislation, once in the letter and once in the spirit."[82] We have already seen, in Chapter 2, that for Gregory the prescriptions of the Law for various kinds of sacrifice had a time-limited pedagogical function, permitting practices in order to draw us to God. Furthermore, for Gregory the Old Testament is to be read according to its "spirit." Thus in Oration 2 Gregory requires that the would-be priest should flee "the antiquity of the letter, that he might serve the newness of the spirit and pass over completely to grace from the Law fulfilled spiritually by the liberation of the body."[83] We may infer, therefore, that in his view the part of the pedagogical value of the Law is merely preparatory for Christ—the literal observance of its sacrificial prescriptions, for example—but that the Law, perhaps even within those same prescriptions, also offered a deeper pedagogy that endures and perhaps anticipates the pedagogy of Christ's commands.

Gregory's appeal to Deut. 22:1-4 in Oration 14 forces us to nuance this conclusion, however. There, seeking to persuade his congregation to love the poor and lepers above all, probably to raise funds for the Leprosarium in Caesarea begun in 368, Gregory resorts among others to this argument:

> A man is not less valuable, O man, than a beast which has fallen into a ditch or wandered away and the Law commands you to raise and return. If [the Law] hides something else, more ineffable and deeper, like the many deep things of the double Law, I do not know but the Spirit who searches and knows all things [does]. What I understand, and what concerns my discourse, is that it is training us from philanthropy in small things to that in more perfect and greater things. For how much more do we owe to our equals in nature and honour what is praiseworthy in respect of irrational beings?[84]

For Gregory, then, the Law harbors a divine intention that has enduring force for Christian readers. It may have many layers of teaching, but what is clear is that the Law intends to exercise us in charity in small matters, to make us capable of greater philanthropy. Here we seem to have a clear example of

---

81. Or. 15.1 (*PG* 35 912A–B).

82. Or. 6.17, *SC* 405, p. 164.

83. Or. 2.97, *SC* 247, p. 216.

84. Or. 14.28 (*PG* 35 896B–C). On the likely original context of this oration see McGuckin, *Saint Gregory of Nazianzus*, 145ff.

divine pedagogy working through a text from the Law in order to inculcate virtue—the love of human beings. In this case, this deeper intent is not remote from what the command enjoins at face value. Rather, it embraces it within a larger logic of moving from the lesser to the greater, or from light to heavy, as the Rabbis called it, for Gregory's exegesis bears strong resemblance to one of their rules for interpreting Torah.[85] Such a pedagogical purpose seems entirely consistent with the pedagogy of Christ in his commandments, and we might again suppose Gregory to think the Word co-responsible with the Spirit for its inspiration, but that divine pedagogy would be available to hearers of the Law before Christ.

The Law, however, anticipates Christ in a second way. Gregory tells us that the first Law "is shadowy, removing demons, but the second clear, resolving enigmas."[86] In Oration 40.6, Gregory calls the Law "a figural (τυπικῶς) light, adumbrating the truth and the great light of the mystery."[87] The suggestion of this last text, especially when read in light of the passage from Oration 15 quoted above, is that there was a dim kind of light present in the Law, figuring forth the one who was to come, so that Christ was present by way of the signification of the figure not only for later generations but for those contemporaries also.

Gregory's exegetical practice frequently exemplifies the consequences of this idea, identifying many Old Testament actions and events as figures of Christ and the sacraments, which in turn prefigure the eschaton.[88] In Oration 38, for example, Gregory describes the manifestation of God in the birth of Christ as a second creation of light dispelling the darkness, a second pillar of light leaving the Egyptians in darkness, and the referent of Isaiah's prophecy of the great light seen by the people living in darkness, adding that with Christ's birth the shadows retire and the truth enters in.

In Oration 45, Gregory identifies the sacrifices of the Law as figurations of Christ. God, he says, did not leave the sacrifices wholly unhallowed or useless or empty save for blood, "but that great and unsacrificeable victim, so to speak, as to its first nature, was mixed with the sacrifices of the Law, and was a purification not for part of the world and for a little while, but for the

85. See "The Exegetical Rules of Rabbi Ishmael and Rabbi Hillel," in Froehlich, *Biblical Interpretation*, 31, 35.

86. Carmen 1.2.34 vv. 185–88. Here and in the following paragraphs I am indebted to the discussion in Demoen, *Pagan and Biblical Exempla*, 252ff. He also notes that Gregory speaks of the two covenants, "the one in shadow, the other in the truth" in Or. 14.27 (*PG* 35 893A).

87. *SC* 358, p. 206.

88. Or. 38.1–2 and Or. 39.1 in respect of Christ's life, Or. 39.17 in respect of baptism.

whole universe throughout all ages."[89] Christ, sacrificed upon the cross for the purification of the world in all ages, was "mixed" with the sacrifices of the Law. There seems to be some kind not only of prefiguring, but a real ontological connection between the sacrifices Israel is commanded to observe with their partial, limited purification, and Christ's complete, universal, and everlasting one.

Such prefigurement was not confined to the details of the Law. In Oration 2, Gregory gives us an example when he invokes a well-established figure of Christ in order to emphasize the demands of the spiritual combat priests must wage: "who is the Moses who triumphs by stretching out his hands on the mountain, so the cross may prevail by being figured forth and being revealed in advance?"[90] Here, on a related occasion in the history of Israel, Moses' physical actions configure the cross by their shape, thus revealing it in advance; and by this prefigurement the cross itself is effective on Israel's behalf. Here, more clearly, figural depiction and ontological connection are closely related: the representation of the cross mediating its reality almost iconically.[91]

These considerations weigh against any suspicion that to describe the practices prescribed in the Law or the events related in the Old Testament as figures empties them of their historical density and specificity. Rather, we have to reckon with Gregory's vision of history where events are both ontologically and semiotically related across time, relative to an eschatological future, and thus have an intrinsically figural character owing to their particular location within a divinely ordered history. Hence, in Oration 45, Gregory reads the Passover as a figure of Christian participation in Christ, which participation is in turn figural of an eschatological and eternal participation in Christ's teaching, so that, as Gregory says, the Passover of the Law was "the figure of a figure."[92] This conclusion only reinforces the implication of the previous passages examined, that figuration, for Gregory, is not antithetical to embodied human life with God in time, but rather an important way by which we, being in time and embodied, may share in divine, intellectual, and invisible things.

89. Or. 45.13 (PG 36 640C).

90. Or. 2.88, SC 247, p. 202. We find this figure for example in Justin Martyr, *Dialogue with Trypho*, 90; *The Epistle of Barnabas*, 12; Irenaeus, *Demonstration of the Apostolic Preaching*, 46.

91. As Frances Young says about typology in Ephrem the Syrian in her *Biblical Exegesis and the Formation of Christian Culture* (Cambridge: Cambridge University Press, 1997), 148.

92. Or. 45.23 (PG 36 654C–656A).

ALLEGORY AND FLIGHT FROM HISTORY?

It is in this light that we need to turn to another passage in Oration 45, where Gregory reminds us that

> [b]efore our time, the divine Apostle declared the Law to be a shadow of the things to come, which are understood by thought. And God, who before that gave audience to Moses, when he legislated concerning these things said: "See that you make everything according to the model I showed you on the mountain." For he set forth the visible things as an adumbration and delineation of invisible things.[93]

Kristoffel Demoen finds here an apparent contrast between the interpretation of the Law as "the adumbration and delineation of things to come," which Gregory cites from Heb. 8:5, and the qualification Gregory adds to it: "which are conceived by thought." He takes the passage as an "allegorical" tendency characterized by a flight from the historically concrete and sensible to the ahistorically abstract and intelligible. [94]

Demoen thus evokes a well-worn discussion in modern scholarship on patristic exegesis, a discussion that revolves around a much-contested distinction between "typology," a modern neologism, and allegory, a term found in Christian literature, but which Demoen, like others before him, gives a precise technical meaning for heuristic purposes.[95] He tells us that "the event or character interpreted in typology refers to a later, historical event or character, firstly to Christ, secondly to the Christian history and eschatology."[96] By contrast, "the moral and 'anagogic' interpretations of the Bible, which switch over from concrete to abstract, from historical to a-historical, from sensible to intelligible, should be called allegorical."[97] On analysis of Gregory's hermeneutics, Demoen finds that Nazianzen holds to a traditional typological conception of biblical salvation history, but also to an allegorical conception of the Bible seen as a text to which history is not important.[98] Such a charge would furnish a serious objection to the argument I am putting forward. At the very least it would mean that part of Gregory's theological hermeneutics is deeply at odds with the overall cast of his theology with respect to history.

Demoen makes his point with reference to a number of passages in Gregory, and I will be returning to it several times in the remainder of this chapter. In respect of the passage just cited from Oration 45, we can find further

---

93. Or. 45.11 (*PG* 36 637A–B).

94. Demoen, *Pagan and Biblical Exempla*, 264.

apparent support for his charge from Oration 28. In Oration 45, one of the visible figures Gregory mentions is the Tabernacle. In Oration 28, he interprets some of its details. He tells us that "the story knows the Tent of Moses is the prefiguration of the whole cosmos, I mean that constituted of 'things visible and invisible.'"[99] Must we, he asks, "go through the first veil, and transcend sensible things, to peer into the Holy Things, the intellectual and heavenly

95. This distinction goes back at least as far as Jean Daniélou's *Sacramentum Futuri: Études sur les origines de la typologie biblique* (Paris: Beauchesne, 1950). There Daniélou identifies typology as a correspondence or analogy between two events in history, which he finds in the New Testament, early Christian liturgy, and the Church Fathers and before them the Old Testament. In the Alexandrian tradition, typology is mixed with the alien practice of allegory, an approach deriving from Philo, which takes biblical stories as images or symbols representing philosophical ideas, a correspondence not between historical events but between the sensible and the intelligible world. Geoffrey Lampe offers a very similar definition in his "The Reasonableness of Typology" in Lampe and K. Woollcombe, *Essays on Typology* (London: SCM, 1957). However, the distinction has been questioned by a number of studies. Henri de Lubac pointed out that Daniélou's use of "allegory" reproduced the polemical usage of the Antiochene school but did not correspond to the wider usage in earlier and later Christian texts going back to Paul; moreover Origen's "Philonic" moral allegory was integral to his understanding of the Christian life and closely connected with what Daniélou called "typology" ("'Typologie' et 'allégorie,'" *Recherches de science religieuses* 34 [1947]: 180–226). R. P. C. Hanson also problematized Daniélou's distinction, seeing a continuum between typology and allegory in early Christianity, with common roots in the rabbinic exegetical practices of Palestinian Judaism, and suggesting that doubts attaching to allegory in light of historical criticism would apply equally to typology. He was prepared, however, to accept that Alexandrian allegory, drawing on Philo and Hellenic philosophical exegesis, introduced a very different, ahistorical allegoresis into Christian interpretation of Scripture (*Allegory and Event* [London: SCM, 1959]). Henri Crouzel argues that the vertical dimension that characterizes "allegory" is proper to the character of human knowledge of God and has a New Testament basis in his "La distinction de la 'typologie' et de l' 'allégorie,'" *Bulletin de littérature ecclésiastique* 3 (1964): 161–74. Frances Young revises the distinction in her *Biblical Exegesis*, viewing typology as a form of intertextuality wherein the type retains its autonomy and integrity while mirroring another event, character, or act, whereas allegory uses words as tokens, arbitrarily taken to refer to other realities by application of a code, so destroying the surface coherence of the text (154–61). Her discussion, however, includes a "vertical" relation to the eternal in typology, and in a later article she argues that Alexandrian and Antiochene "schools" were not divided in method but over particular applications of method where Antiochene concerns were *doctrinally* motivated. See her "The Fourth Century Reaction against Allegory," *Studia Patristica* 30 (Leuven: Peeters, 1997), 120–25. See further the summaries in Elizabeth A. Clark, *Reading Renunciation: Asceticism and Scripture in Early Christianity* (Princeton: Princeton University Press, 1999), 70–78, and Peter W. Martens, "Revisiting the Allegory/Typology Distinction: The Case of Origen," *Journal of Early Christian Studies* 16, no. 3 (2008): 283–96.

96. Demoen, *Pagan and Biblical Exempla*, 247.

97. Ibid.

98. See his conclusions on these points in *Pagan and Biblical Exempla*, 258, 267.

99. Or. 28.31, *SC* 250, p. 170.

nature?" [100]This nature "we cannot see in an incorporeal manner, even if it is incorporeal."[101] The Tabernacle figures forth the whole cosmos; the curtain that divides the Holy of Holies from the rest of the Tent signifies the distinction between the visible world and heaven, the realm of pure spirits. Earlier in the Oration, Gregory says that he cannot see "the first and unmixed nature known to itself, I mean the Trinity, and as much as remains inside the first veil and is covered by the Cherubim."[102] The Holy of Holies represents heaven, the dwelling place of God, who even there is veiled by the Cherubim: the lid of the Ark, where God's presence dwelt between the Cherubim, signifying the dwelling of God in the utter transcendence of his nature.

What the Tabernacle signifies, then, is not exactly eternal realities, but the structure of the cosmos in its relationship to God, both the visible creation and the spiritual creation, and, at its heart, the dwelling of God. There is not really a question of a historical episode being subverted, for the object interpreted is a structure whose pattern was revealed to Moses by God, according to the story, and the interpretation does not deny the historical function of the Tabernacle, but asserts that it showed forth the pattern of the universe.

Moreover, there need be no opposition between this figural function and the historical dimension indicated by Gregory's quotation of Hebrews; that the invisible, intellectual things adumbrated and delineated in the Law are "things to come." For Gregory, we may suppose, is indicating that the Tabernacle is figuring forth the realms to which human beings will have access in the future, so that when the priest enters the Holy of Holies, he prefigures the access to heaven enjoyed by believers in the future. When we see the figuration of intellectual things in terms not of an ahistorical signification of the abstract but the historical figuration of the heavenly and eschatological, the things of God that are still future to Gregory and his readers, Gregory's reading of the Tabernacle seems consonant with his reading of the Passover as a figure of a figure of the heavenly and eschatological Passover that awaits Christians. It will also help us to recall that Gregory does not share the assumption Demoen seems to implicitly attribute to him, namely that there is an antithesis between things conceived in thought and historical events.[103] After all, as we have seen in Chapter 2, God for Gregory is both the source of intellectual light and supreme

100. Ibid.
101. Ibid.
102. Or. 28.3, *SC* 250, p. 104.
103. Frances Young seems to find a very similar phenomenon in Ephrem the Syrian's typological exegesis in her *Biblical Exegesis*, 148ff.

goal of intellectual vision, and yet Gregory holds that in the incarnation God is made manifest to human beings in Christ's birth, as he tells us in Oration 38.[104]

Symbolic Teaching

This understanding of the figuration of both future and eschatological realities in the Law extends, in Gregory's account, to the finer details of the Law (where "Law" here seems to denote the whole Pentateuch, or at least includes the book of Exodus). Each of the objects belonging to the Tabernacle and its use bears deeper significance:

> I am persuaded that none of these things were commanded in vain, none irrationally, none in a grovelling manner, nor are they unworthy of the legislation of God and the ministry of Moses, even if it is hard to find an interpretation ($\theta\epsilon\omega\rho\iota\alpha$) for each of the shadows descending to the finer details, like those concerning the Tent, its measurements, materials, the Levites and Priests who carried them, and concerning the stipulated sacrifices, purifications and offerings.[105]

Gregory goes on to describe the Law as a mode of divine condescension, a condescension signified by God's descent to Sinai in order to give the Law to Moses. The symbolic details of the Law, he tells us, are intelligible ($\theta\epsilon\omega\rho\eta\tau\alpha$), "only to those like Moses in virtue, or closest to him in formation."[106]

> For on the mountain God appears to men, by his ascent from his lofty abode and our ascent from our lowly humility, so that the ungraspable may to some degree be grasped by mortal nature, as far as is safe. For in no other way may the coarseness of a material body and mind imprisoned come into consciousness of God without his aid.[107]

The paradigm of Moses teaches that in order to discern intimations of God in the symbolic details of the Law, God must descend to us, graciously, and we must become like him, as Gregory implies by the language of ascent.

104. Or. 38.3.
105. Or. 45.11 (*PG* 36 637A).
106. Or. 45.11 (*PG* 36 637A).
107. Or. 45.11 (*PG* 36 637A–B).

The configuration of invisible, spiritual realities in visible forms seems to be the expression of that condescension. The real objects and actions that God commands to be made or performed themselves delineate invisible realities that are only properly understood intellectually, in terms accessible to us. The invisible is known by way of the visible, which represents a gracious accommodation of God to our way of knowing things: once again, Gregory understands God to work in a way fitting to our needs and condition. Gregory articulates this principle most explicitly when discussing anthropomorphic descriptions of divine action in Oration 31.22. Sleeping and waking, for example, are ascribed to God in Scripture, yet are activities proper to embodied beings, and not to God.[108] Gregory explains, "we have named the things of God, so as to make them accessible, from what is ours."[109]

In the case of the Tabernacle, such interpretation involves drawing on the symbolic potential of the logic implicit in what is commanded. For example, in the case of the structure of the Tabernacle, Gregory's interpretations in Oration 28 draw on the text's own logic, which is to delineate spheres of increasing holiness relative to the presence of God by means of curtains or veils and the wings of the Cherubim on the Ark lid. Those physical items thus already represent or symbolize both degrees of proximity to and of separation from God and the obscuring of the divine from human sight. It is this symbolic logic that allows Gregory to see in the Tabernacle a physical figure of a spiritual heaven: physical barriers and structures delineate ontological distinctions and degrees of apprehension of reality that share the logic informing the symbolism of the Tent. Thus the deeper meaning is only present by way of a pattern of meaning internal to the text, on which it depends and by way of which interpreters must go.

Gregory finds the authors of Scripture using symbols to depict invisible realities in a number of other respects. Thus in support of his argument that priests must be holy before ministering, and referring to Lev. 21:17-23, he says in Oration 2, "I myself know that the bodily defects of the priest or sacrifices were not exempted from examination, but it was prescribed that perfect men should present perfect offerings, the symbol, I think, of perfection of soul."[110] The physical purity commanded symbolizes the real requirement of perfection of soul; the outward appearance of the priest's body is a representation of the inner quality required of the soul that animates it. This interpretation preserves

---

108. Or. 31.22, where Gregory alludes to Ps. 77:65 (LXX) and Dan. 9:14 respectively (references given in SC 250, p. 316).

109. Or. 31.22, SC 250, p. 316.

110. Or. 2.94, SC 247, p. 212.

the historical function of the command, and recognizes that the holiness of God is at stake, but by reasoning from the symbolic logic of that command draws out its pedagogical force for the Christian reader. In Oration 17, Gregory seems to find a similar symbolic principle at work in Jer. 4:19 (LXX). When Jeremiah laments, "I am pained in my bowels, my bowels, and the senses of my heart are in turmoil," "he names his soul according to the laws of trope."[111]

This understanding of the symbolism at work in the Old Testament Law and prophets indicates that Demoen's charge that Gregory's allegorical tendency sees the Bible as a text to which history is not important is not only inaccurate with respect to history, but overlooks the importance for Gregory of the linguistic, textual mediation of the historical realities he believes the Bible to describe. For, on his account, the sacred text is concerned to describe the details of inherently symbolic entities, just as it elsewhere uses figures of speech to set forth interior or invisible realities.

INSPIRATION

In all these ways, then, we can understand Gregory to find the pedagogical presence of Christ in the Old Testament, reflecting his preexistent pedagogy in Israel. Gregory's concern for the textual mediation of the things of the past that bear that pedagogy brings us to the second of the notions underlying his conception of Scripture as "embodying" Christ's teacherly presence, namely belief in the divine inspiration of Scripture in both testaments. This belief, we should also note, has been linked by R. P. C. Hanson to the dangers of "allegory" in the negative sense used by Demoen and others. He believes that the attempt to discover what the Bible meant was hampered in the early church by the combination of allegory with "an essentially oracular view of the biblical text," a system open to considerable abuse.[112]

There is ample evidence that Gregory held to the common view of the Fathers that all Scripture is divinely inspired. He speaks of "the divine oracles," and "the divine scripture," or more explicit still, the judgments or oracles of God.[113] For Gregory, such inspiration is by no means antithetical to ascribing biblical books to human authors. The basic idea is well expressed at the outset of Oration 2: "let the blessed David begin my discourse, or rather he who uttered

---

111. Or. 17.1 (PG 35 964B–965A): "he names his soul according to the laws of trope."

112. Hanson, "Biblical Exegesis in the Early Church," chapter 13 in *The Cambridge History of the Bible*, vol. 1, ed. P. R. Ackroyd and C. F. Evans (Cambridge: Cambridge University Press, 1970), 449.

through David, and even now still speaks through him." God spoke and still speaks through the speech of the inspired writer.[114]

In some cases Gregory singles out the Spirit in particular as the agent of inspiration.[115] That he should do so is no surprise given, as we shall see, that whereas the Son makes God known, it is the Spirit who enables us to understand things concerning God. Thus by talking of the Spirit he implies an explanation of how the biblical writers came to impart what we shall see he thought of as the teaching of the Word.

Gregory's understanding of the Spirit's inspiration in other contexts explains how he understood the inspiration of the Scripture-writers in greater detail. In Oration 20.5, for example, Gregory explains how Solomon, the putative author of Proverbs, having received unparalleled wisdom from God, could say he lacked wisdom (in Prov. 30:3). "Clearly it is because he has no wisdom proper to himself, since he is energised by a divine and more perfect wisdom."[116] Solomon does not mean to say he does not possess wisdom, any more than Paul, who says "I live, yet not I, but Christ lives in me,"[117] denies that he lives. Paul "is in no way speaking of himself as dead, but as living a life superior to the multitude by his participation in the one who truly lives and is not cut short by death."[118] Just so, Gregory implies, Solomon is wise, yet not from his own independent power but by participation in divine wisdom, which is not to be mechanically manipulated but heightened in rationality and exposure to the truth.

The results of such inspiration, as Gregory understands it, are to be seen in the details of the text itself. As we have already seen, Gregory's account of how the Spirit's intention to furnish lessons for later readers is enshrined in the form of exemplary narratives of cases from which readers may draw lessons for their own lives. By using the term *inspiration* of the texts in question, and then ascribing their purpose in composition to the Spirit, while acknowledging

113. Thus, for example, in Or. 29.16: "let us see your strength from the divine oracles, and whether you may discover something there to persuade us" (*SC* 250, p. 212, and in Or. 31.21, *SC* 250, p. 317) he refers to "divine Scripture." In Oration 8, he praises his sister Gorgonia's openness to "the divine sayings" and her mastering "the judgments of God" (Or. 8.9, *SC* 405, p. 264). He also attests of himself that "the oracles of God pleased me like pieces of honeycomb" (Or. 2.77, *SC* 247, p. 190).

114. Or. 2.1, *SC* 247, p. 84, after a quotation from Ps. 36:7 (LXX).

115. In Or. 14.30, Gregory finds similar expressions of the mystery [of providence] "in divine Scripture although it would take long to enumerate all the expressions of the Spirit that lead me to this conclusion" (*PG* 35 897C). Cf. Or. 2.105, *SC* 247, p. 224.

116. Or. 20.5, *SC* 270, p. 66.

117. Ibid.

118. Ibid.

that the texts had human redactors, Gregory also indicates that the Spirit's care over the details of the text works with, and does not subvert, literary form. It seems then that conventional human literary form is how the energizing of the biblical writer by participation in divine wisdom finds expression. Gregory's belief seems to drive the exegete back to the literary form of the text and, in the case of narrative, the stories' depiction of characters and events as patterns of godly, wise, virtuous, or vicious behavior. We have also seen, in Oration 45, Gregory holds that none of the details of the Law were commanded without a deeper meaning, reflecting a similar belief in the precision of the Spirit's intent in inspiration as that articulated in the passage just referred to from Oration 2. There, as I have argued, the inspired teaching is implied within the symbolic potential of the things the text describes.

Conclusion

Gregory's theology of Scripture, like his theological vision of history, does not share the same attention to the density of historical relativities we find in modern historical consciousness, nor should we expect it to. This difference is most obvious in Gregory's account of inspiration, which does not offer a thick description of the historical location and formation of the biblical traditions and their relations to their historical and cultural contexts. Nevertheless, as a sketch of the main lines for a theology of Scripture that can begin to meet the challenge of historical consciousness, his account has much to offer. In particular, he points us to the potential to be found in locating the character and function of Scripture relative to the history-shaping centrality of Jesus Christ and his presence by the Spirit, to the work of transformation whereby individuals and communities partake of the new historical possibilities opened by Christ, and to the labor of the pastor-exegetes, who share in Christ's pedagogical and therapeutic ministry even as they are themselves transformed by it. His account of the pedagogy of the commandments, the figural character of history theologically viewed, the functions of biblical symbolism, and the transformation of rationality in inspiration is also suggestive. In that next chapter I explore how this account of Scripture informed Gregory's understanding and practice of biblical interpretation, and what these may suggest for our concerns.

5

From Letter to Spirit

All the features of Gregory's theology of Scripture have hermeneutical implications, which Gregory tends to explain in the Pauline terms of letter and spirit, used by so many early Christian exegetes. To do so means recognizing the pedagogical force of the text by following the movement enacted in Christ and the Spirit from the letter of the text to its spirit. Here the hermeneutical differences between Gregory's Christ-centered theological historical vision and a modern historical consciousness become most apparent.

LETTER TO SPIRIT AS AN EXEGETICAL AND SPIRITUAL ACTIVITY

Oration 2 offers one significant example of a very general description of exegesis in these terms, one that reveals that exegesis for Gregory was an act of spiritual insight contingent on the holiness of the reader. There Gregory describes certain scriptural passages that cloak their mystical beauty, which shows itself to the pure, to those capable of ascending from the letter to the spirit.[1]

The spirit of Scripture is here configured variously as the soul within the body, the depth behind the surface appearance, and the beautiful body cloaked in poor clothing. In places, this surface or clothing can mislead the inexperienced and morally weak interpreter to their peril. Hence hard work and a shining life are prerequisites of deeper understanding: the spirit of the text unveils itself and shines forth only to those with these qualities. This account, which speaks of the spirit of the text in erotic, personal terms, makes most sense if by the spirit of Scripture Gregory means the incarnate Word present within, who by the Holy Spirit illumines the virtuous reader to apprehend his beauty within the text. In the Preface to his *Commentary on the Song of Songs*, which may well be Gregory's source, Origen reports the same tradition and specifies

---

1. Or. 2.48.

the texts in question as the first chapters of Genesis, the beginning and end of Ezekiel, where the Cherubim and the Temple are described, and the Song of Songs.

Demoen finds here further evidence for an "allegorical" tendency in Gregory; it is an implicit plea for allegorical interpretation, he claims.[2] If we take allegory in its broad, ancient meaning, as denoting discourse in which there is another meaning or sense to the text besides the apparent one, his point is both incontrovertible and uncontroversial.[3] As we have seen, however, Demoen has a particular concept of allegory whereby a text ostensibly denoting concrete, visible, historical things signifies abstract, invisible, and intellectual realities. Although other ancient writers do use the figures of surface and depth, body and soul, clothing and body to denote meanings that might fall under Demoen's definition of allegory, there is no evidence in this passage that Gregory has such a notion in mind. Demoen also appeals to the passage cited above from Oration 4, where Gregory critiques pagan myth and defends Christian Scripture from those same critiques. There Gregory concedes a similarity between pagan classics and some passages in Christian Scripture: both have a double meaning. His language is very similar to that of Oration 2 and presumably has similar scriptural passages in view: in the passages he has in mind, the hidden meaning is "wonderful and elevated and exceeding bright to those who enter into the depth."[4]

Here Demoen finds an implicit acknowledgment of the "allegorical" method employed by the pagans because it is not challenged as such, and a telling absence of appeal to historicity to distinguish Christian from pagan Scripture.[5] Nazianzen, he claims, here "considers the Bible as a *text* which has to be deciphered." Gregory, he adds, does not emphasize the Bible as "*historically true*."[6] This argument is made from a silence for which other explanations are possible: perhaps Gregory held either that it is reasonable to think fiction might have deeper meanings, which many literary critics would affirm, or that not every text of Scripture concerns historical events, which few modern scholars would dispute.

2. Kristoffel Demoen, *Pagan and Biblical Exempla in Gregory Nazianzen: A Study in Rhetoric and Hermeneutics* (Turnhout, Belgium: Brepols, 1996), 263.

3. See, for example, Quintillian: allegory presents one thing in words, another in sense (*Institutes of Oratory* 8.6.44), or Cicero: allegory is saying one thing and meaning another (*De Oratore* III.iii.203, cited in Jeremy Tambling, *Allegory* [Abingdon, UK: Routledge, 2010], 21).

4. Or. 4.118, *SC* 405, p. 282.

5. Demoen, *Pagan and Biblical Exempla*, 266.

6. Demoen, *Pagan and Biblical Exempla*, 267.

Gregory's emphasis on the text, furthermore, is commendable. It reinforces what we have seen in Orations 2, 14, and 45, that the structure of the text—whether the pedagogical bent of its narrative form, the wider implications of the logic of commandments, or the force of its symbolic logic—conveys its spiritual teaching and must be the starting point for the interpreter. In Oration 2, this emphasis is reflected in Gregory's critique of those who become priests without the proper formation as exegetes, before "they even know the names of the sacred books, before they can recognize the characters and authors of the Old and New [Testaments]."[7] With them, he adds a little later, "the letter is nowhere, and everything must be understood spiritually."[8] By implication, the letter cannot be bypassed in interpretation, and the exegete must know it thoroughly. Above all, the movement from the letter of the text to it, following the intention of the Spirit, takes several forms for Gregory, as his various uses of that terminology show.

Reading the Old Testament

In the first place, Gregory uses a language of exegesis that moves from Old Testament figures to the realities they signify. In Oration 2, Gregory requires that the would-be priest recognize "the kinship and distinction between figures and the truth, separating himself from the former and associating with the latter in order."[9] In light of the analysis above, we can say that such movement in effect follows the movement of history. It conforms to the difference made by the incarnation, at which, as Gregory says in Oration 38, "the letter retires, the spirit gains the advantage, the shadows flee and the truth enters in."[10] If, with the coming of Christ, the significance of the figures is made manifest, exegesis conforms to history when it interprets Old Testament figures in light of Christ.

Next, let us assume we may understand the pedagogical intent of the commandments and stories of the surface of Scripture to be that of the preexistent Word as well as the inspiring Spirit, and that this teaching anticipates the pedagogy of the commandments of the Word incarnate. As we have seen, Gregory thinks of biblical narratives as intended, in their story form, to offer lessons for us in analogous circumstances.[11] In that case, by appropriating the stories by reasoning analogically between their terms and our

---

7. Or. 2.49, *SC* 247, p. 154.

8. Or. 2.49, *SC* 247, p. 156.

9. Or. 2.97, *SC* 247, p. 216.

10. Or. 38.2, *SC* 358, pp. 104, 106.

11. Or. 2.105, analyzed in the previous chapter.

own circumstances, or extrapolating from the commandments to their deeper intentions, reading symbolically where necessary, the readers not only extend the pedagogy of the text in a way consistent with its composition; they realize this pedagogy in a way consistent with God's decisive shaping of history in Jesus Christ, and ordered to the realization of the efficacy of that saving action in their own lives.

Gregory gives an account of his reading of the story of Jonah that illustrates this process. The context is Gregory's ordination, which was forced upon him (he complained) by his father, the bishop of Nazianzus, and after which Gregory, who had desired a life of retreat and contemplation, fled to an estate belonging to the family of his friend Basil of Caesarea, at Annesoi, where Basil was experimenting with the ascetic life. Gregory sought to understand his situation by recourse to the story of Jonah; "Jonah also fled from the face of God, or rather thought to flee."[12] His exposition is too long to examine in full, but the following features stand out.

The first is the sense that Jonah's story adumbrates the pattern of Christ's death and resurrection: Jonah "was stopped by the sea and storm and lot and the stomach of the huge fish and three-day tomb."[13] This tomb, he adds, contains "the figure of a greater mystery." He means that it foreshadows Christ's three-day stay in the grave. The connection had already been made in Matthew's Gospel, where Jesus likens his own stay in the tomb to Jonah's time in the fish, calling the former the "sign of Jonah."[14] Gregory follows this intertextual connection, and so guided, readily finds a plausible figure of Jesus' death, burial, and resurrection in Jonah's descent down to the fish, its swallowing him, his "entombment" in its belly, and his being vomiting forth. Why mention it in this context, though? We should recall that in the Oration Gregory preached at Easter on his return to Nazianzus, he appeals to the day that the risen Christ may renew him by the Spirit.[15] The figure of resurrection seems to be the key: if Jonah was forgiven and in some sense "raised with Christ," might Gregory also be forgiven and renewed, and in which case, on what conditions? It all depends on why Jonah was forgiven: whatever Gregory may learn from the story will depend on interpreting the mysterious behavior of Jonah and of God toward him.[16]

---

12. Or. 2.106, *SC* 247, p. 224.

13. Or. 2.106, *SC* 247, p. 226.

14. Matt. 12:39-41.

15. Or. 1.2, *SC* 247, p. 74.

16. Gregory's conclusion to his exegesis bears this interpretation out, as we shall see.

Second, Gregory's exegesis, which he tells us is informed by what he has read in one of his teachers (probably Origen), centers on resolving an apparent absurdity in the narrative.[17] Gregory's teacher, he tells us, "came, in a not absurd way, to the aid of what is absurd in the appearance and was able to grasp the depth of the prophet" and we, he implies, should do likewise: seek for the depth that will resolve the apparent absurdity of the tale.[18] On the one hand, Gregory opposes the solution that says Jonah was jealous for the status of prophecy. (How could he have been ignorant of God's gracious plan or wish to oppose it?) On the other, he asks whether to believe that Jonah "hoped to hide himself in the sea and escape the notice of the great eye of God by flight is not wholly absurd and ignorant, and not rightly to be believed either of a prophet or of anyone with sense and some measure of awareness of God and his universal power?"[19] As he says later, "he was not ignorant of the powerful hand of God, this Jonah who threatened others with it."[20]

Third, Gregory's solution and interpretation involve attention to the symbolic overtones of Jonah's flight and descent into the sea, the key to which Gregory, following his teacher, finds in a dubious etymology of "Joppa" as "the contemplation of joy."[21] Gregory tells us that Jonah leaves the contemplation of joy, "I mean the ancient elevation and dignity, and throws himself into the sea of grief."[22] For Jonah, Gregory explains, "foresaw the fall of Israel, and sensed the transfer of the grace of prophecy to the Gentiles, for this reason he recoils from proclamation and puts off the thing commanded."[23] (Gregory may well be thinking of, and interpreting Jonah 4:2, where the prophet expresses his knowledge of God's merciful character, which clearly extends to Gentiles.) Jonah's grief explains what follows: "For this reason he is storm-tossed and sleeps and is shipwrecked and is awakened and chosen by lot and confesses his flight and is thrown into the sea and is swallowed by the great fish, but is not killed, but there calls on God and, the wonder, is given up on the third day with Christ."[24] The double meaning of Joppa provides the clue to understanding Jonah's very real flight as both motivated by and symbolically expressive of

17. On the identification of this teacher as Origen, see Bernardi's comment in *SC* 247, pp. 226–27, n. 1.

18. Or. 2.107, *SC* 247, p. 226.

19. Or. 2.107, *SC* 247, p. 228.

20. Or. 2.109, *SC* 247, p. 228.

21. Or. 2.109, *SC* 247, p. 228.

22. Ibid.

23. Ibid.

24. I have followed Bernardi in rendering ἀφείς as "he abandons" (*SC* 247, p. 229).

his grief, not a misunderstanding of God's sovereignty or repugnance at his merciful intentions.[25]

Finally, Jonah functions not as a pattern of discipleship or to provide simple moral lessons, but rather illumines Gregory's situation analogically. For by understanding Jonah's motives, Gregory sees that "there was perhaps some cause of his forgiveness, through that which I have spoken of, for his hesitation from exercising prophecy."[26]

From this conclusion, Gregory has a grasp of the *paradeigma* of Jonah without subverting the interaction of characters and circumstances in it, and while relating the whole to the story of Jesus, literally read. He can now use it as a model to inform his own situation, drawing out the implications analogically. "What reason or what kind of defence would remain for me if I stayed hidden for longer and spurned the yoke of divine service . . . imposed on me?"[27] Without an analogous cause for flight, Gregory cannot justify running from his vocation any longer. The inference is particular to Gregory, but is drawn from what he takes to be the inner logic of the story, which is capable of bearing many other such applications. This exegetical procedure depends on close observation of the story, including incongruous elements that seem to call for symbolic reading but without reducing it to nothing but symbolism. It is perhaps best described in Richard B. Hays's terms as metaphorical reading: where the biblical case is not followed literally, but is allowed to reconfigure and reinterpret our experience, calling for us to reason as to how we might act analogously.[28] In Gregory's case, such reading involves attending to the story in light of the wider shape of history centered in Jesus Christ.

Thus far Gregory's use of letter and spirit with respect to the exegesis of the Old Testament cannot be reduced to a single kind of semiotic relationship but does seem either to conform to or be consistent with his overall vision of history. Here "letter" tends to denote either the Old Testament prescriptions in their literal force, or the past events that signify and partook of the saving reality of the incarnation. Yet Gregory also uses the letter and spirit terminology when discussing the exegesis of the New Testament, and here too we find both diversity with respect to the range of semiotic relations in view, and conformity to his theological vision of history.

---

25. Gregory's procedure bears strong resemblance to that commended by Origen in *Peri Archōn* IV.3.4–5.

26. Or. 2.110, *SC* 247, p. 230.

27. Or. 2.110, *SC* 247, p. 230. I follow Bernardi in translating λετουργία as "divine service."

28. Richard Hays, *The Moral Vision of the New Testament* (New York: HarperCollins, 1996), 302–3.

LETTER AND SPIRIT IN MATTHEW 19

Oration 37 is Gregory's only extant exegetical homily, but it illustrates his hermeneutics and the way they are theologically framed very well. Gregory begins by expounding the opening lines of Matthew 19, in which Jesus leaves Galilee to travel to the region of Judaea beyond the Jordan, followed by large crowds, whom he heals. Gregory understands Christ's motive to be twofold: to gain more for God by visiting them, but also "to sanctify a greater number of places."[29] This motive, he explains, belongs to the wider pattern of action exhibited by the Word incarnate and the deep purpose of his coming:

> He becomes a fisherman, he descends to be with all, he drag-nets all places, in order to bring up from the depths that fish which swims in the unstable, bitter waves of life: the human being. For this reason, now, "when he had finished these words, he left Galilee and went to the regions of Judaea beyond the Jordan."[30]

Christ leaves Galilee for the same reason he descended into our condition, for the same reason he emptied himself of his glory (as Gregory goes on to explain Phil. 2:7, which he echoes here). The same salvific purpose that explains his kenosis leads him to widen his sphere of ministry.

This same purpose explains Jesus' peripatetic ministry and all he does and undergoes: "He dwells nobly in Galilee in order that the people seated in darkness might see the great light of knowledge. He removes to Judaea to persuade them to follow the spirit by rising from the letter."[31] Christ's advent, as we have seen from Oration 38, is the entry of the spirit on the heels of the letter. His ministry is an exercise in illumination and persuasion, to the end that other human beings may conform to this transition in human history that he has effected in himself.

John McGuckin claims that in effect Gregory is making a hermeneutical point here that will govern his exposition of Jesus' treatment of the question of marriage: the compassionate approach that Christ showed to human beings in his ministry ought to be our guiding premise for considering the question of marriage.[32] We may add that Gregory's use of the terms "letter" and "spirit"

29. Or. 37.1, SC 318, p. 270.

30. Or. 37.1–2, SC 318, p. 272. I have followed the syntax of Claudio Moreschini's French translation of the end of the first sentence, which nicely captures the stress of Gregory's prose (SC 318, p. 273).

31. Or. 37.2, SC 318, p. 272.

32. John McGuckin, *Saint Gregory of Nazianzus: An Intellectual Biography* (Crestwood, NY: St. Vladimir's Seminary Press, 2001), 333.

support this reading. They suggest that Christ's ministry establishes a hermeneutical principle for understanding and appropriating his teaching: the reader needs to move, as the Galileans were supposed to, from the letter to the spirit, following Jesus' lead, and this following will be both exegetical and existential. As McGuckin argues, by explaining the purpose of Jesus' ministry as enacting the love of mankind in condescending to us in order to draw us back to God, Gregory supplies from the shape of the incarnation the framework within which to discern the spirit in the letter of Christ's commandments. This inference is borne out in three ways in Gregory's interpretation of Christ's teaching on divorce, which forms the substance of the pericope and the main subject of the Oration.

Gregory comments first on Jesus' proscription of divorce except for unchastity, and the way he introduces his comments further confirms McGuckin's reading: "The question . . . honours chastity, it seems to me, and demands a philanthropic response."[33] In other words, Jesus' teaching must be read in the spirit in which his whole ministry was conducted, in terms of the rationale of the incarnation: love for human beings. At the same time, by focusing on chastity, Gregory takes a step beyond simply reiterating Jesus' prohibition in order to interpret the content of the command in light of its function, the promotion of chastity, which Gregory elsewhere treats as a virtue exercised both in marriage and virginity, whereby reason rules the passions.[34] In effect, he will show us how we are to rise from the letter to the spirit of Jesus' teaching.

Roman law evinced a double standard, allowing greater sexual freedom for men while requiring faithfulness on the part of women.[35] Gregory censures it. Concerning chastity the law is "unequal and uneven."[36] Women are punished for adultery, but men are not, and the latter's interests only are respected in the guardianship of children. Jesus' words, however, give no explicit support for such a critique; if anything, they appear just as capable of being used to support the patriarchy Gregory condemns. To show the equality of men and women in marriage, Gregory first gathers together a number of Old Testament texts on the theme of marriage: "Honour your father and your mother"; "let he who curses a mother or father die a death"; "the benediction of a father establishes a house; the denunciation of a mother uproots foundations."[37] He

---

33. Or. 37.6, *SC* 318, p. 282.

34. Or. 8.8, *SC* 405, pp. 258, 260.

35. E. A. Clark, *Reading Renunciation: Asceticism and Scripture in Early Christianity* (Princeton: Princeton University Press, 1999), 237.

36. Or. 37.6, *SC* 318, p. 282.

sums up their collective force by referring specifically to the accounts of human creation in Genesis, and the salvation brought by Christ: "You see the equality of the legislation: one maker of man and woman, one dust for both, one image, one law, one death, one resurrection. We are born from man and woman alike; one debt is owed by children towards those who beget them."[38] Men and women, he concludes, have bodies "of equal dignity"; how then can men legislate unequally?[39] Women and men, he continues, have an equal share in the fall and redemption alike. Then he quotes Christ: "'The two shall be,' he says, 'one flesh'; let the one flesh have equal honour!"[40]

The underlying hermeneutics here are complex, and in order to follow it I shall make use of Richard B. Hays's understanding of intertextuality as "the embedding of fragments of an earlier text within a later one," which functions to suggest that the later text should be understood in light of a "broad interplay" with the earlier, "encompassing aspects of that earlier text beyond those explicitly echoed."[41] Here, in order to expose the spirit of the text, Gregory follows the intertextual clue Jesus himself gives by quoting Gen. 2:24 along with a string of Old Testament texts that all seem to support the equality of the sexes in marriage implied by the Genesis text, and connects this equality in creation with the equality with which God treats men and women in redemption. In so doing, he implicitly frames this use of intertexts within the larger story of the purpose of Christ's incarnation being to rescue his creature, paralleling and exceeding his creative action (the message also of Oration 38.11–13).

The spirit of the text goes further, however, in its honoring of chastity. First, with many other patristic writers, Gregory infers a ban on second marriages.[42] Second, he elevates virginity over marriage as a superior way of life. It is indeed better not to marry, in view of all the troubles of childbearing and widowhood. Not everyone can accept this teaching, as Christ says, only those to whom it has been given, thus demonstrating the sublimity of chastity, Gregory argues.[43] For not to partake in procreation displays a transcendence of the power of the flesh. Gregory does not simply mean sexual renunciation,

37. Exod. 20:12; Eph. 6.2; Exod. 21:17; Wisd. 3:11 LXX.

38. Or. 37.6, *SC* 318, p. 284.

39. Or. 37.7, *SC* 318, p. 284.

40. Or. 37.7, *SC* 318, p. 286.

41. Richard Hays, *Echoes of Scripture in the Letters of Paul* (New Haven: Yale University Press, 1989), 14 and 20.

42. Or. 37.8, *SC* 318, p. 286; cf. Clark, *Reading Renunciation*, 236.

43. Or. 38.11, *SC* 318, p. 294.

however. Rather, the refusal to marry marks a renunciation of "everything that seems fine to the majority: birth, wealth, throne, power, nor that beauty manifested by the harmony of colours and proportion of limbs, the plaything of time and disease."[44] Sexual desire is actually just one manifestation of a whole economy of desire, which is wrongly ordered in us. Nor does Gregory have in mind a withdrawal from visible creaturely beauty, for elsewhere he teaches that just that beauty leads us to God, and he celebrates it in prose.[45]

We get to the heart of Christ's commendation of chastity, however, when we understand its pedagogical function, which goes deeper than renunciation. As streams of water encased in lead pipes are borne upward by the water pressure to a single goal, so you also "should you bind your desire and attach yourself wholly to God, shall rise up, and not fall down, nor be dissipated, remaining wholly Christ's, until you see Christ your bridegroom."[46] Indeed, if you have made God the sole object of your desire, "then to that extent you have been wounded by the chosen dart, and have perceived the beauty of the husband so that you may speak the words from the drama and Song of marriage: "'You are most sweet and wholly desirable.'"[47] By following the movement of the meaning of Christ's teaching not only with the understanding but with the whole orientation and discipline of one's life, Gregory thus implies, one ascends from the letter to the spirit in the fullest sense, rising from the things of earth to the bridegroom of the soul, Christ himself. The notion of New Testament moral teaching as best appropriated for the function of the education of desire remains a potent one, even if we might not wish to place the weight of emphasis Gregory does on virginity. For it offers a model for the use of those parts of the New Testament intended to inform Christian discipleship that seems both appropriate to that intent and capable of informing life in the everyday into a form that aids the transformation of the self toward God and toward others.

This exegesis also illustrates well two more hermeneutical consequences of ordering one's exegesis around the shaping of history in Jesus Christ. First, it promotes the possibility of a faithfully critical approach to the understanding of biblical teachings, even those of Jesus himself. Gregory's hermeneutic of Christ's kenotic love for humanity provides a critical principle for understanding the pedagogical force of Scripture and resisting regressive readings to which it might otherwise be vulnerable, and a framework within which to exploit intertextual possibilities for readings that accord with that principle. Second,

---

44. Or. 37.11, *SC* 318, p. 294.

45. So Or. 28.16 and Or. 28.22–27, *SC* 250, pp. 132, 134 and 144, and 162 respectively.

46. Or. 37.12, *SC* 318, p. 296.

47. Or. 37.11, *SC* 318, pp. 294, 296.

it anchors the possibility of radical transformations of values and practices that can make an unequivocally normative claim and yet be said to conform to the character of history, theologically understood.

Here, however, we should consider another objection from Kristoffel Demoen, who claims that Gregory's interpretation of Jesus' *logion* about those who make themselves eunuchs for the kingdom of heaven, which, Demoen claims, illustrates "a hierarchy from material to spiritual meaning" that Gregory sees throughout Scripture.[48] Gregory asserts that this saying, "by departing from bodily things, configures higher things through bodily things."[49] Eunuchs are those "whom the Word cleanses by the amputation of their passions."[50] His reason for reading the text thus is that "to limit this saying about eunuchs to bodily things is perhaps petty and very weak and unworthy of it; we must conceive something worthy of the Spirit."[51] But this reasoning needs to be understood within the context just explored above. As with the saying about divorce, so with the saying about eunuchs that follows: Jesus' teaching must be understood according to its spirit, and that means within the framework provided by his incarnation and ministry. So understood, Gregory cannot be taken to advocate an ahistorical approach to the text. On the contrary, he seeks to read this *logion* in accord with the movement that Christ enacts in history. By doing so he finds, in an otherwise highly difficult, apparently impenetrable saying a demanding image that lays down the direction of a path for the transformation of character.[52] The saying about eunuchs effectively continues Jesus' teaching on chastity; it is not removed from bodily things, but it aims deeper than mere renunciation to a transformation of character and desire.

LETTER AND SPIRIT IN CHRISTOLOGICAL EXEGESIS

Another of the competencies Gregory requires of Christian pastors and teachers in Oration 2 is to have traveled "by action and contemplation through the titles and powers of Christ, both the prior and more exalted as well as the humbler latter ones for which we are the reason."[53] Who, he asks, would present themselves for priesthood who "hears these names and realities in vain and does

48. Demoen, *Pagan and Biblical Exempla*, 261.

49. Or. 37.20, *SC* 318, pp. 310, 312.

50. Or. 37.20, *SC* 318, pp. 310, 312.

51. Ibid.

52. Cf. the biblical trope of the circumcision of the heart: Deut. 10:16; 30:6; Jer. 4:4; Col. 2:11; cf. Rom. 2:28-29.

53. Or. 2.98, *SC* 247, p. 216.

not have communion with the Word or participate in him in respect of whom each of these [names] is and is called?"[54] This lived participation in the reality named diversely by Christ's titles is part, Gregory implies, of "learning to speak 'the wisdom of God hidden in a mystery'" and, we may also infer, part of a proper understanding and internalization of the spiritual sense.[55]

Gregory defended this practice, and articulates the hermeneutic it involved against his Eunomian opponents in Orations 28, 29, and 30; here again he uses similar terminology to that of letter and spirit to articulate his hermeneutics. In the proemium to Oration 30, Gregory sums up his efforts in Oration 29. He has, he announced, sufficiently shaken his opponents' reasoning and has destroyed "the obstacles and difficulties from the divine Scriptures, with which those who usurp the multitude and cause disorder on the road of truth by desecrating the letter and despoiling the mind of the texts."[56] Here Gregory thinks of the text in terms of its letter and its mind or sense (νοῦς). We can see how these concepts function in respect of biblical descriptions of Jesus Christ by examining his treatment of objections to a high Christology in Orations 29 and 30.

Gregory articulates his hermeneutical response toward the end of Oration 29. The key to explaining these texts in the most pious way, Gregory asserts, is to attribute the more exalted names to the divinity "and the humbler ones to the composite One who was emptied and became flesh for my sake . . . and was made human and was exalted" that we might learn to exist in a more exalted way and ascend with the divinity, ascending from visible to intellectual things.[57] For, Gregory adds, "the one who is now despised for your sake was once above you and he who is now man, was incomposite: what he was, he remained; what he was not, he assumed."[58] Hence we find that for every lowly creaturely event, experience, or attribute ascribed to Christ, there is also a corresponding and contrasting index of his divinity. How, Gregory asks, "can you trip over what is seen, and not espy what is understood?"[59] How, that is, can you stumble over the letter and miss the mind of Scripture, when you have this hermeneutical key? As with the exegesis of Christ's teaching, so with biblical descriptions of him: the hermeneutical key is provided by the story of his saving and compassionate kenosis in his incarnation.[60] In light of that story, we must understand the coincidence of humble and exalted descriptions of Christ in

54. Or. 2.98, *SC* 247, p. 216.
55. Or. 2.99, *SC* 247, p. 216.
56. Or. 30.1, *SC* 250, p. 226.
57. Or. 29.18, *SC* 250, p. 216.
58. Or. 29.19, *SC* 250, p. 216.
59. Or. 29.19, *SC* 250, p. 218.

Scripture in terms of his identity as the incarnate Son, for because of his saving involvement in our human existence and the path it took, the divine Son is *in addition* the humiliated, suffering, hungry one who prays to the Father who sent him.[61] To use this hermeneutical key is to be able to move from what appears in Scripture to its meaning.

To drive this argument home, Gregory shows the strength of his hermeneutical point by alluding to a great list of scriptural descriptions of Christ, each period beginning with one of Christ's human weaknesses and juxtaposing it with two or three examples, linked variously by metaphorical or literal contrast, of his divine power. For example, "He hungered, but fed thousands, and is the living and heavenly bread."[62] Here Gregory alludes to Jesus' extreme hunger after fasting in the desert after his baptism (Matt. 4:2/ Luke 4:2), and juxtaposes first the feeding miracles, then Jesus' metaphorical description of himself in John's Gospel as the living bread from heaven (John 6:41) so that, following the Johannine Jesus, the theme of miraculous food from God is appropriated to speak of a greater nourishment and the heavenly origin and saving power inherent in Christ. Carefully crafting each phrase to emphasize the contrast and its transposition to a higher place, Gregory effects, through allusion, an interpretation of the scriptural depiction of Christ around the theme of hunger and food.

The underlying conception of the meaning uncovered by Gregory's hermeneutic here is conveyed by another period in the passage: "He gives over his life, but he has authority to take it again, and the veil is taught—for things above are made manifest—the rocks are torn asunder and the dead rise early."[63] In each case, the intention is to bring out the *overall* force or intention of the total scriptural witness (the Gospels especially), over against a forced deductive exploitation of isolated passages, what he calls "profaning the letter and stealing the mind of the scriptures."[64] That mind, for Gregory, is the manifestation of saving, powerful divine reality in Jesus Christ's frail humanity. As Frances Young has shown, Athanasius has a similar concern for the mind of Scripture in his anti-Arian writings, and similar concerns can be traced back

60. Christopher Beeley has drawn attention to Gregory's Christological stress on unity, as well as to the narrative form of this scheme in his *Gregory of Nazianzus on the Trinity and the Knowledge of God: In Your Light We See Light* (New York: Oxford University Press, 2008), 123, 128.

61. As Beeley again rightly notes, for Gregory the more exalted and the humbler statements about Christ in Scripture "refer to the same Son of God, though in different ways." *Gregory of Nazianzus*, 132.

62. Or. 29.20, *SC* 250, p. 220.

63. Or. 29.20, *SC* 250, p. 222.

64. Or. 30.1, *SC* 250, p. 226.

to Irenaeus.[65] As she argues for Athanasius, so also Gregory's exposition of that mind does not fit the main categories invoked in the study of patristic exegesis (literal, typological, and allegorical). Here the deeper sense is, in a sense, deeply historical: for Gregory, Scripture shows that in Jesus Christ heavenly reality has been disclosed in a human life.

This hermeneutic Gregory applies in more detail to some of the more difficult texts contested in the fourth-century doctrinal controversies over Christ. One of the stronger examples is his interpretation of Jesus' cry of dereliction. That cry, Gregory argues, does not express his abandonment by the Father or by his divinity as though retracting from the suffering Christ from fear of death; rather "he images our condition."[66] For, Gregory explains, "we were first abandoned and overlooked, then assumed and saved by the sufferings of the impassible."[67] Assuming that Psalm 21 (LXX) refers to Christ, we can read the cry against the narrative of the saving action of the Logos in becoming human.[68] For Gregory, that becoming human for us extends to Jesus' dereliction on the cross as mimetically signifying that assumption of our condition. Indeed, one could argue that for Gregory, Christ's mimesis of our condition grounds the possibility of our transformation in imitation of him.

Less felicitous are those cases where Gregory appears to distinguish what pertains to Christ's divine and human natures respectively, against the grain of his Christology.[69] Gregory's exegesis here also displays the use of the reading procedures learned in the elementary training of the late-antique orator, and a close attention to the conventions of linguistic usage, as Paul Gallay and Frederick Norris have pointed out.[70] There Gregory remarks, for example, on occasions where Scripture uses tenses differently to their normal sense. He points out, for example, instances of prosopopeia in Scripture; the grammar of the word "until"; the different senses of "to reign"; the polysemy of the verb "to be able to," detailing carefully its different senses according to its

65. Frances Young, *Biblical Exegesis and the Formation of Christian Culture* (Cambridge: Cambridge University Press, 1997), chapter 2.

66. Or. 30.5, *SC* 250, p. 234.

67. Or. 30.5, *SC* 250, p. 234.

68. Gallay, "La Bible dans l'oeuvre de Grégoire de Nazianze le Théologien," in *Le monde grec ancien et la Bible*, vol. 1, ed. C. Mondésert (Paris: Beauchesne, 1984), 323–25; Norris, "Theology as Grammar: Nazianzen and Wittgenstein," in *Arianism after Arius*, ed. M. R. Barnes and D. H. Williams (Edinburgh: T. & T. Clark, 1993), 237–50. See Young, *Biblical Exegesis*, chapter 6, on the wider picture of reference in patristic exegesis.

69. As when Gregory distinguishes talk of Jesus' God and Jesus' Father in this way, Or. 30.8, *SC* 250, pp. 240, 242.

70. On that grammatical training, see Young, *Biblical Exegesis*, 77.

different uses; and *apo koinou* constructions, where one qualifier applies to two parts of a phrase in common.[71] Frederick Norris therefore rightly argues that Gregory thus seems to consider the inspired meaning of words in Scripture to be a function of their use in particular contexts, that is, it is conventional.[72] Exegesis must therefore observe these conventions when interpreting the mind of Scripture, within the wider framework provided by the incarnational narrative.

Gregory closes Oration 30 with an exposition of the meaning and mystical significance of the divine and human names of Christ. The former are explained in terms of the Son's relation to the Father and his divine powers in creation and redemption, the latter in terms of the saving purpose and efficacy of his incarnate existence.[73] The listener is then exhorted, in language recalling Oration 2.98, to "walk through them divinely, as many as are exalted, and with the same attitude, as many as are bodily, or rather in an entirely divine manner, in order to become God by ascending from here below, through him who descended from above for us."[74] In action and contemplation, then, one is either to attend to the Christ's divine identity or imitate the divine virtues manifest in his incarnate life so as to be assimilated to God through participation in Christ.[75] The hermeneutic Gregory applies to his opponents' objections is implicit in this practice, and his purpose in clearing obstacles and clarifying the sense of the texts can now be seen to serve this kind of transformative appropriation of the mind of Scripture.

THE LETTER AND THE HOLY SPIRIT

One more example of Gregory's use of the letter/spirit distinction adds an important dimension to his hermeneutics. In Oration 31, Gregory confronts the

---

71. Or. 29.5, *SC* 250, p. 185; Or. 30.1, *SC* 250, p. 228; Or. 30.4, *SC* 250, pp. 230 and 232; Or. 30.4, *SC* 250, p. 232; Or. 30.10–11, *SC* 250, pp. 242–46, respectively. With regard to the tenses, Gallay points out that Gregory did not identify the real philological reason, which has to do with the way the Septuagint inaccurately rendered the Hebrew conjugation, which marked only whether an action is completed or incomplete and not directly whether it happened in the past or the future ("La Bible dans l'oeuvre," p. 324, n. 45). An example of *apo koinou* Gregory gives is "for God does not give the Spirit out of measure" (John 3:34), where "without measure" applies both to the giving of the Spirit and the one who is given.

72. Norris, "Theology as Grammar."

73. Or. 30.20–21, *SC* 250, pp. 266, 268, 270, 272, and 274.

74. Or. 30.21, *SC* 250, p. 274.

75. See also Beeley, *Gregory of Nazianzus*, 149–51.

charge that teaching that the Spirit is God is unscriptural. Gregory introduces it by saying he will not repeat the labors of those who have already shown the Holy Spirit in both Testaments; those who "have read the divine Scriptures, not with ease or as a hobby, but have gone into the letter and stooped to peer within."[76] They, he says, "were worthy to see the hidden beauty and be illumined by the light of knowledge."[77] This description of those who have demonstrated the divinity of the Spirit from Scripture matches closely Gregory's description of the difficult passages of Scripture and the character of those who may understand them in Oration 2, and seems to convey the same sense of Scripture as composed of exterior and interior, letter and spirit, where the latter denotes something that must be divinely disclosed to the reader. What, then, can we learn from the argument in which Gregory uses these terms here?

Christopher Beeley draws our attention to the significance of the wider argument in Oration 31 to which this discussion belongs. He notes that Gregory begins in Oration 31 by establishing the basis for the divinity of the Spirit in baptismal deification *before* returning to the question of the biblical witness to the Spirit's divinity that he had raised at the outset.[78] It is only in *this* light that Gregory expects his readers to see how the scriptural texts he cites show that the divinity of the Spirit is a scriptural doctrine. "From the perspective of Church's faith-experience of the Holy Spirit, the Bible does indeed declare the Spirit's divinity—according to the Spirit, that is, not the letter."[79] Exegesis of Scripture according to the Spirit, then, "means interpreting it on the basis of the presence and work of the Spirit in the life of the Church and one's own life of purification and illumination."[80] Beeley's argument clearly implies that the experience makes a material contribution to exegesis of these texts on this question (at least). For, he argues, apart from the experience of the Spirit's deifying work in baptism, we could not be sure that biblical attestations of the Spirit doing the work of God do not merely describe the Spirit as an nondivine or semi-divine intermediary through whom God acts rather than as a divine agent. Thus for Gregory, "it is the Christian's actual knowledge of God through the presence of the Holy Spirit within the life of the Church that enables him or her to identify the Spirit as God in the biblical text, and to practice theology at all."[81] Hence the appeal to scriptural texts is only an element in his

76. Or. 31.21, *SC* 250, p. 316.
77. Or. 31.21, *SC* 250, p. 316.
78. Beeley, *Gregory of Nazianzus*, 181.
79. Beeley, *Gregory of Nazianzus*, 181.
80. Beeley, *Gregory of Nazianzus*, 181.
81. Beeley, *Gregory of Nazianzus*, 182–83.

argument. Thus Gregory charges his opponents with being full and far from the Spirit in Oration 31.30. Their resistance to the Spirit prevents them from recognizing his divinity. This feature of Gregory's argument reveals, Beeley concludes, a "hermeneutic of piety" governing Gregory's whole approach to biblical interpretation.[82]

Beeley is surely right to see hermeneutical significance in Gregory's ordering of the argument in Oration 31, and right too to think that placing of the argument from baptismal deification prior to the discussion of biblical exegesis implies some hermeneutical significance to the corporate and individual experience of the Spirit. However, he draws too strong an inference from these observations, one that would seem, by attributing an otherwise fatal ambiguity to the scriptural witness, to weaken the force of Gregory's own appeal to Scripture and to run counter to his theology of Scripture as the texts wherein Christ teaches the truth of Christian doctrine. A reexamination of Gregory's hermeneutical argument will help clarify the issue.

Gregory begins by summarizing the objection. His opponents' blasphemy against the Spirit is provoked, he says, by the claim that the attestation that the name "God" is not clearly or frequently ascribed to the Spirit, as it is to the Father and to the Son.[83] In order to address this problem, Gregory undertakes to discuss an explication of the relation between names and things. Here he distinguishes things that do not exist as such, but are spoken of in Scripture; things that exist but are not spoken of in Scripture; and things that both are and are discussed in Scripture. Into the first category fall anthropomorphic descriptions of God, which figure forth divine action to us in terms we can understand. The second category is the key one.

To demonstrate that there are things that exist but Scripture does not name, Gregory takes an example from his Eunomian opponents, and one from his own party.[84] The Eunomians' key terms are 'ἀγέννητος' (ingenerate) and 'ἄναχος' (unoriginate), properties they ascribe uniquely to the Father. Gregory's party use the term "immortal" for God.[85] As Gregory says, these terms cannot be found in Scripture.[86] What, then, will become of his opponents'

---

82. Beeley, *Gregory of Nazianzus*, 184.

83. Or. 31.21, *SC* 250, p. 316.

84. Eunomius and his followers claimed that Father and Son were unalike, because the Father's nature is ingenerate and the Son's generated. The five so-called "Theological Orations," of which Or. 31 is the last, are directed principally against this position.

85. Or. 31.23, *SC* 250, 318.

86. As Gallay points out, "immortal" in 1 Tim. 1:17 (which Gregory did hold to be canonical) is not the most authentic reading; "incorruptible" is (*SC* 250, 318–19, n. 1).

position? Then he comes to his interlocutor's aid: "Is it not clear that these are [inferred] from those which imply them, even if they are not said?"[87] Gregory has in mind, as examples, God's claims in Isaiah that "I am the first and the last," and that "before me there is no other God, nor will there be after me" (Isa. 41:4; 43:10). For, Gregory explains, "when you admit that there is nothing before him, and that he has no anterior cause, you call him 'unoriginate' and 'unbegotten.'"[88]

Gregory then very briefly discusses things that both exist and are named—God, angels, human beings, judgment—before bringing home the force of his argument. Why, he asks, if there is such a difference between names and things, are his opponents so enslaved to the letter, that is, to insisting on the explicit naming of the Spirit as God?

> For if, in response to your saying "two times five" I concluded "ten," or from your "twice seven" I inferred, "fourteen" or if from your "rational animal, mortal," I concluded "human being," would you think I was raving? How so when I am saying what you are saying? For the words are not the speaker's more than they belong to the one who required them to be spoken. Just as, therefore, here I attend not so much to what you say as to the thoughts, so also if I find something else from the mind of Scripture which is not said or not said clearly, I will not refrain from expressing it.[89]

Gregory's point here, that the exegete should focus on the mind of Scripture expressed through the words rather than the words in themselves, had been made long ago by Origen.[90] His point here is that terms or concepts implied by the scriptural text are properly scriptural, even if not explicitly articulated. That Gregory should make the point by in effect returning to his second category, of things implied but not expressly articulated, seems indicative. It strongly suggests that Gregory sees the Spirit's divinity as clearly implied by Scripture, even if not explicitly expressed.

Gregory then goes on to explain the cause for obscurity in Scripture in a well-known passage that we have already touched on in Chapter 2. Gregory begins by distinguishing three "earthquakes" or decisive transformations of life in human history: that from idolatry to the Law, that from the Law to the

87. Or. 31.23, *SC* 250, p. 318.
88. Or. 31.23, *SC* 250, pp. 318, 320.
89. Or. 31.24, *SC* 250, pp. 320, 322.
90. See Origen, Peri Archon 4.3.15.

Gospel, and that still awaited, from the things as they are now to a condition where they cannot be shaken (an allusion to Heb. 9:3-8).[91] In this way God seeks to persuade, not to coerce, and so brings in changes along with concessions to make them more acceptable. The same process happens but in the opposite way, when it comes to the knowledge of God, he adds, where instead of progress through suppressions, perfection comes through additions.[92] As Gregory explains: "The Old Testament proclaimed the Father clearly and the Son obscurely. The New revealed the Son, and indicated the divinity of the Spirit. Now the Spirit dwells amongst us and provides us with a clearer disclosure of himself."[93] One disclosure prepared the way for the next, or we would have been overwhelmed by the weight of revelation. Instead, by partial additions "and advances and progressions 'from glory to glory,' the light of the Trinity will shine forth in greater splendours."[94] The divinity of the Spirit, Gregory ventures, may have been one of those teachings that Christ did not impart to his disciples before the cross, which was clarified later, "at the time that was ripe for encountering and receiving that knowledge, after the resurrection of the Saviour, when it would no longer be unbelievable, because of that wonder."[95] In other words, we may infer, the reason why the divinity of the Spirit is not explicit is pedagogical: we were not ready to grasp this truth until after the resurrection, until the Spirit had come down upon the church. The difference the coming of the Spirit makes is to enable us to recognize what had already been indicated in Scripture. As Gregory goes on to say, "From the Spirit comes our regeneration, from regeneration our re-creation, and from our re-creation the knowledge of the dignity of the one who re-creates us."[96] It is not that the witness of Scripture is otherwise ambiguous; rather, it is not explicit. It takes the experience of regeneration at the hands of the Spirit to turn our attention to Scripture's clear implication.

For Gregory, this argument takes care of the objection about the Spirit not being named as God in Scripture. He then summarizes the scriptural texts that show the divinity of the Spirit "for those who are not very much in the dark or strangers to the Spirit."[97] The Spirit precedes Christ's entrance into the world, bears witness at his baptism, leads him into the wilderness to be tempted,

91. Or. 31.25.
92. Or. 31.26.
93. Or. 31.26, *SC* 250, p. 326.
94. Or. 31.26, *SC* 250, p. 326.
95. Or. 31.27, *SC* 250, p. 330.
96. Or. 31.28, *SC* 250, p. 332.
97. Or. 31.29, *SC* 250, p. 332.

accompanies him as he works wonders, and takes his place when he goes: in other words, he seems to play a role of equal importance to the incarnate Son. "For what of the great things, and those which God does, can he not do?"[98] Gregory continues. "What of the titles of God [does he not receive], except for unbegotten and begotten?"[99] Gregory then reels off the titles of the Spirit and the actions ascribed to him in Scripture: for example, "The Spirit is the maker, he recreates through baptism and through resurrection. The Spirit knows all things, teaches, blows where and as much as he wills, guides, speaks, sends, sets apart, is provoked, tested, reveals, illumines, gives life, or rather is himself Light and Life, makes us his temples, deifies, perfects, so that he precedes baptism and is sought after baptism."[100] These and those that follow are divine actions and attributes: "He does all that God does."[101] The humble terms applied to the Spirit have to be understood in terms of the Spirit's procession from the Father, whereby the two are distinguished from one another.[102]

What, though, of the problem Beeley identifies, of how to exclude the Spirit from being an intermediary through whom God acts but who need not be divine himself? It is not a problem that Gregory himself recognizes in the Oration, nor one that his argument from baptismal deification appears to resolve, for God may surely be thought to act through the Spirit as an intermediary there also. It seems to be enough for Gregory that a divine activity be properly ascribed to an agent to show that the agent is divine in nature: that is the logic of both his argument from baptism and his argument from Scripture. What the experience of the Spirit in baptism brings, then, is not something lacking in Scripture, but an experience that allows us to attend to what Scripture already implies.

Gregory's account of the scriptural witness to the Spirit and the hermeneutical issues it raises, then, is not quite as radical as Beeley claims. Nevertheless it is highly significant for my purposes. For it shows that Gregory thought of the movement from letter to spirit in respect of this question also to be historically contextualized within the sweep and shape of God's historical pedagogy, with the experience of the Spirit as the hermeneutical key to aid

---

98. Ibid.

99. Ibid.

100. Or. 31.29, SC 250, p. 334, alluding to Ps. 103:30 (LXX); John 3:5; Ezek. 37:5-6, 9-10, 14; 1 Cor. 2:10; John 14:26; John 3:8; Ps. 142:10 (LXX); Acts 13:2, Acts 13:4, Acts 13:2 again; Job 4:9; Acts 5:9; John 16:13, John 14:26 (again), John 6:63; 1 Cor. 3:16 (twice); John 16:13 (again); all given in SC 250, p. 335.

101. Or. 31.29, SC 250, p. 334.

102. Or. 31.30, SC 250, pp. 336, 338.

the interpreter to enter into its interior or mind. Indeed, for Gregory this exegetical movement, like the others we have discussed in this chapter, seems to both conform to and partake of God's saving pedagogy and its historical configuration. Indeed, for Gregory there can be no participation in God's salvation without this encounter with the Spirit, and without the Spirit, no understanding of Scripture whatsoever.

CONCLUSION

Gregory's exegetical procedures, as he describes and exemplifies them, all fall under the common rubric of the movement from letter to spirit, but this movement takes a variety of forms, which cannot be reduced to concepts like typology, allegory, or literalism. What does appear to be true of all these forms is that the procedures all aim at elucidating divine pedagogy in such a way as to further the transformation of this particular reader in terms of the overall shape and purpose of the divine economy that configures history and historical possibilities. What is also true is that this shape and purpose also guide and inform each exegetical procedure. Each procedure in its own way draws on specific characteristics of the letter—its narrative genre or grammatical features, or symbolic potential, or logical form—so that the movement to the spirit is rooted in the possibilities latent in the letter, when seen in light of the whole shape of the divine economy. It is a movement that does not leave the letter behind since it provides the logic to extend into our present or the wherewithal for the imagination to behold Christ or to reconfigure our experience so that we may act aright. Finally, Gregory interprets Scripture by Scripture within that framework, combining intertexts to garner their cumulative force or using them to illumine the spirit of a particular passage in light of Christ, for example. This family group of procedures, then, share some strong resemblances. Those features allow the scriptural text to inform human life in specific circumstances and to draw it toward its divine goal. They also allow the exegete to deal with theologically or morally difficult texts and make them fruitful in sophisticated, complex ways that usually combine symbolic exegesis with placing the text within the wider network of passages in the canon that share a common theme or symbolic resonance.

Our far greater understanding of the letter of scriptural texts (informed by our grasp of their origins and development) makes a simple adoption of Gregory's procedures implausible. Nevertheless, they suggest some features that might characterize exegesis that is attentive to history, theologically understood. Where the text is in some fashion the vehicle for the further participation of human beings in the shape and movement of history centered in Christ, the particular semiotic and literary contents of the "letter," with all their historical traces, may be taken up to further ends and purposes that accord with the character of history, theologically understood, and may bear different relations to one another than merely those entailed by processes of tradition, reception, and redaction. They may become the bases for movements of understanding through which human beings are transformed in conformity with Christ, and their morally and theologically problematic characteristics may be addressed and negotiated so that they may be fruitful and no longer noxious.

The movement from letter to spirit, however, did not end with the exegete, but was to move out through their teaching into the particulars of their hearers' lives. In Gregory's own practice, the vehicles for that distribution were the rhetorical forms and figures of his orations and the interweaving of biblical pedagogies to create a comprehensive, life-shaping texture whose impress would mold the mind and character of listeners, and form a powerful Christian culture.

6

The Rhetorical Deployment of Scripture in Gregory

Gregory never wrote a separate work on biblical interpretation, as Origen and Augustine did. Instead he left us his finely wrought oratory suffused with Scripture, surely intending his use of Scripture there to serve as instruction for future generations. For Gregory, the mediation of scriptural pedagogy was primarily an oratorical affair, a matter of persuasion and formation of the hearer through discourse. His orations illustrate the rhetorical character of his deployment of Scripture: the way the use of the text is shaped by and to the end of moving hearers to partake in the historical possibilities opened by Christ through the Spirit. They conform to his hermeneutics but show them put to work in bringing scriptural pedagogy to bear in the service of the transformation of human beings in their particular historical circumstances. In these ways, examining Gregory's understanding of the rhetorical character of Christian teaching, and his use of Scripture in his rhetoric, helps complete the picture of his approach to the Bible as a premodern model to assist us in addressing the challenges posed by historical consciousness to the theology and theological interpretation of Scripture.

Textuality and Christian Rhetoric in Late Antiquity

To appreciate why Gregory's oratory is the primary vehicle for his biblical exposition, we need to understand a little more about literacy and orality in his context. While some of Gregory's hermeneutical comments do envisage individual readers wrestling with scriptural texts, he usually has teachers in mind, whose scholarship will edify others.[1] And while he envisages private reading on the part of some of the laity—presumably those with sufficient education and wealth to have both ready access to written scriptural texts and the ability to read them fluently—the evidence of his orations suggests he did not think them to be without need of regular teaching in the church.[2] Literacy rates in the ancient world, however, suggest that the large majority of Gregory's congregations would have had no or low levels of literacy, even if we allow for the ability of artisans and other tradespeople to handle correspondence and accounts relating to their business.[3]

Gregory's congregations were, for the most part, likely to have been acquainted with Scripture primarily through the process of catechesis, through the lengthy public reading of Scripture in the liturgy, and through its homiletical exposition.[4] This way of receiving texts, however, is consistent with the oral dissemination of texts in Greco-Roman society to the less literate and illiterate. As Gamble notes,

> Recitations of poetry and prose works, dramatic performances in theatres and at festivals, declamations in high rhetorical style, street-corner philosophical diatribes, commemorative inscriptions, the

---

1. Hence the commendation of Athanasius in Or. 21.6–7, SC 270, pp. 120–24, and the mention in Oration 31 of those who have "read the Divine Writings neither lazily nor as a mere pastime, but have examined the letter and have stooped [and looked] inside," Or. 31.21, SC 250, p. 316. This mention also suggests there were those in Gregory's time who read but without due care and attention. His remarks examined above on the need for formation before undertaking pastoral responsibilities point in a similar direction.

2. Nor could the preacher necessarily count on such people taking the trouble to read the apparently uncultivated writings that comprised Christian sacred literature. It is perhaps for this reason that Gregory wrote paraphrases of key episodes and texts from Scripture in elegant poetry, which may well have been intended for elite correspondents in Constantinople. Gregory also commends Scripture to the readers of his poems in Carmen 2.1.39: the inspired words of God offer "a calm harbour for those who flee the storm" (PG 37 1330).

3. Given what we know of the social composition of early Christian communities and on the basis of work on literacy rates in the ancient world, Harry Gamble estimates that no more than c. 10 percent of any given early Christian community were able to read, criticize, or interpret their Scriptures. See Books and Readers in the Early Church (New Haven and London: Yale University Press, 1995), 5. It is possible, as Jaclyn Maxwell argues of John Chrysostom's congregation in Antioch, that some ability to read texts can be attributed to a variety of nonelite readers on the basis of the availability of lower-prestige schooling, and of the survival of texts in the form of graffiti in Pompeii, or letters from Vindolanda on Hadrian's Wall, or epigraphy in public spaces. See Maxwell, Christianization and Communication in Late Antiquity: John Chrysostom and His Congregation in Antioch (Cambridge: Cambridge University Press, 2006), 100–103. Christian texts were also relatively affordable in the codex format in which most early Christian manuscripts survive (see Gamble, Books and Readers, 49ff.). However, such skills might still fall short of the kind of engagement Gregory speaks to in his more hermeneutical passages, and those who possessed them might lack the leisure for extended reading of biblical passages.

4. Cf. Gamble, Books and Readers, 8.

posting and reading of official decrees, the routine traffic of legal and commercial documents all brought the fruits of literacy before the general population, educating the public in its uses and popularizing its conventions.[5]

Even elite readers were as likely to consume a text by being read to as by reading it for themselves. Indeed, the very nature of textuality was more fluid and intimately connected to orality in this period than we might imagine.[6] Handwritten texts were less stable than modern printed texts, and "virtually all reading, public or private, was reading aloud: texts were routinely converted into the oral mode."[7] Reading out loud, "performing" the written script, was the normal way of reading and indeed an invaluable tool for working out the best interpretation of the seamless flow of characters without spacing or punctuation, which ancient texts presented. Texts, therefore, were as much oral documents as they were written ones, and this rule applied to Christian Scriptures, even for elite readers. Hence when Gregory commends his own sister's deep acquaintance with Scripture, he talks about it in aural terms: she opened the "doors of her hearing" to the divine sayings, he tells the congregation at her funeral.[8]

To appreciate the character of textuality in late antiquity, we need to grasp the importance of memory, as Mary Carruthers has argued. Memory was one of the five divisions of rhetoric, and part of the work of memory was the internalization of literature as the basis for its institutionalization in the language and pedagogy of a group.[9] In ancient and medieval cultures, therefore, books had a subsidiary role, signifying a text whose primary locus was in the mind. As Carruthers writes, in such cultures, a work "is not truly read until one has made it part of oneself—that process constitutes a necessary stage of its textualisation."[10] Such internalization was the basis of oral culture, for the social function of texts. Texts here provide the sources of a group's memory: "Literary works become institutions as they weave a community together by providing it with shared experience and a certain kind of language, the language of stories

---

5. Gamble, *Books and Readers*, 8.

6. Gamble, *Books and Readers*, 30.

7. Gamble, *Books and Readers*, 30.

8. Or. 8.9, *SC* 405, p. 264. Here I take the antecedent ἀκουή θυρας to be the object of the verb ἐνεωξε in this sentence.

9. Carruthers, *The Book of Memory: A Study of Memory in Medieval Culture* (New York: Cambridge University Press, 2008), 11.

10. Carruthers, *The Book of Memory*, 11.

that can be experienced over and over again through time and as occasion suggests."[11] It is in this light that we should understand Gregory's advice, which prefaces his poem on the genuine books of Scripture, to "be always revolving in speech and in mind, / upon the words of God," which offer illumination, conviction of sin, or a means of withdrawing the mind from earthly cares.[12]

Christian preachers operated in a culture in which public rhetoric still flourished and performed a variety of functions and was accessible to and enjoyed by a wide audience. As Jaclyn Maxwell notes, Gregory's pagan contemporary, Themistius, not only held public office and advised emperors, but also attracted criticism for speaking to common people in the theater, which he defended as a way of educating them in philosophy.[13] Rhetorically trained philosophers and sophists "often served as teachers, administrators, and ambassadors to imperial authorities on behalf of their home towns."[14] As well as lecturing their disciples in private, some spoke in public, in theaters and in the streets. They continued to have an active role in late antiquity. Concern for the right mode of addressing popular audiences, criticisms of those who used archaic Attic forms to impress the crowds, critiques of crowd-pleasing popularists among sophists, all attested the important role intellectuals played in the public imagination.

Gregory's self-presentation in his orations and poems indicates that rhetoric was highly valued not only in Constantinople where many of the orations were delivered, but also in his provincial hometown of Nazianzus, and that there was an appetite for his Christian oratory. In his autobiographical poem, *De vita sua*, he is careful to tell us that his teachers and students in Athens, where he studied, wanted to vote him the prize in rhetoric, a remark that assumes that rhetoric is highly prized by the reader.[15] On his return from Athens, he gave a sample of his eloquence to satisfy the demands of the locals. Gregory's disparagement of the "noisy applause . . . showy expressions [and] verbal contortions in which sophists delight amidst crowds of young men" replicates a standard critique of popular speakers on the part of more

---

11. Carruthers, *The Book of Memory*, 14.

12. *Carmen* 1.1.12, 1–7, *PG* 37 471.

13. Maxwell, *Christianization and Communication*, 15. The following paragraph is indebted to her discussion of the Second Sophistic as a context for understanding late-antique Christian preaching.

14. Maxwell, *Christianization and Communication*, 16.

15. *DVS* 255–56, in C. White, *Gregory of Nazianzus: Autobiographical Poems* (Cambridge: Cambridge University Press, 1996), 28.

"philosophical" sophists.[16] Together with the demands made of Gregory on his return, they also indicate the popularity of rhetoric even in rustic Cappadocia.[17]

For Gregory these speeches were, he tells us, preparatory to greater mysteries, presumably the use of his eloquence in the service of Christ. For, even while in Athens, he and Basil had pledged their rhetorical skills to the Word.[18] That theme of Gregory's devotion of his words and rhetorical skill to *the* Word recurs in his Orations, as does that of Christian rhetoric as a form of spiritual nutrition.[19] The former trades on the cultural worth of rhetoric and the latter on an appetite for it on the part of Gregory's congregations. Gregory's praise of Basil as a speaker in Oration 43 tends in the same direction.[20]

It was Gregory's reputation as much for eloquence as for his piety and orthodoxy that led to his calling to assist the small Nicene congregation in Constantinople.[21] There he faced considerable hostility and attracted much criticism, including for his rhetorical success.[22] This success suggests the appetite for Christian rhetoric in Constantinople, which Gregory's criticisms of Maximus the Cynic, the colleague who then attempted to oust Gregory, also indicate; Gregory criticizes Maximus for aspiring to popularity by teaching clever ideas, and describes him as a "sophist." Gregory's own popularity was borne out by the reaction of his congregation when he suggested he might leave them following Maximus' betrayal of him. Their attachment to him was in part due to his preaching skills, his way of speaking as well as his powerful teaching.[23] Gregory contrasts here his gentle, accommodating, moderate persuasion and ascetic concern for truth, with pagan speakers concerned only for display, and with orators who get carried away by the moment or who hide their weakness behind defensive boldness and a "facile and harmful prolixity," speaking of difficult things in theaters, public places, and drinking sessions with unpurified tongues to uninitiated ears.[24] The contrast, although it partakes of a

16. *DVS* 267–69, in White's translation, *Gregory of Nazianzus*, 29.

17. Susan R. Holman claims that due to widespread illiteracy in Cappadocia, rhetorical *paideia* was of even greater social value and the verbal power of the rhetor all the more effective: Holman, *The Hungry Are Dying: Beggars and Bishops in Roman Cappadocia* (New York: Oxford University Press, 2001), 27.

18. *DVS* 481, in White, *Gregory of Nazianzus*, 44–45: a pledge Gregory felt that Basil reneged on in his use of Gregory in episcopal turf wars in Cappadocia.

19. On devoting his *logos* to the Logos, see e.g. Or. 6.4–5, Or. 7.1, and also Or. 38.6 discourse is the appropriate mode of celebrating the incarnation of the *Word*; on Gregory's oratory as spiritual nutrition, see e.g. Or. 6.6, Or. 14.1, and Or. 38.6.

20. See Or. 43.65–66.

21. *DVS* 593ff., in White, *Gregory of Nazianzus*, 54–55.

22. *DVS* 696–720, in White, *Gregory of Nazianzus*, 64–67.

23. *DVS* 1120, 1190–91, in White, *Gregory of Nazianzus*, 98–99.

conventional criticism of popular rhetoric and articulates an ethos of Christian speaking that Gregory enjoins elsewhere, also attests the appeal of Christian rhetoric in the imperial capital. Possession of the bishop's throne, his narrative makes clear, only magnified the interest in him and his words. There are some grounds, then, for seeing Gregory's orations against a context of the popularity of Christian rhetoric, itself of a piece with an appetite for rhetoric in late antiquity. Gregory, however, is concerned to commend a particular vision of Christian rhetoric, in which the teaching of Scripture is central. It will help us understand that notion better if we see it in light of Mary Carruthers's analysis of memory and textualization explored above.

A trained memory was vital to public speaking. In a widespread, ancient, and persistent metaphor in Western cultures, the memory was described as a book or wax tablet.[25] A carefully trained memory, using visual coding, allowed for the storage, ready retrieval, and analysis and synthesis of information and texts.[26] The metaphor of writing in wax indicated the nature of memorization as the inscription of verbal symbols to serve the cognitive purpose of recall, which, because of the partial nature of the symbol, was inherently interpretive.[27] The truth so signified could be variously but never entirely adequately expressed in language, which could be adjusted as occasion demanded.[28]

For Gregory, the Christian teacher too requires a trained memory. In order to be able to deploy the teachings of Scripture, those who teach must already have marked the preacher's own memory: he must have inscribed them threefold on the tablets of his heart—an internalization that was both practically necessary and morally formative.[29] The distribution of the *logos*, he explains in Oration 2, requires adequate comprehension, explication, and understanding—the three parts into which Aristotle analyzed the rhetorical act. [30]Christian pastors as teachers find themselves tossed between three dangers, he continues: in all likelihood either their intellect is not illumined, or their language is weak, or the listening of their audience is not purified, and so the truth will be lamed.[31] Language, for Gregory too, may at best be adequate to the

---

24. DVS 1190–1254, in White, *Gregory of Nazianzus*, 98–102. My paraphrase follows White's translation, 99–103, from which the quotation comes.

25. Carruthers, *The Book of Memory*, 18f.

26. Carruthers, *The Book of Memory*, 22f.

27. Carruthers, *The Book of Memory*, 24–29.

28. Carruthers, *The Book of Memory*, 29–30.

29. Or. 2.96, SC 247, p. 214. Carruthers notes that for the ancients and medievals, memory is basic to moral character: *The Book of Memory*, 11, 14–15.

30. Or. 2.39, SC 247, pp. 140, 142.

realities it signifies where hearing and understanding are intact.[32] For him also, it is a matter of adapting one's language to the needs of the congregation.[33] In addition, the theological content of preaching necessitates the aid of the Spirit "by whom alone God is conceived and explained and understood, for only by purity can we grasp the pure."[34]

Teaching the Christian *logos* which Scripture presents is also a matter of persuasion, as Gregory's account of Basil's preaching confirms. By Basil's homilies on the Six Days of Creation, Gregory was, he tells us, "persuaded not to rest with the letter nor look only to things above, but to advance further and proceed further still from depth to depth, deep calling out to deep and finding light in light until I attain the summit."[35] As we shall see, Gregory too sought to move his hearers to accept certain truths or to behave in certain ways.

However, the end of such persuasion is an enduring formation of the listener. Here again Gregory picks up the metaphor of inscription on wax. He likens the teacher's task to that of a scribe, writing doctrine on the soul; it is easier to write on a fresh soul than to try to efface one script and superimpose another.[36] The teacher seeks to form the memory of his listeners, the very basis for their interpretation of the world and their judgment as to how to act within it. We find the same figure used frequently when Gregory speaks about teaching doctrine.[37] We have already seen that for Gregory the preacher's deployment of Scripture was a medium for the deployment of Scripture's divine pedagogy. Preaching was thus a means by which the movement from letter to spirit by members of the congregation in respect of their own understanding and lives was nurtured, facilitated, and informed, within the encompassing illuminating work of the Spirit in both preacher and listeners. As Carol Harrison has argued, this process of impressing a scriptural seal on the hearts and minds of the hearer was a way of forming a Christian culture, the comprehensive imaginative and intellectual universe that Averil Cameron has argued is so

---

31. Ibid.

32. Or. 28.4, *SC* 250, p. 108.

33. Or. 2.45, *SC* 247, p. 148.

34. Or. 2.39, *SC* 247, p. 140.

35. Or. 43.67, *SC* 384, p. 272.

36. Or. 2.43, *SC* 247, p. 146.

37. See Or. 2.14.3–10, *PG* 424A, where the context is primarily one of moral formation; Or. 6.11, where it is the same faith that, impressed on opposing parties, allows them to be reconciled; and Or. 40.44–45, where Gregory offers to transcribe the faith written upon him, which he has learned and guarded from the beginning, on the baptismal candidates gathered before him. Here he goes so far as to liken himself to Moses, writing the new Law which is the creedal confession of the Trinity on the hearts of the candidates.

instrumental to Christianization in late antiquity.[38] More specifically, it was a way of forming an alternative *paideia*, or educational system based on Christian scriptural classics and aiming at the imitation of Christ, the Image of God.[39]

RHETORIC, HISTORY, AND THE DEPLOYMENT OF SCRIPTURE

The significance of this examination for my wider purposes lies in the occasional character of rhetoric. Gregory's use of Scripture in his orations illustrates another facet of how he thought of Scripture and its exposition in historical terms. Against the background of a theology of history, the teachings of Scripture whereby we are to participate in the living, saving center and flow of history are appropriated to particular audiences in their particular circumstances and crafted accordingly. In this way, as Carol Harrison says of early Christian preaching in general, "Scripture speaks; it . . . becomes a matter of speaking and listening, of communication, conversation—in a real sense it comes alive and enters the realm of time, change and the senses."[40] The auditory context made for immediacy with the scriptural text whereby it could be adapted to the specific needs and circumstances of the congregation, their backgrounds, abilities, hopes, and fears, so that there is an implicit dialogue going on between the preacher and his congregation.[41] The sermon responds with Scripture to the particular situation and dispositions of the listeners, who are in turn invited to respond in particular ways, and whose tacit or verbal response during the delivery of the sermon might in turn influence what was said by the preacher. Such deployment of Scripture perfectly suits Gregory's understanding of the particularizing modality and historical character of God's pedagogy in Christ and through Scripture and its exposition.

The preacher's resources here were drawn from the thought-world and textuality of internalized texts he shared with his audience together with shared expectations and presuppositions. In such a context, Harrison adds, we have to consider "the . . . common memory, or 'symbol-system' shared by those whose conversation we are overhearing: allusions, images, metaphors, passing

---

38. Harrison, "The Typology of Listening: The Transformation of Scripture in Early Christian Preaching," in *Delivering the Word: Preaching and Exegesis in the Western Christian Tradition*, ed. William John Lyons and Isabella Sandwell (Sheffield: Equinox, 2012), 62–79; Averil Cameron, *Christianity and the Rhetoric of Empire: The Development of Christian Discourse* (Berkeley, Los Angeles, and London: University of California Press, 1991).

39. On scriptural exegesis as offering an alternative *paideia*, see Frances M. Young, *Biblical Exegesis and the Formation of Christian Culture* (Cambridge: Cambridge University Press, 1997), 51ff.

40. Harrison, "The Typology of Listening," 66.

41. Harrison, "The Typology of Listening," 67.

references, a name, a person, a story or an event, might well carry a freight of meaning, connotations, and significance which can all too easily elude us."[42] Here, models, images, and patterns were key resources to be creatively and imaginatively employed. These homiletic uses of Scripture fit well Gregory's historical conception of divine pedagogy, and its deployment in scriptural exposition, and with his account of the divine names and of biblical exempla.

Frances Young helps us approach Gregory's way of deploying Scripture on these terms, to shape and inform memory, character, and culture. She reminds us that in ancient literary culture, texts gained status and influence by appealing to the cultural memory of classic texts acquired through education, and did so through mimesis and allusion. In the case of fourth-century Christian leaders, the same move is made by alluding to Christian Scriptures.[43] Young singles out Gregory as an example. His first oration evinces a "highly developed and subtle intertextuality" whereby key passages, without quoting Scripture in full or making explicit citations, depend for their effect on their relationship with scriptural texts.[44] Such allusion, together with the imitation of the classics was, according to ancient rhetorical manuals, a means of suggesting and reinforcing the subject matter and lending it authority.[45]

Young illustrates this function of such intertextuality in patristic writings in five forms, including the following four illustrated by Gregory: reminting biblical language and transferring it to the description of an individual to lend weight to the delineation of their character; use of biblical maxims in moral reflections and in consolation; *synkrisis* or comparison of the subject of panegyric with biblical characters; and the use of quotation and allusion in the form of festival panegyric.

In Gregory's case, Scriptural teaching is imparted in a multifaceted way, richly interweaving its paradigmatic stories and characters, its identifications of God and human beings, the pedagogical force of commandments, prophetic images and descriptions, and other texts in rhetorical figures and structures. The result was a comprehensive, formative texture designed to engage a congregation, to dispose them to see the world in certain ways, to elicit from them forms of action and prayer whereby they might partake in God's saving action in history. The transformative function of scriptural pedagogy, then, was complexly, intertextually, and rhetorically mediated in Gregory's preaching.

---

42. Harrison, "The Typology of Listening," 66.

43. Young, *Biblical Exegesis*, 11 and 97.

44. See also Richard B. Hays's notion of intertextuality cited above in Chapter 5.

45. Young, *Biblical Exegesis*, 99–103.

We have in fact already seen several excellent examples of the rhetorical mediation of scriptural pedagogy through such intertextuality. Chapter 3 provided several examples. There, I quoted a passage from Oration 1.5 that develops the theme of the salvific purpose of the incarnation in a series of kommata combining elements of Christ's human existence with their salvific consequences, often in vivid contrasts of humiliation and deliverance or exaltation, which echoes a number of New Testament texts, most notably Phil. 2:6-11 and 2 Cor. 8:9.[46] I also drew on two powerful passages in Oration 29 (sections 19 and 20), where Gregory refutes his Eunomian opponents by means of a series of antitheses that paired incidents in the Gospels illustrative of the humanity of the Word with contrasting but thematically linked incidents or titles disclosive of his divinity.[47] By way of a skillfully ordered intertextuality, both passages convey a sense of wonder at the condescension of the Word that is intended to displace disbelief in his deity with a richer sense of divine generosity and freedom. And I discussed part of the opening to Oration 38, where Gregory creates a sense of liturgical anamnesis of Christ's birth ("Christ is born, give him glory . . .") as the recapitulation of creation and of salvation history.[48] This aspect of the exordium, which sets up the whole movement of the oration to dispose the hearer to worship and discipleship, works through allusions to texts in Genesis, Exodus, and Isaiah.[49]

In Chapter 4, we have also seen Gregory expound Exodus 12 in the course of his Second Oration on Easter, explaining the details of the instructions about the preparation and consumption of the paschal lamb in terms of Christ's sacrifice and his consumption in the contemplation of Scripture, thus making intelligible the significance of that story for the celebration of the feast in a manner consistent with Gregory's understanding of biblical types and symbols, while at once commending a proper disposition toward the Word and Scripture as the way in which the feast should be kept spiritually. Finally, in Chapter 5 we saw how Gregory turned a homiletical sermon on Matthew 19 into a case for reform of divorce law, where the persuasive effect of his reading derives much of its strength from the way Gregory reads the opening verses of the passage as

---

46. I cite a similar section from Or. 38.13 a little later in the same chapter.

47. Another passage from Or. 2.24 discussed in that chapter shows similar features, relating the circumstances of Christ's human life to his reversal of the fall.

48. Or. 38.1, *SC* 358, p. 104.

49. For a fuller exposition of the rhetorical use of Scripture in Oration 38, see my "Gregory of Nazianzus and Biblical Interpretation," in *Re-Reading Gregory of Nazianzus: Essays on History, Theology, and Culture*, ed. Christopher A. Beeley (Washington, DC: Catholic University of America Press, 2012), 41–48. Similar features pertain to the exordium of Oration 45.

symbolizing the philanthropic purpose of the incarnation. In the remainder of this chapter, I will take one more notable example, Oration 14, and examine the interplay of rhetoric, context, and intertext in more detail.[50]

Oration 14 in Context

Gregory's discourse *Peri Philoptochias*, On Love for the Poor, may well have originated in the campaign led by his friend Basil to establish an institution that would offer care for the poor and especially for those who suffered with leprosy. The project, as Brian Daley has argued, may have originated in Basil's practical response to food shortages during a drought in central Asia Minor, in the summer of 369, and the hoarding of grain by landowners: a development of the soup kitchen he had opened to help relieve the famine and encourage those with supplies to make them available.[51] The institution became known as the "Basileias," and was a complex of guesthouses, shelters, and hospices, located on the outskirts of Cappadocia's provincial capital, Caesarea.[52] Daley argues that Gregory's depiction of large numbers of the homeless poor in his sermons fits the context of a provincial capital, and notes that the sermon depicts the suffering of homeless lepers in terms that he would use again in his panegyric on Basil when describing the condition of those whom Basil's hospice aided (Or. 43.63).[53] This connection confirms, Daley contends, that Oration 14, like Gregory of Nyssa's sermons on love for the poor, had formed part of a campaign of persuasion in support of Basil's new institution. It is difficult to draw firm conclusions on this question. Gregory makes no explicit reference to the Basileias. He clearly envisages a situation in which such provision is lacking, which suggests delivery in a time or context remote from its completion or

---

50. For a somewhat different analysis of Gregory's use of scriptural allusion in Oration 14, see Brian J. Matz, "Deciphering a Recipe for Biblical Preaching in *Oration* 14," in Beeley, ed., *Re-reading Gregory of Nazianzus*, 49–66. While I agree with Matz that Gregory's argument is in large part composed of the words of Scripture, I think there is considerably more art to the way Gregory uses Scripture than Matz seems to suggest.

51. Daley, "Building a New City: The Cappadocian Fathers and the Rhetoric of Philanthropy," *Journal of Early Christian Studies* 7, no. 3 (1999): 441–48. For John McGuckin, the "Basileias" originated in 368, thus *prior* to the emergency of 369: *Saint Gregory of Nazianzus: An Intellectual Biography* (Crestwood, NY: St. Vladimir's Seminary Press, 2001), 145.

52. Daley, "Building a New City," 440.

53. Daley, "Building a New City," 450–55. One could argue, however, that the lack of specific references to famine argues against such a date for Gregory's sermon. See the discussion in Susan R. Holman's excellent *The Hungry Are Dying: Beggars and Bishops in Roman Cappadocia* (New York: Oxford University Press, 2001), 145–46, to which I am much indebted for the discussion of context that follows.

location. It is at least plausible that the sermon was intended to have wider or independent scope and circulation.[54]

So understood, Gregory's oration "On Love for the Poor," like Basil and Gregory of Nyssa's sermons on the subject, should be seen as a rhetorical articulation of a Christian vision of philanthropy.[55] By thus reworking the classical civic virtue of philanthropy and its commendation in the rhetorical tradition in this more radical Christian mode, their orations also formed part of their lifelong responses to the challenge to reshape Hellenic literary and civic culture along Christian lines (to which the Emperor Julian's decree of 362 banning Christians from teaching Greek language and literature was such an enduring provocation, long after his death the following year).[56] In this way too, the Cappadocian Fathers sought to discharge the social vocation that went with their upper-class status in a form shaped by their Christian discipleship, using the most potent tool available to them: their rhetoric.[57] For part of the civic function of rhetoric remained, in late antiquity, to seek to educate citizens in respect of their moral conduct, and the Cappadocians' education, their *paideia* and rhetorical skills, qualified them for local leadership.[58]

In so doing, they sought to reshape civic ideologies and practices of philanthropy and patronage in Christian terms. As members of the class of *curiales* from whom holders of imperial and civic offices were drawn, they were heirs to a whole way of thinking about giving in civic terms, in which the poor were not the primary object of the public service rendered.[59] Such *leitourgia* did not seek to alleviate poverty, but was a form of benefaction or euergetism that entailed an inherently unequal patron-client mutuality between the giver and the civic community, for which the benefactor would expect to receive the gratitude and praise of that community and which asserted their social power.[60]

54. See McGuckin, *Saint Gregory of Nazianzus*, 147, and Holman, *The Hungry Are Dying*, 145–48. I can find no evidence, however, for Holman's claim that Oration 14 was delivered on a feast day—one would expect some clear reference in the exordium and peroration for starters (*The Hungry Are Dying*, 143, 145).

55. So both Daley, "Building a New City," and McGuckin, *Saint Gregory of Nazianzus*, 147.

56. This is Daley's argument in "Building a New City."

57. On rhetoric as the most powerful tool available to bishops seeking to exercise political leadership in respect of the distribution of regional resources, see Van Dam, *Kingdom of Snow: Roman Rule and Greek Culture in Cappadocia* (Philadelphia: University of Pennsylvania Press, 2002), 47ff. In apparent contrast to Daley, Van Dam thinks Basil's initial campaign against the hoarding of grain met with only modest success (pp. 49–50).

58. See Menander Rhetor's comments discussed just below, and Holman, *The Hungry Are Dying*, 26–27.

59. Holman, *The Hungry Are Dying*, 24; Raymond Van Dam, *Kingdom of Snow*, 39.

In general, the poor might participate in such benefits insofar as they were members of the civic community or clients of a particular patron. Particular acts of philanthropy toward them had their rationale in the securing of the good of that patron or of the community. A worthy poor person might benefit in virtue of their place in the wider network of civic relations; famine relief made sense in terms of the self-interest of the elite in taking care of the commons in the body politic in which they both were bound.[61] Destitute beggars might be—indeed must have been—beneficiaries of some giving and might partake of some acts of civic benefaction (feasts, for example) but not in such a way that included them in civic identity.[62] Euergetism, including imperial benefaction, in Greco-Roman late antiquity was a "system of selective patronage which was concerned more with civic identity than with individual poverty."[63] In taking measures to relieve the needs of the poor as such, the Cappadocians were part of a wider phenomenon of Christian bishops in the fourth century tending to the needs of the poor in time of crisis from ecclesial resources.[64] In seeking to co-opt local elites into this project they advanced a new, Christian vision of civic benefaction that included the involuntary poor in civic identity and church worship in a context where local landowners were not averse to exploiting conditions of scarcity in essentials such as warm clothing, or food and water, for profit.[65]

The structure of the oration is well suited to this purpose. Martha Vinson identifies Oration 14 as a *lalia* or "talk": a flexible form of speech recommended by the sophist Menander Rhetor for its utility either for praising a ruler or giving counsel to a city or its governor (as well as more personal purposes).[66] Such "talks" did not conform to a fixed structure, like other forms of oratory, and employed numerous exempla, stories of divine philanthropy, apophthegms, and proverbs, all conveyed in a simple style. As Young notes, literary allusion was therefore an important component of the *lalia* for Menander, which,

60. Holman, *The Hungry Are Dying*, 22, 32–33.

61. Holman, *The Hungry Are Dying*, 35–36. This rationale for famine relief she takes from Dio Chrysostom, Or. 50.3–4.

62. Holman, *The Hungry Are Dying*, 37.

63. Holman, *The Hungry Are Dying*, 38ff. Holman documents some minor exceptions in two of Constantine's laws. Julian's argument that physical care for the poor was an ancient pagan ideal was in fact formed, she argues, by his Christian upbringing.

64. Holman, *The Hungry Are Dying*, 60–61.

65. This way of framing the Cappadocians' rhetorical goal is Holman's. On price-gouging and similar practices in Cappadocia, see Van Dam, *Kingdom of Snow*, 39–52.

66. Vinson, *St. Gregory of Nazianzus: Select Orations* (Washington, DC: Catholic University of America Press, 2003), xviii.

along with changes of tone, would contribute to the sweetness that ought to characterize such discourse.[67] As Vinson says, Oration 14 exemplifies these features in Christian form.[68]

DISTRIBUTING THE COMMAND TO LOVE THE POOR

Gregory's Oration 14 can be fairly characterized as an extended argument urging wealthy Cappadocians to obey the much-repeated biblical command to love the poor by giving materially to those in extreme deprivation, and especially to those suffering from leprosy. Gregory reserves a recitation of the manifold iterations of that command in Scripture for the end of the oration, where he brings forward a catena of texts representative of how all the inspired writers of Scripture urged love for the poor in order that "by unremitting reminding they might make the commandment effective."[69] This command is a constant concern of biblical writers, in Gregory's view, that transcends the particular situations to which it was originally addressed and intends the formation of later readers through its reiteration. The challenge for Gregory as a preacher is to communicate its force as a means of divine pedagogy for the wealthy elite of fourth-century Cappadocia, and his argument is that to obey the command and be formed by it means addressing the needs of the poorest, those marginal to Cappadocian society, and in particular sufferers from leprosy. Leprosy in late antiquity was a term denoting a range of skin diseases that entailed bodily deformity and deterioration and (for fear of contagion) social exclusion, despite medical theories attributing the cause of the disease to an imbalance of humors in the body.[70]

Gregory begins the oration by arguing for the superiority of love as a virtue (sections 2–9), for love of the poor as its preeminent expression, and he advocates for those with "leprosy" as being in greatest need of such love and compassion, as their suffering is especially pitiful.[71] The rest of the oration is taken up with a series of arguments designed to move his listeners

---

67. Young, *Biblical Exegesis*, 102–3.

68. Vinson, *St. Gregory of Nazianzus*, xix.

69. Or. 14.35, *PG* 35 905A.

70. Holman documents the medical description and diagnosis of this condition in *The Hungry Are Dying*, 153–58.

71. In contrast to Holman, I am not persuaded that this argument is best described in rights language, since the appeal is to compassion rather than justice (*The Hungry Are Dying*, 148–53). Later in the oration, the issue of justice forms the basis for one of Gregory's arguments, but it is not predominant overall.

to action. Gregory describes, in harrowing and haunting detail, the plight of those suffering with leprosy and contrasts it, to powerful effect, with the luxury of his listeners (9–17). He portrays their reluctance to help as a spiritual disease for which love is the medicine (18).[72] The ephemerality of worldly goods, the unpredictability of events, and the proximity of death and divine judgment all argue the wisdom of seeking God and caring for the afflicted by way of preparation, for we cannot outgive God (19–22).[73] God's own liberality in creation and providence is further cause, in light of which we must reckon that inequalities in wealth are a product of human sin, not divine intention (23–28). You cannot believe God is your benefactor and fail to use his gifts in service of the poor (29–35). Love for the poor is commanded throughout Scripture (35–39). In visiting, healing, feeding, and clothing the poor, however, we may welcome Christ and give to him that we may be welcomed by him when we depart this world (40).

Gregory thus urges willing obedience to the love command in respect of this group of poor people, drawing on a range of arguments designed to appeal to their listeners in a number of ways, of which the citation of versions of the command is but one, alongside attempts to appeal to the ultimate spiritual interests of the audience and their sense of shame. The rhetorical work of his discourse is a labor to move his listeners beyond an ingrained neglect of these people, a ready acceptance of their status and alienation from society, and a fear of the contagion that might follow from contact with them, to a new form of philanthropy centered on benefit for the poor, rather than honor and prestige.[74]

Understood in the context outlined above, we can also say that Gregory urges the force of the love command for this audience in that context against the tacit backdrop of a practical means for fulfilling that command, namely the project of the hospice in Caesarea (though the oration might equally

72. Hence in Nazianzen's case it does not seem that spiritual healing works through a kind of reverse contagion from the holy bodies of lepers, as Holman suggests of Gregories Nazianzen and Nyssen: *The Hungry Are Dying*, 166–67. For it is Christ who heals through the donor's Christomorphic love, which to be sure involves contact with holy leprous bodies (14.37). There is a suggestion of homeopathy here, but in respect of Christ's wounds. Nazianzen does combat fear of contagion (14.27) but does not seem to use the concept of contagion positively.

73. In this way, Gregory, like his fellow Cappadocians, advances a form of redemptive almsgiving in continuity with earlier Christian tradition, but in which the humanity and agency of the poor gain much greater recognition than was often the case in earlier texts (with some notable exceptions). See Holman, *The Hungry Are Dying*, 49–55.

74. We find these attitudes reflected in Gregory's refutations of them, especially in Or. 14.15–17, 27, and 29. Van Dam describes Basil's efforts to recast philanthropy in these terms. See his *Kingdom of Snow*, 47.

be intended to inspire other similar foundations) and the explicit mention of apparently personal gifts of spiritual teaching, food, and medical care; of keeping them company, offering encouragement and showing compassion; of hospitality and clothing.[75]

This strategy itself is significant in light of my exposition of Gregory's theology of Scripture and its exposition in relation to the question of history. It indicates that in Gregory's practice, the deployment or "distribution" of scriptural pedagogy of this preeminent biblical command functioned in contextually specific ways, by means of a range of supporting arguments designed to move listeners in a number of ways and a practical option (or range of options) to facilitate enaction of the command in their context. This combination of rhetoric, practices, and institutions provided a ready way by which to elicit the "performance" of such texts and so the development of likeness to God, which, by Gregory's account, biblical commands function to promote. This approach thus respects the historical locatedness of the recipients of the divine command and of its mediation through a combination of preaching and ecclesial institutions. In light of Gregory's theology of Christian teaching, we may reasonably suppose that for him these historically situated strategies and practices of mediation were vehicles for God's own teaching action toward human beings in their particular temporal, geographical, and social contexts.

The Rhetoric of Oration 14 and Gregory's Vision of History

It is also significant for my concerns that Gregory's arguments to persuade his listeners to obey the command to love the poor draw on his understanding of providence in general and of God's redemptive action in Jesus Christ in particular. The force of the command turns out, in part, to be rooted in the imperative to imitate God's providential benevolence toward human beings.[76] In this way, Gregory's exposition of the command is informed by his understanding of the mysterious way in which God's creative and ordering power governs and guides the ever-moving course of events and the fragile systems constitutive of the created order, which we explored in Chapter 2. On the one hand, we are to imitate the indiscriminate benevolence of God in bestowing gifts on human beings. On the other, we are to respect the

---

75. Or. 14.27. Van Dam notes another poorhouse funded by an imperial accountant at Amaseia, and that the church in Nazianzus was, according to Gregory's will, a conduit for giving to the poor: *Kingdom of Snow*, 51.

76. Or. 14.23–27.

mysteriousness of the providential ordering of unequal lives and not take it as license to fail to imitate God's generosity toward us.[77] In this way, we may infer, obedience to the love command is to be informed by a sense of the generosity with which God guides and orders human affairs, appropriately chastened by the limits of our capacity to fathom its workings in every particular.

At the same time, Gregory repeatedly returns to Jesus Christ as the paradigm of love for the poor and of Christian living. In this way, his exposition of the command reflects his sense that in Christ human historical possibilities are radically reforged so that Godward transformation is possible in the path he has made in his own life, death, and resurrection for us. First, Christ not only exemplifies many of the virtues Gregory celebrates at the beginning of the oration, but he establishes the pathway to salvation, which one travels through the exercise of virtue, under his guidance. For each virtue is a road to salvation, and what is essential is that one attempts the journey: "[L]et him follow in the steps of the one who guides and directs us well through the narrow way and gate to the wide space of the blessedness thereafter."[78] Second, Christ teaches us that love is the preeminent virtue.[79] In the same vein, Christ supplies, in his own incarnate action, the strongest reason for Christian compassion for the poor. Gregory reminds his listeners, employing terms from 1 Peter 2:9 for the church (holy nation, royal priesthood, chosen people), that the dignity they bear as Christians derives from Christ, who according to a string of biblical descriptions, bore our infirmities, humbled himself in assuming our "dough," became poor in our flesh, and experienced pain that we might be enriched with his divinity.[80] What of us, he asks, who have such an example of compassion and fellow-feeling? Neglect for such people becomes neither his listeners as the flock of the good shepherd who seeks the lost and strengthens the weak, nor their human nature.

Third, Gregory adds to the motive of our fellow-humanity with those who suffer from leprosy the further bond his listeners have with them in Christ. He affirms our common obligation toward the body as our kin and fellow-servant, but then extends this obligation beyond our individual bodies to those of our neighbors, including lepers. His reasoning further amplifies his account of the logic of the command to love the poor. "For we are, all of us, one in the Lord, whether rich, or poor, slave or free, whether healthy or unwell in body; and there is one head of all, from whom all derive, Christ; and what the limbs are to

77. Or. 14.30–33.

78. Or. 14.5, *PG* 35 864B.

79. Or. 14.5.

80. Or. 14.15, *PG* 35 876B–C, alluding to Matt. 8:17, Phil. 2:6-11, and 2 Cor. 8:9.

one another, so are we to each other and all of us to everyone."[81] This is why, he adds, we must not overlook or neglect those who stumble into our common weakness.

Fourth, Gregory defines the primary forms of Christian generosity toward the poor with reference to Christ. The preeminent of these is "lay everything aside for Christ in order that we may truly follow him, bearing the cross, winging lightly to the heavenly world, being equipped with nothing downward dragging, that we may gain Christ before all else, being exalted through humility and enriched through poverty."[82] To renounce wealth is to follow Christ and the deepest possibilities for transformation he holds before us, being transformed through the imitation of his pattern of humiliation and poverty. The second option is to "share our goods with Christ, in order that possessing might somehow, through possessing nobly and sharing with those who have nothing, be sanctified."[83] To share wealth generously with those who lack is to share with Christ: in some way he is present in our neighbor (as Gregory also implies in his peroration), and our giving (or neglect) is a manner of relating to him that may be sanctifying of our mode of existence.[84] In the same way, Gregory can later exhort his listeners to recognize the difference between the fleeting goods of earth and the treasures of heaven, and so practice love for the poor as a way of being crucified to the world with Christ and ascending with him, of following him from earth to heaven; hence he can enjoin them to "follow the Word."[85]

Thus in Oration 14, obedience to the love command is cast in terms of acting in accordance with Jesus Christ in several respects. It conforms to Christ as the pattern and pathway of love for the poor in his incarnation, and by his teaching. It conforms to the mutuality with which Christians are related through their bond with Christ. It responds to the presence of Christ in the poor, and it participates in his own self-giving love. In all these ways, obedience to the command is defined in relation to Jesus Christ, whom Gregory effectively considers central to the whole schema of human history under divine rule. It is for Gregory the preeminent way (after baptism, presumably) of conforming to and participating in the possibilities that Jesus Christ's history opens for human beings in their historical circumstances. In all these ways, Gregory's

81. Or. 14.8, *PG* 35 868A.

82. Or. 14.18, *PG* 35 880C.

83. Or. 14.18, *PG* 35 880C.

84. See also 14.9 (those with compassion for lepers are Christ-lovers and lovers of the poor); 14.37 (compassion to one of Christ's members is reverence to Christ), 14.39–14.40 (see below).

85. Or. 14.21–22, quotation from section 22, *PG* 35 885B.

amplification of the command to love the poor could be said, in his terms, to follow the movement from letter to spirit that is enacted in God's work in history in Jesus Christ and that the reader of Scripture is called to follow and embody. It is also notable, therefore, that this reasoning plays such a substantial role in Gregory's rhetoric. He seeks to persuade his listeners to obey the command by placing it in relation to the central event of history—Jesus Christ—and the way that human vocation and society are reshaped in relation to him. Following Jesus Christ, Gregory's suasion seeks to lead his listeners from the letter to the spirit, in understanding and action, and it is in just this way that the command to love the poor makes deepest sense.

Scriptural Intertextuality and the Rhetorical Amplification of the Biblical Command

In order to draw his listeners to this way of seeing the world and to move them to act accordingly in relation to the most vulnerable and excluded set of people in Cappadocia as he understood it, Gregory drew on both rhetorical tools and scriptural allusions. Both enhance the persuasive potential of the oration in distinct but interrelated ways, of which I will give a few examples here.

Gregory's exordium is an appeal for a generous-hearted hearing. It is his one opportunity to gain their attention and give them reasons to continue to attend to his words and the arguments he will unfold, and to begin the work of persuasion. He does so by linking the generosity of his listeners' response to their spiritual benefit. This appeal depends on a transvaluation of wealth and poverty in order to paint his audience in a position of spiritual need as urgent as the material need he would have them alleviate.[86] Gregory effects this transvaluation with a plethora of scriptural allusions.

While acknowledging that "one may seem more eminent than another, when gauged by our small measure," and so admitting the distinctions of honor and wealth present in his audience, he emphasizes their common spiritual need: they are "brothers and fellow paupers—for we are all destitute and in want of divine grace."[87] To address his audience as brothers (ἀδελφοί) uses familial language in the manner of the New Testament, evoking the leveling of status connoted there in respect of a common bond in Christ. In this one phrase,

---

86. Here "transvaluation" denotes a shift in the identification of what is of value, usually by means of a metaphorical transfer of meaning. I borrow the term from J. D. Y. Peel, who seems to use it in this way in his magisterial *Religious Encounter and the Making of the Yoruba* (Bloomington and Indianapolis: Indiana University Press, 2000); see e.g. 165–66 and 177–78.

87. Or. 14.1, *PG* 35 857A–860A.

Gregory switches from addressing his audiences as συμπένητες, a term for those of limited means who retained their social ties and used for that reason in Christian texts for the spiritual poverty of the wealthy, to πτωχοὶ, the term for extreme poverty more common in the New Testament, and connoting social exclusion.[88]

His wealthy hearers thus find themselves depicted in a position spiritually analogous to those in need of their material benefaction. They may enrich themselves, he argues, by receiving his discourse on love for their fellow-destitute "lavishly, that you may become rich in respect of the kingdom."[89] Gregory thus positions his hearers as beneficiaries of his spiritual patronage, which entails reciprocal obligations upon them. The terms of that mutuality clearly echo Jesus' counsel to the rich young man in the Gospels to give all his wealth to the poor (πτωχοὶ) in order to have treasure in heaven, and appropriate its logic.[90] Gregory, however, does not talk about treasure in heaven but about becoming rich, using the exact term Paul uses in 2 Cor. 8:9 to describe the consequence for believers of Christ's impoverishment in assuming the human condition: πλουτήσητε. The choice is so apt and marked as to indicate a clear echo, and suggests for those familiar with that formula of exchange that Gregory's audience are being offered the saving benefits of the incarnation. These echoes are the lynchpin of Gregory's transvaluation and they frame and implicitly legitimate Gregory's use of biblical feeding miracles—the manna from heaven as described in Ps. 78:24-25, the feedings of the five and four thousand in the Gospels—to describe the spiritual nourishment available through his discourse. Pray with us, he says, that he may break spiritual bread with them, "either by raining down food from heaven, like Moses of old and giving the bread of angels, or by feeding thousands in the desert to satiety with a few loaves, as Jesus did later, who is the true bread and the source of true life."[91] Gregory's allusions to Jesus' counsel and Paul's teaching allow him to employ the symbolic freight of these two feeding miracles with reference to his hearers' spiritual benefit. These allusions are rhetorically powerful for the familiar and authoritative images they employ, ripe for lodging in the memory's storehouse in new connections with new associations of material wealth and spiritual poverty. At the same time, Gregory's allusions also convey

88. According to Susan R. Holman, πτωχός denotes a destitute beggar outside or on the fringes of society, in contrast to a πένης, an individual of limited economic means but whose social ties remain intact; the former is the more common usage in the NT (*The Hungry Are Dying*, 5–6).

89. Or. 14.1, *PG* 35 857A–860A.

90. Matt. 19:21/Mark 10:21/Luke 18:22.

91. Or. 14.1, *PG* 35 857A–860A

with great economy a symbolic reading of both miracles that must be seen in light of his understanding of Old and New Testament types—it is one way in which the letter of biblical texts conveys their spirit, and Gregory uses them accordingly—but which is sufficiently commonplace as a procedure to need no further comment. For his usage relies on a scriptural textuality, a shared language constituted by a rich memorial store of biblical texts.

The next step in Gregory's argument provides our second illustration. Gregory at once evokes an attractive and memorable image to broach the first of a series of arguments in favor of love for the poor. "It is not very easy to discover the victor among the virtues and to give it seniority and the victor's prizes, just as it is not easy in a fragrant meadow of many flowers to find the most beautiful and most fragrant."[92] Each flower "draws to itself our sense of smell and our sight and persuades us to be picked first."[93] These pleasing similes dispose the listener to attend closely to the delights that shall surely follow: a series of portraits of the virtues, each illustrated by biblical exempla and worthy of desire and attainment.

Gregory's audience is treated to a dazzling array of biblical vignettes drawn with economy and style: there is plenty to delight in these terms. At the same time, Gregory sets forth for his audience a rich depiction of the constituents of the Christian life of wisdom, of Christian philosophy. They depict a coherent Christian cultural vision for civic life—composed of faith, hope, love, hospitality, philanthropy, patience, gentleness, jealous zeal, mortification of the body, prayer and watching, chastity and virginity, self-control, solitude and silence, frugality, humility, poverty and contempt for money, contemplation and action—mandated by the Bible, and in which marginalizing the destitute can no longer be normal. The power and detail of that vision lend force to the overall conclusion: that, while each virtue is a path to salvation, and each person should pursue the way of virtue led by Christ, nevertheless love of the poor is the chief virtue and love *for* the poor its most excellent form.

The interplay of rhetorical form and scriptural allusion is again integral to each element of this presentation as well as to its overall effect. The following passage on contemplation and action is a good example:

> Fine are solitude and quietness; so Elijah's Carmel teaches me, or John's desert, or Jesus' mountain, to which he often seems to have withdrawn, to dwell by himself in quietness.

92. Or. 14.1, *PG* 35 860A–B.
93. Or. 14.1, *PG* 35 860B.

Fine is thrift; so Elijah teaches me who rested at the widow's house, John who covered himself with camel's hair, and Peter who survived on a farthing's worth of lupines.

Fine is humility, of which there are many examples from many places, and before all others, the Saviour and Master of all, who humbled himself not only to assuming the form of a slave, nor subjecting his face to the shame of spitting, and being counted with the lawless, who cleanses the cosmos of sin, but washes the disciples' feet in the garment of a slave.

Fine is poverty and contempt for money, so teach Zacchaeus and Christ himself; the former, by offering almost everything when Christ visited him; the latter, by defining perfection in this respect to the rich man.

And to speak more briefly concerning these things, fine is contemplation, and fine is action; the former, in raising us up and conveying us into the Holy of Holies, leading our intellect toward its kin; the latter when it receives Christ and tends him, so demonstrating the efficacy of the lovecharm in its works.[94]

This paragraph displays several features common to others in this section of the oration. The anaphora created by the repetition of καλὸν (fine, beautiful, good, noble) at the start of each kolon conveys a sense of the attractiveness and multiplicity of the virtues in Christianity, so fulfilling the conjunction of the aesthetic and the moral in Gregory's image of the virtues as a meadow of flowers. Each kolon follows a similar formal pattern: the identification of a virtue or pair of virtues as καλὸν, followed by the enumeration of who or what teaches us so, which in some cases is then amplified. This repetition of structure is combined with variations in the number of examples enumerated, or the number of kommata taken to describe them, or whether one or two virtues are praised, creating a pleasing sense of ordered variety at a formal level. The content of the (largely) biblical exempla, which Gregory gives with great economy, adds color in a wealth of varied and vivid detail, together with the pleasure of recognizing the allusions made.

The biblical exempla are the stuff of this revisioning, but the passages to which Gregory alludes are thereby cast as patterns for imitation and linked as exemplifications of Christian virtue, as components in a vision of an encompassing way of life. The exegetical procedure implied by Gregory's use of these texts thus conforms to his understanding of the purpose and function

94. Or. 14.4, *PG* 35 861C–864A.

of inspired narratives and of how they should be used: how the spirit is to be found and followed in the letter. The details Gregory picks out to identify each narrative episode work to illumine the whole episode in these terms so that his manner of allusion is inherently interpretive. Gregory is not offering an exhaustive reading of any one of these passages, but drawing our attention to one aspect of the divine pedagogy they mediate. Elsewhere, for example, he is perfectly aware of the function ascribed to John the Baptist in respect of Jesus in several New Testament texts.[95] Here, however, he focuses in on John's location and dress, detailed in Luke 1:80 and Matt. 3:4, as emblems of the dispositions with which he lived out his extraordinary vocation.[96]

The kolon on Christ's exemplification is an especially skillful weaving of allusions in such a way as to draw out the wondrous conjunction of his divine authority and the humility with which it is exercised: the one who washes the cosmos of sin, according to John 1:29, is the same one who washes the feet of his disciples in John 13:5, the garb of a slave there corresponding to the form of a slave, an allusion to Phil. 2:7, which supplies much of the Christological force of this kolon and indeed of the passage, and is supplemented in turn by allusions to the suffering and identification with sinners of the servant of the Lord in Isa. 50:6 and 53:12. This connecting of texts seems to evince a sense of a common pattern in Christ's action, as related in John's Gospel and Paul's letter and foreshadowed in Isaiah's prophetic figure of the servant. By bringing out the pattern through the intertextuality of this passage in the oration, Gregory highlights the centrality of the action of Christ's incarnation (and his death) in defining Christian virtues and the path by which salvation may be pursued, and he underscores the Christological and (in his terms) historical grounds for the revisioning of culture he is carrying out.

This passage is the last of three describing Christian virtues, and it brings to culmination a rich tableau whose power comes from the way scriptural allusions are deployed. It is therefore in the context of this Christomorphic way of life, so multifarious in its aspects and patterned in so many varied biblical characters and narratives, that Gregory identifies love as preeminent on the basis of good scriptural warrant (Christ's own teaching in Matt. 22:36-40, as well as Paul's in Rom. 13:8), and its highest point as "love for the poor (φιλοπτωχία) and compassion and sympathy for our human kin."[97] This commendation of

---

95. See, for example, Or. 39.14–15.

96. Martha Vinson's translation very helpfully identifies the biblical allusions for us, in her *St. Gregory of Nazianzus: Select Orations* (Washington, DC: Catholic University of America Press, 2003), 41. I am indebted to her for the identification of all the allusions basic to the argument of this section of the chapter.

love for the poor is all the stronger for the wealth of virtues already depicted, and it is likewise grounded in scriptural allusions. Nothing is more akin to God than mercy, whose mercy and truth go before (Ps. 89:14), to whom we must demonstrate our mercy before judging, and who will measure out his compassion to us by the measure of our own toward others (Luke 6:35-38). The scriptural identification of God as merciful warrants Gregory's conclusion that of all the forms of love Scripture commands, love for the poor must be paramount.

Our third example comes from Gregory's argument for the all-encompassing scope of the command to love the poor: that it includes the most destitute and physically and socially repulsive. Part of that argument appeals to our common humanity with them, and part to our common obligation to the body, which Gregory extends to the bodies of our neighbors, including those with leprosy. His reason has to do with the unity and mutuality of his audience with these socially excluded others in Christ's body.

> For we are, all of us, one in the Lord, whether rich, or poor, slave or free, whether healthy or unwell in body;
>   and there is one head of all, from whom all derive, Christ;
>   and what the limbs are to one another, so are we to each other and all of us to everyone.[98]

This argument works by adducing the logic of the arguments of Gal. 3:28 and Rom. 12:4-5. Gregory extends the logic of the former—whereby differences of Jew or Greek, slave or free, male or female no longer pertain or divide "in Christ"—to include the erasure of divisions between those of differing wealth or bodily well-being. He adduces Paul's appropriation of the rhetorical trope of the mutual dependence of the body to argue the obligations of the wealthy to the poor in respect of their bodies, forcing them to imagine themselves in organic contiguity and connection with the suffering, diseased body of the other so that the other's illness is a matter of urgent concern to the healthy. Gregory's usage seems faithful to the logic of each text's rhetoric, but rather than reproduce Paul's acts of persuasion which were directed to particular contexts in the past, Gregory extends that logic into a new context and puts it to work to move his listeners. Such a procedure makes sense when one understands Pauline rhetoric in Gregory's terms, as an instantiation of a living divine pedagogy and eloquence that is capable of entering into successive contexts to transform

97. Or. 14.5, *PG* 35 864B.

98. Or. 14.8, *PG* 35 868A.

human beings there. Gregory takes up that logic within his own argument, thereby putting it to work. The form of his oratory contributes to that re-realization of that logic; in particular, Gregory picks up and repeats the "all" of Gal. 3:28—Πάντες . . . τὰ πάντα . . . πᾶσιν ἅπαντες—driving home the inclusive scope of the logic.

In a complementary rhetorical strategy, Gregory deepens the pathos of his description of the suffering caused by leprosy and the exclusion and dehumanization it brings by placing Job's words from his curse of the day of his birth on the lips of a leper's mother. In one of the most harrowing passages of the oration, Gregory describes how the natural instincts of father and mother are denied them. The father must drive away and grieve for the light of his life; the mother is in childbirth again, lamenting her son as though dead, whom she can no longer recognize and who now must dwell outside society. Gregory has her cry out and weep, both reaching for and shrinking from her child's flesh:

> Why were you formed in your mother's belly, and why did not you not perish at once when you were drawn from her stomach, that your death might concur with your birth? . . . Why did her knees support you? And why did her breasts give you suck, when you were going to live wretchedly a life harder than death?[99]

Gregory has the mother turn Job's curses of his own birth into a lamenting question of the birth of her son, and in so doing she bitterly regrets the childbirth whose pain she relives as grief and the tender nurture that followed it. The effect is both all the more moving for those who recognize the allusion, and all the more powerful rhetorically, for it casts the sufferers in the figure of Job, who suffers despite his upright life. Job is an especially apt figure for these people. If, with Richard Hays, we accept that this kind of intertextuality works by a broad interplay between text and intertext that encompasses aspects of the intertext beyond those explicitly echoed, then we can see how.[100] Not long before Job says these things he has been cursed with boils from head to foot, and has left the city to sit on a dungheap, scraping away the discharge (Job 2:7-8). Job is thus an apt figure for sufferers from leprosy but also one that compels with the recognition of that aptness the recognition also of their humanity and holiness.

99. Or. 14.11, *PG* 35 872A, alluding to Job 3:11-12. See also Or. 14.14, *PG* 35 876A, where Gregory alludes to Job 10:11.

100. Richard Hays, *Echoes of Scripture in the Letters of Paul* (New Haven: Yale University Press, 1993), 20.

> Later Gregory counsels respect for that hallowed disease by
> reverencing those who conquer through suffering, lest somewhere
> a Job should be hidden among the sick, much more worthy of
> reverence than the healthy, even if he scrapes away the discharge and
> suffers day and night in the open, straightened by his wounds, his
> wife and his friends.[101]

Gregory's allusion makes the aptness of citing Job explicit. In context, Gregory
is refuting the argument that the difference between the wealthy and the
desperate sufferers from leprosy evidently reflects God's providential will and
hence should not be altered. Configuring these poor as potential Jobs reinforces
their sanctity (hence leprosy is a disease hallowed by the saints who suffer it).
This move is compounded by a second allusion, this time to the parable of
Lazarus and the rich man.[102] Again, the allusion is apt: Lazarus is a figure of
exclusion who suffers from sores; as Gregory points out, it is not the rich man
that neglected him who rests in Abraham's bosom. In these ways, Gregory can
be seen to employ Job (and Lazarus) in terms that take account of the specifics
of his story, using him in such a way as to promote reflection on his significance
as an exemplum for this particular situation.

The oration evinces many other examples of the employing of the
illocutionary force of particular biblical speech-acts now directed to the
persuasion of Gregory's audience, their pedagogical potential transcending their
particular scriptural contexts yet their usage conforming to the configuration
of history in God's saving economy. Of these, Gregory's final marshaling of
scriptural instances of the command to love the poor deserves analysis here, as
it illustrates the fluency with which Gregory handles allusions to great effect
while dealing with the hermeneutical questions their use provokes.

He introduces a first string of allusions by describing the command to
love the poor as the first, or one of the first, to which "people of the Spirit"
have exhorted us with zeal, using various incitements—exhortations, threats,
reproaches, approval—to make it live in the memory. Gregory sees the biblical
writers as rhetoricians performing a similar role to his own, seeking to persuade
and reinforce and form the memory and thus the character of their listeners in
regard to love for the poor. And so he quotes them, taking their various forms
of persuasion into his own and animating their various illocutions by making
them his own:

---

101. Or. 14.34, *PG* 35 904B, alluding especially to Job 2:8-9.
102. Or. 14.34, alluding to Luke 16:19-31.

It says, "Because of the suffering of the destitute and the sighing of the poor, now I shall arise, says the Lord." Who shall not fear when the Lord arises? And, "Arise, O Lord my God, lift up your hand; do not forget the poor." Let us pray that this uplifting does not happen, and let us not wish to see his hand raised against the disobedient, or still worse, raining blows on the pitiless. It also says, "He does not forget the cry of the poor," and "the destitute shall not finally be forgotten," and "his eyes (better and stronger than 'eyelids') look on the poor"; but "his eyelids examine the sons of men" (the lesser and, so to speak, secondary oversight).[103]

Gregory here quotes from Pss. 12:5 (11:5, LXX), 10:12 (9:33, LXX), 9:12, 9:18, and 11:5 (10:5, LXX), adding after each a comment that emphasizes the illocutionary force of each verse: each divine threat is put directly to the listener before Gregory reminds them of God's vigilance over the poor.[104] Gregory's procedure makes sense as a use of the scriptural text on the supposition that the illocutionary function of these verses, as Gregory understands them, is appropriate not only to their original context, but also to the context of Gregory's listeners, since God's commitment to the poor remains constant and the need to persuade the wealthy to have regard for them remains in very different circumstances. Gregory, however, amasses several such texts here and a little later, and so seeks to reproduce in his own way the rhetorical force of the repetition of the command in the scriptural canon. The repetition of the same message in different forms seeks to shape memory, inscribing on the soft wax of the soul a lesson that will shape judgments and actions.

Gregory's rhetoric is the stronger for anticipating objections, allowing his audience thus to entertain them too and so partake of the process of reasoning that will lead them to his conclusion. The first objection entertained here is that these verses deal with the poor who are victims of injustice, and hence (it is implied) are not applicable to the present case.[105] Gregory's response is to mount an *a fortiori* argument: If we are to rectify the injustices of the poor, how much more to aid them in the first place? Gregory backs up this inference by citing a parallel inference that leads to the same practical conclusion: if, according to Prov. 17:5, he who mocks the poor provokes their maker, then the one who cares for God's creature surely honors the Creator. A second objection

103. Or. 14.35, *PG* 35 905A–B, following Vinson's translation of ἐπαφιεμένην τοῖς σκληροτέροις as "raining blows on the pitiless," in *St. Gregory of Nazianzus*, 68.

104. Gregory does something very similar with a second set of texts in Or. 14.38.

105. Or. 14.36.

raises Prov. 22:2—"rich and poor meet together, and (or 'but') the Lord creates them both"—to justify neglect of the poor, for they are made poor by God. Gregory refutes this inference: the teaching that rich and poor alike are made by God relativizes the "external inequality between them," and should shame the rich into sympathy and brotherly love.[106] In the first case, Gregory seeks to oppose a move to limit the purchase of the text on the present situation: the psalmist's concern for the injustices visited upon the poor argues a love for them that extends beyond righting their wrongs. In the second, he corrects a wrong reading that would license the status quo. The overall argument is the stronger for taking account both of an objection to Gregory's use of Scripture and a counterargument from Scripture. It is not difficult to see, however, that Gregory's refutations gain plausibility from the wider vision he has set forth of divine compassion toward the poor, and hence that such an overarching vision, developed from biblical testimony, is an important framework for handling potentially ambiguous scriptural texts in the service of mediating scriptural pedagogy through rhetoric.

One final intertext deserves comment for its pervasive role in the Oration, which Gregory underlines powerfully in his peroration, namely Jesus' saying in the parable of the sheep and the goats that aid or neglect of his brethren is aid or neglect of him, and will be judged accordingly (Matt. 25:34-46). There are echoes of this text every time Gregory seems to identify the poor with Christ—the most compelling ground, in Christian terms, that Nazianzen offers for showing them compassion.[107] At the end of the oration, Gregory alludes more explicitly to the passage, noting that those Christ rebukes on his left hand are condemned "because they did not heal Christ through the needy."[108] The peroration takes up the implication and makes it the basis of Gregory's final appeal to his "fellow servants of Christ, brothers and fellow heirs."[109] If we have been at all persuaded by him, while there is time,

> Let us visit Christ, let us heal Christ, let us feed Christ, let us clothe Christ, let us receive Christ, let us honour Christ;
>> not with food alone, like some;
>> nor with perfume, like Mary;
>> nor with tomb alone, like Joseph of Arimathea;

106. Or. 14.36, *PG* 35 905C.

107. For references, see above, nn. 82–83.

108. Or. 14.39, *PG* 35 909B.

109. Or. 14.40, *PG* 35 909B.

nor with preparations for the tomb, like Nicodemus who loved
Christ with half of himself;

nor with gold and frankincense and myrrh, like the magi before
these just mentioned;

but since the master of all desires mercy not sacrifice, and a good
heart is worth more than tens of thousands of fat sheep, let us offer
this to him through the needy who are today cast to the ground, so
that when we depart from here, we may be welcomed into eternal
dwellings, in Christ our Lord himself, to whom be glory for ever.
Amen.

The anaphora of the first kolon, which enumerates the actions by which Christ
was shown compassion through his brethren in Matthew 25, and into which
Gregory has inserted others pertinent to the needs of lepers, drives home the
force of those verses in Matthew for this audience in their particular context:
Christ is the explicit object and the leprous poor the implied object of these
verbs. The anaphora of the subsequent kola builds a sense of anticipation: If
not in these reverential actions of biblical characters toward Christ, then how
shall we honor him? Gregory supplies the answer he has already implied in the
previous section—by offering to Christ through the poor—and underlines its
divine sanction with three further allusions, two of which confirm the priority
of compassion in God's perspective and a third that reinforces the logic of the
Christian euergetism for which Gregory has been contending: give to the poor
now, that you may benefit eternally.[110]

Gregory's intertextual use of Scripture is thus shaped by and contributes to
his rhetoric, and so to a radical reenvisioning of late-antique civic euergetism.
In this way he models the rhetorical use of Scripture in a significant cultural
intervention in a cultural system, one whereby the poor gain far greater voice
and humanity than they had hitherto, though they are not socially empowered:
they receive aid on the unequal terms entailed by the patron-client relation.[111]
Even so, not only has Gregory argued that inequality is not the divine will,
and the logic of his vision of euergetism understands that the wealthy's gifts to
the poor are reciprocated not by the obedience of the poor but by the greater,

---

110. Matt. 9:13, Mic. 6:7 (Vinson, *St. Gregory of Nazianzus*, 71, n. 166 and Daley, *Gregory of
Nazianzus*, 218, n. 193 identify the allusion as Dan. 3:39 LXX or 3:40 respectively, but I cannot find
either in the LXX), and Luke 16:9.

111. On the extent to which Gregory humanizes the poor and the limits of this transformation within
civic euergetism, see Holman, *The Hungry Are Dying*, 149–53, 166–67.

eschatological benefaction of God (whose benefaction in fact began long before theirs, in creation, and which they merely imitate).

CONCLUSION

Any account of the theology of Scripture ought to extend its concerns to practices of scriptural use and interpretation in actual churches: to understand them theologically and perhaps recommend reformations, innovations, or critical *ressourcement* from past insights or practices. Any account that seeks to respond to the challenges of historical consciousness will need to address that challenge in this respect also. Gregory's account of Christian teaching as a rhetorical mediation of the pedagogy of Scripture, taken in light of his wider theological commitments, is suggestive in this respect. For Gregory sees God acting to form, heal, and transform human beings through practices of the persuasive deployment of scriptural texts in particular contexts, where the rhetorical art of the preacher is a tool for a divine eloquence that carries into fresh situations the divine pedagogy and rhetoric embodied in the scriptural text.

Gregory's own practice in Oration 14 bears out this account. It illustrates powerfully how the mediation of scriptural pedagogy may be effected through rhetorical means in respect of a particular audience and context and in connection with specific institutional ways of enabling a faithful response. Gregory's example shows that promoting the pedagogy of the commandments involves persuading an audience with a considerable stake in the status quo, with material and social commitments to its neglect of the poor and the channeling of resources toward other priorities, to see themselves and their context in radically different terms, and so transmute their sense of wealth, poverty, and reward. Oration 14 likewise illustrates well how a combination of direct appeal to Scripture, of several uses of comparisons (of love to other virtues, of wealthy and leprous poor), and the refutation of objections all contribute to this reenvisioning, and in particular the rhetorical value of a skillful deployment of scriptural intertexts toward the overall suasion. It shows likewise how in this way what Gregory saw as basic character of exegetical procedure—carefully drawing the spirit from the letter, in accordance with God's work in history and the genre of the text, and embodying it in contemplation and practice—could be mediated to particular listeners through persuasive, contextually nuanced, scripturally intertextual discourse.

Gregory's understanding of teaching Scripture as a rhetorical activity and his practice of using Scripture in his orations cannot simply be transposed into our late-modern context to address the issues raised in this study. Gregory's theology and practice only assist us constructively by suggesting lines along which to work in relation to a much more developed historical consciousness than he could have anticipated, and a complex set of nontheological historical and literary approaches to scriptural texts to negotiate. Nevertheless, his theory and practice are highly suggestive and complete the premodern model he offers as a working sketch from which to draw inspiration and insights to develop in dialogue with Hans Frei's direct engagement with the problem of historical consciousness, to which I now turn.

7

History, Biblical Narrative, and the Shaping of Identity in Hans Frei

Hans Frei belonged to a vaster, more complex world than Gregory's, one removed from late antiquity not only by time but by enormous technological, scientific, economic, social, and cultural change. These changes contributed to the formation of a sense of history of whose significance for theology Frei was acutely aware, having committed himself to working in a modern secular university, the kind of context where the place of theology as an academic discipline has been far more marginal and more institutionally ambiguous than in Gregory's context. Frei's approach to addressing the theological problems posed by historical consciousness offers is no less theological and even more Christ-centered than Gregory's, and integrates providence more closely with Christology and the atonement in such a way as to present a more fully historical vision than Nazianzen's'. At the same time, Gregory's theology is suggestive of ways to flesh out more fully Frei's conceptual description of his theology of history. That theology provides a context in which to examine, in the next chapter, the theology of Scripture it involves.

FREI AND THE CHALLENGE OF HISTORY

The challenges posed by historical inquiry and its vision of reality remain a persistent ingredient in the different ways in which Frei analyzed the critical problems facing modern theologians.[1] The problem emerges clearly in Frei's analysis of the theological background to H. Richard Niebuhr's thought in the

---

1. As Mike Higton has also argued, in *Christ, Providence and History: Hans Frei's Public Theology* (London: T. & T. Clark, 2004), chapter 1. As Higton goes on to show in chapter 2, another part of the background to Frei's concern here has to do with what he thought was the danger in Karl Barth's later theology of not doing sufficient justice to Jesus' humanity.

191

former's earliest published writing in such a way as to shed light not only on Niebuhr but also on Frei's subsequent work.

For nineteenth-century historians, Frei explains, history was the way in which human beings understand themselves. It was the science "of the reflection of man upon mankind in its social intercourse as it develops uninterruptedly through time and in its myriad forms of polity, culture and thought."[2] Despite differences in outlook, historians shared a common method: the presupposition-less scrutiny of original and supplementary sources and evidence critically interpreted by judgments as to the probable nature of happenings. This procedure involves the abstraction, relating, and comparing of events and hypotheses in their interactions. Here Frei identifies two tensions. The first was between particularists (for whom historical understanding is focused on individual, unique phenomena) and universalists (for whom the particulars can only be properly understood in their widest interrelations). The second was between the demand for factuality and objectivity and the demand for historical imagination, empathy, and critical interpretation, made from historically and culturally conditioned perspectives and hence never absolute. The great historians and theorists of history brought these tensions into fruitful interaction so that, for example, for them historical objectivity required an imaginative and empathetic engagement with the past. Frei's was a well-informed account of nineteenth-century historical theory and method, its tensions and subtleties.

The way of looking at the past that historians promoted required theologians to see the church and Jesus of Nazareth within the wider nexus of historical reality, as phenomena whose origins and development must be explained accordingly. Many theologians, Frei explains, responded with Lives of Jesus, which eschewed supernatural or superhistorical explanations but sought to do justice to the uniqueness of Jesus' life and teaching in historical fashion, though the uniqueness that came to light—that of the unifying consciousness underlying his actions and teachings—might be one that transcended historical explanation. To the extent that historical investigation could grasp Jesus, however, his uniqueness and miraculousness could only be that of any other historical phenomenon. To this extent, therefore, it was difficult to reconcile thoroughly historical inquiry into Jesus with claims to his unique divinity. For historical understanding insists, Frei wrote, "that the uniqueness of an event is in no way a denial of its explicability through its interconnectedness with other events."[3] In consequence, if divine providence

---

2. Frei, "Niebuhr's Theological Background," in *Faith and Ethics: The Theology of H. Richard Niebuhr,* ed. Paul Ramsey (New York: Harper & Row, 1957), 21.

only appears in the spiritual uniqueness of every event, explicable in its interrelations with others, it becomes hard to consider Jesus of Nazareth as the focus of a unique divine revelation that is the clue to all history. This is precisely the problem we found in Troeltsch and whose implications for the theology of Scripture we drew out in Chapter 1. Hence arises Frei's question, cited in that chapter: "Is it possible to combine faith in an ultimate Creator and Redeemer, who limits space and time beyond all conceiving, with the 'open-ended' and in its way uniform historical universe which historical consciousness presents to us?"[4]

Frei returns to this issue when he examines Troeltsch's theology toward the end of the essay. Troeltsch appears here as the critic of nineteenth-century German academic theology in its tendency to seal itself off from philosophy and historical method through an agnostic epistemology.[5] As Frei represents him, Troeltsch thought that theology could not avoid contact with historical investigation entirely. Methodologically speaking, both religious knowledge and historical method rest on *a priori* structures in the self, and discover their content in historical particulars. They therefore also share a common focus on these objective historical particulars, from their different perspectives. Troeltsch therefore concluded that historical method was ultimately congruous with the human quest for the infinite and universal through the particular, that is, "through the intuition of each historical-spiritual occurrence."[6] But neither approach, the historical or the religious, can be readily reconciled with Christianity's claim to absolute validity based on historical events of absolute uniqueness. In Frei's view, it was thanks to Troeltsch that theologians have had and continue to have to face this problem. It was a problem of which Frei remained aware at different stages in the development of his writing.

Frei was also aware of some of its implications for the theological reading of the Bible as Christian Scripture. Thus part of Frei's story in *The Eclipse of Biblical Narrative* has to do with the breakdown of premodern ways of reading the Bible as an all-encompassing account of the real world. That breakdown Frei traces to a shift in outlook, going back to seventeenth-century scholars, in which the biblical stories, instead of providing the framework for understanding the world, came to be understood and their truthfulness assessed against an independently constructed schema of history: a shift whose product was historical criticism.[7] Premodern ways of reading the Bible as a unitary

---

3. "Niebuhr's Theological Background," 24.
4. "Niebuhr's Theological Background," 24.
5. "Niebuhr's Theological Background," 54.
6. "Niebuhr's Theological Background," 55.

canon, and the world in light of its witness, became untenable in these new circumstances, and theologians struggled to find new ways of demonstrating the historicity or relevance of biblical stories whose meaning was now thought of primarily in terms of true or false factual reports. In these ways, the shift brought an end to a distinctively Christian and biblical way of understanding history as shaped by God's providence and of understanding the significance of Christ and his work.[8]

A later essay on David Friedrich Strauss provides further evidence of Frei's understanding of the implications of historical consciousness for the theological reading of Scripture, which analysis would seem to lie in the background to many of the writings and lectures of his final years.[9] There Strauss appears as a paradigm of modern historical thinking, for whom historical inquiry generalizes "our present uniform experience of the natural cause-effect connections between natural events."[10] This experience constituted a law, so generalizable that any narrative that violates it could be deemed unhistorical. Strauss prioritized historical science over theology and used criteria of historicity to distinguish factual from mythical narrative in the Gospels and to reconstruct a life of Jesus as a deluded fanatic, who at first considered himself the successor to John the Baptist, later believed himself the Messiah who would inaugurate the kingdom through divine intervention, and finally came to believe that his own suffering and death were necessary preliminaries to this event.[11]

For Frei, Strauss's own work thus pressed the question of the relationship between theology and historical inquiry in respect of the interpretation of the Gospels. The sharpness of that challenge was underlined by Strauss's criticism of Friedrich Schleiermacher's evaluation and exegesis of scriptural sources in his own *Life of Jesus*. Schleiermacher's need to show the compatibility of theology with historical inquiry and the identity of faith in Christ, the source of the believer's awareness of redemption, with faith in the historical figure of Jesus

7. Frei, *The Eclipse of Biblical Narrative: A Study in Eighteenth and Nineteenth Century Hermeneutics* (New Haven: Yale University Press, 1974), 4–5.

8. As described, for example, in *Eclipse*, 31.

9. In the introduction to the Shaffer Lectures that Frei delivered at Yale Divinity School in 1983 and in which he first presented the typology that was to be the preliminary to a much larger work on modern Christology, Frei presents his ideas as a response to the issues of faith and history raised by Strauss with respect to Jesus Christ. See Frei, *Types of Christian Theology*, ed. G. Hunsinger and W. C. Placher (New Haven and London: Yale University Press, 1990), 11.

10. "David Friedrich Strauss," in *Nineteenth Century Religious Thought in the West*, vol. 1, ed. N. Smart, S. Clayton, and S. T. Katz (Cambridge: Cambridge University Press, 1985), 232.

11. "David Friedrich Strauss," 237.

of Nazareth skewed his historical criticism of the Gospels. This need ended up seriously distorting Schleiermacher's historical judgment of the authenticity of sources and their witness to historical events. Strauss's own position was the one that Troeltsch would later give: "a person cannot at one and the same time be an absolutely unique manifestation of the divine life and fully a part of the nexus of history as are other human beings."[12]

As Frei rightly points out, this judgment restates the ancient Christological problematic in terms made more urgent by the questions raised by historical consciousness. Once Strauss had abandoned his own attempt to clarify the philosophical truth wrapped in Christianity's primitive mythical way of thinking, historical criticism became the sole test of the dogma of Christ.[13] On Frei's account, therefore, Strauss presents us with the choice of either accepting the largely mythological and hence largely unhistorical Christ of the New Testament and subsequent Christian tradition, or settling for a historical reconstruction of Jesus' life that bears little resemblance to the divine-human central figure of Christian devotion and doctrine. The Christological problematic in its modern form would be central to Frei's own way of addressing the problems raised by historical consciousness, the problems articulated so clearly by Strauss and Troeltsch. He did not think the options were limited to the unpalatable either-or that Strauss puts to the modern Christian theologian.

The Gospels, Realistic Narrative, and Identity Description

Frei's most significant contribution to addressing these issues is found in his book *The Identity of Jesus Christ* and in the earlier essays on which it is based. Frei describes his project, in a lecture called "Remarks in Connection with a Theological Proposal," as the search for an alternative to what he saw as a modern tradition of apologetic theology focused on anthropology and Christology, then being continued in a form by what he called "the new interest in hermeneutics."[14] Nevertheless, in the course of his thinking, he also developed an alternative way of looking, theologically, at history.

Frei sought a nonapologetic, nonperspectivalist approach to the question of the essence of Christianity, concerned with the logic of Christian belief.[15]

12. "David Friedrich Strauss," 254.

13. See "David Friedrich Strauss," 225–33, 238–41.

14. "Remarks," in *Theology and Narrative*, ed. G. Hunsinger and W. C. Placher (New York: Oxford University Press, 1993), 27. The lecture was originally delivered at Harvard Divinity School in December 1967, as the editors report.

Frei was concerned with the possibility of grounding a description of the logic of Christian belief on a reading of scriptural texts whose character would allow them to yield interpretations normative for Christian faith when approached in terms that did not distort their meaning.

To this end, he proposed starting with what he called "realistic narratives" in the synoptic Gospels. This focus on the Gospels indicates that he is operating with a basically Christocentric orientation to the question of the essence of Christianity, and that it is the centrality of Jesus Christ to Christian faith.[16] When he later comes to examine the eclipse of realistic narrative in modern biblical interpretation, he argues that realism is a feature of "many of the biblical narratives that went into the making of Christian belief," and it is clear as he proceeds that the Gospels are of prime interest because of the centrality of Jesus Christ to that belief.[17] Frei, then, did not simply begin with a theory of narrative, nor did he make it the foundation for his theology; he is rather concerned to describe an important feature of stories central to Christian faith and practice, one that can help reorient modern theology.

These narratives were what Frei also called "aesthetic or quasi-aesthetic texts," which he thought could yield normative interpretations.[18] His use of these terms makes best sense as denoting that which, when we read such a narrative, is given to the imagination as the object for our understanding: that which we first become aware of when we read. Such an appearance is already ordered for us in the structure of the narrative, and hence in this sense Frei asserts that "the formal structure of the narrative itself is the meaning."[19] In this respect, Frei saw a commonality between how meaning and understanding work with respect to the narrative structure of parts of the Gospels and the way they work with respect to narrative structure in nineteenth-century realistic

---

15. "Remarks," 30–31.

16. As Higton and Paul DeHart both rightly point out, we can trace Frei's interest in pursuing a narrative Christology to his praise of H. R. Niebuhr's moral approach to the person of Christ in *Christ and Culture* in his "The Theology of H. Richard Niebuhr," in Ramsey, ed., *Faith and Ethics*, 107–16. See DeHart, *The Trial of Witnesses: The Rise and Decline of Postliberal Theology* (Malden, MA; Oxford: Blackwell, 2006), 10, and Higton, *Christ, Providence and History*, 65–66. The insight that one could take a similar approach and combine it with Erich Auerbach's category of realistic narrative in order to produce a high Christology from the Gospels seems to have been Frei's. Frei may, Higton thinks, also have taken a hint from Barth's treatment of Christ's humanity in his *Church Dogmatics* III/2 and IV/1–2, which Frei commends in the same article.

17. *The Eclipse*, 10.

18. "Remarks," 32. He was, he added a little later, interested in normative or valid interpretation of single texts (33).

19. "Remarks," 34.

novels (like George Eliot's *Middlemarch*) and in historical narrative works.[20] In the structure of all three kinds of narrative, Frei maintained, character, circumstance, and theme emerge in their mutual interaction and not apart from one another.[21] The characters and events are not simply illustrations of a moral theme; the theme cannot be restated in abstraction from the interactions of characters and circumstances; there is no access to the character of historical agents apart from their involvement with others and in the events of the story. (It is worth stressing the limited terms of this comparison with the novel, and highlighting that it stands alongside an equally limited comparison with historical writing, for some have misunderstood Frei to propose the novel as the paradigm for reading biblical narrative.)[22]

What, therefore, is given to the imagination in the reading of such narratives as the object for our understanding is usually sequential interaction of characters and circumstances. In this sense, such narratives are quasi-aesthetic on analogy with the way intuitions, to which thought attends, are related to objects through sensation, and the ordered appearance of the object is its form, according to Immanuel Kant in his account of the Transcendental Aesthetic.[23] Thus while it follows that there can be no meaning apart from readers to receive it, these would be texts in which "the meaning of the text remains the same no matter what the perspective of interpreters may be."[24] In such an instance,

20. "Remarks," 32 and 34. Eliot (Maryann Evans) translated Strauss' *Life of Jesus*. She would seem to embody the missed opportunity Frei senses in that the realistic meaning of the gospel narratives was not recognized in its own right by critics who attended to it, like Strauss, just at the time when realistic narrative was being developed in the English novel. See *Eclipse*, 142ff, 202ff.

21. "Remarks," 34. He gives the same account of realistic narrative in *The Eclipse of Biblical Narrative*, 13–15 and 280–81. Here (vii) he acknowledges the influence of Erich Auerbach's *Mimesis* (Princeton: Princeton University Press, 1953) in his understanding of literary realism.

22. For example, Nicholas Boyle thinks Frei claims eighteenth-century commentators failed to interpret the Bible like a nineteenth-century novel and that premodern readers read the Bible as though it was such a novel. See his *Sacred and Secular Scriptures: A Catholic Approach to Literature* (London: Darton, Longman & Todd, 2004), 60). John Milbank makes a similar point in respect of *The Identity of Jesus Christ* in his *The Word Made Strange* (Oxford: Blackwell, 1997), 149. Frei draws the comparison carefully with due regard for all the differences and denies a comprehensive analogy in "Theological Reflections on the Accounts of Jesus' Death and Resurrection," in *Theology and Narrative*, 59. The perception has been fed by one of the subplots of Frei's argument in *The Eclipse of Biblical Narrative*, namely, the failure of biblical commentators to explore the narrative interpretation of the Bible in the eighteenth century at a time when literary realism was emerging in France, England, and to a much lesser extent Germany. See *Eclipse*, chapters 7–10. He draws the analogy carefully with due attention to the differences in this work on 136–37.

23. *Critique of Pure Reason*, A19/B33–A21/B36.

24. "Remarks," 32.

rather than our interpretation being governed by our categories, we may find that in understanding such a text our categories become "scrambled" in ways we could not have predicted by means of a general theory, but must learn from the encounter with this specific text.[25] Something other to us, found in the text, might thus impinge on our understanding, and shape it.

In this way, Frei pleads in effect for a different priority choice to that advocated by Strauss, which would subordinate historical (and other forms) of inquiry to attention to the narrative as such. At this stage in his thinking, his reasons for this priority have to do with the genre of the texts: "to the extent that the gospel stories are . . . in the form of narratives, let us treat them that way when we ask about their meaning."[26] Later, as we shall see, he would concede that the narrative form of the text is not sufficient justification for this prioritization and would argue instead that Christian faith has particular reasons for making this priority choice. Frei also argues that his aesthetic approach yields a greater stability and normativity of meaning when contrasted with a prioritization of a historical approach with its speculative reconstruction of earlier forms of the gospel traditions (Frei was quite skeptical about the possibility of recovering a thick portrait of the historical Jesus "behind" the gospel portraits).[27] To some extent, the particulars of Frei's argument reflect the prevalence of form criticism in his context at the time of writing, but the observation that historical-reconstructive readings of the Gospels' stories of Jesus are more speculative than the basic structure of those stories is widely applicable even if one is less skeptical than Frei.

To advocate a different priority from Strauss is not necessarily to abandon questions of historicity. Where, though, might this approach leave the question of the historicity of the figure portrayed by the Gospels, or the wider questions raised by historical consciousness for theology? Some hints may be gleaned from *The Eclipse of Biblical Narrative*. There Frei is at pains again and again to argue that the meaning of realistic narratives cannot be reduced to a true or false factual report.[28] This claim, however, has led others to conclude that Frei thinks therefore that biblical narrative bears no relation to reality—that it is "non-referential" text, in Brevard Childs's words.[29]

Part of the answer lies in the particular mimetic qualities of realistic narrative in the Bible, which led Frei to use the term "history-like" alongside

---

25. "Remarks," 32.

26. "Remarks," 41.

27. For Frei's skepticism about the possibility of being able to say much about such the "historical Jesus" in this sense, see e.g. "Theological Reflections on the Accounts of Jesus' Death and Resurrection," in Frei, *Theology and Narrative*, 50.

"realistic" in *The Eclipse of Biblical Narrative*.[30] In *Eclipse*, Frei's descriptions of meaning in realistic narrative add a new dimension to his description in "Remarks," namely that the rendering of events and characters is by way of "the device of chronological sequence."[31] In this way, theme and character are rendered cumulatively. (Frei's use of "to render" here, as David Kelsey explains, means to make something concretely present to the imagination in its unsubstitutability; it is, we might add, a shorthand for the way realistic narratives function as aesthetic texts in respect of their subject matter.)[32] The depiction of characters and circumstances by their mutual interactions through chronological sequence renders a world that resembles the historical world of which we have become aware, with its interweaving of actions and events in a complex, continuous causal web of contingencies. This realism can be evaluated. For example, Erich Auerbach praises the stories of Abraham and others for their "greater depth of time, fate, and consciousness" than Homeric characters, the importance of the biblical characters' sense of their own history and its bearing upon them, and the evocation of their problematic psychological situations.[33] To appreciate these qualities in a story is to relate it to the world in which one lives and, in comparing them, to think about both more deeply.

Another part of the answer lies in the kind of referentiality that Frei ascribes to biblical narrative in *Eclipse*. There he cites Auerbach's characterization of Old Testament narratives as seeking "to overcome our reality: we are to fit our own life into its world, feel ourselves to be elements

28. The terms he uses to make this point are not especially helpful: Frei writes of biblical commentators and theologians confusing realistic meaning with meaning as ostensive reference (reference to a sequence in the spatiotemporal world). Frei does not mean that such thinkers confuse propositional meaning and truth. His point is perhaps better made in these terms: that such thinkers confused realistic narrative in the Bible with the kind of history writing whose propositional meaning is that of a factual claim that is either true or false. His point is that just as we are able to avoid that confusion in respect of another form of realistic narrative, namely the modern novel, so also we ought to be able to do so in respect of biblical narrative.

29. Childs, *Biblical Theology of the Old and New Testaments* (London: SCM, 1992), 19.

30. E.g. *Eclipse*, 10.

31. *Eclipse*, 13.

32. Kelsey, "Biblical Narrative and Theological Anthropology," in *Scriptural Authority and Narrative Interpretation*, ed. G. Green (Philadelphia: Fortress Press, 1987), 131. Paul Schwartzentruber claims Frei's use of the term "render" is evocative, signaling a chastened realism between naïve representationalism and the extravagant theories of the existentially disclosive powers of language in the hermeneutical tradition. See his "The Modesty of Hermeneutics: The Theological Reserves of Hans Frei," *Modern Theology* 8, no. 2 (1992): 187–88.

33. Auerbach, "Odysseus' Scar," in his *Mimesis* (Princeton: Princeton University Press, 1953), 12.

in its structure of universal history."[34] Everything else that happens in the world can only be conceived as an element in this divinely planned sequence. At one point Auerbach seems to affirm what Frei denies when the former says of the biblical stories that "their religious intent involves an absolute claim to historical truth."[35] He is actually expanding on the point just cited in a way that sheds light on Frei's position. The clue is the word "absolute." Auerbach has in mind what he also describes as a claim "to represent universal history."[36] Such a claim is not of the order of the documentation of discrete historical facts: "the world of the Scripture stories is not satisfied with claiming to be a historically true reality—it insists that it is the only real world."[37] In other words, these are texts that, in their particular narrative "realism" do not refer to a world we already think that we know so much as confront us with a new vision of that reality which, they seem to say, is the only or most true perspective. Frei's citation of Auerbach here implies he has this same notion in mind, and this inference is confirmed by the way he describes premodern literal reading: "since the world truly rendered by combining biblical narratives into one was indeed the one and only real world, it must in principle embrace the experience of any present age and reader."[38] Therefore "it was his duty to fit himself into that world in which he was in any case a member."[39] Frei thus recognizes a kind of truth-claim on the part of biblical narratives that distinguishes them from the kinds of truth-claim that might be made by realistic fictional narratives. To see just how Frei thought that claim works, we have to turn back to his constructive work, *The Identity of Jesus Christ* and to the earlier essay that it develops, "Theological Reflections on the Accounts of Jesus' Death and Resurrection."[40]

34. *Eclipse*, 3.

35. *Mimesis*, 14.

36. *Mimesis*, 16.

37. *Mimesis*, 16.

38. *Eclipse*, 3.

39. *Eclipse*, 3. Frei explains that premodern readers responded to this claim on the part of biblical narratives by way of figural interpretation of their experience, something that, we will see, he proposed reviving in *The Identity of Jesus Christ: The Hermeneutical Bases of Dogmatic Theology* (Philadelphia: Fortress Press, 1975).

40. More accurately, *The Identity of Jesus Christ* reproduced an extended version of the argument of "Theological Reflections" that was previously published as "The Mystery of the Presence of Jesus Christ" in *Crossroads*, 1965. "Theological Reflections" was first published in *The Christian Scholar* in 1964. See George Hunsinger, "Hans Frei as Theologian: The Quest for a Generous Orthodoxy," *Modern Theology* 8, no. 2 (April 1992): 103.

THE LIVING ONE: THE IDENTITY AND HISTORICITY OF JESUS CHRIST

In both works, Frei is attacking a range of targets, including proponents of the New Quest for the Historical Jesus, but also looking back to Strauss. His aim is to show that as portrayed in the narrative of Luke's Gospel especially, Jesus' identity emerges most clearly as an unsubstitutable individual in the passion-resurrection sequence. In this identification, Frei will argue, Jesus redefines the messianic and mythical titles and themes attributed to him in a nonmythical way, such is the force of his unsubstitutable individuality. There the question of historicity is pressed and answered in a way that cannot be vindicated by historical argument. Jesus is identified in such a way there as to yield a high Christology, to demand factual assent to his resurrection and to an identity so dense and extensive in its ramifications as to make a claim on every reader in their historical particularity.

Frei thus posits that the theme of the narrative sections of Luke is the identity of Jesus Christ, and he proposes two sets of categories by which to express, formally, that meaning. These are categories called for by the kind of narrative in question. For, he asserts in "Remarks," the interaction of character, circumstance, and theme through chronological sequence in realistic narrative entails a kind of anthropology. It yields characters in whom the "inner" and "outer" cohere, and in whom there is a basic unity to their intentions and actions, to the subject and its objective (for example, bodily) manifestation. This is a unity that cannot be explained (except speculatively) but can be described, up to a point, using certain formal categories.

For that descriptive task, Frei privileges the categories of intention and action because of their obvious fit with narratives that present the connections between intentions and actions in interactions with persons and circumstances, and that do not privilege the former over the latter in their descriptions. In such stories, persons are known "precisely to the extent" that they are what they do and what is done to them.[41] Characters are known to us as agents, and in that sense in a public way, he argues on Christological grounds in "Theological Reflections." We learn what a human being is from the New Testament, he claims, in part from its portrayal of Jesus of Nazareth. Its depiction of Jesus implies that a human being is "what he *does* uniquely, the way no one else does it," whether over a lifetime or at some climactic moment, or both.[42] So we may think, he continues, of some climactic stage in a person's life that either recapitulates a long span of life exhibiting that quality, or resolves several

41. "Remarks," 36.
42. "Theological Reflections," 57.

hitherto ambiguous strands in a clear, decisive way, and we say, here they were most of all themselves. "In that kind of passage from free intention into action, ordering the two (intention and act) into one harmony, a free man gains his being. He becomes what he is; he gains his identity."[43]

Identity is thus something we enact, cumulatively but (potentially) also climactically. To know another's identity is to recognize the individual way in which they hold together and enact their defining qualities.[44] One can identify people in this way, on the basis of their actions, because of the tough bond between the self and its embodied, physical, and social manifestation with particular personal qualities. So much, at least, Frei thought, the Gospels seem to assume. The body is central here as the means for the direct connection of intention and its enactment, which allows this kind of understanding of another.[45] So strong is the bond that to describe an occurrence as an action is to describe an explicit intention; to describe an intention as such—and not just a putative mental "thing"—is to describe it as an implicit action.[46] There comes a point, however, when the categories of intention and action break down but description can continue. For while these categories can describe how an occurrence of another's action comes to figure someone's intentional action, it cannot help us describe how through the interactions of events and characters events become part of characters' identities, something so particular that there is no categorical scheme that can anticipate it: one can only tell the story. In some cases, characters are so uniquely shaped by this tightly woven interaction that we know them through their story, and so it is, Frei claims, with Jesus. "He is who he is by what he does and undergoes," especially in his crucifixion and resurrection.[47] Such description seems appropriate for attending to how realistic narrative renders unique individuals in and through their interactions with others and with circumstances over time: individuals who thus seem to bear analogy with historical particulars as Troeltsch understood them.

This kind of description is not exhaustive. Intentional agents know themselves to precede particular actions and to endure after them without thereby preceding or succeeding *themselves*, so there is more to identity than

43. "Theological Reflections," 57. Frei makes the same point in more formal terms a little later on in the essay: "Identity is essentially the action and testimony of a personal being by which he lays true claim to being himself and the same at an important point as well as over a length of time" ("Theological Reflections," 59).

44. "Theological Reflections," 62.

45. "Theological Reflections," 62–63.

46. Here Frei ("Theological Reflections," 63) cites Gilbert Ryle, *The Concept of Mind* (New York: Barnes & Noble, 1962), 40: "to perform intelligently is to do one thing and not two things."

47. "Remarks," 37.

intention and action: a kind of ultimate yet elusive persistence to which the term "I" is attached. We need a way of describing this "ascriptive subject," but it will have to be indirect and retrospective—we cannot catch the self "in the act," as it were—yet conveying the prospective orientation of the subject.[48] Frei's favored scheme for doing so is the manifestation of the self through a medium that is at once distinct from the self and identical with it. Thus in some utterances, a speaker is wholly present in the words with which he identifies himself, as in performative utterances ("I promise") and some kinds of rhetoric, or, paradigmatically, the use of one's name.[49] The same applies to the body: we speak of "having" a body, implying differentiation between self and body, and yet we identify ourselves routinely with our bodies ("I went to the shops today"). Since no supertheory is available to reconcile these different schemes, we must use both.

"Who is Jesus" is a persistent question in the Gospels, and his identity is profoundly ambiguous. That ambiguity, Frei explains, is resolved in the passion-resurrection sequence. There Jesus' identity as the singular, unsubstitutable human individual that he is comes to sharpest focus. For in the passion sequence we find the climactic summing up of his characteristic intention of love toward his fellow human beings, to perform their good on their behalf, in obedience to God.[50] This is where the unique way in which he holds all his qualities and predicates becomes clearest. For it is only then that Jesus' submission to God's will, beginning at Gethsemane, is irreversibly enacted, as his submission expressed in the Garden implies ("Father, if you are willing, remove this cup from me; yet not my will but yours be done").[51] Here we have a clear statement of Jesus' intention in obedience to God, to which his words at the Last Supper also point, and which we see enacted through the course of his passion.[52]

In the resurrection sequence, Jesus' identity as the ascriptive subject of his story is resolved.[53] In the infancy narratives, Jesus' identity is wholly defined in terms of the people of Israel, for example, in the use of Hos. 11:1 ("out

---

48. "Theological Reflections," 64–65.

49. Frei argues in "Remarks" that speech-acts only make sense in the context of embodied enacted intentions (36).

50. "Theological Reflections," 51 and 57, cf. 59.

51. Luke 22:43.

52. Cf. *Identity*, 111: "To be obedient to God was to pour out his blood in behalf of men." The words of institution in their context in Luke 22:14-23 clearly refer to Jesus' "passion," before which he will be "betrayed," and there he tells us that his body is given for and his blood poured out for the disciples, enacting a new covenant, and according to God's will, for it has all "been determined."

53. "Theological Reflections," 74.

of Egypt have I called my son") in Matt. 2:15.[54] The abundance of legendary material means that here neither historicity nor history-likeness are appropriate categories for understanding these passages, though there is a sense of history in the fulfillment of patterns of meaning summing up Israel's past.[55] From the baptism onwards, Jesus "appears in a limited way as an individual in his own right," as by his deeds and teachings he represents the "direct and immediately pending rule of God."[56] He remains, though, a heavily symbolic figure, identified by his titles in relation to the Kingdom, rather than the reverse. In his preaching and mighty deeds, he embodies and attests the Kingdom in such a way that it defines him.[57] The history-likeness of the portrayal of Jesus' public ministry "raises the question of historical veracity in acute fashion."[58] However, resolving those questions is quite speculative, given how closely Jesus' individual identity is bound up with the Kingdom and in the absence of external, corroborating evidence.[59] Whatever our knowledge of the cultural background, it is difficult to determine what Jesus actually did and said, and how much "is stylized account, illustrative of his representational character and the author's beliefs."[60]

It is the last stage of the story that is most history-like and it is also where the question of historicity arises most sharply. As Frei asserts, "the question of historical likelihood is bound to arise in the case of the most history-like or sharply individualistic reports."[61] That is to say, it makes most sense to ask the questions "did it happen (to him)?" or "did he do it?" where we have a clear idea of who it is we are talking about at least so far as to distinguish the particular event and individuals concerned. It does not follow, of course, that because we have a life-like description of an individual enmeshed in events that the happening carries historical probability, only that we can pose the question more clearly.

In the passion-resurrection sequence that begins with Jesus' announcement that he and the disciples will go to Jerusalem where death awaits him, however, Jesus' individuality is more fully developed: he and the events connected with him "are what they are unsubstitutably and gain all their significance from

54. *Identity*, 128.
55. *Identity*, 132.
56. *Identity*, 130.
57. *Identity*, 131.
58. *Identity*, 132.
59. *Identity*, 132.
60. *Identity*, 132.
61. *Identity*, 141.

being this specific series of linked circumstances and no other."[62] In this sense, this part of the story is the most history-like. Here Jesus is who he is in his interaction with other characters and circumstances, displaying the kind of immersion in a web of contingent events and actions that also characterizes the world seen historically. Jesus is still identified by the Kingdom but in such a way that his own individual destiny begins to displace that theme and problematize the identification. The titles that go with it, moreover, begin to take on an ironic and pathetic cast in application to Jesus as they seem increasingly incongruous to the figure who embodies them, and in this way the focus falls increasingly on him in his singularity.[63] The puzzlement of the disciples at Jesus' turn to Jerusalem to face death and resurrection (Luke 18:34) reflects this new ambiguity in his relationship to the theme of the Kingdom and the titles that went with it.

This part of the story is where the question of historicity can most aptly be asked of the story. It is that "*if* the story or text and history are to coincide directly at any point, then it will have to be in the last stage of the story."[64] It is no objection that the narratives at this point continue to be laced with figural connections to the Old Testament, for as Frank Kermode points out, in the passion sequence the result of these connections still creates an impression of realism, like the apparently fortuitous action of the soldier piercing Jesus' side.[65] They do not, therefore, detract from Jesus' individuality but rather gain specificity from his story, as Frei says of earlier typological connections and christological titles.[66] We should note, then, that whereas Gottlob Frege and others discuss reference in respect primarily of proper names, Frei addresses the issue at the level of the narrative pattern that individuates and identifies Jesus and supplies a description of the content of his name.[67]

What is notable about this last stage of the story, Frei claims, is that Jesus is increasingly closely identified in relation to God, without ever being simply identified with God. This pattern of identity is complex. On the one hand, we have to take account of the coexistence of power and powerlessness in Jesus, that is to say, the coincidence of the circumstances that constrict him,

---

62. *Identity*, 133.

63. *Identity*, 133–34.

64. *Identity*, 141.

65. Kermode, *The Genesis of Secrecy* (Cambridge, MA: Harvard University Press, 1979), 109ff.

66. *Identity*, 135–36.

67. See for example Frege, "On Sense and Reference," trans. M. Black; Bertrand Russell, "Descriptions"; and P. F. Strawson, "On Referring," all in A. W. Moore, *Meaning and Reference* (Oxford: Oxford University Press, 1993).

to the point of death, with his abiding initiative. I have already referred to Gethsemane, where Jesus gives himself up to the will of God and subsequent arrest; the same sense of obedience is also implied at the Last Supper.[68] To this intention also several other sayings attest, like Jesus' declaration of his mission in the words of Isa. 61:1.[69]

The abiding initiative of Jesus is attested, Frei notes, in his response to Pilate's question, are you the King of the Jews.[70] "You have said so," is Jesus' reply, and thereby he actively turns the governor's question into unwitting testimony to himself, the Christ.[71] In Luke's account of the crucifixion, moreover, there are "several sayings that testify to Jesus' abiding initiative in and even over the circumstances that hold him in thrall."[72] The promise to the thief that he should be with Christ, and "his active placing of his spirit in the hands of God (Luke 23:43, 46) are instances of this sort."[73] The Fourth Gospel makes this theme explicit when the writer has Jesus say that he willingly lays his life down and no one takes it from him, and in the triumphant cry on the cross that it is finished.[74] The coexistence of this abiding initiative with powerlessness is attested by the rulers' ironically accurate observation, "he saved others, he cannot save himself."[75]

There is, nevertheless, a transition from power to helplessness, "from a certain liberty of action to an equally certain elimination of it," which is effected as much by Jesus' consent to its beginning as the authorities' prosecution of it.[76] This transition is most clearly seen in Jesus' words in Matthew to the effect that, if he chose, twelve legions of angels would come to his defense.[77] Here power passes "to [Jesus'] accusers and judges, together with all the complicated vested interests they represent."[78] Behind them, moreover, lies "a vast mass of humanity." Together, all these agents constitute "a wide span of what may be called 'historical forces.'"[79] These forces are, in the New Testament, sharply distinguished from "the ultimate, divine origin from which all action derives."

68. See n. 52 above.
69. So Frei, *Identity*, 111, referring to Luke 4:18.
70. Luke 23:46.
71. *Identity*, 112.
72. *Identity*, 112.
73. *Identity*, 112.
74. *Identity*, 112, referring to John 10:17-18 and 19:30.
75. As Frei notes, *Identity*, 115, citing Matt. 27:42.
76. *Identity*, 113.
77. Matt. 26:53-54, cited in *Identity*, 110.
78. *Identity*, 116.
79. The expression, Frei tells us, is Erich Auerbach's.

Yet "there is a mysterious and fascinating coincidence or 'mergence' between divine action and historical forces at their common point of impact—Jesus' judgment and death."[80] According to the story, God's intentions in respect of Jesus are realized through the actions of all these immanent, historical forces, a point that will be important when we consider the meaning of the resurrection.

This coincidence is clear in John, where Jesus tells Pilate he would have no power over him unless it was given him from above. "Something of the same theme," Frei says, "is indicated in Luke's reference to the fact that Christ 'should' have suffered 'these things' and then have entered his glory (Luke 24:26)."[81] All the Gospels and the book of Acts, moreover, "stress again and again that these events were appropriate, for the 'scripture must be fulfilled."[82] On the whole, he concludes, "there is clear indication of the will of God in the rising tide of events."[83]

Thus there is a coincidence of Jesus' intention being enacted by historical forces closely associated with the underlying action and will of God in and through them acting upon him. "Jesus' intentions and actions become increasingly identified with those of the very God who governs the actions of the opponents of Jesus who destroy him."[84] Yet Jesus maintains an initiative of his own, evidenced in the sayings on the cross. In them "Jesus' intentions and actions . . . retain their personal quality and weight."[85] What emerges therefore is "a motif of supplantation and yet identification." [86]Jesus' initiative and actions are superseded by God's, yet this supplantation is the enactment of Jesus' own intention in its abiding integrity.

This complex pattern—where Jesus' identity takes shape through his interaction with complex historical forces, comprising not only other characters and the particular events in which he encounters them, but the wider webs and patterns of interaction that are evoked by the narrative and shape those characters' behavior and the events that transpire—renders an account that is the most history-like of the whole sequence of the story, most akin to the historical world described by Troeltsch. It is a sequence in which contingent particulars are thoroughly interrelated, causally, including human agency, yet yielding unique individuality. Yet the history-like sequence of the passion is

80. *Identity*, 116.
81. *Identity*, 117.
82. Ibid.
83. *Identity*, 117.
84. *Identity*, 118.
85. Ibid.
86. Ibid.

one whose complex contingent interactions in their broad scope and highly particular focus are coincident with divine will. The action of God is veiled.[87] Yet it underlies the contingent events in all their complexity in a mysterious, hidden way. It is, we might say, a kind of activity of a wholly different order to that which coincides with it, with which it is not in competition. It is the action of a God who (as Frei reminds us in a later text) is, as Thomas Aquinas said, beyond genus and species: very much unlike us.[88]

The revolutionary force of this portrayal, however, only emerges with the depiction of the resurrection and the full disclosure of Jesus' identity as a particular person in whom the particular identity of all other historical agents takes shape and force. For the pattern we have just been reviewing is clarified and intensified in the resurrection, where the evangelists' "increasing stress on the rising curve . . . of God's activity over that of Jesus reaches its apex."[89] Here above all, God alone is active and yet in a completely veiled fashion. Only God could have raised Jesus, and only God did so, as Luke has the apostles attest (Acts 10:40; 2:32; 3:15; 4:10).[90] Yet "it is *Jesus* and Jesus alone, who appears just at this point, when God's supplantation of him is complete."[91] In his death, Jesus stands in need of redemption, says Frei. The need is answered in the resurrection; it is, in the story, the same character who dies and is raised. Crucially, "where God alone is active, it is Jesus alone who is manifest," just at the point where his identity is crystallized in the story.[92] Therefore at this point "Jesus of Nazareth, he and none other, marks the presence of the action of God."[93] Just when Jesus is most clearly identified, then, he is most closely identified with and at once distinguished from, God. In the unity and transition from death to resurrection, "Jesus' identity is focused, and the complex relation and distinction between his identity and that of God is manifested."[94]

Frei believes that it is just at the resurrection accounts that the question of historicity arises in the narrative itself, and on its own terms. The resurrection is the "climax" of that story. Therefore the resurrection account, "by virtue

---

87. "Theological Reflections," 80.

88. "Response to "Narrative Interpretation," in Frei, *Theology and Narrative*, 209.

89. *Identity*, 119–20.

90. Hence Mark Bowald's claim that Frei introduces divine agency to bridge the gap between the textual Jesus and the world of the reader in violation of his hermeneutical commitment to the identity of Jesus rendered in Scriptural narrative seems misplaced: *Rendering the Word in Theological Hermeneutics: Mapping Human and Divine Agency* (Aldershot: Ashgate, 2007), 53.

91. *Identity*, 121.

92. *Identity*, 135.

93. *Identity*, 121.

94. *Identity*, 121.

of its exclusive reference to Jesus, and by virtue of its claim that here he was truly manifested in his human particularity, allows and even forces us to answer the question, 'Did this actually take place?'"[95] Remember that in the Gospels, according to Frei, Jesus "becomes who he is in the coincidence of his enacted intention with the train of circumstances in which the story comes to a head."[96] He is "identified as well by his initiation of circumstances, his response to them, and their sheer impingement upon him."[97] Jesus' identity emerges in the very enmeshment with contingent events and others' actions that characterize our own experience of life, and the resurrection does not depart from that pattern, but completes it. So history-like is the narrative, so sharply does it individuate Jesus as a particular human being, that in respect of its climax, we are also forced to come to terms with the seriousness of the narrative: it seems to force the question of the factual status of the meaning of the narrative.

The Gospels, Frei asserts, sometimes portray the identity of Jesus, with fiction-like insight into his person (at Gethsemane) where the question of historicity "is not even pertinent."[98] Nevertheless, "throughout the narrative, and most particularly at the crucial climax of the resurrection, fictional description, providing direct knowledge of his identity in, with, and through the circumstances, merges with factual claim."[99] The narrative is, he adds, fictional in form, historical in intention. Frei frames this intention in a way that deliberately echoes Anselm of Canterbury's double negative description of divine identity: according to the story, Jesus cannot be thought not to be alive. The Gospels, Frei thought, seem to depict Jesus in such a way that "to know *who* he is in connection with what took place is to know *that* he is."[100] It is inconceivable, for these stories, to think of Jesus as anything other than risen. His identity is the one who died and rose again. This claim is implied by the question of the "two men" in Luke 24:5: "Why do you seek the living among the dead?"[101] John's Gospel puts it more forcefully: "I am the resurrection and the life."[102]

The answer as to whether this particular realistic narrative seeks to describe a real event emerges from its own meaning and the force of its identification

95. *Identity*, 140.
96. *Identity*, 104.
97. *Identity*, 105.
98. *Identity*, 145.
99. *Identity*, 145.
100. *Identity*, 145.
101. *Identity*, 146, citing John 11:25.
102. *Identity*, 147.

of Jesus Christ. This answer is particular to the case of Jesus in the Gospels, moreover: there is no general theory of the historical reference of biblical or any other realistic narrative. Frei recognizes the absurdity of claiming that wherever you get highly realistic fictional identity the character identified "ought always to have lived a factual historical life."[103] The coincidence of history-like identity and factuality pertains uniquely to Jesus, whose identity is wholly identical with his factual existence. As Frei notes, the coincidence in Jesus of identity and existence recalls the coincidence of divine identity and existence (or presence) in Exod. 3:14-15: for God, to be the God of Abraham, Isaac, and Jacob is to be "I AM."[104] Likewise for Jesus to be and to be Son of Man and Israel's redeemer are the same thing. It is a similarity that, we might add, befits the inseparability of the identities of Jesus and the God of Israel.

Does Frei then reassimilate these narratives with reports on historical facts? He certainly holds that in the story's own terms "it is more nearly correct to think of Jesus as factually raised, bodily if you will, than not to think of him in this manner."[105] It is also true to say that "because it is more nearly factlike than not, reliable historical evidence *against* the resurrection would be decisive."[106] In other words, it is part of the meaning of the resurrection that it had to happen, and as such, decisive evidence of its nonoccurrence would disprove it. But so to say does not necessarily mean that the gospel narratives are reducible to straightforward factual reports, for just in order to explicate the significance of the real historical event, the evangelists might introduce fictive history-like elements, like the interviews with Pilate or the fate or even character of Judas, or change chronology, as John does with the day of the crucifixion, or apparently supply details just because they fulfill Old Testament figures.[107] Yet these details, whether or not in themselves factual, contribute to the portrayal of the identity of one who must, in that identity, be historical and risen from the dead. Whatever the precise details of his actual passion, it is the details we have that convey Christ's identity to us, and no others. For it is notable that Frei produces an account of Christ's identity that entails a real historical happening that follows a shape given by the narrative in Luke, but that is, as a narrative shape, not necessarily dependent on the factuality of all the details.

To accept the claim of the Gospels that Jesus' identity entails his existence is not a matter of demonstrating historical probability. The Gospels do not

103. *Identity*, 145–46.
104. *Identity*, 149.
105. *Identity*, 150.
106. *Identity*, 151.
107. These examples are all from Frank Kermode, *The Genesis of Secrecy*, 84–99, 109ff.

attempt such a demonstration, nor could there be historical evidence that would make belief in Jesus' resurrection more plausible. For, as Frei asks, "To what historical or natural occurrence would we be able to compare the resurrection—the absolute unity of factuality and identity? None."[108] Rather, such belief is internal to the logic of faith—where that logic is normatively set forth in narrative identification of Jesus. It is a matter of faith attaining understanding. For the believer, Frei says in his "Remarks," the coincidence of the meaning and truth of the story is not a problem in the way it is for the nonbeliever.[109] In the absence of historical evidence to disprove the resurrection, "it seems proper to say that there is a kind of logic in a Christian's faith that forces him to say that disbelief in the resurrection of Jesus is rationally impossible."[110]

The difference of this historical fact-claim from all others is further borne out by the difference involved in affirmation of its truth in another way. Frei says it is not an ordinary fact, not "simply denotative of something in reality, but overwhelmingly affective ("existential"), as befits a unique fact that is unlike other facts in being at the same time an absolute personal impingement."[111] Apprehension of Christ's presence, unlike any cognizance of any other fact, is a matter of complete commitment.[112] For "grateful love of God and neighbor is the proper manner of appropriating the presence, based on the resurrection of Jesus, who in perfect obedience to God enacted men's good in their behalf on the cross."[113] Here faith and assent "by the mind constrained by the imagination" are identical.[114] Thus one answers the question of the historicity of the resurrection in the affirmative by "a kind of thought movement similar to and reiterative of that of the original authors in which grateful discipleship and factual acknowledgment seem to have been . . . one and the same act."[115] The story the Gospels tell delivers to the imagination a rendering of Jesus Christ as one who cannot but live, having died on our behalf, and the faithful imagination "constrains" the mind to factual assent and grateful discipleship marked by love of God and neighbor, in imitation of the obedient love of Christ for human beings. The acknowledgment of Christ's identity as the presence of

---

108. *Identity*, 151.

109. "Remarks," 43.

110. *Identity*, 151.

111. "Theological Reflections," 83.

112. *Identity*, 146.

113. *Identity*, 146.

114. *Identity*, 146.

115. *Identity*, 147.

God and redeemer of Israel and the world entails an ethics of discipleship of the twin love of God and neighbor, by which, we may suppose, the participatory identification of oneself in relation to his identity is worked out in the everyday.

The discipleship entailed by the meaning of the story is affective and volitional, but it is also deeply connected to the believer's cognitive grasp of the story's truth. In his "Remarks," Frei describes the believing reader as a pilgrim, suggesting someone who has yet to reach the destination where everything may become clear and obvious. To such a person, who concedes the story's demand for assent to its factuality—for one who reads in faith, we might say—grasping the possibility of the truth of the story, seeing its deep rationality and plausibility, is more often a matter of "the surprising scramble of our understanding and life that this story unaccountably produces," of the existential commitment that its storied pattern demands.[116] The plausibility and sense of the story emerge as we live out in obedience the demands it makes upon us.

FREI'S CHRISTOLOGY IN *THE IDENTITY OF JESUS CHRIST*

This account of Jesus' identity entails a Christology evincing greater unity and ostensibly as high as Gregory's. Both stress the oneness of Jesus Christ; for both, Jesus of Nazareth is one with God in a unity that is intrinsic to the identity of both. Both, too, share a reticence to try to explain the union of divine and human in Jesus Christ. For Frei, as for Gregory, God matters intensely but is difficult to talk about.[117] For both, the divine action central to their accounts is mysterious and hidden, and transcends other forces in such as way as not to compete with them in causing events.[118] Gregory's sense of the infinity and incomprehensibility of God and so of the partial, fragmentary nature of theological language seems a useful supplement or gloss upon Frei's talk of divine hiddenness.

There are also important differences. Gregory tends to read the narrative pattern of Christ's life in light of a developed theology of the incarnate existence of the divine Word, drawing both on Johannine and Pauline themes and a range of ontological and anthropological concepts to thicken the description.

116. "Remarks," 43–44.

117. So David Ford: Frei's combination of diffidence and definiteness "probably has much to do with his conception of the hiddenness and revelation of God." However it happened, "one tended to come away from any thorough theological engagement with Frei with the impression that God mattered more than anything." "Hans Frei and the Future of Theology," *Modern Theology* 8, no. 2 (1992): 211.

118. So also Ford, "Hans Frei and the Future of Theology," 211.

The oneness of Christ for him pertains to the unity of the Word and his humanity, extended through his actions and sufferings. For Gregory, Christ's oneness with God leads (with an apprehension of the Spirit's divinity) to sustained Trinitarian reflection on the God made manifest in Christ, and the unity and distinctions of the divine hypostases. For Frei, however, Johannine and Pauline Christological material is best understood as commentary upon and hence subordinate to the basic narrative pattern of Christ's identity in the story of his life, ministry, death, and resurrection.[119] Other concepts are likewise to be subordinated to the description of that pattern, rather than to a pattern of the condescension of the incarnate Word for the sake of the exaltation of human beings in him.[120] In *The Identity of Jesus Christ*, Frei eschews Trinitarian reflection, though his account of Christ's identity seems to lead in that direction given the complex pattern of union in distinction between Jesus of Nazareth and the God of Israel. He shows a far greater reticence than Gregory to describe conceptually the theological force of the identity of Jesus.

Frei's concentration on the narrative portrayal of Jesus' identity has distinct advantages in a modern theological context, and yields a pattern of identity in which divinity and historical humanity appear even more inseparable as presented to the imagination than in Gregory. George Hunsinger, however, has questioned whether Frei's emphasis on Jesus' humanity comes at the expense of the attribution of a fully divine identity. Until the resurrection, he argues, the unity of Jesus and God appears to be merely moral, that of a common intention, and is only fully realized in the resurrection, so risking both Nestorianism (God is not the ascriptive subject of Christ's acts) and Adoptionism (Christ becomes God at a point in the story).[121] Though Frei asserts the complex identification of God and Jesus, he is more convincing on their differentiation.

Part of the problem here is the need to bear with what Frei takes to be the way the Gospel narratives identify Jesus, namely, cumulatively. In the synoptic Gospels, as he notes, Christ's ascriptive identity—who he is—remains ambiguous until the resurrection, at which point it is manifested.[122] The ambiguity in question is the ambiguity attaching to the descriptions and prophecies that have hitherto been ascribed to Jesus in the story, such as "Son of Man." In other words, it is an ambiguity about who Jesus has been all along, not about who he will become, and it is resolved through manifestation and not enactment. Hence in *The Eclipse of Biblical Narrative*, in a passage Hunsinger

---

119. "Remarks," 43.

120. See his "Types of Academic Theology" in Frei, *Types of Christian Theology*, 124–25.

121. "Hans Frei as Theologian," 116.

122. "Theological Reflections," 81.

refers to in a footnote, Frei can say that the resurrection is "the affirmation that the whole of Jesus' self-manifestation is in fact the self-manifestation of God," a disclosure that necessarily belongs to the end of the story but embraces all of it retrospectively.[123] For Frei, the resurrection changes our perspective about Christ's ascriptive identity, not who he is in that sense.

Frei's argument that the risen Jesus is the presence of God does not rest on the moral unity of their intentions, but on his analysis of the resurrection. God, whose agency has remained veiled through the passion narrative behind historical forces, acts without secondary causes in the resurrection, but the embodied mode of its manifestation, its presence, is the risen Jesus Christ. In just this way, Jesus' own identity is made fully manifest also. The identity of God and the identity of Jesus are thus closely and inseparably united yet without confusion. It is not immediately obvious, however, why Jesus should be thought of as the embodiment of the divine presence on the basis that God raised him from the dead. The real force of Frei's argument lies in his assertion that the resurrection stories picture Christ as one who cannot be thought not to be alive, as the angels ask the women at the tomb: "Why do you look for the living among the dead?" (Luke 24:5).[124] The angels' reminder of Jesus' prophecy that the Son of Man would be handed over, crucified, and rise again, has more significance, Frei argues, than reprimanding the women for their forgetfulness. "It focuses his identity as one who lives, who is life, and not death. He lives as the one who cannot not live, for whom to be what he is, is to be," which is precisely also to be Jesus of Nazareth, the betrayed and crucified and risen.[125] The sense that Jesus is the manifest embodiment of the divine presence, moreover, is signaled by the narrative in various ways, including what John Webster calls his "odd aloofness" and unfamiliarity to his disciples, an index of his transcendent freedom and strangeness, and not least his announcement of the future proclamation of the forgiveness of sins in his name (who can forgive sins but God alone? Luke 5:21) and the disciples' worship of him (Luke 24:52).[126] Yet the risen Christ is still, the unity of the narrative sequence assures us (as does the risen Christ in Luke 24:39), the crucified Jesus and so still a historical figure, in the sense of someone constituted by what they do and undergo in contingent circumstances.[127]

---

123. *Eclipse*, 315. I owe this reference to Hunsinger, "Hans Frei as Theologian," 127, n. 21.

124. "Theological Reflections," 85.

125. "Theological Reflections," 85.

126. See Webster, "Response to George Hunsinger," *Modern Theology* 8, no. 2 (April 1992): 131.

127. "Theological Reflections," 76.

The result is an analysis of the Gospels' narrative portrayal of Jesus' identity as someone who, against Strauss, is both fully integrated into the nexus of historical causes *and* the manifestation of the absolute. Jesus as identified by the realistic narrative of the synoptics is neither a historical reconstruction constrained by the limits of historical-critical imagination nor a mythological figure, but something else: one who is fully historical (in the sense that Jesus is what he does and undergoes) and yet the presence of God.

We have seen this pattern adumbrated in Gregory's Christology; in Frei the integration of the strands of the pattern is much more complete. Such a portrayal only raises the question of how to reconcile this exceptional figure with our sense of the continuity and interrelated character of historical reality. Frei's way of answering that question is really bound up with his claim that the risen Jesus of Nazareth is the presence of God. It is a claim that asks for thicker description, as Gregory offered of his very similar claim that Christ is God made manifest in human flesh. Such thicker conceptual description will help secure the clarity and consistency of Frei's commitment to divine grace as the condition of atonement effected in and through Jesus of Nazareth, as John Webster rightly argues.[128] Frei's sense of the union in distinction of Jesus and God whereby Jesus can obey his Father in extremes of powerlessness yet be manifest as his presence, full of self-focused authority, requires, as Webster argues, that Frei needs to say more explicitly and forcefully what Rowan Williams says, that Jesus' identity cannot be grasped in its full reality "without allusion to God as *constitutively* significant for it," because his relation to God is constitutive of his whole identity—what he does, says, and undergoes from the beginning to the resurrection, seeing his enacted obedience in light of his divine identity as Son.[129] It requires that we think, with Gregory, of his historical human life as the human life of the Son of God, but press beyond Gregory to say that this historical human life in its *whole* pattern of obedient enactment and suffering as one sent by the Father is therefore a gracious expression of and participation in his Sonship, of the eternal *Logos* of divine love and compassion, which assumes and configures historical human existence as this particular human life that is the presence and Word of God for us. Yet in saying this we must not allow ourselves to think we can now speak of that Sonship independently of or in abstraction from the identity of Jesus of Nazareth; such talk is commentary on that storied identity. Any subordination

128. "Response to George Hunsinger," 130.

129. Williams, "Trinity and Ontology," in his *On Christian Theology* (Oxford: Blackwell, 2000), 156–57. See Webster, "Response to George Hunsinger," 131–32.

of that story to a conceptual description risks mitigating the strengths of Frei's proposal.

THE RISEN JESUS AND THE SHAPING OF IDENTITY

The significance of the resurrection, and of the identity of Jesus manifested there, is all embracing. Without transcending his particularity, it extends to every particular of history. If, according to the Gospels, Jesus must be thought of as alive and present, as the presence of God, then something is being depicted that is of wider significance than an assertion of another historical fact like others we could name: the Black Death, the invention of penicillin, the fall of the Berlin Wall. As Frei had implied in *Eclipse*, so he asserts here of the passion-resurrection sequence of Luke: the meaning of the history-like sequence asserts a claim about the very character and meaning of history, of the contingent interaction of character and circumstance, one that recasts our sense of ourselves, and demands a new way of living in response to it.

Frei develops this significance in a number of stages. The first has to do with the connection between Jesus' identity and his atoning work. As we shall see, Frei presents the risen Jesus Christ as one in relation to whom Israel and every human being is to be identified. Frei thus hints at a complete pattern of particular atonement as something accomplished by God and Christ in respect first of Jesus' own person and thereby on behalf of others: what he calls the "pattern of union through the agonized exchange of radical opposites."[130] He has already indicated this pattern earlier in the book, speaking of how in the Christian story Jesus redeems others by "the congruence or harmony of his helplessness with his perfect obedience, his moral purity," becoming "vicariously identified with the guilty in their need by undergoing their need in innocence and purity," referring to the vicarious suffering of the servant figure of Isaiah 53, and by citing Jesus' own statements to the same effect.[131] The nature of this identification is clear but not that of its vicarious quality, as George Hunsinger has argued.[132] Hunsinger further notes that while Frei talks of the coincidence of power and powerlessness in Jesus' identity, the latter is clearer than the former.[133]

---

130. *Identity*, 162.

131. *Identity*, 58, 69, and 111. I am indebted to Hunsinger, "Hans Frei as Theologian," 115 for these references.

132. "Hans Frei as Theologian," 115.

133. "Hans Frei as Theologian," 115, referring to *Identity*, 112.

In context, when Frei talks in *The Identity of Jesus Christ* of the coexistence of Jesus' power with his powerlessness as illuminating his saving efficacy, he is speaking of his obedience, his abiding initiative reflected in his assent to the accusation of being king of the Jews (Mark 15:2/Matt. 27:11/Luke 23:3), in promising the thief that he will be with him in paradise, and in placing his spirit in the hands of God (Luke 23:43, 46). Frei says of the latter that in this way the very circumstances that hold Jesus in thrall come to be at his service. This power, then, has to do with Christ's abiding obedience and purpose in going through his passion. In part, we can make sense of this power by saying that Jesus' obedience, his moral purity, allows an identification with the guilty that does not entail his own guilt, his own desert of that plight, and hence allows him to be justly delivered from it by the action of God in resurrecting him, a deliverance in which all those with whom he has identified himself are included. In this way Christ's passion becomes, through his obedience, an instrument of his saving work. However, this move does not make sense of the condition of possibility of the vicarious force of that identification. At this point, Hunsinger argues, one would expect some reference to Christ's divinity as what enables him to bear sin and guilt for others in a finished, unrepeatable way since Christian theologians have tended to argue that no merely human being may act on behalf of another in this regard.[134] He finds a more adequate account of the necessary coincidence of human helplessness and divine power in Frei's remark in the earlier "Theological Reflections" to the effect that Jesus' early followers believed that Christ's saving work was the work of omnipotence mysteriously congruent with Jesus' human helplessness.[135] For in that case, Hunsinger argues, God must be the ascriptional subject of Christ's acts and suffering, and Frei is committed to a Chalcedonian Christology.

Leaving aside the disputed question as to what a Chalcedonian Christology might be, Frei does indeed make the divine-human identity of Jesus essential to his saving work, but the way in which omnipotence is shown to work on his analysis of the resurrection narratives is complex, and not as straightforward as simply asserting, say, the infinite satisfaction afforded by his death in view of his divinity. As we have seen, Frei holds that in the Lukan narrative, Jesus is indeed manifest as the presence of God in his resurrection in such a way as to resolve the ambiguity of his identity: this is who Jesus is and has been. However, Jesus in his death is in real need, he suffers real powerlessness; he assents to this, and could at one point have called on God to prevent it, but at the point of death he is entirely subject to others. Yet in his resurrection Jesus is more than redeemed;

---

134. "Hans Frei as Theologian," 117.
135. "Hans Frei as Theologian," citing Frei, "Theological Reflections,"

he is revealed to be the redeemer, the embodiment of the power that raised him, himself the presence of God. It is this identity as the risen one who is the presence of God and yet also the crucified that gives vicarious force and efficacy to his death. His identity as the presence of God is such, so sure, Frei suggests, that the evangelists seem to think it will not allow us to think of human destiny as loss of identity or alienation, for "it is he and none other, Jesus the Son of God, who is the representative man, the second Adam, representative of human identity. . . . Because he has an identity, mankind has an identity, each man in his particularity as the adopted brother of Jesus."[136] The implication is that it is as Son of God, inseparable from who God is, that Jesus is the Second Adam, the representative human whose vicarious identification with us has made each of us his kin, whose destiny defines each of ours.

Hence it is in the first instance that Jesus sums up and brings to fulfillment the identity of Israel: "*That* he is and *who* he is—Jesus of Nazareth who, as that one man, is the redeemer undergoing in obedience all that constitutes the climax and summation of Israel's history—are one and the same thing."[137] Hence he can, after his resurrection, interpret in all the Scriptures the things concerning himself (Luke 24:27) (and hence, we might add, the Gospels introduce elements of the fulfillment of figures and prophecies into their narration). In this way, Jesus gives identity to Israel: "his identity is so unsubstitutable now through the event of resurrection that he can bring it to bear as the identifying clue for the community that becomes climactically focused through him."[138] Jesus as a member of Israel is fully identified with Israel, at once assuming that people's need of deliverance and enacting the obedience to which they were corporately called, who is delivered by God in resurrection and becomes in his own deliverance (and, we might add, justification) the one who gathers that community's identity up in himself as its Lord and God and so reconfigures their identity in relation to his.[139] Reconciliation with God seems to be implied on this account, given the stress on Jesus' vicarious obedience, meeting an implied human condition of sin

---

136. "Theological Reflections," 81.

137. *Identity*, 149.

138. *Identity*, 149, cf. "Theological Reflections," 74, where Frei says that ascriptive subject description "delineates the identity of the human individual, Jesus, at once as the manifestation of the presence of God acting and as the one who, having a true identity of his own, can bestow it without distortion on the community of Israel in which he is a member."

139. The dialectical nature of this reception and bestowal of Israel's identity problematizes David Dawson's suggestion that Frei's thought on this point is strongly supersessionist. See Dawson, *Christian Figural Reading and the Fashioning of Identity* (Berkeley, Los Angeles, and London: University of California Press, 2002), 177–78.

understood as disobedience resulting in death, suffering, and alienation from God.[140]

Hunsinger rightly points out that Jesus' identification with the guilty needs to be balanced by some movement in the opposite direction, in order to explain the saving efficacy of Christ's work. In fact, Frei hints at an application of Christ's own deliverance when he describes him as bringing his finished identity to bear to be the identifying clue for Israel so that it is focused through him. Given that identity is in part a matter of enacted intentions and the things that happen to us, and that identity is a way of describing the reality of characters, the implication of this claim would seem to be that the collective character of the community of Israel comes in some way to be identified—characterized—by Jesus' obedience and his deliverance. To make fuller sense of this language, we might take a clue from Gregory and amplify Frei's account by saying that Israel participates in Christ's own obedience, deliverance, and standing before God. In Frei's terms, however, how would such participation work in a realist, historical fashion? It would have to happen through the history of the community, by a degree of conformity on the part of its members to the pattern of Jesus' own identity. In part this conformity would take place in their own intentional actions and in part it would take place through receipt of some measure of the divine deliverance and justification enjoyed by Jesus in what happens to them.

This pattern of atonement, however, though particular to Israel is not limited to those who claim descent from Abraham, for Jesus' identity is such as to make a claim on *all* human beings: the New Testament asks *all* human beings "to identify themselves by relation . . . to Jesus of Nazareth, who has identified himself with them and for them."[141] This claim indicates the comprehensive scope of this pattern of atonement, to which Frei has already gestured. It begins with Jesus' identification and solidarity with human beings in their plight, thus linking him with them in their need. His singular deliverance at God's hand from that condition in the resurrection manifests him as inseparably one with God, as divine, and consequently those united with him in their need now find themselves called to understand and enact their lives in relation to who he is. His identity has become the clue to their identities. As Frei claims earlier in *Identity*, they find in respect of Jesus' singular identity that "their own specific and unsubstitutable identity becomes sharply accentuated by relation to Jesus' own identity."[142] As with Israel, participation through conformity to Christ's

---

140. To answer Hunsinger's legitimate point that Frei does not explain human sinfulness, "Hans Frei as Theologian," 115.

141. *Identity*, 149.

obedience and to his fate seem to be the missing logic that would help make sense of these claims. Where reconciliation there entailed configuration of the community of Israel, here it also seems to entail the configuration of individual lives in their actions and what they undergo, the deep marking of identities. There is indeed even a sense that individual identity becomes resolved through relation to Jesus: that he became who he is in what he did and underwent in such a unique way that in relation to him we become who we are truly intended to be. One crucial condition of possibility for this relation is that Jesus' own identity is inseparable from that of God and that this inseparability accentuates, rather than subverts, his particular identity as a human being.[143]

This account of atonement in terms of the configuration of identity has begun to indicate that Jesus' strange identity, as portrayed in the Gospels, as both enmeshed in historical contingency and yet the presence of God, is not isolated by its uniqueness so as to constitute a sheer interruption to the historical continuum, but seems to reach into the historical existence of other historical individuals and communities. To this extent Frei seems again to pick up a pattern we have found first in Gregory—including the importance of participatory conformity to Christ through intentional action—yet in a more thoroughly historical, realistic way and with two further advantages: Frei does justice to Christ being the redeemer of Israel, and second, Frei's formulations suggest that none are exempt from the scope of this historical redeeming significance.

To understand this account more fully, both as account of the efficacy of Christ's work and as an account of history and in particular to see how Frei might avoid the appearance of exacerbating the problem of Christ's uniqueness by linking him to other exceptions to the uniformity of historical causes—how indeed, as Hunsinger asks, Christ's finished work realistically can have *cosmic* scope, as Frei claimed it does—we need to turn to his account of providence.[144] In particular, we need to explore the meaning of his claim in his "Remarks" that the Gospels might offer an "incomplete clue" to the rest of history and a necessarily ambiguous clue to the experience of history, since in the Gospels Jesus *is* his story and his story somehow includes the story of God with him and all humanity.[145]

---

142. *Identity*, 133.

143. As I have learned from Dawson's reading of Frei, in *Christian Figural Reading*, 159f.

144. "Hans Frei as Theologian," 115, cf. *Identity*, 63.

145. "Remarks," 42–43.

Providence: Church, History, and the Pattern of Christ's Presence

What Frei means by the story of the gospel being an ambiguous clue to the rest of history becomes a little clearer in the last part of *The Identity of Jesus Christ*, where Frei discusses Christ's presence.[146] To speak of the identity of Jesus, according to the Gospels, is to speak of the presence of God, he reminds us.[147] He then seems to switch his mode of procedure. Having hitherto argued from the narrated identity of Jesus Christ in the Gospels, as the normative basis for understanding the logic of Christian belief, he now seems to switch to general descriptions of ordinary Christian discourse about the presence of Jesus, understood as the presence of the Jesus identified by the Gospels. That normative evangelical description, in other words, seems to become an interpretive guide to the right understanding of that discourse.

Hence when Frei begins to talk about the presence of Christ in between his resurrection and his future return, he talks about the way Christians talk about this presence—in terms of "Holy Spirit," and he explains the meaning of that language with reference to "the complex unity of which we have just spoken—that the unsubstitutably human figure, Jesus of Nazareth, and the presence and action of the God who superseded him [in the passion-resurrection sequence] are given together indissolubly from the climax of the Gospel story onward."[148] Christian believers use the language of Spirit to refer to Christ's presence as indirect: he is present by way of a spatiotemporal basis yet without being constrained by them (he is free in making himself present in this way). At this point, Frei returns us to the New Testament: the indirectness and mysteriousness of Christ's presence now is conveyed by the story of the ascension: Jesus had to withdraw before the Spirit could be given to the community of believers.[149] (Frei's use of the ascension narratives suggests that the rendering of the community of believers in Luke-Acts, the other Gospels, and the rest of the New Testament lies behind Frei's whole account here, in otherwise largely unspecified ways.) However, as David Demson and Mike Higton both argue, Frei's failure to attend explicitly to the narrative rendering of the identity of the disciples in relation to the identity and presence of Jesus in Luke-Acts and the other synoptics obscures something of the specificity of that relation and means his pneumatology and ecclesiology appear

146. As Hunsinger notes, the link from sense to meaningfulness is that from identity to presence, and is provided by Christ's work, "Hans Frei as Theologian," 120.
147. *Identity*, 154.
148. *Identity*, 155.
149. *Identity*, 156.

to emerge out of nowhere.[150] As Higton notes, thematizing Jesus' relationship with his disciples would have led him to be able to relate back other extraneous elements to the main body of his argument—for example, to introduce Word and Sacrament by way of the commissioning of the disciples and institution of the Eucharist; to introduce pneumatology by Jesus' promising and passing on of the Spirit to the disciples.[151]

The presence is really that of Jesus, Frei continues, as confirmed by Christians' understanding of Word and Sacrament as the spatiotemporal bases of his presence, on analogy with a person's verbal and physical presence. Christian talk of the Holy Spirit also names the unity of factual affirmation, commitment, and love "as the appropriate response to the unique unity of presence and identity that is Jesus Christ," discussed above.[152] Reference to the Spirit affirms that Christ's unique unity of identity and presence "calls forth a similarly unique response."[153]

Finally, this talk of the Holy Spirit as the indirect presence of Christ and God refers to the church as the witness to that indirect presence and its public, communal form. Frei's ecclesiology here is only briefly sketched, and complex. The heart of his proposal seems to be the claim that the church is best seen in Israel-like terms; as Israel finds herself and her history summed up, incorporated, and identified in Jesus Christ, so will the church one day. It moves toward an "undisclosed historical summing up," yet to be told in the manifest realization of the Kingdom.[154] Its persistent identity is supplied by the indirect presence of Christ through Word and Sacrament; they allow it a relatively permanent institutional structure necessary for the existence and endurance of communities. Its existence is constituted by its history, following Christ at a distance as a collective disciple, imitating without approaching his pattern of exchange: serving and accepting the enrichment given by its neighbor, the human world.

The church, then, is constituted not only by Christ's presence in Word and Sacrament, but also by his presence in the church's unity with human history.[155] For Christ is also indirectly present, Frei affirms, "in and to the shape of public

---

150. Demson, *Hans Frei and Karl Barth: Different Ways of Reading Scripture* (Grand Rapids: Eerdmans, 1997); Higton, *Christ, Providence and History*, 227–29. For Demson, this lacuna has hermeneutical consequences, as we shall see.

151. *Christ, Providence and History*, 229.

152. *Identity*, 156.

153. *Identity*, 157.

154. *Identity*, 159.

155. *Identity*, 157–58.

events of the world and of human history."[156] And the church so constituted bears witness to Christ as "the ultimate presence in and to the world in its mysterious passage from event to event in public history."[157] That history, and so the pattern of the church's identity, is incomplete, yet to be summed up in some future mode of Christ's presence, as Israel's was in him. This history is public, formed by the pattern of interaction between the church and humanity at large.[158] Christ's twofold presence to history, moreover, "means that history is neither chaotic nor fated, but providentially ordered in the life, death, and resurrection of Jesus Christ."[159] Somehow this particular event conditions all others.[160]

Frei makes similar claims in a later lecture on "History, Salvation-History, and Typology," but with a greater emphasis on the inclusion of the nonhuman world. He advocated that we should maintain a dialectic between the affirmation that God gives freedom to all his creatures and preserves the whole creation from ultimate loss or absurdity and the claim that in fulfillment of that creation and its radical redress in the face of evil, God "has focused his providence in the person of Jesus Christ in whom the reign of God has come near."[161] That reign, he adds, is "foreshadowed, not embodied, in the precarious existence of Christian community."[162] This last claim helps clarify the argument we have been examining: God's providential care is universal and this universal care is focused in Jesus Christ, the embodiment of God's rule, and foreshadowed in the church, which is what makes it a fragile witness to that wider providence. It is this providence, he adds, which embraces the realms of cosmos and history, the revealed unity of whose administration is "Jesus Christ as the all-governing providence of God."[163]

---

156. *Identity*, 157.

157. *Identity*, 158–59.

158. *Identity*, 161.

159. *Identity*, 161.

160. I am not persuaded that it follows therefore that, as Higton claims, the world is historical "*because* it is providentially ordered in Christ. The world is contingent, particular, creaturely, and finite precisely *because* it is the world upheld by the Word spoken in Jesus of Nazareth," and hence Frei can laugh fairly at Strauss because a theology of Christ's identity and figural relation to all that is is the condition of a historical world. See his *Christ, Providence and History*, 174. For the historical quality of temporal existence, theologically speaking, is secured by its being created, even if its actual configuration is Christ-focused.

161. "History, Salvation-History, and Typology" (*YDS* 18-278), 78. From: http://people.exeter.ac.uk/mahigton/frei/transcripts/Frei06-Typology.pdf, accessed 5/11/12 at 20.13.

162. "History, Salvation-History, and Typology," 78.

163. "History, Salvation-History, and Typology," 79.

This last comment suggests that Frei thinks of the providential ordering of history in Jesus Christ as something that pertains to his living to God: a configuration of divine action in respect of contingent creaturely interactions intimated by the scriptural language of Christ's session at the right hand of God's power (Luke 22:69). We seem to be invited to think of Christ, understood as the fully historical embodiment of a divine agency inseparable from that of God yet distinct from it, as the paradigm or governing principle of providential action on account of his atoning work—the representative not only of Israel but of all humanity and indeed the whole cosmos (a significance captured in scriptural language of Christ as second Adam and as recapitulating of all things).[164] For the implication of Frei's Christology is not only that Christ's identity is inseparable from God's, but that God's identity *and action* are now manifestly inseparable from Jesus Christ so that God acts through Jesus Christ in a way that accentuates human identity, that moves individuals as figures of Jesus Christ toward their particular eschatological fulfillments in him, and not only individuals but complex events and social entities.[165] In these claims, Frei in effect turns Troeltsch's principle of correlation on its head: it is true that all events, human and nonhuman, are complexly and contingently interconnected, but this interconnection has a center to which all else is mysteriously related and from which it takes its overall, as yet undisclosed configuration, the event of Jesus Christ.

It is in this sense, then, that the gospel story is an ambiguous clue to the rest of history and the meaning of our experience of it. As Frei goes on to say in *The Identity of Jesus Christ*, we see in a glass darkly here, yet we do see: we may find parables by which to narrate this unfinished pattern, to exhibit something of its order without comprehending the providential action of God. No image or parable can give us *the* clue, however, so various are sequences of events and so unexpected the ways in which they transpire. Frei gives two such parables, patterns that may yield some of the light afforded by the gospel story as an ambiguous clue to the meaning of history.

The first is Paul's sense of a mysterious fitness in the election of the Gentiles through the rejection of his own people, Israel (Rom. 11:29-32), in order finally to be included through that election. In similar vein, it may be that significant events happen among the "Gentiles," the wider human world from whom the

164. See e.g. 1 Cor. 15:21-28 (which links this representative function to Christ's rule of all things); the same connection is made in Eph. 1:1-23. Col. 1:15-20 connects this cosmocratic function with Christ's divinity and preexistence. See also Rom. 5:12-21

165. The point that in Frei's reading a divine agency independent of Jesus is folded back into Jesus' identity I owe again to Dawson, *Christian Figural Reading*, 163.

church as Israel and other, extraecclesial events may "bespeak the presence of Christ" in a more significant way than important ecclesial events.[166] His second parable is taken from Christ's own narrated identity. "Hints of the pattern of union through the agonized exchange of radical opposites do break forth in history."[167] The death of Christ is not simply transcended in his resurrection but remains a once-for-all occasion with its own objectivity. The same is true, Frei adds, "of all terrible sacrifices dimly setting forth the same pattern," so that there is hope if not full realization of the reconciliation, redemption, and resurrection toward which that pattern looks.[168] In some way, Christ will gather up all these appalling "blood sacrifices," without loss of their historical particularity and complexity and horror, and we may glimpse some anticipation of that summation after the events but in advance of its disclosure by analogy with the pattern of exchange exhibited by Jesus himself, in which somehow these events are ordered in connection with the rest of history.[169] This pattern may, for example, be found in the American Civil War—"a nation of brothers fighting a civil war to purge itself of the curse of slavery and so achieve concretely a union previously little more than a contractual arrangement"; the Civil Rights struggle "to complete the unfinished task of reconciliation" of those estranged through racial discrimination; and perhaps, Frei suggests, we may one day live to see it in the Vietnam conflict.[170] Today we might add the struggle for truth and reconciliation in post-apartheid South Africa (within and beyond the commission), and to forge political community in Northern Ireland through and beyond the process that produced the Good Friday Agreement.

This procedure, Frei says elsewhere, is something like the figural reading of history as ordered by a providential design, where figure and fulfillment both have integrity and reality in their own right but where the two are connected in the spiritual discernment of a fit and coherence within a larger, teleological pattern.[171] It is not, Frei made clear, an alternative to social or causal explanation but, as Mike Higton points out, a careful attention to similarities

---

166. *Identity*, 162.

167. *Identity*, 162.

168. *Identity*, 162.

169. I have been helped toward this reading of Frei's account on this point by remarks made by Ephraim Radner in a paper titled "The Life Is in the Blood," given to the Christian Theology and the Bible section of the Society of Biblical Literature at its annual meeting in Chicago, November 2012.

170. *Identity*, 162–63.

171. "History, Salvation-History, and Typology," 82–84. In effect, this is to propose the chastened revival of the premodern figural interpretation of historical experience described in *The Eclipse of Biblical Narrative*, 3 and 24–37.

of pattern.[172] As Higton argues, it exhibits Christian theology's own form of historical consciousness, one akin to that proclaimed by Strauss.[173]

It could, Frei advocates, inform a sense of gracious, universal divine providence upon which theologians might again exercise what he calls a public theology, advocating to historical agencies like nations a progressive course of action appropriate to the times and accordant with the gospel of God's universal reign in Christ.[174] Nevertheless, this parabolic application of Christ's passion and resurrection can only hint at a future mode of Christ's presence wherein its limited power of illumination will be surpassed by a summation in which all historical events will find their place that now we struggle to understand:

> the technological revolution with its present hopes *and* fears, the marvellous secular integrity of the sciences, the fight against poverty and discrimination, the agony of the Vietnamese people, the reunion of the church, the gift of literature and the arts, the horror of overpopulation as well as the fight against it and the despoliation of nature, the search for humaneness and for the care of people's souls—in short, a summing up of the story of humanity within the vast world of nature.[175]

This will be a comprehensive summing up of the whole range of historical experience. For now, the clues we have are only partial, for the future is genuinely open and God acts in freedom and in mysterious coexistence "with the contingency of events," as the story of Jesus attests.[176] No scientific rule or historical law can be discovered to eliminate the need to tell the story. The believer knows that the future summation will be that of God and of Jesus Christ as identified in the gospel story, but cannot say more than this, cannot predict what that future will be on the basis of the past.

Frei pictures the life of the individual believer within this wider ecclesial and providential context in similar terms. We discover the truth of the story, he says, insofar as we hammer out "a shape of life patterned after its own shape."[177] This patterning of our lives after Christ's does not repeat his life, but results in

---

172. "H. Richard Niebuhr on History, Church, and Nation," in Frei, *Theology and Narrative*, 229. See Higton, *Christ, Providence and History*, 172.

173. *Christ, Providence and History*, 173.

174. See "H. Richard Niebuhr on History, Church, and Nation," 214–33.

175. *Identity*, 163.

176. *Identity*, 163.

177. *Identity*, 170.

our lives reflecting his story as in a glass darkly, which is to say that the gospel story is an ambiguous clue to the meaning of individual lives as much as of the larger patterns in history in which they are situated. It is in this way that the story becomes meaningful for us, by being mirrored in our lives: it is a sense and relevance discovered practically in obedient experience. Frei quotes Albert Schweitzer to this effect: to those who obey him, wise or simple, Christ will reveal himself "in the toils, the conflicts, the sufferings which they shall pass through in His fellowship."[178]

Like the church, we follow Christ at a distance, discovering a new path of life (Rom. 6:4) and "a new way of governing our bodies" (Rom. 6:12-14) in adopting an intentional pattern of action partially corresponding to Christ's identity.[179] The individual believer also is bound to the wider human world, to their neighbor, because Christ is found there. In his Princeton lectures, delivered in 1978, Frei ventures with Kierkegaard the claim that "we have not met the textual Jesus until we have also met him . . . in forgetfulness of himself or incognito in a crowd."[180] In this sense Frei quotes Schweitzer again. Christ "comes to us as One unknown, without a name, as of old, by the lake-side, he came to those men who knew him not."[181] It is an account of discipleship fully concordant with Frei's account of history and entailing, surely, a practice of discernment linked to love of neighbor in one's everyday encounters.

I will turn to a fuller comparison of Frei and Gregory in a moment, but before doing so there are three observations worth noting. The first is to note a broad similarity between these theologians' sense of the availability and presence of Christ as the pattern for our participatory discipleship, and as somehow present in the poor and the stranger. In Frei, this presence is more firmly universal in scope and more closely connected with the shaping of history in all its complexity. In Gregory's case, we saw that a reasonable way of making sense of that availability in light of his theology would be to suppose that the Word holds together his whole human existence and makes it available by his Spirit, who incorporates us into him. For Frei, the risen Christ is the historical Jesus, and the drift of his argument is that Jesus Christ is the embodiment and form of God's providential rule. Part of the conditions of possibility for this availability have to do with the character of Christ's risen life: that, as Frei says with Paul (Rom. 6:9-10), he lives to God and hence not in our

178. *Identity*, 171, citing Schweitzer, *The Quest of the Historical Jesus* (New York: Macmillan, 1956), 403.

179. *Identity*, 171.

180. Frei, "The Encounter of Jesus with the German Academy," in *Types of Christian Theology*, 136.

181. *Identity*, 171–72, citing *The Quest of the Historical Jesus*, 403.

time, not, we might infer, in such a way as to be temporarily or spatially near or far from us, but remote by the difference of his life to God, a difference that does not impede but enables his presence.[182]

Part of those conditions has to do with the work of the Spirit in relating us to Christ. Frei's pneumatology in *The Identity of Jesus Christ* understands the Spirit as the presence of this Christ and so the mode of his indirect presence, shaping church, disciple, and history in its various patterns. His insistence that this providential governance is at one with the limited but free agency of creaturely agencies might be better supported, however, by distinguishing the Spirit more adequately from Jesus Christ's presence as one who draws us into conformity with him by energizing and exciting our own understanding, volition, longing, and agency. Such an incorporative pneumatology, in which the Spirit perfects and sanctifies creatures through energizing their own enacted identities in conformity with the form of Jesus of Nazareth, might be drawn from Pauline passages like Rom. 8:9-30 and 1 Cor. 2:9-11. It might allow for a more realistic sense of creaturely agency and immanent dynamics in the distinction and conformity that Frei's figure of the disciple following at a distance is intended to convey, as well as with the Christ-focused teleology Frei ascribes to divine providence.[183]

Turning back to Gregory's perspective, we might also be prompted to consider whether, in Frei's more thoroughly Christ-focused, expansive yet realistic vision, there might be a place for a notion of divine pedagogy and persuasion. One of the dimensions of discipleship is precisely learning, and the Gospels seem designed to take account of our need to learn who Jesus is and what that means for us; we might see this learning, following the Gospels, as an activity in response to the teaching of the risen Christ, helping us see who he is and understand the truth of his story as we pattern our lives accordingly. With Gregory, we might imagine a persuasive dimension to this pedagogy: without imagining that our learning is something we are capable of independent of the Spirit, nevertheless our desire and curiosity and hope are

---

182. On this and the next point, cf. the conclusion to my "Feeding and Forming the People of God: The Lord, His Supper and the Church in Calvin and 1 Corinthians 11:17-34," in *New Perspectives for Evangelical Theology: Engaging with God, Scripture and the World*, ed. Tom Greggs (London: Routledge, 2010), 93–107.

183. For two different examples of such incorporative pneumatology, see Sarah Coakley, "God as Trinity: An Approach through Prayer," in *We Believe in God: A Report by the Doctrine Commission of the General Synod of the Church of England* (London: Church House Publishing, 1987), 104–21 (among many places). See also Daniel W. Hardy, "The Foundation of Cognition and Ethics in Worship," in his *God's Ways with the World* (Edinburgh: T. & T. Clark, 1996), 25–30.

involved in our decisions to attend, to learn, to essay obedience. Something of the very strangeness of Jesus Christ, the weight of his identity as we learn to discern it, its illuminatory power for our own living and acting, draws us in, and all along the way we are persuaded into a deeper conformity.

Finally, one wonders, in light of Gregory's thought, whether the figure of following Christ at a distance ought alone to govern the logic of creaturely participation in Christ. It expresses a radical distinction between Christ and the disciple necessary to the gracious efficacy of his unique identity, including the mutuality and reciprocity it establishes between human beings, as Gene Outka observes.[184] It also, however, connotes a remotion foreign to the sense of friendship and mutual inherence between Christ and his disciples, which in John's Gospel is bound up with their mutual love, for example, and to the presence of Christ in the stranger that Frei affirms.[185] As David Dawson observes, this figure thereby also seems to limit the scope for the disciple's transformation.[186] The risen Christ does indeed live to God, as Frei affirms with Paul (Rom. 6:9-10), and the life he lives to God is not in our time sequence.[187] He lives to God; his relation to God now characterizes him not only comprehensively but immediately, we might infer, and hence he is life. Yet while we cannot span this difference by time or imagination or experience, it remains true, as Frei affirms, that his life is ours "only in him."[188] Surely, we may say, being conformed in some measure to Jesus' identity involves some conformity to the relation to God that is constitutive of his human existence, his Sonship, by way of adoption, as Paul says, and hence some kind of limited, graced sharing of the life he lives to God even if largely in a manner veiled now to us and awaiting full consummation in the resolution of our identities.

Conclusion

Frei's account of providence is thus closely connected with his understanding of the identity of Jesus Christ and his atoning work. History in all its contingent complexity, together with cosmos, is providentially ordered in Jesus Christ, and the pattern of exchange found in him gives us a partial clue to discerning the lineaments of the final pattern of the history we live through, so as to inform our discipleship, our love of neighbor, and the pursuit by church and theologian of

184. Outka, "Following at a Distance: Ethics and the Identity of Jesus," in *Scriptural Authority and Narrative Interpretation* (Philadelphia: Fortress Press, 1987), 149–53.

185. See e.g. John 15:1-17; 17:20-26.

186. Dawson, *Christian Figural Reading*, 206.

187. *Identity*, 172.

188. *Identity*, 172.

the kind of cautiously circumscribed progressive politics that fits both a realism about human sin *and* about the mysterious, universal, and gracious rule of a loving God focused in Jesus. It is just at this point that we can see the full scope of the alternative historical consciousness Frei finds in Christianity, with its own realism, its own sense of the mutual interaction of historical particulars and the significance of human agency in response to particular circumstances; a consciousness centered upon the action of God focused in Jesus Christ, acting through other agencies without diminishment of their freedom. It is a vision that does not preclude explanatory historical analysis but does resist the reduction of history and so of political wisdom to what historical inquiry can explain.

Frei thus offers an account of history that evinces several similarities with the lines of development suggested by Gregory with regard to loving providential ordering of creaturely systems and interactions, of the strangeness of divine action, the centrality of Christ, and the universal scope of his significance, appropriated historically by the disciple. Frei's, however, has a more fully realistic, historical (in his sense) vision of Christ, the disciple, and history more generally. In his account, moreover, Christ's identity, atoning work, and God's providential rule are much more closely intertwined than in Gregory, which, notwithstanding Gregory's own progressive interventions in civic and imperial politics, lead to a much greater and more hopeful commitment to engagement with the temporal order of things on the basis of a more unambiguously universal scope to the atonement, to the inclusion not only of all human souls but of historical events and other creaturely phenomena. It is a vision, as we have seen, that bears supplementation, even correction from Gregory and others in the ways just suggested. It is also an account that, as we shall see in the next chapter, entails and requires a theology of Scripture that Frei only sketches in the briefest terms, but affords the terms in which to develop a theology of Scripture that takes historical consciousness seriously.

8

History and Holy Scripture in Hans Frei

Frei's theological account of history requires a theology of Scripture, and he supplies one, or at least the outline of one. Despite being criticized for not being theological enough about Scripture, for prioritizing theories of narrative or the church as a social entity over a dogmatic account of the Bible, his central concerns with the identity and presence of Jesus Christ led him to say enough about Scripture to indicate a truly theological account of its nature. This account, taken as a whole, in turn makes sense of his understanding of what he calls the literal sense of the synoptic Gospels and of the scriptural canon constituted as a whole in relation to them. Most importantly for my purposes, it is an account that, taken with his theology of history, points the way to a theology of Scripture that can address the issues raised by historical consciousness. Historical consciousness makes it difficult to think of God intervening in the world, so that (1) thinking of Scripture as an instrument or vessel of divine action or presence becomes problematic, (2) the world of the text is distanced from historical reconstructions of the past it attests and from the world of the reader, (3) its normative function in Christian community becomes hard to sustain imaginatively or intellectually, and (4) it in turn becomes subject to ethical scrutiny as a diverse set of historically conditioned documents set against a larger history of human values. For all that his theology of Scripture is not as developed as it might be, the value of Frei for the contemporary pursuit of the theology and theological interpretation of Scripture lies in his capacity to help us with these questions.

Faith Seeking Understanding, the Identity of Jesus, and the Theology of Scripture

It is easy to read Frei's early or later work and conclude that his accounts of realistic narrative, or later, of Christian reading practices, because of their prominence, are meant to warrant the way he reads biblical texts. Such a conclusion would be unfair, however. In his earlier work, Frei turns to the Gospels as texts authoritative for Christian faith on grounds that Christians hold Christ to be present thereby, in some way. His analysis of Christ's identity is intended to clarify that notion of presence, and so the procedure can be described as one of faith seeking understanding. In his later work, the same procedure is there, only it is more explicit and thoroughgoing: the meaning as well as the truth of Christian narrative turns on the way Christians have believed Christ to be present in relation to these texts.

As we have seen, Frei selected the Gospels in the essays that became the material for *The Identity of Jesus Christ* because of their centrality to Christian belief, and indeed the passages that bear most weight in his analysis, the passion and resurrection sequences, have been of particular importance to the practice and expression of Christian faith through the varied history of Christian traditions. This reason for his choice belongs very much to the mode in which Frei believed theology should be done.

At first glance, Frei seems to locate his analysis in *The Identity of Jesus Christ* outside dogmatic theology. He will not, he tells us in the Introduction, use faith as a convenient assumption and expand its implications for Christians by reasoning from their faith in Christ's presence.[1] What he means by this denial is that he will not be simply "unfolding" Christian beliefs as expressed in dogma, perhaps by deduction or inference from dogmatic propositions.[2] Nevertheless, he adds that what he will write "constitutes a reflection within belief."[3] He will explore one order for thinking about the component parts of belief in Christ's presence: namely that it matters—not least for the interpretation of the gospel—that we think about Christ's presence in light of his identity because the reverse procedure leads us away from both Christ and his presence. This exercise, for the believer, is "a pleasurable exercise in . . . ordering his thinking about his faith and—in a certain sense—a praise of God by the use of his analytical capacities."[4] In this context of reflection within faith, it is entirely natural for Frei to announce that he will turn to the New Testament in order to examine the identity of Jesus.[5] Of similar import is Frei's comment in his earlier Harvard "Remarks," explaining his approach to these same issues, that for him as

---

1. Frei, *The Identity of Jesus Christ: The Hermeneutical Bases of Dogmatic Theology* (Philadelphia: Fortress Press, 1975), 1.

2. *Identity*, 3.

3. *Identity*, 4.

4. *Identity*, 5.

5. *Identity*, 16.

for Karl Barth, theology begins with the actuality of Christian truth, rather than arguing for its possibility. This position strongly suggests that implicit in Frei's focus on the Gospels and the passion-resurrection sequence is the rendering of Jesus Christ as the actuality of the core of Christian truth in normative form.

Therefore Frei's discussion of that sequence in terms of its aesthetic qualities as realistic narrative belongs to a context framed by the task of thinking through Christian belief in Christ's presence, suggesting at the least that the authority of these texts for that task is assumed. Frei was quite clear that the realistic qualities of the texts were not the grounds for their authority but a condition of its possibility: the unity of text and meaning here "does not itself bestow authority, but without it there can be no authority."[6] Some kind of authority is assumed, therefore, and Frei's discussion of the problem of Christ's presence makes it clear that in Christian belief that authority is related to the presence of Christ, though there is controversy as to how. If, then, the character of Scripture's authority and the nature of Scripture on which it rests is bound up with Christ's presence, then it makes some sense to do as Frei did and postpone fuller comment upon it until the question of Christ's presence has been more fully analyzed.

That analysis leads, as we have seen, to the claim that Jesus' identity uniquely entails his presence as the one who cannot be thought not to be present, who is life itself, inseparably united with God and the embodiment of his presence. Such is "the testimony of the New Testament and, hence, the understanding of believers."[7] For the believer, Frei explains, there is no problem with this truth-claim "and, therefore, its meaning in formal aesthetic description *is* its truth."[8] Belief in Jesus' resurrection, therefore, "is more nearly a belief in something like the inspired quality of the accounts" than in a theory of their historical probability, for what is attested cannot be related to any measure of historical probability, there being no historical analogues for it.[9] Nevertheless, he continues, belief in the inspiration of the descriptive contents of the stories and belief in their factuality would have to coincide with respect to the resurrection, only this is a fact-claim that cannot be adjudicated like any other; assent to it is not based on factual evidence. In other words, the way the New Testament identifies Jesus Christ as bodily risen and hence present requires a clarification of its authority not in terms of historical judgments about

<hr>

6. "Remarks," in *Theology and Narrative: Selected Essays*, ed. G. Hunsinger and W. C. Placher (New York: Oxford University Press, 1993), 42.

7. *Identity*, 149.

8. "Remarks," 43.

9. *Identity*, 150.

evidence but in terms of the action of God in relation to these texts, for apart from something like God's inspiration of the writers it is difficult to see how a claim of this order could be set forth truthfully in a human text.

Frei elaborates his theology of Scripture, or at least of the scriptural texts in question, a little further when he discusses the pattern of Christ's presence with respect to the church. As we have seen, his account of the church sees it as a subject constituted by the indirect presence of Christ, by way of its spatiotemporal bases in Word and Sacrament enacting its identity and existence in its engagement with the wider human world. This Word, it becomes apparent, comprises primarily "the feeble, often naive and simple word of written Scripture," what Frei elsewhere describes as "testimony" and here as "a witness," but also "its usually pathetic, clumsy interpretation in the spoken word."[10] On analogy to the way Jesus Christ himself as witness is attested, according to John's Gospel, by the Father and Spirit to whom he bears witness, so this witness of the Word—Scripture and exposition—becomes a "true witness, yet more than a witness."[11] For it actually witnesses to what it is not, "the presence of God in Jesus Christ," and at the same time God witnesses to it, making himself present to it so that it may become the temporal basis of the Spirit who is the presence of God in Jesus Christ.[12] Here we have the lineaments of a theology of Scripture resembling that of Karl Barth, which I shall explore in more detail below. For now we may note that, in light of the foregoing, Frei's analysis begins to clarify the character of scriptural authority and the nature of Scripture in terms of Christ's presence understood in light of his identity. Its position toward the end of the argument does not mean that belief in Christ's presence by way of Scripture has been conjured somehow from an argument that began with a nontheological theory about realistic narrative. Rather, what we have at the end of the argument is an analysis of a belief presupposed at the beginning of the exercise, as is proper to the analytic circularity that Frei ascribes to his endeavors.[13]

CHRISTIAN READING PRACTICES AND THE THEOLOGY OF SCRIPTURE

The objection that Frei's early theology began with a theory of realistic narrative and built a theology of Christ's presence, including his presence via

10. *Identity*, 165. For examples of Frei describing Scripture or the New Testament specifically as "testimony," see *Identity*, 103, 149

11. *Identity*, 165.

12. *Identity*, 165.

13. See *Identity*, 5.

Scripture, on top of it finds apparent support from Frei's own critique of his earlier position in a paper first delivered in 1983 and titled "The 'Literal Reading' of Biblical Narrative in the Christian Tradition: Does It Stretch or Will It Break?"[14] Frei's principal concerns here are about the capacity of philosophical hermeneutics, especially that exemplified by Paul Ricoeur's work to date, to sustain a Christian reading practice that Frei terms "literal reading" or the *sensus literalis*, at the heart of which is the move to take the Gospels to be stories about Jesus of Nazareth rather than having something more ultimate as their true subject matter. However, a number of developments seem to have caused Frei to question his own position.[15] Having examined difficulties with hermeneutical philosophy as a hospitable theory for literal reading, Frei turns to "a recent proposal" about the relationship between realistic narrative and historical fact-claim in respect of biblical narrative, and the synoptic Gospels especially.[16] He clearly has his own approach in *The Eclipse of Biblical Narrative* and *The Identity of Jesus Christ* in mind, as he acknowledges.[17]

Here he finds in respect of the category of meaning a low-powered but nevertheless general theory that locates the texts in question within a larger class called literary texts and a smaller subcategory of these called "realistic narrative."[18] On this account, as in the literary theory of the New Critics, Frei says, the meaning of the text is held to be pure and normative apart from any factual reference or authorial intention or readerly reception. Such an account involves a kind of general theory: "[t]he Gospel narratives 'mean' realistically because that is the general literary class to which they belong."[19] It

---

14. Reproduced in Frei, *Theology and Narrative*, 117–52. For the date, see Higton, *Christ, Providence and History: Hans Frei's Public Theology* (London: T. & T. Clark, 2004), 262.

15. Frei's decision to turn his attention to this question may well have much to do with the critique of New Criticism, with which Frei had identified his own proposals in *Identity*, a critique that was prosecuted in the late 1960s and early 1970s, and in which literary theorists at Yale University, where Frei taught, were prominent. He aligned himself with the New Critics in his "Remarks," 33. Christopher Norris in his *Deconstruction: Theory and Practice* (London and New York: Methuen), 1–17, details the criticisms being made of New Criticism at this time, and the role of Geoffrey Hartman and J. Hillis Miller, who both taught at Yale in that period. In the argument of "The 'Literal Reading,'" Frei's allegiance with New Criticism is the focus of his self-critique. He attributes to the New Critics of the notion of the autonomous sacrosanct text, distinct from critical writing. His criticism of that idea resembles the criticisms Norris details and the desire of the Yale theorists to go "beyond formalism." Brevard Childs (*pers. comm.*) has drawn my attention to the significance of this context for explaining Frei's change of direction in his later writings.

16. "The 'Literal Reading,'" 139.

17. "The 'Literal Reading,'" 151 n. 27.

18. "The 'Literal Reading,'" 140.

is a perilous general theory to which to be yoked, however. For both the claim that the text is self-referential and that it is almost self-interpreting are equally "artificial"; they refuse quite proper and serious questions about referentiality and the mutual implication of interpretation, or reading and textual meaning or textuality. Worse still, this theory does for Christian meaning what Frei had in earlier writings accused apologetic theologies and hermeneutical approaches of doing for Christian truth. They ground the actuality of the coincidence of meaning and truth of the synoptic narrative of Jesus' identity in a general account of the possibility of this coincidence in respect of realistic narrative, whereas in fact it is only the actuality of divinity and humanity in Jesus Christ that is the basis for the coincidence of meaning and truth in the Gospels. This actuality may only be affirmed by faith, not rational demonstration, a condition that extends to the very meaning of the dogma of Christ, for the unity of Christ's person is not fully explicable in this life. The New Critics have thus taken this specific case of Christ and the Gospels and turned it into a general theory, of which the doctrine of the incarnation is only one of the items in which one may or may not believe. Frei's own procedure of taking the synoptic Gospel narratives and their partial redescription in terms of the doctrine of the Incarnation as instances of a general category of realistic narrative, then, puts the cart before the horse, cuts the lines, and claims "the vehicle is self-propelled," as Frei put it.[20]

Frei's self-critique here seems a little unfair insofar as the gestures he makes toward a theology of Scripture in *The Identity of Jesus Christ* seem to make the coincidence of meaning and truth in the Gospels a unique affair bound up with the unique coincidence of identity and presence of Jesus Christ. His appeal to realistic narrative in that text, and in the earlier "Theological Reflections" and "Remarks," seems to lack the kind of extravagant claims made on behalf of the whole genre of realistic narrative that he here ascribes to the New Critics.[21] Nevertheless, we may concede that his appeal to the account of meaning in realistic narrative, while relatively minimal, at least risks confusing the matter by placing the Gospels within a larger category of texts that share a common aesthetic quality. It fails sufficiently to do justice to the insight in whose service those categories are invoked, namely that the texts render the unsubstitutable identity of Jesus Christ as one whose identity, uniquely, entails his presence.

19. "The 'Literal Reading,'" 141.

20. "The 'Literal Reading,'" 142–43.

21. Frei may be a little more culpable in respect of *The Eclipse of Biblical Narrative*, where the genre of realistic narrative does more work.

Frei's argument in "The 'Literal Reading'" is that the practice of literal reading is more likely to be visible and will look stronger and more flexible when rooted in "its primary and original context, a religious community's 'rule' for faithful reading."[22] For when specific cases like this are analyzed in terms of general theories, their claims look "inescapably ambiguous or problematic" in philosophical terms.[23] Instead, therefore, of an explanatory theory of meaning grounding discussion of the possibility of a specific case under its auspices, Frei commends the description of the *sensus literalis* as a reading that "governs, and bends to its own ends whatever general categories it shares—as indeed it has to share—with other kind of reading": categories such as meaning and truth and their relation.[24] It is case-specific and belongs primarily in the sociolinguistic communal context of the religion of which it is a part, understood following Clifford Geertz's account on analogy with a text as a "determinate code in which beliefs, ritual and behavior patterns . . . come together as a common semiotic system, and also as the community which is that system in use."[25] The appropriate critical procedure here is what Geertz calls "thick description": description of details as parts in the whole semiotic system and from the participant's perspective. In such description, congruence between internal and external perspectives is possible without the need to ground it in a general explanatory theory. Understanding is a matter of attending to the meanings things have in their usage in the cultural system and is like understanding a joke, proverb, or allusion.

Is Frei here repeating his alleged mistake and grounding his account of Scripture in a sociological or ethnographic account of religion rather than in a theology of Scripture? We need again to beware being misled by the prominence of this account in his argument, and pay closer attention to the role it plays. Frei's concern is clearly to avoid any kind of move that would impose an alien explanatory theory onto the specific practices of Christian faith and the specific meanings they have; these are best described by the appropriation and alteration of specific terms borrowed from theory and fitted to the description of this or that specific case. The role of the account of religion as a cultural system and theology as "thick description" serves to clarify this argument. Frei's presentation of the account in this piece does, nevertheless, suggest that he has substituted one low-level "sacramental" general theory of

22. "The 'Literal Reading,'" 139.
23. "The 'Literal Reading,'" 144.
24. "The 'Literal Reading,'" 143–44.
25. "The 'Literal Reading,'" 146, citing Geertz, *The Interpretation of Cultures* (New York: Basic Books, 1973), 13, 27.

textual meaning for another low-level, pragmatic general theory of religious meaning. Elsewhere, however, Frei makes the same basic move in terms more of an analogy than identification. Theology understood as an aspect of the self-description of Christianity as a religion rather than of theology as a general class, and inquiring into the coherence and appropriateness of given instances of the use of Christian language in light of its normative articulation (however that norm is identified) "is closer to the social sciences than to philosophy, though certainly not identical with them."[26]

However proper it is to seek to describe Scripture in theological terms, if we want to have a discussion, as Frei did, about that approach as compared with the alternatives to an audience who do not necessarily share the same basic theological commitments in common, then we will need some language with which to map and relate the alternatives. The benefit of the analogy with social scientific description to which Frei moved for that purpose was the focus on the specificity of Christianity, the priority, as he saw it, of the participant's perspective and the move to understand the meaning of beliefs and practices in relation to one another against appropriate norms. These moves in principle privilege a truly theological account of Christian faith. As Frei explains, alluding to David Kelsey's account of the uses of Scripture in modern theology, theology here "may be said to be working from a number of ultimate and perhaps ultimately different 'visions' or designs concerning the manner of God's presence implied by this religion and its sacred texts—visions that have much more of an imaginative and aesthetic than philosophical character."[27] Theology, in other words, is concerned with God and sees everything in relation to God in a way that is primarily a matter of imaginative vision, and explicates Christian beliefs in light of it. Frei's own theological description of the *sensus literalis*, in "The 'Literal Reading,'" is theological in just this way, and in a fashion that can be seen to be in accord with much of the Christological analysis of *The Identity of Jesus Christ* and its antecedents. To show this much will take two steps.

The first is Frei's description of the practice in question. What he calls "plain" readings of sacred texts in religious communities—of which literal reading is an example—are warranted, he says, not by general theories but by agreement with the community's rules for reading the sacred text.[28] Like

26. "Theology and the Interpretation of Narrative: Some Hermeneutical Considerations," in *Theology and Narrative*, 95–96.

27. "Theology and the Interpretation of Narrative," 95, citing Kelsey, *The Uses of Scripture in Recent Theology* (Philadelphia: Fortress Press, 1975), 162ff.

28. "The 'Literal Reading,'" 144.

many others on the topic, Frei is indebted to Raphael Loewe's analysis of literal or plain sense interpretation in Jewish tradition, as Frei acknowledges elsewhere.[29] The literal sense is a plain, natural, or obvious way of reading the texts, he says there quoting Charles Wood, which the community of faith has normally acknowledged as basic.[30] The rules for reading amount to the content of this very minimal, largely informal, and very flexible consensus. The commonality involved here is only that enjoyed by those who can understand one another enough to have meaningful arguments with one another, who share a consensus wherein these people "by and large *agree* with one another enough so that they can *disagree*."[31] He is not asserting that when Christians have read the Gospels they have come to the same conclusions about Jesus of Nazareth; he means only that there is a significant commonality and continuity in the manner of their reading. Nor is he claiming that this kind of reading is what Christians have always called "the literal sense"; the use of the term is his own. These rules specify that, first, Christian reading of Christian Scriptures must not deny the literal ascription to Jesus of all that is associated with him in the stories in which he plays a part and other New Testament texts in which he features; second, that Christian reading may not deny the unity of the two Testaments or the congruence of that unity with the ascription to Jesus of the things said about him in the New; and third, that any readings not in principle in contradiction with the first two rules are permissible. Frei's account of this minimal consensus thus describes an informal agreement to read Scripture in a way that is focused upon the figure of Jesus of Nazareth variously rendered by the texts of the New Testament.[32]

What in turn grounds this minimal ruled consensus, Frei says, quoting Charles Wood, is "the community's own experience with the text."[33] In similar terms, Frei argues, what viability literal reading has will follow "excellently from the actual, fruitful use religious people continue to make of it in ways

29. Loewe, "The 'Plain' Meaning of Scripture in Early Jewish Exegesis," in *Papers of the Institute of Jewish Studies in London* (Jerusalem: Magnes, 1964), 1:140–85. Frei cites this article in "Theology and the Interpretation of Narrative," 105. The paper's argument made a big impression in Yale (Childs, *pers. comm.*). Childs cites it in his important article, "The Sensus Literalis of Scripture: An Ancient and Modern Problem," in *Beiträge zur alttestamentlichen Theologie: Festschrift für Walther Zimmerli zum 70. Geburtstag*, ed. H. Donner et al. (Göttingen: Vandenhoeck & Ruprecht, 1977), 81, itself an important source for Frei. So too does Kathryn Greene-McCreight, *Ad Litteram: How Augustine, Calvin and Barth Read the "Plain Sense" of Genesis 1-3* (New York: Peter Lang, 1999), 10.

30. "Theology and the Interpretation of Narrative," 104, quoting C. Wood, *The Formation of Christian Understanding: An Essay in Theological Hermeneutics* (Philadelphia: Westminster, 1981), 43.

31. Frei, *Types of Christian Theology*, ed. G. Hunsinger and W. C. Placher (New Haven and London: Yale University Press, 1992), 56.

that enhance their own and other people's lives."[34] It would seem reasonable to suppose that, in Christian communities, this experience has had something to do with what participants would describe in terms of the presence of Jesus Christ, for only some such description would make sense of the consensus in question. How, then, should that presence be understood?

When it comes to describing the meaning of the Gospels when so read, Frei argues, the Christian tradition proceeds by way of faith seeking understanding, even in respect of the very meaning of the dogma. Here the fact of the unity of divine and human in Christ (which, we may suppose, is presented to the imagination when the stories associated with him are read as stories about him) yields the implicit rule of religious use that governs the use of other categories, such as the category of "nature." The unity of divine and human natures as a description is dependent on the actuality set forth in the scriptural portrayal of Jesus Christ. From the perspective of this rule of faith and its interpretive use in Christian tradition, therefore, the realistic novel is an appropriate if somewhat puzzling and incomplete analogue of "the coherence between linguistic or narrative and real worlds rendered in the Gospel stories."[35] For in that tradition of reading the Gospels within a framework of belief that acknowledges the actuality of the unity of divine and human in Jesus Christ, "the ascriptive literalism of the story, the *history-likeness* if you will, of the singular agent enacting the unity of human finitude and divine infinity, Jesus of Nazareth, is taken to be itself the ground, guarantee, and conveyance of the truth of the depicted enactment, its *historicity* if you will," if those are the right categories for talking about meaning and truth today.[36] In consequence the linguistic, textual world is both necessary and sufficient for our orientation in the real world: as Frei notes, this is not the kind of claim from which plausible general theories are made!

32. The rules Frei specifies are so minimal and formal that his appeal to rule-following on this specific point seems less vulnerable to Kathryn Tanner's critique of postliberal appeals to that notion than is George Lindbeck's theory of doctrine. See Tanner, *Theories of Culture: A New Agenda for Theology* (Minneapolis: Fortress Press, 1997), 138ff. One could demonstrate the historical continuity Frei appeals to here across considerable variation in belief, practice, and church doctrine.

33. Frei, "Theology and the Interpretation of Narrative," 104, citing C. Wood, *The Formation of Christian Understanding*, 43.

34. "The 'Literal Reading,'" 119. Nicholas Wolterstorff has drawn my attention to the importance and wisdom of this passage in Frei in his *Divine Discourse: Philosophical Reflections on the Claim That God Speaks* (Cambridge: Cambridge University Press, 1995), 181–82.

35. "The 'Literal Reading,'" 143.

36. "The 'Literal Reading,'" 143.

It is not difficult to see here the conclusions of *The Identity of Jesus Christ* about the coincidence of identity and presence in Jesus Christ as rendered by the Gospels reiterated in different terms. Here, however, they are framed in relation to first a widespread consensus in Christian practice about the ascription of the attributes of Jesus of Nazareth to that character, and second to a particular tendency in Christian tradition, namely that which accepts the claim of the text so read that the one depicted cannot not be present, so that the risen Lord Jesus Christ is understood to be the one who makes the coincidence of meaning and truth actual and possible in regard to these particular texts. This extraordinary claim is clearly profoundly theological and appears unimpeded by the largely maieutic work of Frei's appeal to ethnographic description; on the contrary, that procedure for locating theology has allowed him to foreground Christian faith and a theological understanding of Jesus Christ's identity as the clue to the peculiar theological character of this portion of Christian Scripture.

We find the same theological justification for the unique unity of meaning and truth in the textual portrayal of Jesus Christ in other pieces Frei wrote after this "turn" to think about the meaning of the Gospels and about theological description in relation to the social practices and the cultural "texts" of Christian communities. These also bear out still more strongly the continuity with his earlier arguments in *The Identity of Jesus Christ*, but without the earlier emphasis on the category of realistic narrative.

The Word Written: Textual Mediation, Divine Condescension, and Human Transformation

In 1985, the evangelical theologian Carl F. H. Henry gave a series of lectures at Yale, one of which critiqued "narrative theology," taking Frei's work as one of its principal exemplifications.[37] Among other questions, Henry pressed those of the factuality of the witness of biblical narratives to historical events, of their relation to a divinely revealed referent transcending the texts, that is, to God, and to the divine authorship and inerrant authority of Scripture.[38] He took Frei radically to disjoin Scripture from revelatory external history outside the text and revelatory propositions in Scripture. The approach Frei exemplifies "is so open to realistic theological fiction that it readily obscures historical fact and clouds the foundations of a stable faith," since the gospel is dependent upon a divine saving act in space and time.[39] It encourages skepticism by separating the

---

37. As Placher and Hunsinger tell us, *Theology and Narrative*, 207.

38. Henry, "Narrative Theology: An Evangelical Appraisal," *Trinity Journal* 8 (1987): 11–14.

truth-claims of literary authority of the story from historical-critical scrutiny, for unless open to such scrutiny the events attested by the text are not historical, however divinely enacted.[40] By failing to ground itself in the divine authorship of Scripture, he alleged, Frei's approach gives us no warrant for affirming unambiguously the objective truth of its testimony as divine revelation.[41]

Henry's criticisms voice common concerns about Frei's position, but also a (not uncommon) failure to pay close attention to the argument of his early texts, and of *The Identity of Jesus Christ* in particular.[42] Henry depicted Frei as foregoing the revelatory status and objective truthfulness of the text in favor of its narrative meaning. In response, Frei claimed that we do refer "*by means* of that story," but in a complex way that is not so easily stated as Henry thinks, which does not marry up with a particular philosophical account of knowledge and truth, but which is thoroughly theological.[43] The text is a witness to the Word of God, historically and otherwise and in either case is sufficient for our reference; it is, in this sense, "the Word of God written."[44]

There seem to be several components to Frei's position here as he struggles to articulate it. He asserts clearly that the scriptural witnesses really do refer to a transcendent and (at times) historical referent, including and especially the claim that God was in Christ reconciling the world to himself, and that this Christ was crucified and risen. Yet the demand that one clarify exactly and univocally *how* such reference occurs is not one the theologian can or ought to satisfy. In part, as in "The 'Literal Reading' of Biblical Narrative," this reluctance has to do with a concern about the viability of philosophical schemes as means of securing Christian affirmations. We need to use philosophical concepts to articulate Christian truth, but we do so eclectically and provisionally because philosophical schemes prove less enduring than the church's witness in language to God in Christ. Once we spoke of Christ in the terminology of Chalcedon and this language was partly adequate, partly inadequate, and certainly not neutral; now we tend to talk in terms of historicity and factuality, and in those

---

39. "Narrative Theology," 13.

40. "Narrative Theology," 11.

41. "Narrative Theology," 13.

42. See, for example, Francis Schüssler Fiorenza, "History and Hermeneutics," in James Livingstone, Francis Schüssler Fiorenza, Sarah Coakley, and James H. Evans, *Modern Christian Thought: The Twentieth Century* (Minneapolis: Fortress Press, 2006), 376; Mark I. Wallace, *The Second Naiveté: Barth, Ricoeur, and the New Yale Theology* (Macon, GA: Mercer University Press, 1990), 104–9; Francis Watson, *Text, Church and World* (Edinburgh: T. & T. Clark, 1994), 25–29.

43. "Response to 'Narrative Theology': An Evangelical Appraisal," in *Theology and Narrative*, 209f.

44. "Response," 209.

terms Frei would want to affirm the factuality of Christ's death and resurrection. Those categories are not *a priori* or theory-neutral but convey assumptions that do not sit easily with the truth-claims they are being used to articulate. Is Jesus Christ, the eternal Word made flesh, Frei asks rhetorically, "a 'fact' like other historical facts?"[45] Like creation *ex nihilo*, Jesus Christ is a reality for which there is no analogy in our historical experience.

Hence Frei's refusal to tie the affirmation of the truth to the scriptural witness is not solely to do with the fragility of philosophical schemes but with the strange conditions that pertain to talking of God and of divine action. The analogical way we have of talking about God qualifies every positive statement with a host of denials, Frei reminds us: there is, he says, not only a *via eminentiae* but also a *via negativa* in Christian language, because God is unlike us. We are not able, therefore, to say how such language might truly name God. We cannot place it within the frame of a larger explanatory theory of language and truth, even if one were available, because the referent does not fit within any of our categories of understanding. Hence, as Frei goes on to say, the scriptural narrative is referential, but that does not mean we have an adequate theory of *how* its witness refers.[46]

We are, rather, bound to the story itself, read as a story concerning Jesus of Nazareth. The textuality of Scripture is, for Frei, the inescapable medium of its witness and referentiality. However much it is true to say that all human thinking is only by way of language, our talk of the God of Jesus Christ is inescapably so with reference to the gospel story because we have no independent alternative for thinking about its truth, because the truth it attests is so unlike the things we think we can explain—beyond genus and species, as Aquinas said—in a manner that the term "supernatural" is wholly inadequate to clarify.[47] Thus what Frei here calls "the language pattern, the meaning-and-reference pattern" of the gospel story to which literal reading attends (in contrast to taking the story as referring metaphorically to a "limit experience") is our means of access to its referent: we are bound to it and it is sufficient.[48]

---

45. "Response," 211.

46. "Response," 210. I am here conflating what Frei says about the scriptural witness and about Christian language-use in its (very) broad continuities over time. For him, Christians speak of God on the basis of the literal reading of the gospel story ("Response," 209) and adapt their language to that story and its Old Testament prefiguration (210), so that one can reasonably take what he says about the truth conditions of Christian language as applicable to Christian Scripture since the meaning and truth of the former depend on the meaning and truth of latter.

47. "Response," 209, alluding to ST 1a 3.5 *resp.*

48. "Response," 209.

The rationality of being bound to the story, and the sufficiency of the story, indeed of the wider witness of Scripture, requires a theological rather than a philosophical basis. As Frei says at the end of his response, "Jesus Christ" in scriptural witness refers ordinarily "only by the miracle of grace," which means we do not know how it refers.[49] Frei's reserve about how much we can say about the way in which the text is true is entirely theologically proper, given that the relevant cognitive truth condition is the crucified and risen Jesus Christ whose identity is inseparable from that of God.

Indeed, what the truth of the scriptural witness (and Christian language-use more generally) involves here is more complex than a question of correspondence to the "facts." It entails talking about the truth conditions of that witness in terms that begin to look Trinitarian. Christian use of "God" on the basis of the literal reading of the Gospels and the figural reading of the Old Testament—and hence that scriptural witness—is not only true by way of a reference to reality, but also by being true "to the way it works in one's life, and by holding the world, including the political, economic and social world, to account by the gauge of its truthfulness."[50] Hence we have to talk about God in cognitive, descriptive terms as wholly other but also "obediently or trustingly" as Holy Spirit, as the ground of truthfulness of what we mean by "God" that we discover through discipleship and prophetic critique of the world.[51]

Missing in his "Response" is a clearer sense of the divine grace by which Scripture's witness is made adequate alongside its truthfulness in the shaping of human living and the critique of human society. We can find further clarification in a lecture Frei gave at Princeton Theological Seminary in 1986, titled "Conflicts in Interpretation: Resolution, Armistice, or Co-existence?"[52] Here Frei outlines what he sees as a pervasive conflict in contemporary biblical scholarship. On the one hand, there are those, he claims, who stand in a long modern tradition of consensus around the unity of meaning and truth, a tradition that spans historical critics, those whom they opposed, and hermeneutical thinkers like Gadamer and Bultmann. Up until recently, readers of the Bible in the West disagreed on a common basis. Now, however, new ways of reading seem to abandon that consensus in unsettling ways, for whom interpretation proceeds from the divorce of meaning and truth. To the extent that such structuralist and post-structuralist readers force us to hesitate before the transition from meaning to truth, and not make too hasty a transition, Frei

---

49. "Response," 212.

50. "Response," 210.

51. "Response," 210.

52. See Hunsinger and Placher's editorial introduction in *Theology and Narrative*, 153 for the context.

expresses a cautious and qualified agreement: the textuality of the text is to be distinguished (though not divorced) from its truth, and neither should be prioritized over the other.[53]

Frei's reason for distinguishing meaning and truth with respect to the scriptural text is a theological one. He invokes what he sees as Karl Barth's interpretation and appropriation of the Reformer's doctrine of Scripture. For Barth, the text is the Word of God in the sense that it is sufficient for us. We are, here too, bound to the text in that there is no alternative access to God: beyond the text lies the *Deus absconditus*, the hidden, destructive God who may well be simply a human projection, a dangerous idol.[54] However, the sufficiency of the text is not due to any inherent qualities, as though it could point to its subject matter in some extraordinary way beyond its literal sense (as a historical fact, perhaps, or limit experience). Hence, Frei claims, the Reformers say that we should not worship the text. In so saying they implied what Barth says explicitly: that the text is a witness to the Word of God whose authority derives from that witness to the Word who is truth, ontologically transcendent and historically incarnate, rather than from any "inherent divinized quality."[55] What makes the text adequate is not its own capacities to make God present, but divine grace. In talking of that graced referentiality, Christians must be suspicious of any categories that would disallow "the condescension of the truth to the depiction of the text—to its own self-identification with, let us say, the fourfold story of Jesus of Nazareth, taken as an ordinary story."[56] "The textual world as witness to the Word of God is not identical with the latter, and yet, by the Spirit's grace, it is 'sufficient' for the witnessing."[57] (Frei does allow a secondary role for a "tentative" historical argument for the resurrection from the evidence of the empty tomb, but it is no more plausible than its contrary and, we may add, does not get us to the divine-human truth of the risen Christ.)[58]

This is a bold account of the relationship between the Word and Scripture's human testimony. In the earlier "Theology and the Interpretation of Narrative," Frei was bolder still in his formulation of the Reformers' bibliology. For them, he says, "The text did not refer to, it *was* the linguistic presence of God, the fit

53. "Conflicts in Interpretation," in *Theology and Narrative*, 162.

54. "Conflicts," 163.

55. "Conflicts," 163.

56. "Conflicts," 164.

57. "Conflicts," 164.

58. In a piece titled, "Of the Resurrection of Christ" (originally written in 1987 for an edited volume on the Thirty-Nine Articles of the Church of England) in *Theology and Narrative*, 203–4. As in *The Identity of Jesus Christ*, so here the empty tomb is a negative condition for the truth of the resurrection.

embodiment of one who was himself 'Word,' and thus analogous to, though not identical with, Incarnation."[59] Frei's other remarks, earlier and later, on the frailty of the human text suggest this passage should be read in light of those already examined. By appealing to the Reformers in this way, Frei does not mean to identify the scriptural text and its truth here but to affirm the extent of the condescension of the Word to the story, which renders the story the embodiment of its truth so that, as Frei says, there is no question of a translinguistic reference since the reality "is given linguistically; it is linguistic for us."[60] His concluding remarks in "Conflicts in Interpretation" make clear that for him as for the Reformers the "fit" between text and truth is "realized in the constant reconstitution of the Church where the word is rightly preached and where the sacraments are rightly administered."[61] It takes place there, without any guarantees, he adds. We might best sum up his position by saying Frei sees the text as the (only) true verbal icon of the Word by the gracious, free presence of the same in the administration of Word and Sacrament, as a specific claim about Holy Scripture seen in Christian terms.

Frei understands the relationship between meaning and truth, therefore, theologically in terms of the condescension of the Word of God, Jesus of Nazareth, by way of the Spirit, to the fourfold story that, on a literal reading, identifies him. His account of Scripture in his later writing accords very much with that of *The Identity of Jesus Christ*, but now with a greater emphasis on the graced linguistic mediation of the Word by the text. It is an account explicitly and evidently indebted to that of Barth. Frei reproduces in both earlier and later work Barth's dialectic between the fallible, historically and culturally conditioned humanity of the various textual witnesses, incapable in themselves of presenting God to us, and the revelation of God in Jesus Christ that they do in fact attest and re-present, and the unity without confusion of the two in the event by which Christ, the divine Word, condescends so that God speaks through these words now as once he did.[62] In both accounts, Frei clearly distinguishes between the frail, fallible (often fragmentary and confusing) human text as witness and the truth for which it is made adequate by the presence of the Word.[63] The text is not identical with the truth. Yet in

59. "Theology and the Interpretation of Narrative," 108.

60. "Theology and the Interpretation of Narrative," 104.

61. "Conflicts," 166.

62. See *Church Dogmatics* I/2, §19, ed. G. W. Bromiley and T. F. Torrance (Edinburgh: T. & T. Clark, 1956) (henceforth *CD* I/2). Mike Higton has noted Frei's Barth-like doctrine of the Word in his "Hans Frei," in Justin S. Holcomb, *Christian Theologies of Scripture: A Comparative Introduction* (New York: New York University Press, 2006), 231.

virtue of the Spirit, it is nevertheless the linguistic medium of the presence of the Word. In this sense the text becomes the written Word: the textual medium of the gracious presence of the risen Lord. Frei has a more specific account of the textuality of the Gospels, but the effect of the witness of the Word to the human witnesses of Scripture is the same: we are bound to these texts yet cannot force them to be the Word of God, we can only orient ourselves to them in prayerful expectation.[64]

The presence of God in Christ by way of the text, on Frei's account, is grounded in the resurrection and the freedom of the risen Christ in his life to God. The textual presence of Christ is thus one specific form of the presence of the risen Christ. Hence for Frei, as for Barth, the witness of Scripture stands and falls with the declaration of Christ's divine sonship in the resurrection.[65] It is a presence that Frei approximates to the verbal presence of a speaker, yet does not involve a full or static identification of human words with the divine Word. Elsewhere Frei distinguishes between semiotic signifier, semiotic signified, and the referent of human language.[66] On his account of Scripture, the narrative identification of Jesus Christ, the signifier, is taken in Christian reading to really be about Jesus Christ, the signified. It is that human sign which God appropriates as divine effective speech by his Son, the incarnate Word, uniting himself to it. As for Barth, but with specific reference to the gospel narratives, the result is that this human narrative signifier becomes the very voice of God: the Word himself.[67] It is an intense unity that quite properly falls short of deifying the text or extending the incarnation to the text of Scripture. Though there is an analogy here with the incarnation, with Barth Frei observes the differences between the unity of divine and human in Jesus Christ and in Scripture: there is no personal union of the human words and the divine Word.[68] The text is the Word of God in a miraculous event of God's free grace on the occasion of the use of the text in Christian community (and hence more as language than as object).[69] It is not an analogy, therefore, that should be pressed too far or allowed to exert independent critical authority.

---

63. Frei speaks of the resurrection accounts in particular as "fragmentary and confusing" in "Of the Resurrection of Christ," *Theology and Narrative*, 203.

64. For Barth, see *CD* I/2, 492.

65. *Church Dogmatics* I/2, §19.2, 485–86.

66. *Types*, 78–79.

67. See *CD* I/2, §19, and esp. 532.

68. Both theologians' use of the language of witness secures this point; Barth is most explicit on it: see *CD* I/2, 499–500.

69. Cf. *CD* I/2, 502ff., 513.

The distinction of human testimony in Scripture from the presence of the Word which freely graces it allows Frei, like Barth before him, to acknowledge the human, historically and culturally conditioned character of the texts and the flaws and limitations that they bear as a result without these becoming obstacles to the authority that the text bears as the vessel of divine presence.[70] It is for this reason, presumably, that he does not simply identify Scripture with divine speech, an option of which he was well aware.[71] Indeed, Frei's following Barth's theology of Scripture when viewed in light of his analysis of the synoptic narratives allows us to distinguish between the cumulative force of the narrative sequence in its identification of the unsubstitutable identity of Jesus as one who cannot but be present, and a variety of materials taken up in the service of that identification.[72] Their contribution to the story's overall effect is sufficiently qualified that that identifying force may be sustained despite our recognition of mythical elements, or cultural values, theologoumena or ideologies at odds with the deepest logic of the story, or inconsistencies of description. Indeed, on Frei's account, that identifying force lends specificity and resolution to the ambiguous use of cultural materials throughout the narrative, requiring us to read them in light of the resurrection, whereby they may be demythologized or perhaps even subverted; a transformation that precludes simply identifying them with the divine voice apart from the movement of the narrative.

The identifying force of the narrative, gathering up and ordering its component materials, is the primary bearer of Christ's gracious presence.[73] Indeed, this position seems to fit with the very logic of those stories, as Frei understands it. The synoptics do not present themselves as God's speech, but

---

70. Compare *CD* I/2, 507–11.

71. *Identity*, 18–19.

72. This distinction does not seem to amount to the "separation" between revelation and culture that Dawson ascribes to Frei, for the narrative pattern that identifies Jesus is composed of cultural materials woven to a particular logic. See Dawson, *Christian Figural Reading*, 185.

73. In this way, Frei could answer one of Geoffrey W. Bromiley's concerns about Karl Barth's account of scriptural authority, namely that it inadvertently undermined the objective authority of the text. Frei's account of the truthfulness of this rendering of Christ's identity helps address Bromiley's worry that Barth's refusal to countenance biblical inerrancy left the reliability of the Bible's witness in doubt, and his sense of the iconic function of the gospel portrayal of Jesus Christ helps specify how the text bears divine authority while distinguishing it, as witness, from the Word it becomes. See Bromiley, "The Authority of Scripture in Karl Barth," in *Hermeneutics, Authority and Canon*, ed. D. A. Carson and J. Woodbridge (Leicester: InterVarsity, 1986), 290ff. For a robust defense of Barth on some of these questions, see Bruce L. McCormack, "The Being of Holy Scripture Is in Becoming: Karl Barth in Conversation with American Evangelical Criticism," in *Evangelicals & Scripture: Tradition, Authority and Hermeneutics*, ed. V. Bacote, L. C. Miguélez, and D. L. Ockholm (Downers Grove, IL: InterVarsity, 2004), 55–75.

tell good news about Jesus Christ; they bear witness to one whose resurrection discloses him as one who cannot but be present. In resurrection, the story attests, it becomes clear that Jesus is God's presence or, as John's Gospel describes him, God's own Word, and other words reported in the Gospels, whether human or divine, belong to the disclosure of *that* Word and are presumably effective in that regard in virtue of *his* presence. By Christ's condescension to the narrative identification of him, we might say, God speaks the whole sign: the human signifier and the divine-human signified in a representation of the cumulative utterance that is Jesus Christ.

This quasi-iconic theology of the text as the linguistic medium of Christ's presence echoes in a different idiom Gregory's account of the text as the embodiment of the incarnate Word. Frei's eschatological reserve about the possibility of specifying exactly *how* the story is true also recalls Gregory's apophatic reserve about the interpretation of divine names and is similarly grounded in the unlimited otherness of the God who has drawn near in Jesus Christ.

Frei, however, with a much fuller sense of the human weakness of the scriptural text, offers a rather different account of inspiration. Instead of Gregory's oracular account where the participation of the Scripture writers' intellects in the divine Word by the Spirit made the Spirit as much author of the text in themselves as the writer, Frei's account of inspiration places the emphasis firmly on the present moment in which the Word realizes the witnessing force of the text but is not directly identifiable with it as such. His chastened distinction between divine and human elements here seems necessary in light of a deeper, more critical understanding of the human qualities of these texts than was available to Gregory.

Following Barth, Frei might extend this account of inspiration to include the original composition of the texts as something equally graced. Following the suggestion of David Demson that Frei's account needs this supplementation, we might say that the specific way in which Scripture attests itself as Word of God has to do with the particular identities of the first witnesses of God's revelation who speak there, whether those prophetically anticipating Jesus Christ or those bearing witness to his first advent.[74] For, as Barth argues, their identities and perspectives as witnesses have shaped the form of that witness, by which Christ is now present to us also. Of these identities, Barth gives various elements of a description in *Church Dogmatics* I/2, citing the accounts

---

74. See *CD* I/2, 486f. and D. Demson, *Hans Frei and Karl Barth: Different Ways of Reading Scripture* (Grand Rapids: Eerdmans, 1997).

of the calling, commissioning, and sending of the apostles by Jesus Christ in the Gospels and in Paul's self-descriptions, with the effect that the apostles are closely identified with Christ's own voice and presence, proleptically in the synoptic narratives as well as in Acts and in Paul's own self-presentation (and that of the author of 1 John), and speak in his name, with the ability he gives them.[75] These identities in turn correspond to the pattern of identification of prophets in the Old Testament, whom the witnesses of the New recognize, in the light of the resurrection, as heralds of Jesus Christ.[76]

In *Church Dogmatics* IV/1, Barth's comments on the disciples suggest a more developed narrative analysis of their identity, which falls into four distinct phases. The first pertains to Christ's ministry, where the disciples are the most direct objects of Christ's direct self-disclosure and participants in his ministry.[77] Yet his identity is not revealed to them; the perception is closed to them.[78] Despite their privileged proximity to Christ, they are as unwitting as the rest of Israel.[79] In the second phase, the passion sequence, this lack of perception continues, and the implicit way that Christ has been set over against even the disciples with whom he has lived is worked out in Gethsemane, where he is left alone while they sleep.[80] This separation seems intrinsic to the pattern of exchange Barth traces out. For Christ seems to come as judge, even of the disciples, who reveal their lostness together with the rest of Israel in their common desertion of him, and yet he ends up bearing the judgment on their behalf.[81] So far, we might say, on Barth's analysis the disciples are distinguished from the rest of Israel by their proximity to Christ only to fail to perceive or stand by him like all the rest. They are only distinguished by the prominence of their failure, and are the object of his saving action along with everyone else.

With the resurrection, the disciples, on Barth's account, seem to gain greater individuality and focus in a way that is in continuity with what went

75. *CD* I/2, 487–88, citing Matt. 3:14 and 2:14 (both proleptic of the commissioning of the disciples in the resurrection); Eph. 4:11 and Gal. 1:1-15 on the calling and commissioning of the apostles; Luke 10:16, Matt. 10:40, John 20:21, John 17:20, and Matt. 16:18f. on the hearing and receiving of Christ in his apostles; Matt. 10:19f., Acts 1:8, John 14:26, John 16:13, and Acts 2:1ff. on the empowerment of the apostles to bear witness; and the assimilation of the apostles to Christ in the *analogia fidei* as reflected in Acts 3:4ff., Matt. 28:20, and 2 Cor. 5:20.

76. *CD* I/2, 488–91.

77. *CD* IV/1, 178.

78. On the perception being closed to them, see *CD* IV/1, 301–2.

79. Barth takes Peter's confession of Christ at Caesarea Philippi to be anticipatory of the revelation of Christ in his resurrection, *CD* IV/1, 301–2.

80. *CD* IV/1, 267.

81. *CD* IV/1, 226, 235.

before and lends it sharpness. In the resurrection they are enabled to perceive what they had witnessed as revelation.[82] The forty days of Christ's appearances form a perspective from which the disciples view the whole life and death of Jesus with enlightened perception of the act of God in that life and death and of how it determines their own existence and that of the whole world. These appearances constituted their commissioning to go out with the *kerygma* to Jerusalem and beyond. This period forms the basis for the disciples' missionary impulse and the founding of the community, but there is a transition to that foundation in the ascension, whereby Christ's presence alters in mode from being direct and perceptible to being unavoidably mediated through recollection, tradition, and proclamation.[83] Only with the advent of the Holy Spirit is the faith of the disciples revealed so that it becomes a historical factor as they bear the *kerygma* into the world.[84]

The New Testament texts themselves belong to this last phase, the time of the community in the world, grounded on the foundation of the apostles and prophets, and they bear its characteristics, looking back to the life, death, and resurrection of Jesus and forward in their light to their own time and those that follow.[85] It is from this perspective that the primitive church remembered, collected, and composed the accounts of Christ's sayings and acts: they are recalled for the present force and significance in light of the resurrection. Thus they take their form and content from the way in which the identities of the first witnesses were shaped and transformed in relation to Jesus Christ, through the resurrection-Pentecost sequence, and the implication of Barth's account is that the perspective of those first witnesses—their witness—shaped its reception down to the composition of New Testament texts.

Such an account, however, would need to do greater justice to the integral part evidently played by human creativity in that process of reception (and indeed on the part of the first witnesses), not merely recognizing it in dialectical relation to the divine Word, but making its evocation by that Word more intelligible. Here the incorporative pneumatology that informs Gregory's account of inspiration may be suggestive insofar as it encourages us to think of the activity of witnesses, tradents, and redactors as creative in virtue of a participation in the incorporative action of the Spirit, whose gifts and operations are manifold, so that we may begin to reconcile their various individual (or

---

82. *CD* IV/1, 302.

83. *CD* IV/1, 318.

84. *CD* IV/1, 338.

85. *CD* IV/1, 319–20.

communal) contributions to the shaping of the written witness as responses to the presence of the One to whom the witnesses pointed.

Frei also brings a much stronger relation of the theology of the Word to the historical existence of Jesus Christ than Gregory. However, Gregory's theology of the Word can benefit Frei's in respect of the former's understanding of the relation between Word and Spirit. Here, again, an incorporative understanding of the Spirit would help address a difficulty in Frei's theology of Scripture by opening a way to a clearer account of the union between the risen Christ and the texts that identify him. What is difficult about Frei's account is how to think of that union, and of how the text thereby becomes divine speech, while maintaining his emphasis on the undiminished creatureliness of the textual witness. On an incorporative account of the Spirit, creaturely realities are drawn into fuller participation in the Word of God. For the grammar of participation is that the participating depends upon the participated and is wholly characterized in virtue of it without sharing to the extent of identity with it, and that such participation is not necessarily reciprocated, so allowing for the radical distinction between the Word and human words to be maintained. The term "Word," like the Johannine title "Light," indicates that the risen Lord Jesus Christ is maximally intelligible, as befits Frei's understanding of him as the focal center of providential action, in whose future mode the sense of all history will be resolved. We may specify the presence of Christ as Word by way of the text more closely, then, by saying that the human witness is caught up into the event of God's Word uttered in the human flesh of Jesus of Nazareth so that its witness partakes of him and of his "Wordliness"—his fully actual representation and embodiment of what Daniel W. Hardy calls the infinite density of meaning of the divine, which brings identity and coherence to everything—thus, by the Spirit, rendering the Word in human language.[86]

For Frei, our cognitive knowledge of the truth is complemented by the Spirit's work of conforming the disciple to its truth and helping them see the world truly. The presence of the Word by the text is met, as it were, by the action of the Spirit in the shaping of the life of the reader. Here there seems to be an allusion to the account in *The Identity of Jesus Christ* of the unity of apprehension of Christ's identity with love of God and neighbor, to the notion there and in Frei's "Remarks" that in part we discover the truth of the story as we pattern our lives after it and in part an anticipation of the later piece on H. Richard Niebuhr on the progressive political engagement to which theologians are called, now more explicitly as part of what it means to

---

86. See Hardy, "Reason, Wisdom and the Interpretation of Scripture," in *Reading Texts, Seeking Wisdom*, ed. David F. Ford and Graham Stanton (London: SCM, 2003), 85.

receive and experience the truth of Scripture's testimony.[87] Frei's account here also fills out a little further the Trinitarian shape of his theology of Scripture. To make sense of the claim that God is truly named with reference to Jesus Christ as identified by the fourfold gospel story, we have to think about the text in relation to Jesus Christ as the Word of God; to make sense of how this truthfulness is not only cognitive but lived, life-shaping, and prophetic, we have to talk about the Holy Spirit who is at once God and distinct from God. We could extend Frei's account one step further by saying that since, as he says, we have to hold together the first claim with the second on account of the inseparability of the cognitive and existential-prophetic dimensions of God as truth, so we must hold that this inseparability derives not from us but pertains to the truth itself as the source of our knowledge and experience of God. In this way, Frei seems to gesture here to something like a Trinitarian theology of revelation of a very restrained kind, where the triunity of God in revelation discloses the divine triunity *in se*; an account that bears some resemblance to that of Karl Barth in *Church Dogmatics* I/1.[88]

The Presence of the Word, the Priority of the Story of Jesus Christ, and the Shape of the Canon

Not only is Frei's account of Scripture properly theological, his theology of Scripture also makes sense of how he thinks Scripture should be read, in ways that are more robust than sometimes thought. In his lecture on "Conflicts in Interpretation," it is on the properly theological grounds of the graced condescension of the Word to the story that Frei pleads "for the textuality of Scripture, the importance of its linguistic-descriptive shape this side of metaphor" or rather the priority of its meaning under the literal sense.[89] In the first instance, as Frei's procedure in *The Identity of Jesus Christ*, the rules for literal reading enumerated above, and Frei's remarks on the theology of

---

87. Hence Gary Comstock is wrong to argue that what Frei means by saying the texts are true is opaque, in his "Truth or Meaning: Ricoeur versus Frei on Biblical Narrative," *The Journal of Religion* 66, no. 2 (April 1986): 117–40. Full clarity is inappropriate for theological reasons, but Frei's account is still a recognizable combination of coherence (the logic of the story requires its truth), correspondence (therefore Jesus really is risen and alive), and function (the text is true in the way it works in one's life), but reshapes each of these notions around the reality of God's presence to us in Christ. See also Frei's letter to Comstock of November 5th 1984, *YDS* 12-184. To this extent, Frei anticipates Bruce Marshall's treatment of the topic in his *Trinity and Truth* (Cambridge: Cambridge University Press, 1999).

88. Specifically in §§8–9.

89. "Conflicts," 164.

Scripture from his later writings all make clear, this textuality denotes the narrative rendering of the identity of Jesus Christ in the synoptic Gospels.

This decision anchors Christian reading in features of the text that retain sufficient objectivity and integrity to provide a norm over against the reader's understanding and categories, and to make possible its authoritative function. Although in his later writings, Frei qualified heavily his appeal to the category of realistic narrative, which helped him make this claim in respect of the passion-resurrection sequence of the synoptic Gospels, in his later writings he retains an insistence on these texts' power of resistance to the theories and categories we bring to the interpretation of them. Explicating Barth on the subordination of reading schemes to Scripture in his final Schaffer Lecture, as published in *Types of Christian Theology*, Frei affirms with him that "the text is not inert but exerts a pressure of its own on the inquiring reader who is bound to bring his or her own pre-understanding and interests to the reading." [90] He adds, citing Frank Kermode, that "a 'good enough' text . . . has the power to resist; it has a richness and complexity that act on the reader."[91] The features of the text, he adds, provide a common reference point by which to adjudicate readings, and by these we may take him to mean the very "narrative structures" he refers to in earlier writings, in particular the direct interaction of character and circumstance.[92] Such statements indicate a more general principle: that to the extent that the theme and formal features are interwoven, respect for that complexity in the use of the text provides the measure of good interpretation. The richer and more complex the text, the greater the constraint they place on interpretations, and the smaller the scope of interpretations that most readers will judge the text to be patient of bearing. Their intricacy and wealth of features provide a check on interpretation and a criterion—simply stated in the abstract but complex in application—by which to assess differences in interpretation. For Frei, the synoptic narratives are, in Frank Kermode's terms, good enough texts, those with the capacity "to subvert obvious expectations and manifest senses."[93] They resist a total interpretation. Hence Christian reading of Scripture must be, to borrow a term from Valentine Cunningham, "tactful," denoting a careful, attentive "touching" of the text in reading.[94] To this end, and subordinate to this priority, it would be consistent with Frei's approach to

90. *Types*, 86.

91. The reference is to Kermode, *The Genesis of Secrecy: On the Interpretation of Narrative* (Cambridge, MA: Harvard University Press, 1979), 14.

92. *Types*, 87.

93. *Types*, 106.

94. V. Cunningham, *Reading After Theory* (Oxford: Blackwell, 2002), 155ff.

adduce a wide range of critical tools, textual, historical (see below), redactional, rhetorical, and literary.[95]

The primary reason, however, for the primacy of the literal ascriptive reading of the narrative sequence of the Synoptics is theological, as we have seen. That theological account of the presence of the risen Lord Jesus Christ as Word also grounds the primacy of these stories so read over both other genres of discourse in the Gospels and over other texts in the Christian canon, and warrants a relative primacy to narrative in that canon. It is also a role to which these texts are suited. Frei agrees with Barth that the story of Jesus, while not a salve for all ambiguities, is "more perspicuous than others and therefore more conducive to agreed-upon interpretation—or 'plain reading.'"[96] It is thus capable of functioning as "a kind of loose organizing center for the whole."[97] The story of Jesus as a loose organizing center while bringing relative perspicacity suggests both flexibility and tolerance for a fair degree of ambiguity and opaqueness in the discernment of the unity of the witness of Scripture. Without developing a full account of what canonical reading might look like for him, Frei offers several clues as to how the priority of Jesus' story might function in this way.

First, as we have already seen, it prioritizes the narrative sequence over Christological titles taken in abstraction from it. In Frei's own reading, those titles contribute to the ambiguity of the early parts of the story, but when their sense is clarified with the resolution of Christ's own identity, they also contribute to the overall rendering of who Jesus Christ is.[98] Second, Frei also advocated reading the parables in Jesus' preaching in light of the passion-resurrection sequence, as part of the narrative identification of Jesus Christ. They are indirectly metaphorically descriptive of the identity of the one who spoke them "with authority."[99] Third, in his accounts of the literal sense, Frei takes the narrative identification of Jesus to have priority over the prescriptive

---

95. C. Kavin Rowe demonstrates the fruitfulness of applying textual and redactional criticism to a narrative analysis of Christ's identity in Luke's Gospel in his *Early Narrative Christology: The Lord in the Gospel of Luke* (Grand Rapids: Baker Academic, 2009).

96. *Types*, 87.

97. *Types*, 87.

98. For an excellent development of this approach to the Gospel of Luke that supports Frei's reading of a high Christology there through an analysis of Luke's use of *kurios* in the context of his narrative, see C. Kavin Rowe, *Early Narrative Christology*. In Rowe's analysis, the title *kurios* does irreplaceable work in expressing fundamental aspects of Luke's Christology, not least the intertwining of Jesus' historical existence with its revelatory force disclosed in the resurrection (217–18), yet without blurring historical realism in the portrayal of the pre-Easter Jesus (cf. 216), and in such a way as to make sense of the unity of his agency with God's in the book of Acts (202).

dimensions of the Gospels.[100] In other words, insofar as the Gospels lay down a way of life for a community, the identity of Jesus is the clue to the meaning of those regulations.

Fourth, this complex narrative identification of Jesus Christ serves as the center for reading the wider New Testament witness. Frei is cautious here: there is no easy way to describe or show the unity of the canon. His plea in his "Remarks" was to take the narrative identification of Christ in the Gospels as an "*incomplete* clue to the rest of Scripture."[101] With respect to the New Testament, no single hermeneutical device could cover its variety of texts. Nevertheless, by starting with the narrated identity of Jesus Christ in the synoptics, one could move, for example, to John and Paul seen as commentary on this story (or the sequence of events it relates). A number of studies have demonstrated the central role played by the story of Jesus Christ as the "substructure" on which Paul reflects in several key passages in his letters, including paranetic passages.[102] These analyses suggest the fruitfulness of Frei's suggestion as a hermeneutical move for reading Pauline texts theologically that might in turn enrich our grasp of Jesus' identity and its ramifications for us and our world, not least in respect of the concept of participation in Christ in the Spirit.[103]

With respect to the Old Testament, Frei's caution and qualification of the illumining power of the gospel narratives is all the more in order. There can be no easy reduction of what Christians call the Old Testament to Christian meanings or Christological witness. Nevertheless, that the story of Jesus Christ informs the way Christians ought to read the Scriptures they share with Jewish readers follows from its rendering of his identity. For in his passion and resurrection, Frei tells us, Jesus Christ is the Christ of Israel who "in his own singular identity and unsubstitutable history, sums up and identifies the history

---

99. "Conflicts," 165. Frei thought this approach represented a consensus in Christian tradition ("Theology and the Interpretation of Narrative," 104, 110–11); a claim that could certainly be supported from much premodern exegesis of the parables.

100. "The 'Literal Reading,'" 120, where admittedly his point is wider.

101. "Remarks," 42–43. The emphasis is Frei's.

102. Richard B. Hays, *The Faith of Jesus Christ: The Narrative Substructure of Galatians 3:1–4:11* (Grand Rapids: Eerdmans, 2002) [originally published in 1983]; Stephen E. Fowl *The Story of Christ in the Ethics of Paul: An Analysis of the Function of the Hymnic Material in the Pauline Corpus* (Sheffield: JSOT, 1990); N. T. Wright, *The Climax of the Covenant: Christ and the Law in Pauline Theology* (London: T. & T. Clark, 1993), 200–214; Douglas A. Campbell, "The Story of Jesus in Romans and Galatians," in *Narrative Dynamics in Paul: A Critical Assessment*, ed. B. Longenecker (Louisville: Westminster John Knox, 2002), 97–124.

103. Which, as Richard Hays notes, a narrative approach to Paul tends to highlight. See his "Is Paul's Gospel Narratable?," *Journal for the Study of the New Testament* 27, no. 2 (2004): 228–30, 235–36.

of the whole people."[104] It is, in other words, the consequence of the vicarious atoning work that is so bound up with his identity: he assumes and transforms the identity of Israel so that Israel and her history are identified in relation to him. Hence it is that the risen Lord, on the road to Emmaus, interprets "in all the scriptures the things concerning himself."[105] For those who believe in the risen Lord, the meanings of the Old Testament are now firmly related to Christ as their fulfillment.[106]

In his later writing, Frei speaks in terms of the choices made in early Christian tradition about the applicative use of the story of Jesus with reference to other scriptural texts, a choice that, we have seen him argue, is grounded in a belief about the presence of Christ that Frei's own theology of the Word explicates. The narrative identification of Christ became the basis for combining "that disparate set of stories from Jewish and Christian Scriptures" which we now term "salvation history" into one sequence.[107] Frei recognizes a range of procedures for this combinative reading, an activity that he traces back to the New Testament witnesses themselves. The Gospels and the Pauline epistles provide paradigms for this procedure.[108]

Of the several modes of this procedure practiced in premodern interpretation, Frei clearly favors figural or typological interpretation; where earlier events are taken as real in their own right, earlier meanings are complex and meaningful in themselves, but these are in some way incomplete in such a way that their incompleteness is resolved by the story of Jesus (or the whole story of salvation) so that they become figures of it in a relationship that is at once temporal as well as literary or metaphorical.[109] For this approach, as exemplified by Calvin, did not evacuate Old Testament texts of their own meaning and integrity, but "extended" it by discerning a connection in terms of providential design between its subject matter and its temporal fulfillment, and where interpretation as a spiritual act merely supplies the comprehension

---

104. *Identity*, 137.

105. Luke 24:26-27, cited by Frei in *Identity*, 136.

106. Cf. *CD* I/2, 489-90.

107. "Theology and the Interpretation of Narrative," 110.

108. As Richard Hays has shown with respect to Paul. See his *Echoes of Scripture in the Letters of Paul* (New Haven: Yale University Press, 1993). As he says elsewhere, "the story of Jesus Christ . . . becomes for Paul the ordering framework that imparts unity and directionality to all other stories, including the stories of Israel's Scripture," in his "Is Paul's Gospel Narratable?," 224. See also Ben Witherington III, *Paul's Narrative Thought World: The Tapestry of Tragedy and Triumph* (Louisville: Westminster John Knox, 1994), and A. Katherine Grieb, *The Story of Romans: A Narrative Defense of God's Righteousness* (Louisville: Westminster John Knox, 2002).

109. "The 'Literal Sense,'" 121–22.

of their connection without prejudice to the concrete reality of the figure.[110] In this way, on Frei's account, figural reading is not a reading that resolves figures to their Christological fulfillment without remainder and so that no other reading of them is possible; it discerns a partial relationship between two patterns of meaning that is not necessary except for those who accept Christ's identity in the resurrection, and that sends us back into both stories.[111] As the examples of the Gospels, the Pauline epistles, and Karl Barth's practice also show, the process of reading Christ as the fulfillment to the figures of Israel's Scriptures also illumines the identity and significance of Jesus Christ, providing the terms in which it is made intelligible.[112] To this extent, Frei advocates the disciplined recovery of a procedure we also see exemplified in Gregory, shorn of its symbolic exegesis and eschatological references, which might yet bear careful recovery when ordered under the literal sense.

Frei only sketches the implications of his theology of Scripture for the configuration of the canon, and significant (but not fatal) questions can be raised in respect of it: How, for example, do texts of genres like wisdom or apocalyptic relate to the story of Jesus? It also has at least one telling weakness insofar as Frei does not explain or emphasize the relation of the story of Jesus to the eschatological elements of New Testament texts (though Frei's eschatology is important for his own theology). Nevertheless, it is an attractive vision that has room for degrees of dissonance and awkwardness of fit, for Old Testament texts to retain their particular strangeness in relation to the strangeness of Jesus Christ, and not to be swallowed up by that relation. There is no attempt here to construct a simple sequential narrative into which all texts could fit, although Frei does envisage a larger narrative shape from creation to eschaton with the story of Jesus Christ at the center. Nor does Frei attempt to make all the canonical texts fit a common master category or theme. Instead, an individual is made central but not in such a way as to bend other texts toward him against their grain. The relations between his identity and their patterns of meaning may be discerned, partially and provisionally, but not forced.

---

110. *Eclipse*, 28ff. For an excellent account of how Frei's notion of figural reading dissolves an opposition of figural to literal by grounding the integrity of figures in Jesus' identity being resolved through divine action in the resurrection, see Dawson, *Christian Figural Reading*, and esp. 163.

111. In *Eclipse*, viii, Frei points us to Barth's figural exegesis in *CD* II/2, 340–409 as exemplifying this approach. For an analysis, see Mike Higton, "The Fulfilment of History in Barth, Frei, Auerbach and Dante," in *Conversing with Barth*, ed. M. Higton and John C. McDowell (Aldershot: Ashgate, 2004), 120–41, to whom I owe the point about figural reading sending us back into both narrative poles of the figure.

112. For Barth, see *CD* II/2, 340–409. For Paul, see the references in n. 106.

In terms of Frei's theology of Scripture, this central role of the story of Jesus Christ in the canon follows from his identity as disclosed in the resurrection. One obvious way to extend his theology of the Word to encompass explicitly more of the canon would be to argue that other scriptural texts may become bearers of the gracious presence of the Lord Jesus Christ as Word as he condescends to be identified in relation to them. We might go further, picking up on the Lukan story of the risen Lord exegeting Israel's Scriptures (Luke 24:25-27), and say that in respect of those texts Christ, through his presence in the relation of his story to them, comes as the expounder of Israel's Scriptures for those who would attend to the connections. In respect of New Testament reflection upon his identity and its significance for particular Christian communities or Christian discipleship in a first-century context, we might say with Gregory that Christ condescends to be present through the allusions to his story in the mode of teacher and rhetor, who once by the Spirit elicited such reflection, and by means of that paradigmatic reflection seeks to elicit it once more for other readers in respect of their particular contexts. In short, it would seem consistent with Frei's Barth-like theology of the Word taken together with his account of Jesus' identity to see Christ's gracious presence via the narrative renderings of that identity, not only as the organizing center of the canon but the heart of the way God exercises authority through the canon.

At this point, however, we may note an objection to Frei's account, namely that his emphasis on textuality will not suffice to sustain the authoritative function he attributes to the texts in question. Nicholas Wolterstorff raises the problem of Scripture as a "wax nose," which can be twisted any which way according to the ideologies we bring to the text: a problem, he notes, with which Frei was preoccupied throughout his career.[113] His concern seems to be that Frei, by making the meaning of the texts subject to the interpretative decision of the church, does not alleviate the anxiety, for he has merely replaced the malleability of the text to the individual interpreter with the specter of its manipulation by the community.[114] He does not establish a ground for the community's interpretation. While the anxiety can never wholly be alleviated, the best way to minimize it is to understand the Bible as divine discourse: God's appropriation of authorially intended meanings. For such meanings have the requisite fixity, and we should assume that God intends to say the same thing with the same words unless we have good reason, grounded in a scriptural doctrine of God, for doing so—and with the proviso that we may be wrong.

---

113. *Divine Discourse*, 226–30.

114. *Divine Discourse*, 235.

Wolterstorff mistakes Frei's position in number of ways. He portrays Frei as consistently rejecting authorial intention as determinative of meaning and of not thinking about Scripture in terms of divine discourse.[115] We have already seen that the latter is inaccurate: there is a sense in which the Bible becomes divine speech for Frei. The former is untrue also. Frei holds that texts have determinate features because they are authorially intended. Texts do not write themselves, Frei says, but "the author's intention is not a separable mental entity or action from the consecutive activity of working out his action."[116] Intentions are implicit actions; actions are explicit intentions. To attend to authorial intention is precisely to attend to what authors have *done* in respect of all the features just named (and more).[117] Frei was by no means opposed to considerations of authorial intention so long as it is a matter of attending to what an author did rather than speculating about motives or an authorial consciousness located "behind" the text.[118]

At the same time, in his later writings Frei admitted more of a role for the reader and for reading communities. Wolterstorff's argument anticipates any simple, final appeal to the authority of reading communities to address his complaint and shows its inadequacy.[119] While some communal authority is involved in the notion of literal reading, we have seen that its basis lies in the consistent apprehension of the presence of Christ by way of the stories about him. It is quite true to say that therefore the communal way of reading rests on a belief, but the same can be said of Wolterstorff's account of divine discourse. The strength of Wolterstorff's position lies in the overlap it posits between authorial communicative intentions and divine communicative intentions. However, this move involves a problematic degree of abstracting both communicative actions from their specific historical contexts, whereas taking these into account might problematize the very overlap Wolterstorff needs. Surely God's communicative intentions toward any given church community today with respect to the Corinthian correspondence is not identical to Paul's, having in view as it does a very different community in a very different context.[120] Frei's position is arguably more flexible, in that there is nothing to stop us thinking of the presence of the risen Lord Jesus Christ as Word

---

115. *Divine Discourse*, 223, 231.

116. *Eclipse*, 281.

117. It is quite possible, of course, that the results of authorial intentions may exceed what was consciously purposed.

118. See "Remarks," 33 (cf. *Eclipse*, 268–89).

119. The obvious candidate here would be Stanley Fish's account in his *Is There a Text in This Class? The Authority of Interpretive Communities* (Cambridge, MA: Harvard University Press, 1980).

by way of the text as directed to specific circumstances in various ways. But precisely because the community recognizes that presence in respect of texts' formal features that resist readerly manipulation, as we have seen, it is at least no less robust as a necessary condition for scriptural authority.[121] Literal reading actually fosters a binding of the reading community to features of Scripture that exert a counterpressure to their categories, ideologies, and habits, the features that make possible its normative function.[122]

THE THEOLOGY OF SCRIPTURE AND THE THEOLOGY OF HISTORY

Having explicated and defended Frei's theology of Scripture, it is time to examine its import for the challenges posed by historical consciousness to the theological interpretation of Scripture. That challenge, as we have seen, has at its heart the problematizing of divine action in a historical world and pertains to seeing the text as an instrument of divine action, to the bifurcation of its witness and both the historically reconstructed past and the present of the historically conscious reader, to the consequent relativizing of its authority, which entails its exposure to ethical questioning as another historically conditioned religious textual tradition. By taking Frei's theological account of Scripture in relation to his theology of history, we may begin to see a way of addressing these challenges.

First, for Frei, divine action in respect of Scripture is not simply an interruption of contingent events that disturbs the historical continuum. Because it is a matter of the presence of the risen Lord Jesus Christ as Word, it is the presence of one in whom history is mysteriously and providentially configured. For in him, as the focus of God's mysterious, loving rule, human and cosmic history in their contingent complexity are providentially ordered, an order realized through the configuration of other agencies after his future form yet without prejudice to their creaturely freedom. His presence by way of Scripture is an intensified manifestation of a presence that is coextensive with and inclusive of the extensity of the historical continuum and with the manifold complex, contingent interactions of which it is constituted. That manifest presence in Word and Sacrament has a particular purpose relative to the whole of human history, for it constitutes the church as a social body whose

120. It might be better to think of an analogy of communicative intentions instead, though this introduces a little more room for anxiety!

121. We should also recall that the literal sense is not exactly a communal interpretation of the text as an informal rule about how it may be read.

122. As Mike Higton has pointed out to me (*pers. comm.*).

unity derives likewise from Christ and which, in its frailty and fallibility, bears witness to the wider human world regarding the One in whom human history and human identities will ultimately find meaning and resolution. On such an account it becomes very difficult to see how one could sustain the objection that in the end Frei's account of Scripture tends to isolate the text from its relations to reality. On the contrary, that relation is deep and maximally extensive by way of the extensity of the presence of Jesus Christ. In so linking the theology of Scripture to Jesus Christ as the shaping center of human and cosmic history, Frei echoes and furthers Gregory's connection of these elements with greater complexity and realism of historical vision.

This connection with Frei's theology of history casts further light on the account of the origins of Scripture developed above, for it makes the handing down, collation, and redaction of the testimony of the first witnesses in the early church a process within a wider nexus of cultural, economic, and social interactions in the first-century Mediterranean (as indeed they appear to be in the New Testament), whose shaping by the impact of that witness is entirely in accord with its universal historical import. Indeed, the formation, preservation, dissemination, and piecemeal ecclesial recognition of what became the New Testament texts, which combine frail, fallible words with testimony to Jesus Christ as Lord and their subsequent recognition and in particular in the combination of these various frail, fallible texts with the Scriptures of Israel, we might discern another echo of the pattern of the unity of divine and human identity to which the stories bear witness with respect to Jesus Christ, and hence a fragmentary, partial, obscure anticipation of the final form of his presence: the stuff of an eschatologically chastened bibliology. For these events also are ordered providentially in Jesus Christ.

This account might be further extended to the implicit practical consensus about the reading of the gospel narratives as stories about Jesus Christ that Frei calls the literal sense. I have already argued that it is the experience in Christian community of Christ's presence in the narratives of the Gospels read in literally ascriptive fashion that explains that consensus theologically. In the continuity of this rule amidst great variations of cultural practices, including enormous variations of reading practices, in widely differing contexts, we might discern a sign of the constancy of Christ to the Christian communities in their continuity over time around his contested identity; a sign of the unity of the diverse cultures and the future reconciliation of their warring parties and denominations. For, as the logic of the story as continued in the book of Acts implies, the Lord Jesus is active in the practices of the church that bears his name.[123] A more incorporative pneumatology would help here too, as the grace mysteriously at work in the human agency of the members of these communities in their interactions with their own circumstances serves not only to maintain this rule, but at various times and places makes it the basis for fresh adaptations, negotiations, and improvisations—with cultural materials to hand and inherited Christian forms in new and changing contexts.

The World of the Text and the History It Renders

Frei's account does not require that the history-like world portrayed in Scripture be always or even largely reconcilable with a critical reconstruction of the history of ancient Israel, Jesus of Nazareth, or the primitive Christian communities. What matters most for Frei's purposes is the portrayal of the identity of God and his people in their engagement with the wider human world in its cosmic context, in which the rendering of the identity of Jesus Christ and his disciples is central and lends specificity and clarity to the whole. For that purpose, on Frei's account, the claim of the Gospels that Jesus was the kind of man he is portrayed to be is a historical claim but not one that requires that every saying be authentic or every pericope traceable to a putative reconstruction of the "historical Jesus," nor one that can be settled definitively. For in the gospel narratives, his identity is not fully resolved until the passion-resurrection sequence. One might be able to trace degrees of likeness and dissimilarity with Jewish figures, practices, institutions, and ideas we know of from first-century Palestine; we may be able to make speculative judgments about the likely historicity of certain episodes, both negative and positive; we may be able with some confidence to assign some to a first-century wandering Jewish teacher, miracle worker, and apocalyptic preacher and others to the communities that identified him as the Messiah of Israel and Lord who was and is to come. However, we will not yet have really attended to the identity of the Jesus Christ the Gospels render until we look where his most characteristic intentions are enacted and where he comes most sharply into unsubstitutable focus. All historical judgments are provisional, for the Christian, until we do, for on the passion-resurrection sequence turns the meaning of the whole story and its components.

When we do, we discover one whose identity is inseparable from the identity of God, precisely as a history-like figure, who lends definition to all the ways in which he had been characterized in the story hitherto. Whether we can accept this historical claim, which stretches the conceptuality of "fact"

---

123. So Rowe, *Early Narrative Christology*, 202.

and demands that we reorient our historical sensibilities around Jesus Christ, is a matter of faith, Frei says. The empty tomb is a negative criterion of its truth, but the reality is of an order at once historical and transcending all historical analogies, not as an exception from the historical continuum but the focal center from which it takes its order.

Accepting this claim will have consequences for how we read the story. For now it must be seen primarily as a bearer of the identity of one who is graciously present by way of it. Such a state of affairs does not preclude the kind of historical judgments mentioned above, but it will inflect the terms upon which they are made and their importance. If we accept that Jesus is as the Gospels render him, in Frei's sense, then making historical judgments on the assumption of his nonresurrection or a sharp discontinuity between the pre-Easter Jesus and the faith of the post-Easter community will no longer be an option. To go a little beyond Frei, it seems consistent with the claim of the Gospels to exercise the historical imagination in drawing tentative analogies between Jesus as identified in his death and resurrection and other things we know about his Jewish first-century context, but these cannot yield or govern his unsubstitutable identity rendered definitively in the passion-resurrection sequence. We may properly detect elements of myth or fiction even in that sequence, but as contributing to the history-like rendering of an identity rather than as signs of an unhistorical mentality. Nor can we definitely rule out miracle stories.[124] Given Frei's understanding of the resurrection, we might understand such figures not as interruptions to the historical order but anticipations or manifestations of the presence of the risen Christ which orders all history.[125] Similar considerations might be extended backward to the story of Israel and forward to that of the primitive church, so long as the relationship between the meaning of the relevant texts to the story of Jesus Christ is upheld as primary.

124. Frei once wrote that he would interpret signs, wonders, or miracles in the gospels as types or figures of the resurrection. He may well have meant types or figures in a merely literary sense, but his notion of figural meaning would admit of a relation here between two concrete historical events. See Letter to William Placher, March 24th, 1974. *YDS* 4-78.

125. It is striking in this respect that Frei can use the language of miracle to talk about the resurrection, the inclusion of human beings in Christ's saving work, his evoking of our faith in him, and the truthfulness of the gospel narratives in rendering the risen Jesus Christ. See, for example, "Of the Resurrection of Christ," 203, 205, and "Response," 211–12.

The World of the Text and Its Readers in a Historical World

For Frei, the story of Jesus Christ identifies one who, in virtue of his vicarious identification with us in our need and the manifestation of his historical identity as inseparable from God's identity, configures the identity of every human being. As this one, he will one day sum up all human and cosmic history in himself in the future mode of his presence. In his narrated identity lies the partial clue we have for discerning tentatively the pattern of his presence in the church, in our neighbors, and in the events of our history all seen as figures of him. We are summoned by his presence to follow him at a distance, to pattern our lives after his identity, recognizing his presence in the text and the world with a combination of faith and love of God and neighbor, in whom we may encounter him *incognito*; we are called likewise to a discernment of the patterns of his presence shaping human history and on this basis and the belief that the gospel of God has much to do with a "carefully circumscribed progressive politics," to contribute to public discussion about the goods, ends, and forward direction of institutions, communities, and nations.[126] Frei's theology of Scripture, through its connection with his theology of history, thus allows us to see how Scripture might be the vehicle of divine address to historically conscious human beings, for the heart of that address is the story of one in whom our history is shaped and in the crepuscular light of whose identity we are called to live. Where this story is at the heart of our applicative reading of Scripture, governing the way we relate to and learn from its texts, the meaningfulness of Scripture generates a historical sensibility that is like Troeltsch's in its sense of contingency and immanent causal interconnection, yet thoroughly theological.

In light of Frei's theology of Scripture, we may see this summons as the force of Christ's presence by way of his story, and borrowing from Barth describe that force in the language of command.[127] The presence of the risen Lord Jesus Christ as Word by way of the story that identifies him comes to believers as the command of God, requiring their conformity to the pattern of his identity in their love of God and neighbor, whether the near neighbor of one's immediate life circumstances or the wider social and political neighborhood of community and nation and the organizations and institutions vital for its flourishing.

The obedient love Christ commands in himself is, for Frei, bound up with a true recognition of the Word present by way of the text, and this unity

---

126. "H. Richard Niebuhr," 232.
127. See *CD* II/2, 509ff.

of re-cognition and loving response to God and neighbor is grounded in the inseparable unity of the Spirit with the Word and with God. Here again an incorporative pneumatology would help address a problem in Frei's account. For, on his account, it is difficult to distinguish between the presence of Christ as Spirit by way of the text and the Spirit who evokes the faith and loving obedience called for by that presence. To say that Christ's presence evokes its own response seems to offer no place for the subjectivity, cognition, desire, and will of disciples. Frei, by saying that we need the language of Spirit alongside that of God and Word to hold together the correspondence and the existential ways in which the text is truthful, seems to recognize the inadequacy of that move. An incorporative pneumatology assigns to the Spirit a dynamic that cannot be collapsed back into Christ's presence nor separated from it, but gathers up disciples into ever-greater conformity with and participation in Jesus Christ, and includes an orientation toward God in him that allows for the disciples' subjectivity in (re-)orientation toward Christ. Similarly, Gregory's account of the many *logoi* that inhere in the one Logos, and that provide ways for finite, temporal beings to participate in him is also suggestive for Frei, for whom all human identities are somehow "contained" in Christ and ordered by him. The Christ "embodied" in the gospel narratives, the crucified and risen Lord who is God's Wisdom, we might say, is at once a historical figure and as such the ordering principle of all historical lives and forms. In the infinite density of his identity so understood, there is a kind of capaciousness for a multitude of disciples to find the clue to their own vocations in the everyday as figures of his truth.[128]

Such reading is at once, for Christians, a spiritual and rational practice and lies at the heart of their historical sensibility. It is also doxological, as we have seen in the previous chapter. There is something like Gregory's concern for contemplation of Christ here, now oriented more firmly to his narrated identity. Since the Word is linguistic for us in the Gospels, and those who may read or hear the story are linguistic animals, we may take inspiration from Gregory's account of consuming the Logos in the text and say that the Word is present in such a way that the process of attentive understanding is doxological because in this way the Word is rendered patient of participation through reading and analysis. Following and redescribing the story then becomes contemplative and participative of the One thereby present, a consuming of the Lamb. For Frei, such contemplation is inseparable from

---

128. As are the elect (and the rejected) in Barth's account of the election of individuals, *CD* II/2, 306ff., esp. 353–54.

practice since the truth of Scripture involves the reader's obedient love of God and neighbor.

The presence of Christ by way of his narrative rendering in the Gospels thus becomes the focus and reference point of the life of discipleship and for the task of public theology through its figural application to the immediate and the wider world. Here a fuller specification of the identity of the figures of the disciple and the Christian by closer attention to their renderings in the New Testament would help to inform a thicker sense of what such conformity and participation involve. It might in part give greater clarity and grounding to the sense of Christ's presence as a commanding presence, directing human beings down new avenues in concrete modes of partaking in him. It might suggest that one important way in which we are to receive the commanding presence of Christ in the relation of his story to non-narrative parts of the canon is as eliciting reflection on his identity and its implications for us and for our world, and to see the practical challenges of Christian and secular civic communities in light of this way of imagining the world. Dominical instruction in the synoptics and John, the deliberations depicted in Acts, and Pauline paranesis, for example, all help us learn to discern the directing force of Christ's commanding presence for the particulars of our lives, communities, and circumstances.

In rendering this world and training us to respond to the command issued there in the person of Jesus Christ, what part might the Old Testament play? Frei's argument in *The Eclipse of Biblical Narrative* celebrates premodern exegetes for whom the Old Testament prefigured not only Jesus Christ but human history after him, and he commends Barth's figural interpretation in his account of the elect and rejected in *Church Dogmatics* II/2, which examines Old Testament characters not only as figural clues to Jesus Christ but also as guides to what it is to live out one's election as elect or rejected. These clues suggest it would be consonant with Frei's position to see in the Old Testament history, which Jesus Christ sums up, figures not only of him but of what it might be to follow him, to partake of his presence, to live as a community in interaction with the wider human and nonhuman spheres. In so doing we would be following the paradigm for reading the Old Testament offered by Paul in his letters, according to Richard Hays's analysis: that, as Paul's practice in 1 Cor. 10:1-13 vividly illustrates, the church is to learn its own identity and path from the story of Israel it has inherited and in which God's eschatological action in Christ and the identity and vocation of the church are prefigured.[129] This approach supplies, in effect, a way of realizing the

---

129. See Hays, *The Conversion of the Imagination: Paul as Interpreter of Israel's Scripture* (Grand Rapids: Eerdmans, 2005).

community-shaping potential in the canonical shaping that Childs finds in the Old Testament. To take it would be to resume, with more restraint and a firmer sense of the rich integrity and proper alterity of the meanings of Old Testament texts in their own right, an imaginative approach to the Old Testament text that we find in Gregory along with so many other early Christian writers.

In so doing we have to recognize again that such instructions are part of the human witness of Scripture to Jesus Christ and not identical with his presence, and that they may be highly contextually specific, and will bear the traces and influence of aspects of the cultural milieu in which they were innovated and issued. They might be seen, then, not as timeless imperatives but as indications and paradigms of what it is to pattern human living after the identity of Jesus Christ, what it is to respond with loving obedience to his sovereign presence as Word. In short, Frei challenges us to see the meaningfulness of other canonical texts in and through their relations with the story of Jesus Christ, whether by way of commentary or figuration, to understand their authority as functioning by way of that relation, in virtue of which Christ graciously condescends to use such texts to conform our minds and action to himself. It is in this way that their "force" for Christian readers might best be understood. From Gregory we might also take the cue to see in the Word's gracious presence in the text and in the Spirit's drawing of the church, world, and the reading disciple (with their agencies and interiorities) into conformity to Christ, a kind of divine training, education, and persuasion of human beings in their histories and contexts that make use of just these indications and paradigms as governed by the pattern of his identity. Thus we might say that Christ trains us by way of his story and these other textual resources to recognize his presence and to learn to follow him. By such recognition and obedience in the spirit, it seems fair to Frei and consistent with Gregory to say, Christ leads us deeper into both cognitive and enacted participation in his own identity and life.

The textual condition for this kind of address of the text to readers in a historical world remains the history-likeness, the realism of the New Testament, whether in narrative or other forms: the various ways in which disciples are rendered as fully immersed in their interactions with others and with their circumstances and just so as figures of Jesus Christ in the Spirit. The story renders, Frei is still prepared to say in his later writings, "the same kind of world as ours, the world in which persons and circumstances shape each other and their stories cannot be told without that interaction."[130] The truth condition of the address of the text, however, and the reason its portrayal of a history-like

---

130. "Theology and the Interpretation of Narrative," 111.

world can have compelling force for us in our time, is because of the history-wide significance of Jesus Christ's identity. To this extent, Frei again echoes a strategy we have seen in Gregory: it is the universal historical significance of Jesus Christ, the *Logos*, which grounds the applicability of the biblical texts and its pedagogy for the reader enmeshed in historical circumstances. For Frei, though, that claim is made with more thoroughgoing realism. It is Christ's identity as one who is present to and in history, to and in the lives of historical individuals, and to and in the church and the disciples who compose it, as the focal center of God's providential action by which all those realities are ordered so that they become figures of him—it is this identity that unites the world of the text with our world. It makes, to use Frei's language in *The Eclipse of Biblical Narrative*, the world of the text the real world we inhabit: not in the sense that it is a photocopy of our world in its baffling complexity but that it renders by way of its central story and related texts a way of seeing that world truly, as mysteriously configured by the action of God in Christ in and through its contingent interactions of its free agents, circumstances, and events.

Hence theological reading (and presumably all Christian literal reading) involves what Frei calls *applicatio*, the skill of relating the story to the context, and the judgment as to whether we share a common world with it and with the community that has read it in this way. It is an existential appropriation of the story, what Frei elsewhere describes as a discovery of its truthfulness in the experience of being patterned after it through everyday life. As Wayne Meeks says, "the hermeneutical circle is not complete until the text finds a fitting social embodiment," which may be other than what the text itself envisages.[131] For the theologian, such reading extends to critical examination of the community's forms of speech (and life) and to the contemporary world. In all these modes, the move from the identity of Jesus Christ to the lives of believers and the wider life of human communities and nations is made in virtue of their relation to Jesus Christ as the center of human (and cosmic) history, and hence, as in Gregory of Nazianzus, the move from letter to spirit is a history-shaped one. As in the previous chapter, however, we might after Gregory see this move in relation to the incorporative action of the Spirit rendering human beings participants in Jesus Christ.

Finally, Frei's prioritization of the identity of Jesus Christ, narratively rendered, as the linguistic presence of God's Word in the event of its being read and expounded, provides a way of taking up one further strategy of Gregory of Nazianzus. Today theologically trained readers are, on the whole,

---

131. "A Hermeneutic of Social Embodiment," *Harvard Theological Review* 79, no. 1-3 (1986): 183–84.

highly alert to the challenges that follow from placing biblical texts in their wider historical contexts not only to see their resemblance to past cultures but also to see their negative rhetorical force for subsequent contexts and cultures right down to the present, for a whole range of people making up the larger part of humanity (not to mention the nonhuman sphere). The susceptibility of these texts to being employed to further the subjugation, denigration, social exclusion, suffering, and dehumanization of human beings who are other to those with power—whether by gender, sexuality, ethnicity, or bodily impairment—is an ongoing cause for vigilance.[132]

To the extent that Gregory, like other patristic interpreters, was alive to the problem of texts with apparently or potentially immoral meanings (including misogynist meanings), his solution lay in reading biblical texts within the framework of the story of the incarnate Word's loving condescension to human beings in the life, death, and resurrection of Jesus Christ, and where necessary looking to figure and allegory to provide alternative ways of reading those texts so that they speak of Christ and his love as the pattern for our own action. Frei's prioritization of the narrated identity of Jesus Christ over other elements of the Gospels and other texts in the canon allows for a similar move now made in light of a much fuller understanding of the depth and extensity of the problem. In this way, when the text is read with a chastened awareness of its own rhetorical trajectories and deployments, the focal normative force of Jesus' identity as the one who enacts the good of all human beings without distinction on any grounds allows for something like an internal critique of Scripture on the basis of the very source of its authority. This source is none other than the presence of the risen Lord as Word by way of his narrated identity as the one who enacts the good of all human beings, Jew and Gentile, slave and free, male and female, such that other markers of identity, separation, and exclusion between human beings become relativized and patient of critique even as in the church human beings are reconciled in new bonds of solidarity and mutuality, a transformation that gives a clue to the progressive politics mandated by the gospel.[133] Indeed, so read, the internal critique of Scripture by Scripture might be generative of the critique of similar patterns of oppression in our history.[134]

132. See, for example, Phyllis Trible, *Texts of Terror: Literary-Feminist Readings of Biblical Characters* (London: SCM, 2003); Adrian Thatcher, *The Savage Text: The Use and Abuse of the Bible* (Chichester: WileyBlackwell, 2008).

133. I follow Frei here in using Gal. 3:28 to describe the inclusive force of Christ's redemptive work. See *Types*, 126–27, where Frei replaces "Jew" and "Gentile" with Eastern communism and Western capitalism, and 135 where it becomes clear that this inclusiveness does not efface the particularities of those included. I owe these observations to Dawson, *Christian Figural Reading*, 179–80.

Conclusion

In these ways, Frei's theology of Scripture, developed and extended with insights from Gregory of Nazianzus, points the way toward a theological account of Scripture and its interpretation that is capable of addressing the challenges put to it by Troeltsch's account of historical consciousness, whether in respect of divine action through the text, the history the text relates, the way the text speaks to us in our history, or the ethical evaluation of the text as a historically conditioned document. It remains to gather up the threads of this argument and make one final connection between Gregory and Frei—that between Gregory's emphasis upon and practice of the rhetorical mediation of the Word and Frei's narratival theology of the threefold Word.

134. Phyllis Trible's reading of "texts of terror" in connection with the Suffering Servant passages of Second Isaiah, the synoptic depictions of Gethsemane, and Paul on the Lord's Supper in 1 Corinthians suggests the possibility of seeing such problematic passages in relation to the identity of Jesus Christ without subsuming them into his identity so as both to raise awareness of such abuse in the world of the reader and—what Trible refuses—a hope of a kind of redemption that further delegitimizes such suffering.

9

Conclusion
Divine Eloquence

In all our attempts to repair Christian theology in the relatively hospitable climate afforded by some educational contexts in recent years in the late-modern West, and in all our efforts to reappropriate the wisdom of the premodern past in service of that reparative labor, it is important that we do not lose sight of the scale of the challenges raised to theology by modern thought. Ernst Troeltsch was an eloquent exponent of one of the most significant of those challenges, the challenge of modern historical consciousness. It is a challenge that goes to the heart of Christian theology. In the current revival of the theology and theological interpretation of Scripture, it is a challenge we need to keep before us and factor into our understanding and our practice. I have sought here to offer one way of beginning to address that challenge, drawing on both premodern wisdom and late-modern insight from Gregory Nazianzen and Hans Frei.

In this study, Gregory and Frei offer respectively a sort of premodern figure and late-modern partial "fulfillment" of an answer to the problems Troeltsch's account of historical consciousness raises for Christian theology in general and specifically in respect of Holy Scripture. Figure and fulfillment have not matched neatly and yet there are surprising resonances and possibilities of supplementation. While Frei's position in many ways goes well beyond Gregory's in addressing the challenge, there are strong similarities of strategy—ways in which Frei works, in his own fashion, along lines we see suggested by Gregory. While Gregory's theology and practice belong very much to their own time, yet there is enough commonality of purpose between the theologians—given their common preoccupation with the same divine-human subject—to allow not only for his insights to be echoed in Frei's more developed thinking on the question of history and Scripture, but for him to suggest possibilities of supplementation and correction to Frei's thought, especially in respect of pneumatology and the conceptuality used to describe Jesus Christ and his presence.

In Chapter 1, I explicated Troeltsch's account of the challenges posed by historical consciousness for the theology and theological interpretation of Scripture, and showed how, in varying degrees, a number of important recent proposals failed adequately to address those challenges (though some offered significant insights reiterated or developed through the reading of Gregory and Frei in later chapters). Those challenges centered on the problem of how to think of divine action in a world viewed historically. They problematized thinking of Scripture as the vehicle or instrument of divine action, the unity of the text and the reality it attests, and the capacity of the text to address the world of the reader and so to sustain its normative function in Christian community. They also placed scriptural texts within a wider spectrum of ethical thinking as historical relativities that may be judged in light of other historical highpoints of the expression of human values. We can sum up the rest of the foregoing argument in terms of three moments of thought developed in respect of each of the core problems and each of these particular issues for the theology of Scripture: strategies and lines of reflection suggested by Gregory; Frei's answer to the issue beyond Gregory; and how that answer might be developed in light of Gregory's thinking undeveloped by Frei.

I

The basic problem of divine action in a historical world, as Troeltsch frames it, was not part of Gregory's intellectual milieu. Nevertheless, Gregory's general account of the relation of God and world offers some suggestive ways forward. His understanding of God as exceeding every creaturely limitation, analogy, or conception clears space to see divine action in noncompetitive relation with the complex creaturely interactions it orders providentially, even in respect of human cognition and action. His understanding of human beings as rational, desiring agents ordered to an end in God allows us to begin to see them historically and teleologically as immersed in historical contingencies yet oriented to something that transcends them. These notions combine in an understanding of history as the field of a divine pedagogy proceeding in steps, which accommodates divine action to the limits of historical creatures while accustoming them to ever-deeper conformity to God. Gregory's account of Jesus Christ and our participation in him in the Spirit suggests we think of the incarnate Word as a historical particular who conditions the whole of history and the individual and social possibilities for historical human agents in anticipation of a more fundamental transformation; possibilities between the times that communities and individuals may realize and embody through the incorporative action of the Spirit.

It is this line of thinking that we find echoed in Hans Frei's approach to the problem of history for theology. The identity of Jesus Christ narrated by the synoptic Gospels, on his account, is of an unsubstitutable historical individual in whom, as the representative in whom all things are gathered, God's ordering of all history in its contingent complexity is exercised and whose narrated identity provides a partial, provisional clue to its unfolding sense, so informing discipleship and a progressive politics. Frei thus offers a realistic Christian historical consciousness fleshed out in the figural reading of secular history. It exceeds Gregory's account in its scope and integration of Christology, atonement, and providence and realism, while quietly presupposing something like the noncompetitive account of divine action Gregory indicates.

Gregory's account, nevertheless, suggests more than one supplementation of Frei. First, an incorporative pneumatology like his would enable Frei better to do justice to creaturely agency and desire. Second, he invites us to consider the possibilities for divine pedagogy and persuasion in providence so understood: if we may partially discern, on occasion, lineaments of the pattern of providential action and on this basis urge certain courses of political action, a fully theological account of such discernment and counsel would surely appeal to God as the ground not only of the providential action but of the discernment suasion to which it gives rise. Third, he encourages us to think that in our conformity to Christ the radical distinction Frei secures with the motif of distance might be reconcilable with unity and a fuller sense of participation in Christ's sonship.

II

In respect of Holy Scripture, Gregory connects the nature of Scripture to Jesus Christ and so grounds the reality of Scripture in the figure who lies at the heart of God's ordering of human and cosmic history. The presence of Jesus Christ as Logos in the scriptural text is instantiated in teachings of divine wisdom and human praxis that offer ways of transformation for human beings into fuller participation in God. The shaping of history in Jesus Christ and the Spirit then informs the movement in Gregory's hermeneutics and exegesis from letter to spirit, so that the exposition of the text unfolds transformative divine teaching in a manner consistent with the character of history, without sacrificing the specifics of the letter of the text but realizing the possibilities they indicate. Gregory's approach allows him to make morally or theologically problematic texts fruitful for this transformative purpose, aided by a combination of the strategic use of intertexts and symbolic interpretation. It is a mode of interpretation completed in its embodiment in the hearers of the exegesis, furthering their participation in Jesus Christ.

Frei's approach to Holy Scripture repeats this linkage of Scripture with Jesus Christ as the center of God's shaping of history. His is a thoroughly theological account of Scripture in Barth-like terms as a fallible human witness to Jesus Christ, realized as the written Word of God by the accommodating condescension of the Lord Jesus as Word to his textual identification, whereby his story becomes the organizing center of Scripture's coherence and of the exercise of God's authority through it. His notion of witness can be specified more closely with respect to its origination and form through Barth's remarks on the identity of the disciples. The capacity Barth's dialectic between human witness and divine-human Word affords for respecting the historicity of the former is supplemented by Frei's clarification of how the human witness may identify Christ and yet be composed of fallible materials drawn from its historical context—in effect they are reconfigured around Jesus Christ. The truth of the text, as Jesus Christ, involves something like factual reference but also exceeds it, because its primary referent is constituted by divine action, and because it involves an existential dimension requiring a Trinitarian description of truth.

Frei's account, by centering the truth and authority of Scripture upon the presence of the risen Lord Jesus Christ as Word, connects divine action through Scripture with the one through whom God providentially orders human history in and through its contingent interactions and without prejudice to human freedom. Divine action through Scripture in constituting the church thus becomes an intensification or peculiar form of a history-shaping presence whose extensity is universal. It is thus instrumental in the formation of a Christian historical consciousness centered upon Jesus Christ as one who cannot but live, who precisely as historical requires us to alter our sense of history, and whose identity becomes the clue to our own historical identities. Frei's approach allows for a nuanced, flexible approach to the relation of biblical texts to historical realities around the central story of Jesus Christ, which urges its own historicity at just the point where it depicts one who has no historical analogue. In consequence, the scriptural depiction of Jesus Christ, and of others in relation to him, becomes formative of a Christian historical consciousness rather than something at odds with a historical vision of the world, and allows us to begin to see our world as somehow shaped in him, in a way yet to be fully disclosed but sufficiently intimated to inform our discipleship and politics. The meaningfulness of Scripture, the commanding or directing force of Christ's identity, is thus to be embodied, as in Gregory, in the patterning of human lives and communities. Frei's prioritizing of the storied identification of Jesus, finally, allows for an internal critique of scriptural materials in relation to Jesus Christ. Such an approach acknowledges the critical questions raised by the historicity of the texts yet grounds its critique in one who in his very historicity is the presence of God, the one in whom all relativities are configured. It is, in other words, an expression of an alternate historical consciousness to the one Troeltsch describes rather than a refusal of historical contextualization and the ethical challenges it brings to sacred texts.

Frei's theology of the Word thus makes the same connection as Gregory, and produces a quasi-iconic notion of the presence of the Word that echoes Gregory's understanding of the Logos as "incarnate" in Scripture, which appeals to a sense of the transcendence of divine actions we have seen in Gregory. Frei's is the more thoroughly historical account, yet Gregory offers, again, several suggestive supplementations. An incorporative pneumatology like Gregory's together with the category of participation would help Frei articulate the integrity of the human witness of Scripture and those active in its production and reception, and a fuller notion of the transformation of Christian readers. Gregory's theology of Scripture invites us to think of Christ's presence via his story and scriptural figures of his identity and commentary upon it in pedagogical and rhetorical terms as the presence of the capacious focus of divine providence, a form of divine rule of infinite density, allowing for multiple modes of participation by way of diverse historical human identities, like the *logoi* inhering in the Logos.

III

The proposals to which this argument gives rise must await fuller substantiation beyond this book. My hope has been to present a coherent vision that shows one way in which the issues posed by historical consciousness for the theology of Scripture might begin to be addressed. In concluding, I want to return to one strand of the argument that does not figure prominently in the above summary, but is vital in relation to the practical embodiment of a Christian historically conscious approach to the theological interpretation of Scripture. The foregoing account suggests several core practices, namely contemplative attention to the narrative renderings of Christ's identity (and to reflections upon it and its significance) in its manifold relations with other biblical texts (drawing on a wide range of critical tools where possible), and attention to and love for one's neighbor and to the wider human world in light of that identity—a kind of figural reading. Just as central, however, to such an approach precisely in its historical consciousness is the rhetorical nature of this reading of the text and of the world, understood as a partial, fallible, penultimate participation in the divine eloquence enacted in Jesus Christ.

We have seen where the case for such an argument begins in Gregory. For him, the divine pedagogy embodied in Scripture is primarily mediated through its deployment by Christian teachers, who are being sanctified through their own engagement with the manifold pedagogy of the text and may access its depths. Gregory characterizes that activity in rhetorical terms, as an act of persuasion that is fallible and frail, but also graced. For him, God acts through such rhetorical mediation of scriptural pedagogy to heal and train human beings through practices of the persuasive deployment of scriptural texts in particular contexts. Here, the human rhetorical art of the preacher is a tool for a divine eloquence that carries into fresh situations the divine pedagogy and rhetoric embodied in the scriptural text. His own practice in Oration 14 illustrates this rhetorical mediation of scriptural pedagogy. Here Gregory urges a particular way of realizing the pedagogical force of scriptural commands to love the poor, and does so by incorporating scriptural allusions into arguments designed to move his audience to see themselves and the leprous poor differently and to be differently disposed toward them—disposed, in fact, in just the way the commands require.

Hans Frei does not offer us a comparable account of the rhetorical exposition of the scriptural story of Jesus, or other scriptural texts. Like Karl Barth, however, he does, however, make human exposition of the text integral to his theology of the Word. In *The Identity of Jesus Christ*, Frei extends Christ's gracious presence via the text to human proclamation based upon it, which fits with what he says in later writings about the truthfulness of Christian talk of God and of Jesus Christ in general. In effect, he thus appropriates Barth's three forms of the Word, where Jesus Christ is the Word of God in the primary sense, and Scripture and preaching "become" that Word by way of his presence, a way of speaking that marks the contingency of the texts' revelatory sufficiency on the gracious freedom of God in Christ (as Frei's own formulations clearly indicate).[1] Frei's later remarks on the theology of Scripture also locate the literal reading in the Christian community in its worship, in the "Word" that is

---

1. *CD* I/1, §§4–6.

complemented by the Sacrament. It presupposes a repeated privileging of the gospel stories and especially of the passion-resurrection sequence in worship throughout the year, and makes the sermon or homily of particular importance. To this extent Frei is in accord with Gregory, only with a more explicit and firmer focus on the synoptic narratives as central to Christian communal reading and exposition of Scripture. We may, however, go a little further in light of Gregory's account.

For one strand of my argument has been that it is a legitimate and consistent extension of Frei's position to see Christ's gracious presence by way of his story and the texts related to it in Christian reading as a pedagogical and persuasive presence, training us in forms of attention and eliciting certain ways of understanding and acting in light of who Christ is and who we are in relation to him and to the world. After all, among the identifying themes that crystallize around Jesus of Nazareth in the synoptics are those of the teacher and prophet, whose authoritative words draw on Scripture and yet whose meaning is bound up with his destiny in the passion-resurrection sequence. So in Luke 4, Jesus preaches in the synagogue at Nazareth, interpreting the scroll of Isaiah as speaking of himself in gracious words and yet who will not be identified with reference to his hometown, but in hinting of the extension of his ministry to the Gentiles narrowly avoids a lynching in a prefigurement of his passion. Public, persuasive speech also typifies the apostles in Acts, from Peter's sermon at Pentecost forward (see especially Acts 2:40), where their bold speaking is at times identified with "the word of God" (Acts 4:31; 12:24; 13:8) or "the word of the Lord" (Acts 8:25), suggesting its close connection with not only God's presence but the unity of that presence with the presence and identity of the risen Jesus, in whose name they speak and argue (Acts 9:28-29; 13:44, 48-49; 15:35; 19:10, 20).[2] Much of this argument is from the Scriptures (Acts 2:14-36; 4:8-12; 7:2-53; 8:32-35; 13:16-41; 18:25-27). Paul, for all his eschewal of human eloquence, typifies himself in broadly rhetorical terms in his self-presentation in 2 Cor. 5:20ff. These descriptions suggest that the first witnesses of Jesus Christ are to be seen as exercising a Spirit-empowered rhetoric centered on Christ's identity and its implications for their hearers, and they indicate that all such testimony on the basis of the Scriptures will have a similarly persuasive goal.

To see the exposition of Scripture as a work of persuasion, taking up scriptural texts and using them in arguments that realize their directing force for human communities and their members, is proper to the historical character of the performance of Scripture. For, on the one hand, attending to Jesus

---

2. Assuming that, in light of the use of *kurios* in Luke's narrative, we cannot read that term without hearing a reference to Jesus Christ here, as well as to God.

Christ and the world and discerning how to act in light of his identity and its partial illumination of that world involve dealing with texts that resist totalizing interpretations and realities that remain stubbornly ambiguous and obscure and so admit of different interpretations, so that exposition becomes a matter necessarily of argument. More fundamentally, it belongs to the character of human beings in their historicity to be moved to action by a combination of factors not simply logical but also appealing to deeper intuitions and ways of seeing the world. The transformation of human beings who are historical in being shaped by certain cultural practices and the values they instantiate involves transforming practice, and transforming practice involves shifting the landscape of our sense of reality and of value in which they make sense. It is therefore appropriate that the transformation of human beings in conformity and participation in Jesus Christ, the focal center of history, as something that does not overcome our relative freedom, agency, and historical locatedness, should engage our attachments and imaginations and habits of mind and will by way of rhetoric conceived as broadly as Gregory practiced it—as an attempt to move the whole person. Such movement, theologically understood, is attempted in hope of the Spirit's action to energize the motion of others from certain ways of seeing and acting to those that conform more closely, more fully, to Jesus Christ as present to us through Scripture and hence to our clearest clue to the final shaping of our reality. It seems entirely appropriate, then, to God's condescension to our historical world in Jesus Christ, and to the use of Scripture to direct our lives, that its suasion and pedagogy should be mediated, with the help of the Spirit, through fallible, provisional human arguments that take up scriptural texts ordered around Jesus' identity into their suasion.

On Gregory and Frei's accounts, such rhetoric would be primarily a matter of public teaching and preaching, presumably by those recognized in Christian communities as called and gifted for that task. Yet we might extend the notion a little more widely to include other kinds of discursive interaction in Christian communities between all kinds of participants; insofar as we seek to offer one another versions of discernment of what it would mean to follow Christ in this or that circumstance, we should seek to persuade, to appeal to the whole person, rather than coerce. As Charles Campbell argues, preaching after Frei embodies the pattern of Jesus' identity in a coexistence of powerlessness and the power of God.[3] Authority is not left behind by such argument, but the way Christian rhetoric appeals to authority, if it is to be persuasive, will not be authoritarian—the laying down of ultimatums, a rhetorical coercion. Rather,

3. Charles Campbell, *Preaching Jesus: New Directions for Homiletics in Hans Frei's Postliberal Theology* (Grand Rapids: Eerdmans, 1997), 216.

it will appeal most of all to the authority intrinsic to the identity of Jesus Christ, which speaks, as it were, for itself and which lays the speaker open to its authority as much as the interlocutor, secondarily to models of reasoning and discernment of following Christ normed in Scripture, and thirdly to the lived experience of those who have followed this path in the past—the saints, broadly construed. Authority so construed accords with God's affirmation of our historicity in Jesus Christ by giving time to our learning and consent, by encouraging a taking of time with the text, by allowing space for disagreement, and by relating authority to our relation to God who works through persuasion.[4]

So understood, the rhetorical deployment of Scripture would not entail simply expounding given meanings. Rather, in the first place setting forth Jesus Christ as identified by the gospel narratives, with a wealth of illumining parables, titles, and figures.[5] Second, and not least, performatively by means of figuration (as in Gregory's festal orations), it incorporates us into his story, projects our identities as identified in relation to him.[6] Third, it refashions cultural images and values under the pressure of Christ's identity.[7] Fourth, it would involve incorporating in one's discourse, through allusion and echo as much as explicit appeal, the various patterns of reasoning, the logics, of biblical texts and their imagery taken in light of the pattern of Christ's identity, in the service of ad hoc arguments urging ways of following Christ in respect of particular circumstances.[8] As in Gregory, the condition of the practice of such rhetoric must surely be—not privilege or elite status, but —the pursuit of holiness, of being transformed by the depth or density of meaning disclosed in Jesus' narrated identity, and on the part of listeners as well as speakers, a pursuit that in turn presupposes the kinds of community and communal practices that can help sustain that pursuit.[9] The goal of such rhetoric is a cultural performance that helps furnish such an environment for lived holiness

---

4. See Angus Paddison, "The Authority of Scripture and the Triune God," *International Journal of Systematic Theology* 13, no. 4 (2011): 459–61. On taking time with the text, see also Rowan Williams, "The Discipline of Scripture," in his *On Christian Theology* (Oxford: Blackwell, 2000), 44–60.

5. Campbell, *Preaching Jesus*, 193

6. Cf. ibid., 250ff.

7. And so opposes "historical forces" in human society; so ibid., 216.

8. Cf. the description of exegesis as a rhetorical practice in David S. Cunningham, *Faithful Persuasion: In Aid of a Rhetoric of Christian Theology* (Notre Dame: University of Notre Dame Press, 1990), 219–38, who also appeals to late-antique models, among others.

9. Campbell, *Preaching Jesus*, 241ff.

by training and shaping Christian communities as Christ's collective disciples in the wider world.

Frei's account of the public vocation of theologians suggests, finally, that such rhetoric may not be confined to intraecclesial conversation and discourse. His invocation of Lincoln's Second Inaugural Address, in a conference lecture honoring Jürgen Moltmann and Elisabeth Wendel-Moltmann, is suggestive, as are his allusions in another place to what he clearly found a problematic but suggestive public rhetorical practice, the Puritan Jeremiad.[10] There he suggests the possibility of taking the civil community as a figure, a variable antitype of a biblical original that one assumes is Israel and the church, in view of the dialectic that pertains between the universal scope of God's saving providential action and the particular focus of that action in Jesus Christ, whose reign is foreshadowed in the "precarious existence of Christian community."[11] Such figural reading, a particular form of the practice he commends in *The Identity of Jesus Christ*, would be a form of the careful discernment of providence informing a proposed political course of reconciliatory, reparative action, as in Lincoln's address. We might, therefore, imagine in some contexts at least, where scriptural language has purchase or where it can be explained simply, and in the hope perhaps that the presence of Christ in the human sphere extends to shaping contingent human rationalities, for public, social forms of this kind of rhetoric, making Christian reasonings public by employing their scriptural paradigms in order to urge progressive political courses of public policy.[12] Along with its ecclesial counterpart, we might, after Gregory, see such rhetoric as a participation in a divine eloquence that belongs to a pedagogical dimension of God's providential anticipation of the reconciliation of all things in Jesus Christ.

10. See Frei, "God's Patience and Our Work" (*YDS* 18-268), 101 (accessed from http://people.exeter.ac.uk/mahigton/frei/transcripts/Frei07-Patience.pdf), and his "History, Salvation History and Typology" (*YDS* 18-278), 87 (accessed from: http://people.exeter.ac.uk/mahigton/frei/transcripts/Frei06-Typology.pdf).

11. Ibid.

12. I adapt the notion of making religious reasonings public from Nicholas Adams, "Making Deep Reasonings Public," *Modern Theology* 22 (June 2006): 385–401, where it has particular reference to the practice of Scriptural Reasoning.

Bibliography

THE WORKS OF GREGORY OF NAZIANZUS

GREEK EDITIONS

Patrologia Graeca, vols. 35–37. Edited by J.-P. Migne. Paris: 1857–1862.

SOURCES CHRÉTIENNES

Grégoire de Nazianze. Discours 4–5. Edited by J. Bernardi (*SC* 247). Paris: Éditions du Cerf, 1983.

Grégoire de Nazianze. Discours 27–31. Edited by P. Gallay and M. Jourjon (*SC* 250). Paris: Éditions du Cerf, 1978.

Grégoire de Nazianze. Discours 20–23. Edited by J. Mossay (*SC* 270). Paris: Éditions du Cerf, 1980.

Grégoire de Nazianze. Discours 32–37. Edited by C. Moreschini (*SC* 318). Paris: Éditions du Cerf, 1985.

Grégoire de Nazianze. Discours 42–43. Edited by J. Bernardi (*SC* 384). Paris: Éditions du Cerf, 1992).

Grégoire de Nazianze. Discours 6–12. Edited by M. A. Calvet-Sebasti (*SC* 405). Paris: Éditions du Cerf, 1995.

Lettres Théologiques. Edited by P. Gallay (*SC* 208). Paris: Éditions du Cerf, 1974.

OTHERS

St Gregory Nazianzus. Poemata Arcana. Edited by C. Moreschini. Oxford: Clarendon, 1997.

De vita sua (Carmen II.i.11). In C. White, ed., *Gregory of Nazianzus: Autobiographical Poems.* Cambridge Medieval Classics 6. Cambridge: Cambridge University Press, 1996, pp. 11–154.

In suos versus (Carmen II.1.39). In C. White, ed., *Gregory of Nazianzus: Autobiographical Poems.* Cambridge Medieval Classics 6. Cambridge: Cambridge University Press, 1996, pp. 2–9.

TRANSLATIONS

Wace, P., and P. Schaff, eds. *Gregory of Nazianzus: Select Orations*. In Nicene and Post-Nicene Fathers VII. Oxford: James Parker, 1894.

Daley, B. E. *Gregory of Nazianzus*. London: Routledge, 2006.

Gilbert, P. *Of God and Man: The Theological Poetry of St. Gregory of Nazianzus*. Crestwood, NY: St. Vladimir's Seminary Press, 2001.

Meehan, D. M. *Saint Gregory of Nazianzus: Three Poems*. Washington, DC: Catholic University of America Press, 1987.

Vinson, M. P. *St. Gregory of Nazianzus: Select Orations*. Washington, DC: Catholic University of America Press, 2003.

Wickham, L., and F. Williams. *On God and Christ: St. Gregory Nazianzus: The Five Theological Orations and Two Letters to Cledonius*. Crestwood, NY: St. Vladimir's Seminary Press, 2002.

OTHER ANCIENT AUTHORS

The Exegetical Rules of Rabbi Ishmael and Rabbi Hillel. Translated by K. Froehlich. Biblical Interpretation in the Early Church. Philadelphia: Fortress Press, 1984, pp. 30–36.

Origen, On First Principles: Book 4. In K. Froehlich, ed., Biblical Interpretation in the Early Church. Philadelphia: Fortress Press, 1984, pp. 48–78.

Origen, and R. J. Daly, ed. *Treatise on the Passover and Dialogues of Origen with Heraclides and His Fellow Bishops, on the Father, the Son, and the Soul*. New York: Paulist, 1992.

Origen. *Origen: Homilies on Leviticus 1–16*. Translated by G. W. Barkley. Washington, DC: Catholic University of America Press, 1990.

WORKS OF HANS FREI

Frei, Hans W. "Niebuhr's Theological Background." In Paul Ramsey, ed., *Faith and Ethics: The Theology of H. Richard Niebuhr*. New York: Harper & Row, 1957.

— *The Eclipse of Biblical Narrative: A Study in Eighteenth and Nineteenth Century Hermeneutics*. New Haven and London: Yale University Press, 1974.

— *The Identity of Jesus Christ: The Hermeneutical Bases of Dogmatic Theology*. Philadelphia: Fortress Press, 1975.

— "David Friedrich Strauss." In N. Smart, P. Clayton, P. Sherry, and S. T. Katz, eds., *Nineteenth Century Religious Thought in the West*, vol. 1. Cambridge: Cambridge University Press, 1985, pp. 215–60.

— *Types of Christian Theology*. Edited by G. Hunsinger and W. Placher. New Haven and London: Yale University Press, 1992.

— *Theology and Narrative: Selected Essays*. Edited by G. Hunsinger and W. Placher. New York and Oxford: Oxford University Press, 1993.

— *Unpublished Pieces: Transcripts from the Yale Divinity School Archive*. Edited by M. Higton, 1998–2004. Available at http://www.library.yale.edu/div/fa/Freiindex.htm, and at http://people.exeter.ac.uk/mahigton/frei/transcripts.html

OTHER WORKS

Adams, N. "Making Deep Reasonings Public," *Modern Theology* 22 (2006): 385–401.

Adler, W. "Early Christian Historians and Historiography," from Susan Ashbrook Harvey and David G. Hunter, eds., *The Oxford Handbook of Early Christian Studies*. New York: Oxford University Press, 2008, pp. 584–602.

Barr, James. "Revelation through History in the Old Testament and in Modern Theology," *Interpretation* 17, no. 193 (1963): 193–205.

Barr, James. *The Bible in the Modern World*. London: SCM, 1973.

Barr, James. *The Scope and Authority of the Bible*. London: SCM, 1980.

Barth, K. *Church Dogmatics* I/1. Edited by G. W. Bromiley and T. F. Torrance, 2nd ed. Edinburgh: T. & T. Clark, 1975.

Barth, K. *Church Dogmatics* I/2. Edited by G. W. Bromiley and T. F. Torrance. Edinburgh: T. & T. Clark, 1956.

Barth, K. *Church Dogmatics* IV/1. Edited by G. W. Bromiley and T. F. Torrance. Edinburgh: T. & T. Clark, 1956.

Barton, S. "New Testament as Performance," *Scottish Journal of Theology* 52, no. 2 (1999): 179–208.

Beeley, C. "Cyril of Alexandria and Gregory Nazianzen: Tradition and Complexity in Patristic Christology," *Journal of Early Christian Studies* 17, no. 3 (Fall 2009): 388–94.

Beeley, C. *Gregory of Nazianzus on the Trinity and the Knowledge of God: In Your Light We See Light*. New York: Oxford University Press, 2008.

Bernardi, J. *Saint Grégoire de Nazianze: Le Théologien et son temps (330–390).* Paris: Éditions du Cerf, 1995.

Billings, J. Todd. *The Word of God for the People of God: An Entryway to the Theological Interpretation of Scripture.* Grand Rapids: Eerdmans, 2010.

Bouteneff, P. C. *Beginnings: Ancient Christian Readings of the Biblical Creation Narratives.* Grand Rapids: Baker Academic, 2008.

Bowald, M. A. *Rendering the Word in Theological Hermeneutics: Mapping Human and Divine Agency.* Aldershot: Ashgate, 2007.

Boyle, N. *Sacred and Secular Scriptures: A Catholic Approach to Literature.* London: Darton, Longman & Todd, 2004.

Braaten, Carl E., and Robert W. Jenson, eds. *Reclaiming the Bible for the Church.* Edinburgh: T. & T. Clark, 1995.

Bromiley, G. "The Authority of Scripture in Karl Barth." In D. A. Carson and J. Woodbridge, eds., *Hermeneutics, Authority and Canon.* Leicester: InterVarsity, 1986, pp. 275–94.

Byassee, J. *Praise Seeking Understanding: Reading the Psalms with Augustine.* Grand Rapids: Eerdmans, 2007.

Campbell, C. L. *Preaching Jesus: New Directions for Homiletics in Hans Frei's Postliberal Theology.* Grand Rapids: Eerdmans, 1997.

Campbell, D. A. "The Story of Jesus in Romans and Galatians." In B. Longenecker, ed., *Narrative Dynamics in Paul: A Critical Assessment.* Louisville: Westminster John Knox, 2002, pp. 97–124.

Cameron, A. *Christianity and the Rhetoric of Empire: The Development of Christian Discourse.* Berkeley, Los Angeles, and London: University of California Press, 1991.

Carruthers, M. *The Book of Memory: A Study of Memory in Medieval Culture.* New York: Cambridge University Press, 2008.

Chapman, M. D. *Ernest Troeltsch and Liberal Theology: Religion and Cultural Synthesis in Wilhelmine Germany.* New York: Oxford University Press, 2001.

Chesnut, Glenn F. *The First Christian Histories: Eusebius, Socrates, Sozomen, Theodoret, and Evagrius.* Macon, GA: Mercer University Press, 1986.

Clark, E. A. *Reading Renunciation: Asceticism and Scripture in Early Christianity.* Princeton: Princeton University Press, 1999.

Childs, B. *Biblical Theology of the Old and New Testaments.* London: SCM, 1992.

Childs, B. "The *Sensus Literalis* of Scripture: An Ancient and Modern Problem." In H. Donner et al., eds., *Beiträge zur alttestamentlichen Theologie: Festschrift für Walther Zimmerli zum 70. Geburtstag.* Göttingen: Vandenhoeck & Ruprecht, 1977, pp. 80–93.

Coakley, S. "Why Three? Some Further Reflections on the Origins of the Doctrine of the Trinity." In Coakley and D. A. Pailin, eds., *The Making and Remaking of Christian Doctrine*. Oxford: Clarendon, 1993, pp. 29–56.

Coakley, S. "God as Trinity: An Approach through Prayer." In *We Believe in God: A Report by the Doctrine Commission of the General Synod of the Church of England*. London: Church House Publishing, 1987, pp. 104–21.

Comstock, G. "Truth or Meaning: Ricoeur versus Frei on Biblical Narrative," *The Journal of Religion* 66, no. 2 (April 1986): 117–40.

Corrigan, K. "Essence and Existence in the *Enneads*," and Michael F. Wagner, "Plotinus on the Nature of Physical Reality." In Lloyd P. Gerson, ed., *The Cambridge Companion to Plotinus*. Cambridge: Cambridge University Press, 1996, pp. 105–29.

Crouzel, A. *Origen*. Translated by A. S. Worrall. Edinburgh: T. & T. Clark, 1989.

Crouzel, H. "La distinction de la 'typologie' et de l' 'allégorie,'" *Bulletin de littérature ecclésiastique* 3 (1964): 161–74.

Cunningham, D. S. *Faithful Persuasion: In Aid of a Rhetoric of Christian Theology*. Notre Dame: University of Notre Dame Press, 1990.

Cunningham, V. *Reading After Theory*. Oxford: Blackwell, 2002.

Daley, B. "Walking Through the Word: Gregory of Nazianzus as a Biblical Interpreter." In J. Ross Wagner et al., eds., *The Word Leaps the Gap*. Grand Rapids: Eerdmans, 2008, pp. 514–31.

Daley, B. "Divine Transcendence and Human Transformation: Gregory of Nyssa's Anti-Apollinarian Christology," *Modern Theology* 18, no. 4 (2002): 497–506.

Daley, B. "Building a New City: The Cappadocian Fathers and the Rhetoric of Philanthropy," *Journal of Early Christian Studies* 7, no. 3 (1999): 431–61.

Daniélou, J. *Sacramentum Futuri: Études sur les origines de la typologie biblique*. Paris: Beauchesne, 1950.

Dawes, G. *The Historical Jesus Quest: The Challenge of History to Religious Authority*. Louisville: Westminster John Knox, 2001.

Dawson, J. D. *Christian Figural Readers and the Fashioning of Identity*. Berkeley, Los Angeles, and London: University of California Press, 2002.

DeHart, Paul J. *The Trial of Witnesses: The Rise and Decline of Postliberal Theology*. Oxford: Blackwell, 2006.

Demoen, K. *Pagan and Biblical Exempla in Gregory of Nazianzen: A Study in Rhetoric and Hermeneutics*. Turnhout, Belgium: Brepols, 1996.

Demson, D. *Hans Frei and Karl Barth: Different Ways of Reading Scripture.* Grand Rapids: Eerdmans, 1997.

Evans, C. S. *The Historical Christ and the Jesus of Faith: The Incarnational Narratives as History.* New York: Clarendon, 1996.

Fish, S. *Is There a Text in This Class? The Authority of Interpretive Communities.* Cambridge, MA: Harvard University Press, 1980.

Ford, D. F. "Hans Frei and the Future of Theology," *Modern Theology* 8, no. 2 (1992): 203–14.

Fornara, Charles W. *The Nature of History in Ancient Greek and Rome.* Berkeley, Los Angeles, and London: University of California Press, 1983.

Fowl, S. *Engaging Scripture: A Model for Theological Interpretation.* Oxford: Blackwell, 1998.

Fowl, S. *Theological Interpretation of Scripture.* Eugene, OR: Cascade Books, 2009.

Fowl, S. *The Story of Christ in the Ethics of Paul: An Analysis of the Function of the Hymnic Material in the Pauline Corpus.* Sheffield: JSOT, 1990.

Fowl, S., and L. G. Jones. *Reading in Communion: Scripture and Ethics in Christian Life.* London: SPCK, 1991.

Frege, G. "On Sense and Reference." In A. W. Moore, *Meaning and Reference.* Oxford: Oxford University Press, 1993, pp. 23–42.

Froehlich, K. *Biblical Interpretation in the Early Church.* Philadelphia: Fortress Press, 1984.

Fulbrook, M. *Historical Theory.* London and New York: Routledge, 2002.

Fulford, B. "Gregory of Nazianzus and Biblical Interpretation." In Christopher A. Beeley, ed., *Re-Reading Gregory of Nazianzus: Essays on History, Theology, and Culture.* Washington, DC: Catholic University of America Press, 2012, pp. 31–48.

Fulford, B. "Divine Names and the Embodied Intellect: Imagination and Sanctification in Gregory of Nazianzus' Account of Theological Language," *Studia Patristica* L. Leuven: Peeters, 2011, pp. 217–31.

Fulford, B. "Feeding and Forming the People of God: The Lord, His Supper and the Church in Calvin and 1 Corinthians 11:17-34," *New Perspectives for Evangelical Theology.* London: Routledge, 2010, pp. 93–107.

Gallay, P. "La Bible dans l'oeuvre de Grégoire de Nazianze le Théologien." In C. Mondésert, ed., *Le monde grec ancien et la Bible*, vol. 1. Paris: Beauchesne, 1984, pp. 313–34.

Gallay, P. *La vie de saint Grégoire de Nazianze.* Paris: Emmanuel Vitte, 1943.

Gamble, H. *Books and Readers in the Early Church.* New Haven and London: Yale University Press, 1995.

Grant, R. *A Short History of the Interpretation of the Bible.* London: A. & C. Black, 1965.

Greene-McCreight, K. *Ad Litteram: How Augustine, Calvin and Barth Read the "Plain Sense" of Genesis 1–3.* New York: Peter Lang, 1999.

Grieb, A. K. *The Story of Romans: A Narrative Defense of God's Righteousness.* Louisville: Westminster John Knox, 2002.

Hanson, R. P. C. "The Interpretation of the Bible in the Early Church." In R. P. C. and A. C. Hanson, *The Bible without Illusions.* London: SCM, 1989.

Hanson, R. P. C. "Biblical Exegesis in the Early Church." In P. R. Ackroyd and C. F. Evans, eds., *The Cambridge History of the Bible,* vol. 1. Cambridge: Cambridge University Press, 1970.

Hanson, R. P. C. *Allegory and Event.* London: SCM, 1959.

Hardy, D. W. "Reason, Wisdom and the Interpretation of Scripture." In David F. Ford and Graham Stanton, eds., *Reading Texts, Seeking Wisdom.* London: SCM, 2003, pp. 69–88.

Hardy, D. W. "The Foundation of Cognition and Ethics in Worship." In his *God's Ways with the World.* Edinburgh: T. & T. Clark, 1996, pp. 25–30.

Harrison, C. "The Typology of Listening: The Transformation of Scripture in Early Christian Preaching." In William John Lyons and Isabella Sandwell, eds., *Delivering the Word: Preaching and Exegesis in the Western Christian Tradition.* Sheffield: Equinox, 2012, pp. 62–79.

Harrisville, R. and W. Sundburg. *The Bible in Modern Culture: Baruch Spinoza to Brevard Childs,* 2nd ed. Grand Rapids: Eerdmans, 2002.

Harvey, V. *The Historian and the Believer: The Morality of Historical Knowledge and Christian Belief.* London: SCM, 1967.

Hays, R. B. *The Conversion of the Imagination: Paul as Interpreter of Israel's Scripture.* Grand Rapids: Eerdmans, 2005.

Hays, R. B. "Is Paul's Gospel Narratable?" *Journal for the Study of the New Testament* 27, no. 2 (2004): 217–39.

Hays, R. B. *The Faith of Jesus Christ: The Narrative Substructure of Galatians 3:1–4:11.* Grand Rapids: Eerdmans, 2002.

Hays, R. B. *The Moral Vision of the New Testament.* New York: HarperCollins, 1996.

Hays, R. B. *Echoes of Scripture in the Letters of Paul.* New Haven: Yale University Press, 1993.

Henry, C. F. H. "Narrative Theology: An Evangelical Appraisal," *Trinity Journal* 8 (1987): 3–19.

Higton, M. A. "Hans Frei." In Justin S. Holcomb, ed., *Christian Theologies of Scripture: A Comparative Introduction.* New York: New York University Press, 2006, pp. 220–39.

Higton, M. A. "The Fulfilment of History in Barth, Frei, Auerbach and Dante." In Higton and John C. McDowell, eds., *Conversing with Barth.* Aldershot: Ashgate, 2004, pp. 120–41.

Higton, M. A. *Christ, Providence and History: Hans Frei's Public Theology.* London: T. & T. Clark, 2004.

Holman, S. R. *The Hungry Are Dying: Beggars and Bishops in Roman Cappadocia.* New York: Oxford University Press, 2001.

Hunsinger, G. "Hans Frei as Theologian: The Quest for a Generous Orthodoxy," *Modern Theology* 8, no. 2 (1992): 103–28.

Jeanrond, W. *Text and Interpretation as Categories of Theological Thinking.* London: Gill & Macmillan, 1986.

Jenson, A. *Theological Hermeneutics.* London: SCM, 2007.

Kelsey, D. "Biblical Narrative and Theological Anthropology." In G. Green, ed., *Scriptural Authority and Narrative Interpretation.* Philadelphia: Fortress Press, 1987, pp. 121–43.

Kennedy, G. A. *New History of Classical Rhetoric.* Princeton: Princeton University Press, 1994.

Kennedy, G. A. *Greek Rhetoric under Christian Emperors.* Princeton: Princeton University Press, 1983.

Kermode, F. *The Genesis of Secrecy.* Cambridge, MA: Harvard University Press, 1979.

Krentz, E. *The Historical-Critical Method.* London: SPCK, 1975.

Lamberton, R. *Homer the Theologian: Neoplatonist Allegorical Reading and the Growth of the Epic Tradition.* Berkeley, Los Angeles, and London: University of California Press, 1986.

Lampe, G. "The Reasonableness of Typology." In Lampe and K. Woollcombe, *Essays on Typology.* London: SCM, 1957, pp. 9–38.

Lash, N. "Performing the Scriptures: Interpretation through Living," *The Furrow* 33, no. 8 (August 1982): 467–74.

Lauro, E. D. *The Soul and Spirit of Scripture Within Origen's Exegesis.* Leiden: Brill, 2005.

Levenson, J. D. *The Hebrew Bible, the Old Testament, and Historical Criticism.* Louisville: Westminster John Knox, 1993.

Levering, M. *Participatory Biblical Exegesis: A Theology of Biblical Interpretation.* Notre Dame: University of Notre Dame Press, 2008.

Lindbeck, G. A. "The Story-Shaped Church: Critical Exegesis and Theological Interpretation." In S. E. Fowl, ed., *The Theological Interpretation of Scripture: Classic and Contemporary Readings.* Oxford: Blackwell, 1997, pp. 39–52.

Lindbeck, G. A. *The Nature of Doctrine: Religion and Theology in a Postliberal Age.* Louisville: Westminster John Knox, 1984.

Loewe, R. "The 'Plain' Meaning of Scripture in Early Jewish Exegesis," *Papers of the Institute of Jewish Studies in London,* vol. 1. Jerusalem: Magnes, 1964, pp. 140–85.

Louth, A. *Discerning the Mystery: An Essay on the Nature of Theology.* Oxford: Clarendon, 1989.

de Lubac, H. "'Typologie' et 'allégorie,'" *Recherches de science religieuses* 34 (1947): 180–226.

Marshall, B. D. *Trinity and Truth.* Cambridge: Cambridge University Press, 1999.

Martens, P. M. "Revisiting the Allegory/Typology Distinction: The Case of Origen," *Journal of Early Christian Studies* 16, no. 3 (2008): 283–96.

Matz, B. J. "Deciphering a Recipe for Biblical Preaching in *Oration* 14." In Beeley, ed., *Re-reading Gregory of Nazianzus,* pp. 49–66.

Maxwell, J. L. *Christianization and Communication in Late Antiquity: John Chrysostom and His Congregation in Antioch.* Cambridge: Cambridge University Press, 2006.

McCormack, B. L. "The Being of Holy Scripture Is in Becoming: Karl Barth in Conversation with American Evangelical Criticism." In V. Bacote, Laura C. Miguélez, and D. L. Ockholm, eds., *Evangelicals & Scripture: Tradition, Authority and Hermeneutics.* Downers Grove, IL: InterVarsity, pp. 55–75.

McGuckin, J. A. *Saint Gregory of Nazianzus: An Intellectual Biography.* Crestwood, NY: St. Vladimir's Seminary Press, 2001.

Meeks, W. A. "A Hermeneutic of Social Embodiment," *Harvard Theological Review* 79, no. 1-3 (1986): 176–86.

Milbank, J. *The Word Made Strange.* Oxford: Blackwell, 1997.

Auerbach, E. *Mimesis.* Princeton: Princeton University Press, 1953.

Murphy, F. A. *God Is Not a Story: Realism Revisited.* Oxford: Oxford University Press, 2007.

Noble, T. A. "Gregory Nazianzen's Use of Scripture in Defence of the Deity of the Spirit," *Tyndale Bulletin* 39 (1988): 101–23.

Noble, P. *The Canonical Approach: A Critical Reconstruction of the Hermeneutics of Brevard S. Childs.* Leiden/New York/Köln: Brill, 1995.

Noll, M. "History." In Kevin J. Vanhoozer, Craig G. Bartholomew, and Daniel J. Treier, eds., *The Dictionary for the Theological Interpretation of the Bible.* Grand Rapids: Baker Academic, 2005, pp. 295–99.

Norris, C. *Deconstruction: Theory and Practice.* London and New York: Methuen, 1982.

Norris, F. W. "Gregory Nazianzen: Constructing and Constructed by Scripture." In P. Blowers, ed., *The Bible in Greek Antiquity* (Notre Dame: University of Notre Dame Press, 1997), 149–62.

Norris, F. "Theology as Grammar: Nazianzen and Wittgenstein." In M. R. Barnes and D. H. Williams, eds., *Arianism after Arius.* Edinburgh: T. & T. Clark, 1993, pp. 237–50.

Outka, G. "Following at a Distance: Ethics and the Identity of Jesus." In *Scriptural Authority and Narrative Interpretation.* Philadelphia: Fortress Press, 1987, pp. 144–60.

Paddison, A. "The Authority of Scripture and the Triune God," *International Journal of Systematic Theology* 13, no. 4 (2011): 448–62.

Paddison, A. *Scripture: A Very Theological Proposal.* London: T. & T. Clark, 2009.

Pannenberg, W. "Redemptive Event and History." In Pannenberg, *Basic Questions in Theology*, vol. 1. London: SCM, 1970, pp. 15–80.

Peel, J. D. Y. *Religious Encounter and the Making of the Yoruba.* Bloomington and Indianapolis: Indiana University Press, 2000.

Pépin, J. *Mythe et Allégorie: Les origins grecques et les contestations judeo-chrétiennes.* Paris: Études Augustiniennes, 1976.

Plagnieux, J. *Saint Grégoire de Nazianze Théologien.* Paris: Éditions Franciscaines, 1951.

Plantinga, A. "Two (or More) Kinds of Scripture Scholarship." In C. Bartholomew, C. S. Evans, M. Healy, and M. Rae, eds., *Behind the Text: History and Biblical Interpretation.* Carlisle/Grand Rapids: Paternoster Press/Zondervan, 2003, pp. 19–57.

Portmann, F. *Die göttliche Paidagogia bei Gregor von Nazianz. Eine dogmengeschichtliche Studie.* St. Ottilien, Deutschland: Eos Verlag der Erzabtei St. Ottilien, 1954.

Radner, E. "The Life Is in the Blood." Paper given to the Christian Theology and the Bible section of the Society of Biblical Literature at its annual meeting in Chicago, November 2012.

Rae, M. *History and Hermeneutics*. London: T. & T. Clark, 2005.

Rebillard, S. A. "Historiography as Devotion." In C. Beeley, ed., *Re-reading Gregory of Nazianzus: Essays on History, Theology and Culture*. Washington, DC: Catholic University of America Press, 2012.

Ricoeur, P. *Interpretation Theory Discourse and the Surplus of Meaning*. Fort Worth: Texas Christian University Press, 1976.

Rowe, C. K. *Early Narrative Christology: The Lord in the Gospel of Luke*. Grand Rapids: Baker Academic, 2009.

Ruether, R. Radford. *Gregory of Nazianzus, Rhetor and Philosopher*. Oxford: Clarendon, 1969.

Russell, B. "Descriptions." In A. W. Moore, *Meaning and Reference*. Oxford: Oxford University Press, 1993, pp. 46–55.

Schenck, K. *A Brief Guide to Philo*. Louisville: Westminster John Knox, 2005

Schneiders, S. *The Revelatory Text: Interpreting the New Testament as Sacred Scripture*. Collegeville, MN: Liturgical Press, 1999.

Schüssler Fiorenza, F. "History and Hermeneutics." In James Livingstone, F. Schüssler Fiorenza, Sarah Coakley, and James H. Evans, *Modern Christian Thought: The Twentieth Century*. Minneapolis: Fortress Press, 2006, pp. 341–85.

Schwartzentruber, P. "The Modesty of Hermeneutics: The Theological Reserves of Hans Frei," *Modern Theology* 8, no. 2 (1992): 181–95.

Špidlík, T. *Grégoire de Nazianze: Introduction à l'étude de sa doctrine spirituelle*. Rome: Pont. Institutum Studiorum Orientalium, 1971.

Springs, J. A. *Towards a Generous Orthodoxy: Prospects for Hans Frei's Postliberal Theology*. Oxford: Oxford University Press, 2010.

Strauss, D. F. *The Life of Jesus Critically Examined*. Translated by G. Eliot. Edited by P. Hodgson. London: SCM, 1973.

Strawson, P. F. "On Referring." In A. W. Moore, *Meaning and Reference*. Oxford: Oxford University Press, 1993, pp. 56–79.

Struck, P. *Birth of the Symbol: Ancient Readers at the Limits of Their Texts*. Princeton: Princeton University Press, 2004.

Stuhlmacher, P. *Historical Criticism and Theological Interpretation of Scripture*. Translated by R. Harrisville. London: SPCK, 1979.

Tambling, J. *Allegory*. Abingdon, UK: Routledge, 2010.

Tanner, K. *Theories of Culture: A New Agenda for Theology*. Minneapolis: Fortress Press, 1997.

Thatcher, A. *The Savage Text: The Use and Abuse of the Bible*. Chichester: WileyBlackwell, 2008.

Tilley, T. *History, Theology and Faith: Dissolving the Modern Problematic.* Maryknoll, NY: Orbis, 2004.

Topping, Richard R. *Revelation, Scripture and Church: Theological Hermeneutic Thought of James Barr, Paul Ricoeur and Hans Frei.* Aldershot: Ashgate, 2007.

Torjesen, K. J. *Hermeneutical Procedure and Theological Method in Origen's Exegesis.* Berlin and New York: Walter de Gruyter, 1986.

Treier, Daniel J. "What Is Theological Interpretation? An Ecclesiological Reduction," *International Journal of Systematic Theology* 12, no. 2 (2010): 144–61.

Treier, Daniel J. *Introducing Theological Interpretation of Scripture: Recovering a Christian Practice.* Nottingham: Apollos, 2008.

Trible, P. *Texts of Terror: Literary-Feminist Readings of Biblical Characters.* London: SCM, 2003.

Troeltsch, E. "Historical and Dogmatic Method in Theology." In James Luther Adams, ed., *Religion in History.* Edinburgh: T. & T. Clark, 1991, pp. 11–32.

Troeltsch, E. "The Significance of the Historical Jesus for Faith." In Robert Morgan and Michael Pye, eds., *Ernst Troeltsch: Writings on Theology and Religion.* Louisville: Westminster John Knox, 1990, pp. 183–207.

Troeltsch, E. "The Significance of the Historical Jesus for Faith." In Robert Morgan and Michael Pye, eds., *Ernst Troeltsch: Writings on Theology and Religion.* Atlanta: Westminster John Knox, 1990, pp. 182–207.

Troeltsch, E. *The Absoluteness of Christianity and the History of Religions.* Translated by D. Reid. London: SCM, 1972.

Troeltsch, E. "Historiography." In J. Macquarrie, ed., *Contemporary Religious Thinkers: From Idealist Metaphysicians to Existential Theologians.* New York: Harper & Row, 1968.

Van Dam, R. *Kingdom of Snow: Roman Rule and Greek Culture in Cappadocia.* Philadelphia: University of Pennsylvania Press, 2002.

Vanhoozer, K. J. *Remythologizing Theology: Divine Action, Passion, and Authorship.* New York: Cambridge University Press, 2010.

Vanhoozer, K. J., et al., eds. *The Dictionary for Theological Interpretation of the Bible.* Grand Rapids: Baker Academic, 2006.

Vanhoozer, K. J. *The Drama of Doctrine: A Canonical Linguistic Approach to Christian Theology.* Louisville: Westminster John Knox, 2005.

Vanhoozer, K. J. *First Theology: God, Scripture and Hermeneutics.* Downers Grove, IL/Nottingham: IVP Academic/Apollos, 2002.

Vanhoozer, K. J. *Is There a Meaning in This Text? The Bible, the Reader and the Morality of Literary Knowledge*. Leicester: Apollos, 1998.

Wallace, Mark I. *The Second Naiveté: Barth, Ricoeur, and the New Yale Theology*. Macon, GA: Mercer University Press, 1990.

Ward, G. "Allegoria: Reading as a Spiritual Exercise," *Modern Theology* 15, no. 3 (1999): 271–95.

Watson, F. *Text, Church and World*. Edinburgh: T. & T. Clark, 1994.

Webster, J. *Holy Scripture: A Dogmatic Sketch*. Cambridge: Cambridge University Press, 2003.

Webster, J. "Response to George Hunsinger," *Modern Theology* 8, no. 2 (1992): 129–32.

Wilken, R. L. "In Defense of Allegory." In L. Gregory Jones and James J. Buckley, *Theology and Scriptural Imagination*. Oxford: Blackwell, 1998, pp. 35–50.

Williams, R. D. *On Christian Theology*. Oxford: Blackwell, 2000.

Winslow, D. F. "Christology and Exegesis in the Cappadocians," *Church History: Studies in Christianity and Culture* 40, no. 4 (1971): 389–96.

Witherington III, B. *Paul's Narrative Thought World: The Tapestry of Tragedy and Triumph*. Louisville: Westminster John Knox, 1994.

Wolterstorff, N. *Divine Discourse: Philosophical Reflections on the Claim That God Speaks*. Cambridge: Cambridge University Press, 1995.

Wood, C. *The Formation of Christian Understanding: An Essay in Theological Hermeneutics*. Philadelphia: Westminster, 1981.

Woolverton, John F. "Hans W. Frei in Context: A Theological and Historical Memoir," *Anglican Theological Review* 79, no. 3 (1997): 369–93.

Work, T. *Living and Active: Scripture in the Economy of Salvation*. Grand Rapids: Eerdmans, 2002.

Wright, N. T. *The Climax of the Covenant: Christ and the Law in Pauline Theology*. London: T. & T. Clark, 1993.

Wright, N. T. *The New Testament and the People of God*. London: SPCK, 1992.

Young, F. M. "The Fourth Century Reaction against Allegory," *Studia Patristica* XXX. Leuven: Peeters, 1997, pp. 120–25.

Young, F. M. *Biblical Interpretation and the Formation of Christian Culture*. Cambridge: Cambridge University Press, 1997.

Young, F. M. *The Art of Performance: Towards a Theology of Holy Scripture*. London: Darton, Longman & Todd, 1990.

Index of Subjects and Names

Lightning Source UK Ltd.
Milton Keynes UK
UKHW022049181022
410698UK00010B/157